Immigration Offences

A Practical Guide

Immigration Offences

A Practical Guide

Daniel Bunting
Barrister, 2 Dr Johnson's Buildings

Bloomsbury Professional

LONDON • DUBLIN • EDINBURGH • NEW YORK • NEW DELHI • SYDNEY

BLOOMSBURY PROFESSIONAL
Bloomsbury Publishing Plc
50 Bedford Square, London, WC1B 3DP, UK
1385 Broadway, New York, NY 10018, USA
29 Earlsfort Terrace, Dublin 2, Ireland

BLOOMSBURY and the Diana logo are trademarks of Bloomsbury Publishing Plc

British Library Cataloguing-in-Publication Data

A catalogue record for this book is available from the British Library.

ISBN: PB: 978 1 52652 551 2
Epdf: 978 1 52652 553 6
Epub: 978 1 52652 552 9

Typeset by Evolution Design and Digital (Kent)

To find out more about our authors and books visit www.bloomsburyprofessional.com. Here you will find extracts, author information, details of forthcoming events and the option to sign up for our newsletters

Preface

Criminal and immigration law are both complex and fast-moving, areas of law where a year with only one new piece of legislation to grapple with is a quiet one. The aim in publishing this book is to provide a framework for anyone whose practice brings them into the intersection of those two areas of law. Whilst it is focused on assisting practitioners (barristers, solicitors, police station representatives and immigration advisors) and the judiciary, it is hoped that it may prove useful to a wider group of people (such as students, academics and third sector organisations).

Not only does the book deal with immigration offences, it goes further and deals with foreign national offenders in general. It is hoped that it will provide support at all points in a criminal case, from the busy police station rep faced with an unfamiliar offence to someone advising long after conviction as to whether there may be an avenue of appeal.

Whilst the book is split into 12 chapters, it can be seen as having five (unequal) parts. Firstly, there is an introduction to immigration law, and to criminal law, for those unfamiliar with either aspect. Then, secondly, there are five chapters that focus on the main (as well as the uncommon) immigration offences, before chapters on two areas that are fraught with difficulty; the specific defences relating to refugees and the victims of trafficking, and sentencing (including deportation). Lastly, there are three chapters on procedure and evidence (including investigatory powers) that are of general application.

The pace of change continues unabated. This was brought home to me in the week before the first draft was submitted where there was a new announcement or case every day that meant a re-write. It is hoped that, whether because of the constant changes or otherwise, there are no errors in the text (or, perhaps the most that any writer can hope for, the errors are as few and harmless as possible).

I would also like to thank everyone at Bloomsbury Professional, friends, family, colleagues, members of the judiciary and opponents who have helped get the book to print, and especially to Jo, Paul, Hannah and Adam who have been such immense support.

Daniel Bunting
August 2023

Contents

Table of Statutes

[All references are to paragraph numbers.]

Table of Statutory Instruments

[All references are to paragraph numbers.]

Table of Other Material

[All references are to paragraph numbers.]

Table of Cases

[All references are to paragraph numbers.]

S

1 Immigration law for criminal lawyers

Introduction

1.1

This chapter provides an introduction for criminal lawyers to immigration law. Of necessity, it can only provide a brief, and incomplete, overview on what is a vast area of law where the Immigration Rules themselves cover many thousands of pages.

Historical overview

1.2

Until the beginning of the 20th century[1] there was remarkably little by way of immigration control. The Aliens Act 1905 is often seen as the historic starting point of the modern regulation of the movement of people into the United Kingdom. This was passed following a Royal Commission in 1903 amid concerns of increasing immigration fuelled by increasing persecution of Jews in Eastern Europe and the greater mobility afforded by developments in boat and train travel. The post of the Immigration Officer, with the power to inspect (certain) ships and aliens, and to refuse entry to would be migrants, was created and for the first time there was a formal structure whereby the Home Secretary could deport an alien (albeit only after recommendation by a court following a conviction for a criminal offence, or a finding that an individual was a charge on the rates). It also formalised the concept of asylum into aliens' legislation, although it had already been present in law since the Extradition Act 1870 which prohibited the return of people charged with an offence which is 'one of a political character'.

1 Prior to then, there was very little formal control on immigration. For example, the Aliens Act 1793 created a requirement for 'aliens' to register with the local Justice of the Peace and gave wide ranging powers of deportation (that were not generally acted on). Until 1836, that law was repealed and re-introduced depending on the political climate (the regulations were repealed in 1814, but brought back in 1816 due to the Napoleonic wars and changed again in 1826). In 1836, the Registration of Aliens Act was passed which further relaxed controls. Whilst there was (as the name implies) a requirement for aliens to register, there was no formal mechanism to either expel them or to prohibit their entry at a port. The only other piece of legislation in the nineteenth century was some minor modifications in 1848 following the political turmoil in Europe, but this was allowed to lapse after a short period of time as tensions on the Continent ended. For a good overview, see Winder, R., *Bloody Foreigners*, (Abacus, 2004).

1.3

Over the course of the 20th century there has been an ever-increasing number of measures, which has continued at pace into the 21st century. The legislation has become ever more lengthy and complex over time, as well as being increasingly difficult for even immigration lawyers to keep up to date with[2].

1.4

The legislative foundation of current immigration law is still the (much amended) Immigration Act 1971 (IA 1971). This is supplemented by a number of other statutes that include the following that a practitioner may have to consider at one point or another[3]:

- British Nationality Act 1981 (BNA 1981)
- Asylum and Immigration Act 1996 (AIA 1996)
- Immigration Act 1988 (IA 1988)
- Immigration and Asylum Act 1999 (IAA1999)
- Nationality, Immigration and Asylum Act 2002 (NIAA 2002)
- Asylum and Immigration (Treatment of Claimants, etc) Act 2004 (AI(TC) A 2004)
- Immigration, Asylum and Nationality Act 2006 (IANA 2006)
- UK Borders Act 2007 (UKBA 2007)
- Immigration Act 2014 (IA 2014)

---

2 In *ZA (s 58(9) – Abandonment – Date of grant) Ethiopia* [2004] UKIAT 00241 the Asylum and Immigration Tribunal said (at [14]) that, in relation to a Commencement Order under the NIAA 2002:
'… It would be quite impossible to make the assumption of rationality and non-absurdity which Ms Anderson suggests underlies the statutory scheme. We do not need to make any large comments about the drafting of the numerous statutory changes to the immigration, asylum and human rights appeal system that have been introduced in the last few years. Such comments have been made with great frequency and are undoubtedly well merited. It suffices for present purposes to consider the Commencement Order before us. It is admittedly so badly drafted that it has been the subject of three Amendment Orders (SI 2003/1040, SI 2003/1339 and SI 2003/2993). We believe that the introduction of even one Amendment Order to a Commencement Order is almost unknown: so the present Order has some claim to be the worst-drafted Commencement Order ever passed by Parliament.
This has continued to the present day, with an (unreported) example being *SSHD v Kabir* (2023) UI-2022-002538 where the Upper Tribunal essentially gave up on an attempt to interpret the EU Settlement Scheme as (at [21]):
Although we could attempt a more detailed analysis citing all the different definitions that one might need to turn to within the wording of paragraph (b)(ii) and Appendix EU, we conclude that it is not a proportionate use of court time. Having spent many hours considering this part of the rules one finds that there is nothing natural or plain about the wording that might reveal its intended meaning. A repeated reading of paragraph (aaa), the associated definitions within the Appendix, and the policy guidance only leads to a 'curiouser and curiouser' situation. Like Alice in Wonderland one falls down a rabbit hole and stumbles across a circular race, with the Eaglet exclaiming: "Speak English!… I don't know the meaning of half of those long words, and what's more, I don't believe you do either!".'

3 Interpretation Act 1978, Sch 1 states that the 'The Immigration Acts' (plural) are those Acts set out in UK Borders Act 2007, s 61(2). This lists all these Acts as well as Asylum and Immigration Appeals Act 1993 and Immigration and Social Security Co-ordination (EU Withdrawal) Act 2020.

- Immigration Act 2016 (IA 2016)
- Nationality and Borders Act 2022 (NABA 2022)

1.5

This is before other statutes (such as the Identity Documents Act 2010) that create criminal offences relevant to immigration law are considered. Added to this will be the Illegal Migration Act 2023 which received Royal Assent on 20 July 2023, although very little is in force[4].

1.6

The Immigration Rules are at the heart of the immigration system, although they occupy an unusual position legally. Whilst they are referred to in the IA 1971, s 3(2) they are not statutory instruments, being a statement of the policy of the Home Secretary as to how they will exercise their powers[5]. They have been described as 'quasi-law' and holding a 'unique' position[6], but it is now settled that 'any requirement which, if not satisfied by the migrant, will lead to an application for leave to enter or remain being refused is a rule within the meaning of the IA 1971, s 3(2)'[7] and must be laid before Parliament.

1.7

It is unlikely that a criminal practitioner will need to consider the intricacies of this point. It is likely that all parts of the Immigration Rules are 'immigration law' for the purpose of the IA 1971, s 25 offence, at least as it relates to the admission of foreign nationals to the United Kingdom[8].

1.8

As with other areas of immigration law, a common complaint amongst practitioners and judges was articulated by Aikens LJ, 'The Immigration Rules are voluminous and they change with dizzying frequency'[9].

1.9

Whilst the Rules are supposed to be a 'complete code', there is a residual discretion for the Home Secretary to grant leave to remain outside of the Rules in a suitable case.

4 Section 64(4), which is in force, adds the Illegal Migration Act 2023 to those Acts listed in UK Borders Act 2007, s 61(2).

5 During the passage of the 1971 Act attempts were made to amend what is now s 3(2) to make the Rules secondary legislation, but these were unsuccessful (see, by way of example and for explanation, the speeches of Lord Windlesham at HL Deb 12 October 1971 vol 324 cc319-333).

6 *Pankina v SSHD* [2010] EWCA Civ 719, [2011] 1 QB 376.

7 *R (Alvi) v SSHD* [2012] UKSC 33, [2012] 1 WLR 2208 at [94].

8 *Mohamed* [2023] EWCA Crim 211 at [75], [2023] 2 Cr App R 2.

9 *R (MM (Lebanon) v SSHD) and Others* [2014] EWCA Civ 985, [2014] 1 WLR 1073, at [2].

Who's who

1.10

The Home Secretary is the person who is in overall charge of the immigration and visa regime in the United Kingdom. What was called the UKBA (UK Border Agency) was dissolved in 2013 and replaced with three different agencies. These are: UK Visas and Immigration (dealing with, as the name suggests, applications for visas to come to the UK as well as with applications to stay in the UK, asylum cases, applications for citizenship and applications from business and educational institutions that seek to sponsor foreign nationals); 'Immigration Enforcement' and the 'Border Force' (both dealing with enforcement).

1.11

As stated, the position of Immigration Officer has its origins in the Aliens Act of 1905[10], although they are now appointed by the Secretary of State under the IA 1971[11], and they are civil servants rather than office holders under the Crown[12]. In exercising their functions they are bound to act in compliance with the Human Rights Act 1998, and must comply with the provisions of the Equality Act 2010. They have a primary role in examining all foreign nationals who arrive at a UK port and determining who should be granted leave to enter at that point, although the power to give leave to remain in-country remains with the Secretary of State[13].

1.12

They have powers of arrest and detention which are considered in more detail below, although only certain officers ('Designated Immigration Officers') are trained in PACE. In addition, Immigration Officers may use reasonable force to (lawfully) exercise any power under the Immigration Acts[14].

EU Law

1.13

Running in parallel with the system of leave to enter and remain was, until recently, the system of free movement under EU law. This was distinct from 'domestic' law[15], which has caused problems in criminal proceedings[16].

---

10 The role, along with those of a medical inspector, was created by virtue of Aliens Act 1905, s 6.
11 IA 1971, Sch 2, para 1(1).
12 *R v Secretary of State for the Home Department, ex parte Oladehinde* [1991] 1 AC 254.
13 IA 1971, s 4(1).
14 IAA 1999, s 146.
15 IA 1988, s 7(1).
16 In *Boateng* [2016] EWCA Crim 57, [2016] 4 WLR 70, the appellant was indicted under IA 1971, s 24A(1) – obtaining leave to enter by deception, but the conviction had to be quashed as what he had obtained was an EU residence permit.

1.14

Following the UK's departure from the EU and the implementation of the Withdrawal Agreement (on 1 February 2020[17]) the free movement law, as it existed previously, ceased, as did the rights of EEA nationals. To replace it the Government set up the EUSS (European Union Settlement Scheme) with the intention being that this would be an application scheme (referred to as a constitutive scheme) rather than a declaratory one. The consequence would be that whilst someone who has not got status may be able to apply for it, this will be a new grant of leave to remain rather than a recognition of an existing right. However, in *R (Independent Monitoring Authority for the Citizens' Rights Agreements) v Secretary of State for the Home Department*[18] the Administrative Court (Lane J) ruled that the EUSS was unlawful as being contrary to the Withdrawal Agreement, at least in the requirement for those with pre-settled status to subsequently make a further application for Indefinite Leave to Remain[19].

1.15

There are now a large number of cases going through the system and the position in relation to the EUSS is in a state flux, with any statement of law being likely to be out of date very rapidly. Although the United Kingdom formally left the EU on 31 January 2020[20], practitioners will still need to be aware of the situation prior to then. This will not just be as it not uncommon for an alleged deception to come to light many years after the event, but it is likely that there will remain a level of complexity with some individuals having retained rights under EU law, which may impact on the lawfulness of their presence in the United Kingdom and the requirements to obtain leave to enter or remain.

1.16

Where an issue arises as to the impact of the fact that a person is or was an EEA national, or a relative of an EEA national, at the relevant time, specialist immigration advice should be sought.

Coming to the United Kingdom

Who requires permission?

1.17

Anyone who has a 'right of abode' is entitled to come to the United Kingdom without permission. This was a status created in the IA 1971 and is held by any British citizen, as well a small category of other people who were British

17 There was then a transitional period, called the Implementation Period, that lasted until 1 January 2021.
18 [2022] EWHC 3274 (Admin).
19 The Home Office have subsequently confirmed that they will not be appealing this.
20 In practice there was a transitional period until 31 December 2020 under the Withdrawal Agreement ('Agreement on the withdrawal of the United Kingdom of Great Britain and Northern Ireland from the European Union and the European Atomic Energy Community').

subjects or Commonwealth citizens with historic links to the United Kingdom. Since 1983 the only people who have a right of abode are British citizens and those who had retained the historic right. Those are the only people who can come to the UK as of right.

1.18

The situation of Irish citizens is different from other foreign nationals, in that they are normally exempt from the general regime of leave to enter and remain, unless there is specific action taken against them personally[21].

1.19

With a small number of exceptions, every other foreign national will require permission to enter and live in the United Kingdom.

Entry clearance v leave to enter

1.20

The Immigration Rules contain a list of foreign nationals who need an 'entry clearance' to come to the United Kingdom[22] for whatever reason. This means that they will have to apply in advance of coming (and may be committing a criminal offence if they do not do so[23]).

1.21

Foreign nationals who do not always require an entry clearance may apply at a port of entry to visit the UK for six months or less, but will generally require entry clearance for longer stays. It is still open to the person to apply for an entry clearance, even if this is not required.

1.22

An entry clearance must be applied for outside the UK and will typically be made to the British Embassy or Consulate of the person's home country. Various documentation will need to be submitted along with the application form and, if the proposed stay is longer than six months, then biometric data must be provided. The person may be called for an interview with an Entry Clearance Officer.

1.23

Even when an entry clearance is granted, that does not guarantee that the person will be admitted to the United Kingdom, although it is likely that in most cases the only checks conducted at the port will be to establish the person's identity.

21 IA 1971, s 3ZA.

22 Currently this is at Appendix VN 1.1. This includes anyone who is stateless. There are a number of exceptions in relation to some countries at 2.1-3.3 for holders of certain passports from those countries, or those who have an Electronic Visa Waiver Document for certain countries.

23 IA 1971, s 24(D1) – see Chapter 4.

1.24

Foreign nationals who do not require an entry clearance can apply for leave to enter at the port of arrival, showing that they satisfy the requirements of the Immigration Rules, although in many cases this will be a short-form process.

1.25

The United Kingdom is developing an 'Electronic Travel Authorisation'[24], which will be similar to the 'ESTA' issued by the United States. This will be piloted with nationals of Qatar from 15 November 2023[25], rolling out to the other Gulf Cooperation Council states (and Jordan) from 22 February 2024 and then to all other nationalities subsequently[26].

1.26

Foreign nationals who do not have to apply for an entry clearance will have to apply for authorisation to arrive prior to coming to the United Kingdom (the exact details will be set out in the Immigration Rules when the provision is brought fully into force). It will be a criminal offence to arrive in the UK with the relevant authorisation[27].

Avenues to come to the United Kingdom

1.27

There are a large number of different ways to apply to come to the United Kingdom, with the main categories being as a family member, a student, a worker or a visitor.

1.28

Each route comes with a large number of rules that need to be satisfied. The application forms are on the gov.uk website and care must be taken in drafting the application, which is why many people will seek legal help. There are a variety of different fees depending on the application. These are often high, which is a further reason legal advice is often sought[28].

---

24 This is set out under IA 1971, s 11C which was inserted by NABA 2022, s 75.

25 Electronic Travel Authorisation (ETA) Guidance, 9 March 2023 (available at https://www.gov.uk/guidance/electronic-travel-authorisation-eta) and Statement of Changes in Immigration Rules, HC 1160 (09 March 2023).

26 Ibid, and Electronic Travel Authorisation (ETA) scheme factsheet (7 June 2023), Home Office News Team.

27 Criminal Justice Act 2003, s 24(E1).

28 These are set out on the gov.uk website, and updated from time to time. These often run into several thousands of pounds.

Extension of leave/3C leave

1.29

When somebody who has current leave to remain applies in-time for an extension of leave then it will take time for this to be considered (in some case many years). In order to prevent such a person from being an overstayer (and therefore committing a criminal offence) there is provision for their current leave to be extended until the application is determined and the period of time for an appeal expires (and, if applicable, until any appeal is determined). Any conditions attached to the existing leave will automatically continue (unless they are varied in the same way as initial leave is). This is referred to as '3C leave', coming from the IA 1971, s 3C.

Entry for the purposes of giving evidence

1.30

There are a number of different ways of giving evidence from abroad remotely, which have increased in frequency since the start of the Covid-19 pandemic[29]. However, where someone is required to give live evidence in England and Wales they will have to meet the requirements of the Immigration Rules in the usual way.

1.31

There is always a residual discretion to waive the requirement of the Rules, which can be done in an exceptional case if the person is unlikely to qualify for a visa but there are clear reasons why it is in the public interest for them to attend court. This is unlikely to be straightforward, and should be done well in advance of any trial. A similar procedure would apply for someone currently in the United Kingdom with leave, but whose leave is shortly to expire.

Entry as a defendant

1.32

There is no provision in the Immigration Rules to grant entry for someone who is a defendant in a criminal case to come and answer the charge. Someone in that position will have to make an application in the usual way. Where someone has been deported or removed whilst criminal proceedings are ongoing, although

29 Criminal Just Act 2003, s 51 (introduced by Police, Crime, Sentencing and Courts Act 2022, s 200) sets out a general power for a witness to give evidence abroad by audio or video link. This should be read subject to 'Live Links in Criminal Courts – Guidance' issued by the LCJ in July 2022 (in particular para 18). There are potentially important points of policy and international relations – see *Agbabiaka (Evidence from Abroad: Nare Guidance: Nigeria)* [2021] UKUT 286 (IAC), [2022] INLR 304. Unsurprisingly, the Immigration Courts have dealt with the bulk of the cases that raise this issue.

there is no jurisdictional bar on proceeding in their absence, it may well be an abuse of process to do so[30].

Making an asylum claim

1.33

The question of 'who is a refugee' is a complicated one, which will be considered in more detail in Chapter 8. An asylum claim can only be made from within, or at, the borders of the United Kingdom[31]. There is no general provision in the Immigration Rules for an asylum claim to be made from abroad, nor is there any provision for a person to lawfully travel to the United Kingdom in order to claim asylum. If a claim is made at the border, then this can be done by approaching a Border Force official and the person stating that they wish to claim asylum. They will then be 'screened' (with an interpreter if necessary).

1.34

A claim can be made inside the UK, either because the circumstances giving rise to the claim have only just arisen[32] (such as a change of government in the home country) or the person had reasons (good or bad) to not claim asylum at the border. The procedure in-country is that the person must call the 'Asylum Intake Unit' based in Croydon[33] to register the claim, and an appointment will be arranged[34].

1.35

The first step will be an Initial Contact and Asylum Registration Questionnaire, generally called a Screening Interview. In this, the person will be asked basic details about themselves, including their journey to the United Kingdom. This will not be a full examination of their asylum case. As part of this, they may be asked to complete a 'Preliminary information questionnaire', which will be given to them at or after the Screening Interview and should be completed within 20 days. As well as administrative questions, this asks questions to obtain an overview of the asylum claim.

1.36

They will also have their fingerprints taken and be issued with an Asylum Registration Card (an 'ARC'). Once this has been completed, there will be a

---

30 *Gavin & Tacsie* [2010] EWCA Crim 2727, [2011] 1 Cr App R (S) 126 at [36]–[40]. This was in relation to confiscation proceedings, but the arguments in relation to a trial are stronger.

31 *R (European Roma Rights Centre) v Immigration Officer at Prague Airport* [2004] UKHL 55, [2005] 2 AC 1. There have been a limited number of resettlement schemes that have operated such as the Syrian Vulnerable Person Resettlement Programme. However there is no such thing as an 'asylum visa' for people to come to the United Kingdom to have their claim determined.

32 This is called a '*sur place*' claim.

33 Formerly called the 'Asylum Screening Unit' (ASU).

34 An overview is set out in the Home Office document 'Information booklet about your asylum application' (21 October 2022).

full asylum interview that will go into the asylum claim in detail. It is open to an applicant to submit a statement prior to then, but whether or not to do so is a tactical question (weighing up the benefits of not having to give an account in a stressful situation where there is the risk of confusion or omission, versus the risk of being effectively cross-examined on inconsistencies and giving the Home Office something to 'hang' a negative credibility finding on). A decision on the claim will not be made there and then. There was previously a 'service standard' of deciding the claim within six months, but this was abandoned and there is no timeframe, with many decisions taking considerably longer than that[35].

1.37

A lawyer representing a client who has made an asylum claim (where that is part, or potentially part, of the narrative of the criminal case) should ensure that they have these documents well in advance of trial, not least to check the consistency (or otherwise) of the account.

1.38

The Home Secretary will consider the claim and may accept that the person is entitled to refugee status[36]. At one point refugees were granted ILR (Indefinite Leave to Remain), although recently it would be a grant of leave for five years, following which an application for ILR could be made. Following NABA 2022, this had changed for people claiming asylum after 28 June 2022, but this has now been abandoned[37]. If the Home Secretary does not accept that the person is a refugee, then they will go on to consider whether to will grant 'Humanitarian Protection'[38]. This will typically be for people who would be at risk of persecution in their home country, but not for a convention reason.

Applications by people in criminal detention/with an ongoing criminal case

1.39

The fact that someone is remanded in custody on a criminal charge makes, in theory, no difference to the processing of a claim[39]. In reality, there are often logistical difficulties for someone remanded in custody in getting in touch with

35 A small number of people will be screened out of the general process by the National Asylum Allocation Unit, this includes unaccompanied children and those who are subjected to an 'accelerated process'. See the Home Office publication 'Asylum screening and routing' (v8.0), 03 February 2023.

36 The test is set out at para 334 Immigration Rules.

37 Under Nationality and Borders Act 2022 there was a distinction drawn between 'refugee permission' and 'temporary refugee permission', with the latter category being worse off in a number of respects including the fact that they will be granted 2½ years' permission to stay. However, it was announced on 8 June 2023 that this would be stopped. This was formally changed on 17 July 2023 (Statement of Changes HC 1496) but has retrospective affect.

38 The test for this is set out at para 339C Immigration Rules.

39 See 'Asylum screening and routing' (v8.0), 3 February 2023 at p32.

the relevant person to lodge a claim. Further, even where someone has made it clear that they wish to claim asylum, there is often then a delay before the process is started.

1.40

There is specific Guidance produced[40] that confirms that 'there is no specific time frame within which a decision on a person's asylum claim must be made in circumstances where there is a criminal prosecution pending against them, either in the UK or abroad', although where it takes more than six months then the applicant should be informed of the delay[41]. Further, it 'is preferable to make an asylum decision once all relevant facts are available. Therefore, claims from those with a prosecution pending are normally held for as long as required'.

1.41

Whether an asylum claim is put on hold pending the resolution of the criminal case is fact specific. However, given the current backlog it is unlikely that a decision will be made prior to any trial being heard.

Fresh applications in asylum cases

1.42

It is not at all uncommon for someone who has been refused asylum (whether or not they have unsuccessfully appealed) to make a further application at a later date, usually on the basis of there being fresh evidence to support his claim.

1.43

There is no bar to this, but there is obviously a risk of abuse with attempts to delay removal by making multiple claims. However, it is also the case that a fresh claim will sometimes succeed where a previous one did not for a multitude of different reasons[42].

1.44

The procedure is that when the fresh claim is submitted it will be considered by the Home Office who will make an assessment of whether the material is new and whether, taken with everything previously submitted, there is now a realistic prospect of the claim succeeding.

---

40 Pending Prosecutions in asylum cases – v2.0 (Jan 2023).

41 This is a general requirement for all applicants under para 333A Immigration Rules.

42 Common examples would be a change in country conditions meaning someone not previously at risk now would be, further compelling evidence, and a new representative presenting a better case or collecting evidence which should previously have been obtained.

1.45

If the Home Secretary decides that the test is not met, then that is the end of the matter with the only remedy being a Judicial Review (although there is nothing to stop further fresh claims)[43]. There is no bar on removal at this point.

1.46

If the Home Secretary decides that the test is met, then it does not mean that they will grant asylum (although that may be the outcome). However, if the claim is refused, there is then a right of appeal as if this was the first claim. At that hearing, assuming (as is almost invariably the case) that there was a previously unsuccessful appeal, the Immigration Judge will approach the case in accordance with the *Devaseelan* principles[44]. This strikes a balance between the general desire for finality in litigation and the requirement that a person has one opportunity to put forward their case with the requirement for fairness and flexibility in cases where fundamental human rights are at stake.

Appeals

What decisions are appealable[45]?

1.47

Whilst it might be thought that someone who applies under the Immigration Rules for a visa, or for further leave to remain and is refused, would have a right of appeal on the grounds that a decision is wrong (for example because it was contrary to the Immigration Rule under which it was made), the situation is not that straightforward.

1.48

Generally, the rights of appeal are against an immigration decision (typically a decision to refuse leave to enter the UK, or remain here having entered, but there are a number of other possible decisions including a decision to revoke someone's British citizenship or a decision to refuse an application under the EUSS) with the main grounds being set out in the NIAA 2002, s 84[46]:

> **'84 Grounds of appeal**
>
> (1) An appeal under section 82(1)(a) (refusal of protection claim) must be brought on one or more of the following grounds—

43 *R (Ali Akber) v SSHD (paragraph 353; Tribunal's Role)* [2021] UKUT 260 (IAC).

44 From the case of *Devaseelan v SSHD* [2002] UKIAT 00702. This has been approved on a number of occasions by the higher Courts. See, as recent examples that also set out an overview of the principles, *BK (Afghanistan) v SSHD* [2019] EWCA Civ 1358 and *SSHD v Patel* [2022] EWCA Civ 36.

45 The Illegal Migration Act 2023 makes a number of changes to the appeals regime. It is not known when this will be brought into force,

46 In addition there are EEA appeals where the right of appeal is in different instruments 2002 (depending on a variety of factors including the date of the application) or BNA 1981, s 40A (for deprivation of citizenship appeals).

(a) that removal of the appellant from the United Kingdom would breach the United Kingdom's obligations under the Refugee Convention;

(b) that removal of the appellant from the United Kingdom would breach the United Kingdom's obligations in relation to persons eligible for a grant of humanitarian protection;

(c) that removal of the appellant from the United Kingdom would be unlawful under section 6 of the Human Rights Act 1998 (public authority not to act contrary to Human Rights Convention).

(2) An appeal under section 82(1)(b) (refusal of human rights claim) must be brought on the ground that the decision is unlawful under section 6 of the Human Rights Act 1998.

(3) An appeal under section 82(1)(c) (revocation of protection status[47]) must be brought on one or more of the following grounds—

(a) that the decision to revoke the appellant's protection status breaches the United Kingdom's obligations under the Refugee Convention;

(b) that the decision to revoke the appellant's protection status breaches the United Kingdom's obligations in relation to persons eligible for a grant of humanitarian protection.'

1.49

So, as an example, if someone wishes to apply to come to the UK as a spouse of a British citizen then there are a large number of different requirements of the Immigration Rules that they have to comply with, including a minimum income from the spouse and accommodation requirements.

1.50

However, if the application is refused, then they cannot appeal on the basis that the Home Secretary 'got it wrong', or that the decision was not in accordance with the Immigration Rules. However, it can be argued that the decision is unlawful under the Human Rights Act 1998 as to refuse the person's visa would breach their right to a family life under Art 8 of the ECHR.

1.51

Whilst that may be straightforward in the case of a spouse, it does mean that some people (for example prospective visitors) may not have a right of appeal

47 There is power to revoke somebody's protection status (whether as a refugee or someone else in need of protection) in a number of different scenarios set out at paras 338A and 339A-339BC Immigration Rules for asylum cases and paras 339G and 339GA-339GD. Examples of situations when this would be done include a fundamental change in the risk profile of the person or the circumstances of the home country, or due to their actions (eg, serious criminality) the person should be excluded form protection.

and would have to use Judicial Review proceedings to overturn a wrong decision.

1.52

However, on an appeal, the fact that a judge concludes[48] that the appellant does, in fact, meet the Immigration Rules then this will be positively determinative of that person's article 8 appeal, provided their case engages Art 8(1), for the very reason that it would then be disproportionate for that person to be removed.

1.53

The outcome will therefore be effectively the same as it would be if there was an appeal under the Immigration Rules.

Non-suspensive appeals/no right of appeal

1.54

Most appeals are 'suspensive' in the sense that the person cannot be removed from the United Kingdom whilst the appeal is pending. However, the Home Secretary has power to certify a claim as being 'clearly unfounded' which meant that there was no in-country right of appeal. The NABA 2022 removed the right of appeal entirely in cases that are certified on or after 28 June 2022[49].

First-tier Tribunal

1.55

An appeal to The First-tier Tribunal (FtT) will be heard in the Immigration and Asylum Chamber (IAC). This will typically be a judge sitting alone to determine the appeal[50].

1.56

Whilst there will be grounds of appeal, an appeal is a full hearing on the merits and is as of right. The Home Office will be represented by a Presenting Officer ('HOPO') or sometimes a barrister, although it is not uncommon, particularly in more straightforward cases, for the Home Office not to attend. If they do not, then the case will usually still proceed and the appeal will be heard on the merits[51].

48 *TZ (Pakistan) and PG (India) v SSHD* [2018] EWCA Civ 1109.

49 See Certification of protection and human rights claims under NIAA 2002, s 94 (clearly unfounded claims), v5.0, 28 June 2022.

50 The Tribunal Procedure Rules, along with a number of pieces of Guidance, are on the FtT website on the Judiciary website (currently – https://www.judiciary.uk/courts-and-tribunals/tribunals/first-tier-tribunal/first-tier-tribunal-immigration-and-asylum-chamber/first-tier-tribunal-immigration-and-asylum-chamber-rules-guidance-and-forms/).

51 *SSGA (Disposal without considering merits; R.25 Iraq)* [2023] UKUT 12 (IAC).

1.57

Particularly where the appellant is represented, there will often be a full trial bundle with witness statements (which are supposed to stand as evidence in chief, although it is routine for there to be relatively wide-ranging oral evidence after the statement is adopted), and other papers. This should be obtained by any criminal practitioner reviewing the case at a later stage, or dealing with an allegation where the asylum claim may be relevant.

1.58

There will be a Home Office Refusal Letter (often abbreviated to RFRL) which should set out a full overview of the appellant's case and the reasons for the decision.

1.59

Decisions will normally be reserved and given in writing at a later date. The burden of proof is generally on the appellant and, in immigration matters, is the usual civil standard. In protection cases, due to the issues at stake, the burden of proof has been a lower one. This is variously described as there being a 'reasonable likelihood', a 'serious possibility', a 'reasonable degree of likelihood', or a 'real risk'[52].

1.60

The hearings are generally held in public (although there is power for them to be held in-camera[53]), although it is common for an anonymity direction to be made in asylum appeals[54]. The judgement will not routinely be published.

Onward appeals

1.61

Either party may appeal the First-tier Tribunal's decision to the Upper Tribunal on the grounds of there being an error of law, although there is no automatic right and permission must be granted.

1.62

An application for permission to appeal goes to the First-tier Tribunal first, where it will be considered by a judge from a different Hearing Centre on the

52 In assessing the question of a convention reason and past matters NABA 2022, s 32 changes (or purports to change) the standard of proof to the balance of probabilities. This came into force on 28 June 2022, although is unlikely to go unchallenged.

53 Tribunal Procedure (First-tier Tribunal) (Immigration and Asylum Chamber) Rules 2014, r 27.

54 Guidance is contained in Anonymity Orders and Directions in the First-tier Tribunal (Immigration and Asylum Chamber).

papers[55]. If the judge grants permission, then the case proceeds to the Upper Tribunal. If permission is refused, then it can be renewed to the Upper Tribunal. This will likely be decided on the papers, although there is provision for an oral permission hearing.

1.63

If permission is granted, then the case will generally proceed to an oral hearing (although there is provision for cases to be decided on the papers if requested). If the appeal is successful then it may be allowed outright or, depending on the reasons for the error of law and the circumstances of the case, sent for a fresh hearing which may be either back at the First-tier Tribunal or it may be kept in the Upper Tribunal.

1.64

Either party can appeal to the Upper Tribunal. All the judgments are published on the Tribunal Decision website, with the more significant ones on BAILII as well (there is a system for cases that raise an important point of law or practice to be reported). From there, there is a restricted right of appeal to the Court of Appeal (Civil Division) and the Supreme Court. Although very few cases get that far, the Supreme Court takes a relatively large number of cases.

1.65

Due to the subject matter of many immigration appeals (that involve allegations of likely mis-treatment in the person's home country that would amount to a breach of Art 3 of the ECHR and/or the question of whether removal would breach an individual's family or private life under Art 8 of the ECHR) there are again a relatively high number of cases that are considered by the European Court of Human Rights.

1.66

Since the Tribunals, Courts and Enforcement Act 2007, the Upper Tribunal has a judicial review jurisdiction and now deals with the majority of immigration and asylum judicial review cases, although there are a number of cases that can only be heard in the High Court:

- the validity of the immigration rules or legislation;
- the lawfulness of someone's detention (as opposed to the decision to grant bail);
- a sponsor not being included on the register of sponsors maintained by UK Visas and Immigration;
- a decision to refuse British citizenship;
- a decision to refuse asylum seeker support;

55 See https://www.judiciary.uk/wp-content/uploads/2019/08/PTA-guidance-August-2019-1.pdf for guidance.

- a decision made by the UTIAC;
- a decision made by the Special Immigration Appeals Commission;
- a declaration of incompatibility under section 4 of the Human Rights Act 1998;
- a decision that has been certified as in the interests of national security; and
- a decision by a competent authority in respect of being a victim of trafficking.

1.67

There is a cost regime in place in the Tribunal, but this is rarely used in the First-tier Tribunal. The Upper Tribunal is more willing to impose costs, although this is usually when exercising its Judicial Review jurisdiction rather than acting in an appellate capacity.

Detention and bail

Introduction

1.68

There is a common perception amongst criminal practitioners that someone who is in the country illegally (whether or not they are an asylum seeker) will be detained by the authorities until their immigration claim is determined and then, if unsuccessful, until they are removed. This is, however, not the case. The Illegal Migration Act 2023 makes a number of changes to the detention and bail framework, although it is not known when these will be brought into force.

1.69

Whilst there is a power to detain someone, this should be used 'sparingly', and for a specific purpose. There are a vast number of cases dealing with the use of detention, but practitioners will often see reference to the *Hardial Singh* Principles[56] that form the springboard for the current law on detention. The following summary was approved by a nine-judge division of the Supreme Court in 2011[57]:

> '(i) The Secretary of State must intend to deport the person and can only use the power to detain for that purpose;
>
> (ii) The deportee may only be detained for a period that is reasonable in all the circumstances;

56 From *R (Hardial Singh) v Governor of HMP Durham* [1984] 1 WLR 704.

57 *Lumba v SSHD* [2011] UKSC 12, [2012] 1 AC 245. This also sets out the history of the 'presumption of release' at [11]. The question of what is a reasonable period of detention is complex and fact specific. A summary of factors to take into account is at [104], but a period of time that is clearly unreasonable in pre-trial detention would not necessarily be so in an immigration context.

(iii) If, before the expiry of the reasonable period, it becomes apparent that the Secretary of State will not be able to effect deportation within a reasonable period, he should not seek to exercise the power of detention;

(iv) The Secretary of State should act with reasonable diligence and expedition to effect removal.'

Initial detention

1.70

The framework for the detention and examination of new arrivals is at the IA 1971, Sch 2[58] with the main provisions on bail being at the IA 2016, Sch 10.

1.71

Anyone who arrives in the United Kingdom can be examined by an Immigration Officer[59] to see if they are a British citizen (or can enter without leave as they have a right of abode) and, if not, whether they have existing leave to enter[60]. If that is the case, the Immigration Officer can determine whether that leave should be curtailed or honoured. In other cases, the Immigration Officer can determine whether or not leave to enter should be granted.[61] This includes a power to require a further examination.

1.72

Attached to the power to examine, is the power to detain for examination (or further examination)[62]. Someone detained at this point will be given an IS81 Form[63] which will set out the reason for the initial detention. This will often be detention at the port for a short period of time (no longer than is necessary, but no more than 12 hours) whilst enquiries are made, rather than detention in a prison or detention centre. There is a power to search the individual at that point[64].

58 There are different rules that apply to children and to vulnerable adults (including those who have been victims of torture).

59 There is also provision under the Act for medical examinations, which will not be considered in this chapter.

60 Where the leave to enter comes from an entry clearance, the powers to examine and review is under IA 2016, Sch 2, para 2A(2A).

61 IA 2016, Sch 2, para 2. For guidance, see 'Irregular or unlawful entry and arrival' v.2 (8 July 2022) at pages 26-27.

62 IA 2016, Sch 2, para 16. There are powers to detain for other purposes such as to fingerprint someone or refer them for a medical examination.

63 IS stands for 'Immigration Service', with this IS81 being one of a number of forms that are issued. It is entitled 'Notice to Person Required to Submit to Further Examination'. This must be issued by an Immigration Officer. Guidance is at 'Irregular or unlawful entry and arrival' v.2 (8 July 2022) at pages 28-29.

64 IA 2016, Sch 2, para 18A.

1.73

Someone who claims asylum at the port can be detained pending the resolution of their claim[65]. However, this is unusual, and most will be released on immigration bail[66]. In the case of someone who does not have leave to enter and can be removed, they can be detained pending a decision as to whether they should be removed, as well as pending removal[67].

1.74

When someone is detained beyond the initial immigration, they should be given an 'IS91R' (an equivalent form – an IS91 – is given to the person who is in charge of detaining them), which will contain reasons for their detention, and other written information about how to apply for bail. A Prison Officer can serve a form on behalf of an Immigration Officer.

1.75

The form contains a tick box list of the reasons for detention and a separate one for the factors that the Home Secretary has taken into account. Detainees must be given further written reasons for their continuing detention on a monthly basis.The review of someone's ongoing detention is at a much higher level than for a criminal defendant remanded in custody.

1.76

Administrative matters and the conditions of detention are set out in the Detention Centre Rules 2001. Practitioners will sometimes hear reference to a 'Rule 35' report.This relates to r 35 of the Rules, and ensures that someone who is particularly vulnerable (often because they are a victim of torture) is identified and appropriate steps taken in relation to their wellbeing.

1.77

There is power to hold a person subject only to immigration detention in the prison estate, but that is generally only where there is a need for a higher level of security (for example, people who present a risk to national security).When that is the case, then the person should be held in the same conditions as a remand prisoner[68].

---

65 Under NAIA 2002, s 62.

66 Prior to 2018 most asylum seekers were given 'temporary admission' as an alternative to bail.This was a status that allowed them to be lawfully present in the UK, despite them not having leave to remain. Over the years there have been a number of 'fast track' schemes where asylum seekers are kept in detention pending the resolution of their claims. In this area it is especially important to ensure that a client has immigration lawyers in place. In addition, the Illegal Migration Act 2023 will make a number of changes. To date, ss 30–37 (restricting frture grants of leave to enter, entry clearance or an ETA, and restrictions on future applications for British citizenship) is the only one of these in force.

67 IA 2016, Sch 2, paras 10 and 14 and NAIA 2002, s 62.There is also power to detain family members under IA 2016, Sch 2, para 10A.

68 PSI, para 2.66. A person can be permitted to remain in a prison which does not normally hold remand prisoners provided that they give written consent.

1.78

There is a separate power to detain under the NIAA 2002, s 62 where the Secretary of State can set removal directions. This goes alongside the power in the IA 1971, Sch 2, para 16 to detain someone where there are reasonable grounds to suspect that they can be removed from the UK until a decision is made as to whether they can be removed, and to detain them until they are removed. This power can be exercised outside of a port[69].

1.79

In relation to those who are subject to deportation proceedings, or liable to be, the powers of detention are in the IA 1971, Sch 3, para 2 and the UKBA 2007, s 36. This includes a power to detain pending a decision by the Home Secretary.

1.80

There is no maximum period of detention, but generally detention can only be used for the purpose it is initially intended. The ongoing decision to detain must be kept under review.

Detention after a criminal prosecution

1.81

A further widespread perception amongst criminal lawyers is that the fact that someone has committed an immigration offence (or that they are a foreign national without status who has committed a criminal offence) will mean that they will be detained under immigration powers once they have completed their sentence. However, this is not the case and, if they are detained, this will not happen automatically. The basic principle is that someone can only be detained if there is legal authority to hold them (this will likely be the IS91 form). Therefore, once someone is bailed by the criminal court or their sentence finishes, they have to be released whatever their immigration status[70], unless positive steps are taken to detain. That is the case even if they are sentenced and the sentence is one that attracts automatic deportation, or the court made a recommendation for deportation.

1.82

Therefore, in a criminal context, whilst someone who has arrived illegally will be eligible to be detained, that will only give rise to a lawful detention where a decision has been made to detain. Sometimes they will have been detained under immigration powers, but this is not always the case (for example, if they are arrested under the criminal law prior to consideration for detention) and so an IS91 may not always be in place. Without that, there is no power to

69 There are additional powers in IA 2016, ss 28A-28H.
70 PSI 52/2011, para 2.32

detain and the person must be released. Shortly before the sentence expires, the prisoner should be served with an IS91 if a decision to detain has been made and one not already served.

1.83

This is also the case with someone who was on remand and acquitted, or sentenced to a non-custodial sentence. or a custodial sentence allowing for their immediate release.

1.84

Where someone is detained under the Immigration Acts, and subsequently remanded in custody by a criminal court, then they can be granted immigration bail to reside at the prison where they are remanded.

Immigration bail

1.85

Following the implementation of the IA 2016, someone who is liable to be detained can be released on immigration bail as an alternative to detention. Even where the grounds for detention are not made out (because, for example, there is no realistic prospect of removal within a reasonable time), someone can still be subject to bail.

1.86

There is no power to have unconditional bail. For someone not being detained pending deportation[71], there must be at least one of the following conditions[72]:

(a) a condition requiring the person to appear before the Secretary of State or the First-tier Tribunal at a specified time and place;

(b) a condition restricting the person's work, occupation or studies in the United Kingdom;

(c) a condition about the person's residence[73];

(d) a condition requiring the person to report to the Secretary of State or such other person as may be specified;

(e) an electronic monitoring condition (see paragraph 4); or

---

71 IA 2016, Sch 10, paras 1(1)(b) and (d) and 2(2). For such a person, there must be an electronic tagging condition (unless the exceptions in para 2(5)-(9) apply) as well as one of the other conditions in (a)-(d) and (f).

72 IA 2016, Sch 10, para 2(1). This is subject to an overall requirement that a tagging condition would not lead to a breach of Arts 3 and/or 8 (see the Home Office publication 'Immigration Bail', v15.0 (27 January 2023), especially at pages 30-35).

73 This generally does not apply where the person is being accommodated under IAA 1999, Part VI as an asylum seeker.

(f) such other conditions as the person granting the immigration bail thinks fit.

1.87

Any condition imposed under (f) must be reasonable. It is also possible to have a 'financial condition'. This is effectively a surety that the person will comply with bail conditions (not just that they will attend as directed). This can be provided by the person themselves, or by another person.

1.88

In deciding whether to grant bail and, if bail is to be granted, what conditions should be imposed, the Secretary of State (and the FtT on a bail application) must have regard to[74]:

(a) the likelihood of the person failing to comply with a bail condition,

(b) whether the person has been convicted of an offence (whether in or outside the United Kingdom [and whenever it was committed])

(c) the likelihood of a person committing an offence while on immigration bail,

(d) the likelihood of the person's presence in the United Kingdom, while on immigration bail, causing a danger to public health or being a threat to the maintenance of public order,

(e) whether the person's detention is necessary in that person's interests or for the protection of any other person,

(ea) whether the person has failed without reasonable excuse to cooperate with any process—

 (i) for determining whether the person requires or should be granted leave to enter or remain in the United Kingdom,

 (ii) for determining the period for which the person should be granted such leave and any conditions to which it should be subject,

 (iii) for determining whether the person's leave to enter or remain in the United Kingdom should be varied, curtailed, suspended or cancelled,

 (iv) for determining whether the person should be removed from the United Kingdom, or

 (v) for removing the person from the United Kingdom, and

(f) such other matters as the Secretary of State or the First-tier Tribunal thinks relevant.

74 IA 2016, Sch 10, para 3(1) and (2).

1.89

A grant of bail can be conditional on the requirements in the grant being met[75].

Practical matters for criminal lawyers

1.90

As stated above, immigration law is a highly specialist area and unless the firm instructed in the criminal matter also does immigration, it is important that the client is signposted to an immigration firm as soon as possible.

1.91

For someone who is arrested for a criminal offence and either released under investigation, the process of immigration detention and bail can proceed as normal.

1.92

Where someone is remanded into custody, the fact that they are a foreign national is not a bar on getting bail from the criminal court. For the above reasons, the perception that someone will remain in immigration detention if granted bail is incorrect. For that reason, it would not be correct for a bail application to be made on the basis that it would be 'technical bail'.

1.93

Where the prosecution relates to an offence on arrival, and the client does not have an address (most likely provided by friends or family) it will be necessary to liaise with the Home Office to ensure that accommodation is in place if a bail application is made.

1.94

An asylum seeker will often be provided with support (including accommodation) under the IAA 1999. A typical condition from the criminal court would be to 'live as directed by the Home Office' as this will allow for the person to be moved by the Home Office without repeated application to vary bail.

1.95

The Home Office has the power 'to enable [a] person to meet bail conditions'[76] by providing accommodation and travel costs if there are exceptional circumstances[77].

---

75 IA 2016, Sch 10, para 3(8).

76 IA 2016, Sch 10, para 9.

77 See *R (Humnyntskyi & others) v SSHD* [2020] EWHC 1912 (Admin), [2021] 1 WLR 320 for discussion of this provision.

1.96

The same applies where a criminal case has finished. If arrangements are not made, then there is a risk that the client will be released from prison homeless, and with no means of support.

1.97

Practitioners should be aware that, in contrast to criminal bail, it is a criminal offence to breach a bail condition without reasonable excuse[78].

Challenging a decision to detain

1.98

As well as a power to ask the Home Secretary, there is power to apply to the First-tier Tribunal (Immigration and Asylum Chamber) for a grant of bail[79].

1.99

The Secretary of State will provide a 'Bail Summary' which will be a useful document for the criminal practitioner to see as it will set out an overview of the case and the Home Office's position. If a bail application is refused, then it can be renewed after 28 days, or after a change in circumstances. The Tribunal will not be able to consider the underlying lawfulness of the detention. If this is to be challenged, then it would have to be by Judicial Review.

1.100

Somewhat surprisingly, for a criminal lawyer, is that the Tribunal cannot grant bail unless the Secretary of State gives consent where there are removal directions in place, and these are to take effect within 14 days[80].

Legal aid

1.101

Whilst legal aid is available in immigration cases, it is very limited in scope compared to criminal cases. Subject to means, it will be available in asylum cases[81] as well as, generally speaking, in the following cases:

---

78 IA 1971, s 24(1)(h). This is summary only with a maximum sentence of 6 months.

79 See Part V Tribunal Procedure (First-tier Tribunal) (Immigration and Asylum Chamber) Rules 2014 or the relevant procedure rules.

80 IA 2016, Sch 10, para 3(4).

81 Including protection cases where there would be a breach of Art 3 on return, even if the person is not a refugee. However, whilst it is available, there can be difficulties finding firms that will be able to take on cases given the number of providers who have ceased operating (including the Refugee Legal Centre and the Immigration Advisory Service – two charities who went into administration in 2010 and 2011, citing the unviability of legal aid work), or ceased doing legal aid work.

- Applications for bail by those in detention;
- Applications for asylum support;
- Applications by under 18s who are looked after by the local authority;
- Victims of trafficking applying for leave to remain on that basis;
- Victims of domestic violence applying for leave to remain on that basis[82]; and
- SIAC[83] cases.

1.102

This leaves a large number of cases which are out of scope, although it is possible to apply for Exceptional Case Funding.

1.103

The merits application is relatively straightforward at the initial application stage[84], although once an application is refused, the previous funding does not carry through to an appeal, and it has to be assessed that there is a greater than 50% chance of success. As with most criminal cases, legal aid pays a fixed fee rather than an hourly rate.

1.104

In relation to means, someone in receipt of asylum support is passported through. For other people, the situation is more complicated and depends on a number of factors (including the number of dependents). Broadly, they will need to earn less than £2,657 and have a capital less than £3,000.

Victims of trafficking

1.105

For obvious reasons there is an overlap between foreign nationals accused of involvement in immigration offences, and victims of trafficking.

1.106

Practitioners will need to be aware of the framework that exists for the protection of victims and potential victims of trafficking. There is a specific defence in certain circumstances for victims of trafficking. Both are considered in more detail in Chapter 8.

---

82 For an application under the 'Domestic Violence Concession', an application for Exceptional Case Funding will be needed. However, an application for ILR as a victim of domestic violence will be in scope.

83 Special Immigration Appeals Commission – the body that deals with appeals in national security cases.

84 With the test being whether the case clears the threshold of being 'clearly hopeless'.

2 Criminal law for immigration lawyers

Introduction

2.1

This chapter provides an overview for non-criminal lawyers as to how the criminal justice system operates.

2.2

It is not intended to be a complete guide to the criminal law, and is not a substitute for a more comprehensive practitioner text, to which reference should be made if fuller details are required. In particular, it should be noted that this does not deal with the position of youths, who are often dealt with very differently to adults.

Jurisdiction of the criminal courts

Classification of offences

2.3

With a few exceptions, all criminal offences can be split into one of three categories – 'indictable only', 'either way' or 'summary only', depending on which court they can be tried in.

2.4

The most serious offences (such as serious sexual and violent offences) are indictable only, meaning that they have to be tried in the Crown Court. Less serious are the 'either way offences', ones that (as the name suggests) can be tried either in the Crown Court or the magistrates' court. Finally, there are those offences that can only be tried in the magistrates' court. These form the vast majority of offences (and prosecutions) that are pursued in England and Wales.

Who can prosecute?

2.5

Almost all prosecutions will be started in the name of the King (and so be referred to as *Rex v Smith* or, in older cases, *Regina v Smith*). This will include all the ones that are likely to fall within the scope of this book.

2.6

The Crown Prosecution Service is the body that is the principal agency for prosecuting criminal cases in England and Wales. It is a relatively recent creation, only starting operating in 1986[1], although the origins are. It is headed by the Director of Public Prosecutions[2] ('DPP'), which is a position that dates back to the 19th Century. The Attorney-General ('AG') exercises supervision over the CPS although is generally not involved in individual decisions.

2.7

Some offences require specific consent (usually from the AG), which is considered further in Chapter 10.

2.8

Whilst the Home Office may take the lead on a number of immigration prosecutions in terms of the investigation, it will generally be the CPS that prosecutes the case[3]. In addition, the DPP has the duty to 'to give, to such extent as he considers appropriate, advice to immigration officers on matters relating to criminal offence'[4].

2.9

As well as a number of other government bodies, prosecutions are sometimes brought by local authorities and non-governmental bodies (such as the RSPCA). In addition, it is possible for anyone to bring a private prosecution for most offences[5] (although this is rare).

Code for Crown Prosecutors

2.10

The CPS are not required to prosecute in every case. In deciding whether to prosecute, a prosecutor must have regard to the 'Code for Crown Prosecutors'[6]. This mandates a two stage approach (the 'Full Code Test'). Firstly, there must be an assessment of whether there is sufficient evidence to provide a reasonable prospect of conviction. A prosecutor must take account of all the evidence (including assessing whether it would be admissible in court, as well as its

1 As implemented by the Prosecution of Offences Act 1985, which is still the source of much of the law relating to prosecutions.
2 Some older cases in the law reports will be written as *DPP v Smith*.
3 Prosecution of Offences Act 1985, s 3(2)(aa) states 'It shall be the duty of the Director … to take over the conduct of any criminal proceedings instituted by an immigration officer (as defined for the purposes of the Immigration Act 1971) acting in his capacity as such an officer'.
4 Prosecution of Offences Act 1985, s 3(2)(ec).
5 In cases where consent is needed, this will need to be sought by the person seeking to prosecute. In practice the CPS will then review the case and either take it over the case and prosecute it itself if it meets the Full Code test. If it does not, then consent will not be given, and the case will not be able to proceed.
6 This is published on the CPS website and reviewed at regular intervals. It is currently published online at – https://www.cps.gov.uk/publication/code-crown-prosecutors.

reliability and credibility) and the account of the suspect, and ask themselves whether a jury (or magistrates' court) is more likely than not to convict.

2.11

It is only if this test is met that the prosecutor goes on to the second stage – the public interest test. However, just because there is sufficient evidence to prosecute does not mean that a prosecution must follow. There will be many cases where it would not be in the public interest for a prosecution to be started.

2.12

At para 4.14 of the Code there are eight different questions to be asked (along with specific factors that should be applied when answering them :

(a) How serious is the offence committed?

(b) What is the level of culpability of the suspect?

(c) What are the circumstances of and the harm caused to the victim?

(d) What was the suspect's age and maturity at the time of the offence?

(e) What is the impact on the community?

(f) Is prosecution a proportionate response?

(g) Do sources of information require protecting?

2.13

It is only when both the evidential sufficiency and the public interest test is met that a prosecution can go forward. This would normally be assessed when all the lines of enquiry that could be pursued have been.

2.14

The exception is when someone is arrested and interviewed and it cannot be concluded at the time whether the Code is met (because, for example, the evidence is incomplete), but it is not appropriate to bail the suspect as an immediate decision is required. An example would be where the person is a flight risk, and liable to flee the country if they were not remanded in custody.

2.15

In those circumstances, prosecutors can apply the 'Threshold Test'[7]:

(a) There are reasonable grounds to suspect that the person to be charged has committed the offence,

(b) Further evidence can be obtained to provide a realistic prospect of conviction,

---

7 The Code elaborates on these factors at paras 5.3-5.10.

(c) The seriousness or the circumstances of the case justifies the making of an immediate charging decision,

(d) There are continuing substantial grounds to object to bail in accordance with the Bail Act 1976 and in all the circumstances of the case it is proper to do so, and

(e) It is in the public interest to charge the suspect

2.16

When this is the case, a charging decision can be made, although this should be kept under review.

2.17

Whether the decision to prosecute is made under the Full or Threshold test, practitioners are able to make representations to the CPS both before a decision to prosecute is made, as well as during the currency of the case.

2.18

Where a person who has made an application for leave to remain is subject to a criminal investigation then there is power for the Secretary of State to defer consideration of the application until the conclusion of the criminal investigation, although this power must be exercised lawfully particularly having regard to the question of whether the investigation will conclude in a reasonable time[8].

At the police station

2.19

Many cases, and certainly most immigration offences, will start life with an arrest by an Immigration Officer or Police Officer. Even if an arrest is made by an Immigration Officer, the suspect will still likely be taken to the police station to be processed.

2.20

When someone arrives at the police station a 'custody record' will be opened. This is an electronic log that details the detainee's details, as well as any interaction that they have with the police. The conditions, and length, of detention are governed by the Police and Criminal Evidence Act 1984 (universally called 'PACE') and there are specific Codes of Practice, with Code C ('Code of Practice for the detention, treatment and questioning of persons by Police Officers') being the one that a practitioner will most likely need to refer to[9].

---

8 *R (oao X and othrs) v SSHD* [2021] EWCA Civ 1480, [2021] 4 WLR 137.

9 The most recent version is from 31 July 2018 and is available online (as will any amended versions) – https://www.gov.uk/guidance/police-and-criminal-evidence-act-1984-pace-codes-of-practice

2.21

Code C has a specific section[10] dealing with interpreters, with there being a requirement that someone who needs, or appears to need, an interpreter is provided with one. Where an interpreter is used for a consultation between a detainee and a lawyer, then the interpreter will be covered by legal privilege[11]. One consequence of this is that there should be a different interpreter at trial than was at the police station, unless there are good reasons otherwise (such as an unusual language with very few interpreters)[12].

2.22

Where someone requiring an interpreter is remanded to the magistrates' court from the police station, then it is the duty of the police to arrange for an interpreter to attend. Otherwise, the court will arrange this, although both CPS and defence should be alive to ensuring that the court are aware of the need for one, and that the correct one is booked.

2.23

In addition, a foreign national is entitled to have their High Commission, Consulate or Embassy informed of their arrest and the location of their detention, and to be able to speak to a relevant official[13]. There are a number of countries which operate a mandatory notification procedure, so that the UK will automatically inform the relevant Embassy of the arrest[14]. However, there is a safeguard for people who are at risk in their home country:

> 'Notwithstanding the provisions of consular conventions, if the detainee claims that they are a refugee or have applied or intend to apply for asylum, the custody officer must ensure that UK Visas and Immigration (UKVI) (formerly the UK Border Agency) is informed as soon as practicable of the claim. UKVI will then determine whether compliance with relevant international obligations requires notification of the arrest to be sent and will inform the custody officer as to what action police need to take.'

2.24

Someone arrested will almost always be interviewed[15]. This will be recorded (on a digital system). The suspect will be entitled to free legal advice (regardless

---

10 Code C, Section 13.

11 *R (Bozkurt) v Thames Magistrates' Court* [2001] EWHC 400 (Admin), [2002] RTR 15.

12 The Law Society provides a useful guidance note on the use of interpreters in criminal cases – https://www.lawsociety.org.uk/topics/criminal-justice/use-of-interpreters-in-criminal-cases. Reference can also be made to the Code of Professional Conduct produced by the National Register of Public Service Interpreters. The Home Office also produces a Code of Conduct, as well as 'Criminal investigations: use of interpreters' v7.0 (26 September 2022).

13 Code C, 7.1-7.4.

14 A list of countries (which is dated 2013) is currently held by the FCDO here – https://assets.publishing.service.gov.uk/government/uploads/system/uploads/attachment_data/file/246235/Table_of_Consular_Conventions_and_Mandatory_Notification_Obligations.pdf

15 The Home Office public guidance to their staff is at 'Interviewing suspects' v7.0 (10 February 2020).

of means) from their nominated solicitor (provided that they have a legal aid contract with the LAA), or from a duty solicitor scheme. At the start of the interview the suspect will be cautioned, and warned that they do not have to say anything, but it may harm their defence if they do not put an account forward at that stage then that may count against them later.

2.25

Once an interview has been conducted, the suspect will either be charged (and then bailed or remanded to court), subject to no further action or, as is increasingly frequent, bailed or 'Released Under Investigation' (released without any conditions) for further investigation, or for the Crown Prosecution Service (CPS) to decide whether the suspect should be charged.

Victims of trafficking

2.26

The police station is one area where a victim of trafficking (or potential victim) should be identified, although it will often be missed. There is guidance for police provided by the College of Policing (as well as further guidance published by individual forces), as well as for solicitors and police station representatives published by the Law Society (all available online).

2.27

A representative should be alive to the fact that someone arrested for a criminal offence may be a victim of trafficking and should be careful to explore this with a client. It is important to not necessarily take a statement from someone that they are not a victim at face value for a variety of reasons (including fear on behalf of the victim and the fact that they have been 'coached' by traffickers). If someone is identified by a lawyer as a potential victim, then they should ensure that this is noted on the custody record, which should ensure that the police investigate the claim, and make a referral into the National Referral Mechanism (NRM). For further details on this, see Chapter 8.

Criminal procedure

The Criminal Procedure Rules

2.28

Once a case has reached court, overriding guidance is given by the Criminal Procedure Rules (CPR) and the Criminal Practice Directions 2015. For someone used to civil proceedings, the CPR are not enforced in the way that the Civil Procedure Rules are, although they are still the basis for the way that a case will (or, at least, should) be conducted.

First appearance at court

2.29

A suspect can be bailed to court, so released on an obligation to attend the magistrates' court on a set date. This can be with or without conditions (typical conditions being to reside at a certain accommodation and report to a police station on a certain day). Alternatively, the person can be remanded in custody (kept in the police station overnight) to a court appearance the next working day[16].

2.30

If the case is indictable only, then it will be sent straight to the Crown Court, although a bail application can be made if they are in custody.

2.31

If summary only then a plea will be taken and, if it is guilty, the court will proceed to sentence or adjourn for a Pre-Sentence Report (a report prepared by a Probation Officer who has spoken to the person and is intended to give a rounded view of them, along with a recommendation). If the plea is not guilty, then a trial date will be fixed and the court will engage in case management. Typically, there will not be another hearing before the trial.

2.32

Where the offence is either way then the person will be asked whether they intend to plead guilty or not guilty. If they indicate a not guilty plea, then the court will decide whether it is suitable for trial in the magistrates' court or if it should be tried in the Crown Court. This would normally be because the sentencing powers of the magistrates' court are insufficient, or the case is so complex it should be tried in the Crown Court.

2.33

If the magistrates (or the District Judge) conclude that the case should be heard in the Crown Court then it will be sent there. If not, then the case will be tried in the magistrates' court unless the defendant wishes to have a trial with a jury, in which case they can 'elect' for a Crown Court trial.

2.34

If the defendant pleads guilty then the magistrates will proceed to sentence them or, depending on how serious it is, commit it for sentence to the Crown Court. The magistrates' court can also commit a case for sentence to the Crown Court after convicting someone of an either way offence, even if they have previously accepted jurisdiction.

---

16 See 'Bail and refusal of bail by criminal courts and police officers', v5.0 (21 April 2020) for guidance from the Home Office to staff.

2.35

If a person faces more than one offence, then the process will be guided by the more serious one. So, if there is an indictable only offence and an either way offence, then the magistrates' court will send the either way offence to the Crown Court with the indictable only one. Where the summary only offence cannot be tried in the Crown Court, it will still be sent with the others for the judge to deal with after the end of the Crown Court case.

Trial

2.36

The basic outline of a criminal trial is the same in both the magistrates' and Crown Court, although there are obviously differences.

Magistrates' court

2.37

In the magistrates' court the case will either be heard by a 'lay bench' or a District Judge. A lay bench is formed of three (or occasionally two), people who are not qualified lawyers, but sit with a legal advisor. Magistrates act on a voluntary basis. A District Judge is a qualified lawyer who works full-time or part-time as a judge. They will sit alone and, if hearing a trial, will both decide on the facts as well as the law.

2.38

This means that they will deal with matters of admissibility of evidence themselves, with the consequences that they have often seen the disputed material before they rule on it.

2.39

The trial will start with the prosecution 'opening' the case (explaining what it is about) before calling witnesses. Although witnesses' statements are prepared and served on the defence, the court will not have them and there is full evidence in chief before the witness is cross-examined. The District Judge or lay bench can ask questions, but should be careful to not cross the line and 'enter the arena'.

2.40

As part of the prosecution case, there can be admissions[17] (agreed facts) or witness statements that are uncontentious being read by agreement (often called 's 9' from the Criminal Justice Act 1967, s 9, which is the power under which

---

17 The power comes from Criminal Justice Act 1967, s 10.

witness statements can be read). The police interview (or a summary of the police interview) will often be read at this time.

2.41

After the prosecution case has finished, the defendant can make a 'submission of no case' – an argument that there is not sufficient evidence on which a court, properly directed, can convict. This is a high test and such applications are rarely made (and even more rarely succeed)[18]. Following that, there will be the defence case, which may involve the defendant giving evidence himself, although he does not have to.

2.42

At the end of the defence case there will be closing speeches from both sides (prosecution and defence), which is the opportunity to comment on the state of the evidence and providing reasons in support of their case.

2.43

A District Judge will typically give their verdict then and there, whereas a lay bench will retire and consider the verdict, before returning to court to deliver it. They will receive advice as to the law from a legally qualified Legal Adviser. Reasons, albeit not in any great detail, are required to be given orally (as they would be for any sentence passed). There is no transcript made or, generally, written reasons given.

Crown Court

2.44

A trial in the Crown Court will be heard by a judge sitting with a jury of 12 people. They do not have to be unanimous – there is provision for majority verdicts of 11-1 or 10-2. A judge will sit alone to deal with all the pre-trial hearings and, if applicable, to sentence. Whilst it will be the same judge who hears the trial that sentences the person, there is no requirement for it to be the same judge who hears all the pre-trial hearings. Where the case is concluded with a guilty plea there is more flexibility as to whether it would be the same judge that passes sentence.

2.45

The timetabling is similar to the magistrates' court, although there will often be arguments relating to the admissibility of evidence before the trial starts. This will generally be before the jury is sworn and the Prosecution open the case

---

18 It will sometimes be called the 'Galbraith' test (from *Galbraith* (1981) 73 Cr App R 124), or a 'half time submission' as it is made half-way through the trial.

to them. The jury will not be present when legal issues arise during the trial (including for any submission of no case to answer).

2.46

After the evidence there will be speeches from both prosecution and defence. The modern procedure is that a judge will conduct a 'split summing up' with a summary of the law before speeches, and a summary of facts afterwards. The jury will then deliberate in private (although they can send a note to the judge for help on the law or the facts) before coming back to court to give their verdict. This will just be guilty or not guilty, with no reasons being given.

Defendants with mental health difficulties

2.47

People who are asylum seekers that are suspected of immigration offences are often vulnerable, with a higher level of mental health difficulties than in the general population. This can often be due to a history of torture in their home country. This will present particular difficulties to representatives, especially given the impact of a diagnosis of PTSD, depression or anxiety disorder can have on a person's ability to fully engage with their lawyer.

2.48

Practitioners will need to be aware of this and consider whether further investigation will be needed, even if a client has no diagnosis or is denying any mistreatment.

2.49

At the extreme, it may be that this will impact on the person's ability to engage in legal proceedings at all. If that is the case, then it will be necessary to consider whether they are 'fit to plead'[19]. This will be decided by the judge on the basis of the medical evidence provided. If the person is unfit to plead, then a jury will be empanelled to consider whether they did the act or omission charged (not whether they are guilty or not). There is no specific procedure for fitness to plead in the magistrates' court.

2.50

In the Crown Court, as well as verdicts of guilty or not guilty, a jury can also find a special verdict of 'not guilty by reason of insanity', if they conclude that at the time of the alleged offence the defendant, due to a defect of reason from a disease of the mind, did not know the 'nature and quality' of their action, or did not know that it was wrong. That is not a complete acquittal as the court

19 See the Criminal Procedure (Insanity) Act 1964 and the case of *Pritchard* (1836) 7 C &P 303.

has a number of different mental health disposals available. In the magistrates' court there is no special verdict, and so someone in those circumstances will be entitled to a complete acquittal.

Sentencing

2.51

There are a number of different sentences that can be passed by a court. The most common would be a prison sentence or a community order.

Sentencing powers

2.52

For many years it used to be the case that the maximum sentence that could be passed in the magistrates' court was six months (unless there was more than one either-way offence being sentenced at the same time). This changed in May 2022 to make the maximum sentence that can be imposed for one either-way offence 12 months[20]. However, this was then changed back to six months as of 30 March 2023[21].

2.53

The maximum sentence for a summary only offence is set by the statute that creates the offence, but will be no more than six months. However, many summary only offences are non-imprisonable. The maximum sentence in the Crown Court is life imprisonment, or the maximum as set by the statute (for example the sentence for murder, an offence under the common law, is life imprisonment, whilst that for theft is seven years[22]).

Pre-Sentence Report

2.54

Prior to sentence a judge or magistrate will often want to know more details about the offender before deciding what sentence to pass. In those circumstances, a Pre-Sentence Report (PSR) will be directed[23]. This is prepared by a Probation Officer who has access to the prosecution papers and has spoken to the defendant and will often contain a recommendation. It is often the case that there will be an adjournment for three or four weeks whilst this happens,

20 Sentencing Act 2020, s 224.

21 Sentencing Act 2020 (Magistrates' Court Sentencing Powers) (Amendment) Regulations 2023, SI 2023/298, reg 2.

22 Theft Act 1968, s 7.

23 The legislative framework is now set out at Sentencing Act 2020, ss 30–33. A report is mandatory unless 'unless, in the circumstances of the case, it considers that it is unnecessary to obtain a pre-sentence report'.

although it is possible in some cases for an oral report to be given on the day, often called a 'stand-down report. This is more likely where the judge is inclined to pass a non-custodial sentence (or a suspended sentence) but they need to confirm the person's suitability or resolve a narrow issue, although the fact that a judge, although where the judge does follow that course of action it is not guaranteed that a non-custodial sentence is passed.

2.55

The need for a report is particularly strong where the case is such that it is on the cusp between a non-custodial and custodial sentence, but one will also be called for even where a long sentence of imprisonment is going to be passed as the report can be relevant to the length. A report is more likely to be directed where the offender is young and/or has no previous convictions (or at least has not been to prison before). One will often also be produced if the judge is considering passing a life sentence or an extended sentence.

Custodial sentences

2.56

A custodial sentence will take effect immediately on being passed. The rules are more complicated for youths (people under 18), but for an adult the sentence can be of any length up to the maximum sentence.

2.57

Any time spent on remand in prison will count towards any prison sentence that is passed. This will be calculated automatically and deducted. Where someone is bailed with a condition of electronic monitoring and a curfew of at least nine hours per day (a 'qualifying curfew'), then that will count as half a custodial day, but this will have to be recorded in court by the judge[24]. So, as an example, if someone spends 30 days on a qualifying curfew, and receives a sentence of 12 months, then that sentence will be reduced by 30 days (meaning that the custodial part of the sentence will be reduced by 15 days from six months).

Release provisions

2.58

How long someone will actually serve in prison depends on the nature of the sentence that is passed. This will be the sentence as stated by the judge in court. The court will issue an order of imprisonment which will almost always be reliable. The police have a central database of all convictions and sentences on the Police National Computer and it is commonplace to see a 'PNC' – a

24 Sentencing Act 2020, s 325.

printout from that database. That is generally reliable, but it is not uncommon at all for there to be some errors on it, so if someone disputes the entry this should be checked. The PNC should include details of any pending prosecutions.

2.59

It used to be that there were effectively two forms of sentence that could be passed; a determinate sentence (measured in a fixed number of years) or an indeterminate sentence (at the time this was just life imprisonment). However, over the years there have been an increasing number of different types of sentencing and different release provisions.

Determinate Sentences

2.60

With a number of exceptions, for a 'normal' (determinate) sentence, half the sentence will be served in prison and then the person will be released automatically (ie, without anybody having to direct release)[25].

2.61

If the determinate sentence was imposed in relation to a 'terrorist prisoner' (one serving a sentence for an offence listed in the Criminal Justice Act 2003, Sch 19ZA, Pt 1 or 2 or one listed in Part 3 **and** the offence has a 'terrorist connection as defined in the Sentencing Act 2020, s 69[26]), then their case will be referred to the Parole Board for consideration of release after serving two thirds of the sentence[27]. If release is not directed, then the person will be released automatically after they have served the full sentence.

2.62

Where someone is serving a determinate sentence of seven years or more for certain serious sexual or violence offences[28] that carry a maximum sentence of life imprisonment, then they will not be automatically released until they have served two thirds of the sentence[29]. This will apply if the sentence is passed after 1 April 2020 irrespective of the date of the offence.

25 Criminal Justice Act 2003, s 244(1).

26 Criminal Justice Act 2003, s 247(7A).

27 Criminal Justice Act 2003, s 247 – this applies to people serving a sentence whenever it was imposed, provided that they were in custody serving that sentence on 26 February 2020. That was when the Terrorist Offenders (Restriction of Early Release) Act 2020, the Act that introduced s 247, came into force. This was passed in a response to the attack on Fishmongers Hall by Usman Khan and a further incident where Sudesh Amman attacked passers-by with a knife. Both had been released automatically.

28 Implemented by Release of Prisoners (Alteration of Relevant Proportion of Sentence) Order 2020, SI 2020/158. The relevant offences are those listed in Criminal Justice Act 2003, Sch 15.

29 Criminal Justice Act 2003, s 244ZA(4).

2.63

For a sentence of at least four years, but less than seven years, that is passed after 28 June 2022 for a serious sexual of violent offence[30], then the prisoner will not be automatically released until they have served two thirds of the sentence.

2.64

For other determinate sentences there is a specific provision for the Secretary of State for Justice to block a person's automatic release[31] in cases where they believe on reasonable grounds that the person would present a significant risk of serious harm to the public by committing murder or other serious violent offences[32]. This then means that the case is referred to the Parole Board for a decision as if the case was one where the initial decision to direct release was taken by them[33].

2.65

In all other cases, the person will be automatically released having served half the custodial sentence.

Sentences of particular concern

2.66

For people convicted of certain sexual[34] and terrorist offences[35], whenever they were convicted, then if a judge imposes a determinate sentence, but does not pass a suspended sentence, then the sentence passed has to be a 'special sentence' where there is an additional licence period of one year on top of the determinate sentence. Further, there is no automatic release. Instead, the case must be referred to the Parole Board after the person has serviced two thirds who will decide if the person is eligible for release[36]. If they do not do so, then the person must be released at the end of the custodial period, but will remain on licence until the end of the full sentence.

30 This is defined in Criminal Justice Act 2003, s 244ZA(7) as any sexual offence in Criminal Justice Act 2003, Sch 15, Pt 2 where the maximum sentence at the time was life imprisonment, as well as a limited number of violent offences in Part 1 (manslaughter, soliciting murder, s 18 wounding/GBH, and inchoate offences relating to murder, manslaughter, solicitor murder or s 18 wounding/GBH).

31 Criminal Justice Act 2003, s 244ZB(3).

32 The offences are listed Sentencing Act 2020, s 306, Sch 18and are the offences for which an extended sentence can be passed.

33 Guidance can be found on the Parole Board website – https://assets.publishing.service.gov.uk/government/uploads/system/uploads/attachment_data/file/1126237/Standard_Determinate_Sentence_Power_to_Detain_Information_Note_August_2022_external.pdf.

34 The offences listed in Sentencing Act 2020, Sch 13, Pt 2 (and like repealed offences) which are penetrative sexual offences of victims under 13.

35 The offences listed in Sentencing Act 2020, Sch 13.

36 Criminal Justice Act 2003, s 244A. If sentenced prior to 28 June 2022 then the period will be one half rather than two thirds, but this will not apply if the person is a 'terrorist prisoner'. In that case, the provisions of Criminal Justice Act 2003, s 244A will, and the person's case will only be referred to the Parole Board after the person has served two thirds of the custodial sentence.

2.67

As an example, if someone receives a sentence of six years for rape of a ten-year old girl then instead of being released automatically after three years, they will be eligible for release by the Parole Board after three years and, if not released early, then they will be released automatically after six years. Whenever they are released, they will remain on licence until the end of the six-year period, but plus an extra year at the end.

Extended sentences

2.68

Where an extended sentence has been passed (typically because the person is considered dangerous, but not given a life sentence), there will be a total sentence made up of a custodial element and an extended licence period. The person will be eligible for release after serving two thirds of the custodial part of the sentence, but can only be released at that point if the Parole Board direct their release. If that does not happen, then they will be released automatically at the end of the custodial period, and then will remain on licence (and therefore liable to be recalled – being sent back to prison because of a breach of their licence conditions) until the end of the extended licence period.

2.69

As an example, if someone receives a sentence of 12 years, made up of a nine-year custodial term and a three-year extended licence, then they will be eligible for early release after six years, they will have to be released after nine years but, whenever they are released, they will be on licence until they have served 12 years.

Indeterminate sentences

2.70

The most serious sentence that can be passed is one of life imprisonment. This will only be available for an offence where the maximum sentence is designated as life imprisonment. Although there is a power to pass a life sentence for any such offence[37], in practice the power will be exercised for certain serious offences set out in the Sentencing Act 2020[38]. This will normally only be passed where the person poses a significant risk of serious harm to the public by the commission of further serious offences and the seriousness of the offending is such as to justify a life sentence.

---

37 *Saunders* [2013] EWCA Crim 1027 where it was said [12] that such a sentence would be 'rare' but possible, with the example of 'repeated offences of very serious drug supplying' being given, at [11].

38 See Sentencing Act 2020, Sch 19.

2.71

There are some refinements. Someone convicted of murder is in a special category as the only sentence that can be passed is one of life imprisonment (although the 'tariff' will depend on all the factors in the case).

2.72

Where someone is being sentenced for certain serious offences[39], and has previously been sentenced to at least ten years (or a life sentence with a five-year tariff) for a serious offence (not necessarily the same one) then, if the current offence merits a sentence of ten years or more, a life sentence must be imposed unless it would be unjust to do so. A life sentence is also required for the manslaughter of an emergency worker unless there are exceptional circumstances[40].

2.73

The judge will set a tariff, which is the minimum period of time which the person will have to spend in prison before being eligible for release. Whether they are released will be a decision for the Parole Board at the time of any application. Whilst some people are released 'on tariff', it is not unusual for people to be in prison many years past their 'Tariff Expiry Date'.

2.74

In practice, whilst there are immigration offences for which a life sentence is eligible (such as IA1971, ss 25 and 25A), it is not believed that any such sentences have been passed. Whilst it is unlikely that one would be, it may be that following *Saunders*, someone who has repeatedly arranged the facilitation of people in inherently dangerous circumstances (such as on a 'small boat' or sealed in a lorry where there is a clear risk of death) such a sentence would be upheld.

2.75

Given the complexity of sentencing law, advisers should be aware that it is not that unusual for an unlawful sentence to be passed.

Suspended sentence

2.76

If a court is going to pass a sentence of imprisonment on anyone aged over 21 (or detention of between 21 days[41] and 2 years if aged between 18 and 21) of between 14 days and 2 years then, instead of it taking effect immediately the

39 As set out in Sentencing Act 2020, Sch 15.

40 Sentencing Act 2020, s 258A.

41 By virtue of Sentencing Act 2020, s 263(2) the minimum sentence of detention is 21 days.

judge can order it to be suspended for a period of between six months and two years[42]. There are a number of conditions that can be attached to this sentence. These are part-punitive (such as unpaid work of up to 300 hours) and part-rehabilitative (such as drug rehabilitation).

2.77

Suspending a sentence means that it will not take effect immediately, and it will not do so at all unless the offender commits a further offence or breaches a condition within the operational period. If that occurs then the suspended sentence can be activated, in whole or in part (but the sentence cannot be longer than the term originally listed). A list of the possible conditions is set out at the Sentencing Act 2020, s 287, Sch 9.

Community Order

2.78

A further sentence that can be imposed is a Community Order. This can only be imposed for an offence which carries a prison sentence[43] and involves the judge ordering the offender to comply with a number of conditions as set out in the Sentencing Act 2020, s 201 (similar to those that can be attached to a suspended sentence).

2.79

If the conditions of the order are breached, or there is further offending, then the judge can re-sentence for the original offending. Unlike a suspended sentence, the judge can pass a prison sentence of any length. For that reason, although a community order is less serious than a prison sentence, there are sometimes advantages for an offender in having a suspended sentence as it caps the maximum sentence in case of a breach.

Particular issues relating to foreign nationals

2.80

There is no reason why a suspended sentence or community order cannot be imposed for an immigration offence, although if someone has no status in the UK (and especially if they are detained or likely to be detained, under the Immigration Acts) there is a practical limitation of how likely a community order (or suspended sentence with some conditions) is to be imposed.

42 Sentencing Act 2020, ss 286–288.

43 There is a power in s 204A to impose a community order on someone who has been fined on three occasions for a non-imprisonable offence, but this is not yet in force.

2.81

A foreign national serving a prison sentence will be referred to as a Foreign National Prisoner (FNP). If they are detained under immigration powers following the conclusion of their custodial sentence, then they are referred to as a Foreign National Offender (FNO), although these terms will often be used interchangeably by most people.

2.82

A prison must facilitate a detainee in obtaining legal advice in relation to immigration matters. As well as private solicitors, there are organisations that detainees can be referred to such as PAS (Prisoners' Advice Service) and BID (Bail for Immigration Detainees).

Appeals

From the magistrates' court

2.83

Someone convicted in the magistrates' court has an automatic right of appeal to the Crown Court against sentence and (if they did not plead guilty) against conviction. This will be a re-hearing. Alternatively, a defendant (or the prosecutor) can appeal on a point of law to the Divisional Court.

From the Crown Court

2.84

An appeal lies for an appeal against conviction and/or sentence, with permission, to the Court of Appeal (Criminal Division)[44]. The deadline for appealing is 28 days from conviction or sentence, with separate time limits running for each (so if a person is convicted and adjourned for sentence, then the 28 days runs from the date of conviction, so it is not possible to wait until sentence is passed to decide whether to appeal the conviction).

2.85

There is no absolute right to appeal – reasons must be given as to why the applicant considers that there was an error in the original decision.

2.86

On an appeal against conviction, the test is whether the conviction is 'unsafe'. This is a wide provision, and is capable of covering a number of different

44 There are some exceptions, such as when a trial judge certifies that the case is fit for appeal or where the CCRC refers a case.

possibilities. Typical grounds would be that the judge gave the jury a wrong direction or that evidence was admitted that should not have been.

2.87

In immigration offences there are often particular issues that have caused difficulties such as the meaning of 'enter' in the facilitation offence[45], the difference between leave to enter and the dates of the offences meaning that the offending is charged under the wrong legislation[46].

2.88

Normally an appeal against conviction will follow from a trial, although a large number of immigration offences that have been considered by the Court of Appeal have come about in the context of appeals following guilty pleas. This is not a legal bar on an appeal against conviction, although it often will mean that there are evidential difficulties in pursuing an appeal.

2.89

The test on an appeal against sentence is whether the sentence is manifestly excessive or wrong in principle. The Court of Appeal are relatively flexible in an appeal against sentence, and are often willing to step back and look at the sentence imposed and whether it was a proper one in all the circumstances.

Appeals out of time/CCRC

2.90

There are strict time limits on appealing although, given the importance of what is at stake there is provision for appealing out of time. When someone no longer has the right to appeal to the Court of Appeal, then they can apply to the Criminal Cases Review Commission (CCRC). Both areas are given further consideration in Chapter 10.

Paperwork

Record keeping

2.91

In the Crown Court, all proceedings are recorded, and it is generally possible to get transcripts of a whole trial if needed. To obtain a transcript it is necessary to complete and submit an EX107 Form (the MoJ provides guidance notes, and there are a number of different transcription companies). The cost depends on how long the transcript required is, as well as how urgent it is and whether it has

45 See, inter alia, *Kakaei* [2021] EWCA Crim 503 and *Bani* [2021] EWCA Crim 1958.
46 *Boateng* [2016] EWCA Crim 57, [2016] 4 WLR 70.

previously been transcribed (in whole or in part). The transcript can be obtained quickly (within 24 hours if there is a need for urgency). The availability of a transcript is separate to the question of funding and, at the stage of an appeal out of time, the LAA will generally not pay for a full transcript of the evidence and it would be limited to the summing up[47].

2.92

Magistrates' court hearings are not recorded, but it is still possible to apply to the court for some information about the case[48]. In practice, the best way of finding information will be to obtain the file from the previous solicitors dealing with the case.

2.93

It is possible to make a Subject Access Request ('SAR') for a client to the CPS[49] and the police.

2.94

Finally, with cases that are heard in the Court of Appeal or Divisional Court there will almost always be a written judgment that is available through one of the legal reporting services.

A criminal file

2.95

Over time the criminal courts have moved away from paper towards a more digital way of working.

2.96

This has the advantage in meaning that there can be a much higher level of confidence that the papers that are obtained are complete. However, advisors who are advising clients who were convicted many years ago may face difficulties in ensuring that they have all the material needed.

DCS (Digital Case System)

2.97

Almost all Crown Court cases will now use the 'DCS'. This is a digital platform that can be used by the judiciary, defence and prosecution, as well as

47 See, in relation to CCRC cases, Standard Crime Contract 2022, para 11.23.
48 CPR r 5.9.
49 Currently to the Information Access Team (IAT@cps.gov.uk).

other court users (such as Probation Officers). This makes the case of a new representative much easier, as they will then have direct access to most of the papers. This will contain a lot of material that relates to the procedural aspects of the case. As well as the case-management forms, there is a 'side bar' which contains comments from the judge and the advocates as to the procedure of the case.

Unused material

2.98

Every criminal case will have 'unused' material. This is material generated during a police investigation, but not used by the prosecution (examples would be witnesses spoken to but not called, CCTV, etc). The law is that this material must be retained and considered. A summary will be put into a schedule and that material that is capable of undermining the prosecution case or assisting the defence case must be disclosed. This is an ongoing process, with one of the purposes of a Defence Statement being to obtain more by way of disclosure from the CPS. Depending on the age of the case, this material may be on the DCS.

2.99

A police investigation will generate a 'Crime Report' (sometimes called a CRIS – Crime Reporting Information System), which is a log of all actions taken by the OIC (Officer in the Case – the police officer designated to be in charge of overseeing the investigation). With an immigration case that is investigated by the Home Office, it will likely be overseen by an Investigator from Immigration Enforcement. The same obligations of disclosure will apply, although the recording systems are different. Immigration Officers use 'CLUE 3' as an electronic management system. It is generally called 'CLUE' and is used by a number of different agencies (including some police forces) to process data relating to criminal investigations.

2.100

The Home Office also use PRONTO ('Police Report and Notebook Organiser) which is now generally used as a mobile phone 'app'. It is a form of electronic 'pocket notebook' that will be used to log actions, searches, etc, during an investigation. For example, a conversation with a suspect should be logged on PRONTO in a way that a police officer in days gone by would have done so in their pocket notebook[50].

50 Further guidance on the use of PRONTO (and the investigation of criminal offences generally) can be found in 'Dealing with potential criminality (ICE teams), v.2 (23 February 2023).

Defence file

2.101

A defence solicitor will still have a separate file relating to a criminal case that contains correspondence, file notes, etc. This should certainly be requested by a new firm instructed on a criminal matter, but it may well be useful to a practitioner dealing with an immigration matter. Especially as many criminal appeals will involve a waiver of privilege, it is important that practitioners are fully aware of what material has been collected.

Legal aid

2.102

Legal aid is available in criminal case in a far more comprehensive way than in other areas of law (due, in part, to the obligations imposed by Art 6 of the ECHR). An applicant must satisfy both the merits and means test. In order to be able to provide legal aid, a firm needs to have a contract with the LAA.

2.103

At the police station on arrest there is no means test regardless of the person's income or savings. This is due to the short period of time that people can be held, which would cause a large number of difficulties given the potential complexities in resolving entitlement. A person is, of course, entitled to pay privately, although this will be more likely to happen where someone attends by appointment (or for a second interview) and have had time to arrange this.

2.104

There is a merits test, but any imprisonable offence (other than drink driving related ones) will automatically qualify[51]. Even then, there are a number of exceptions that will bring the case within scope.

2.105

There is a Duty Solicitor scheme that operates 24 hours a day throughout the year, and can provide a solicitor (or qualified Police Station Representative) to provide telephone or in-person advice. A person can request a duty solicitor, or a representative from a nominated firm with a criminal contract. Part of the responsibilities of the police on detention is to help facilitate the provision of legal advice.

---

51 See paras 9.8–9.13 Standard Crime Contract Specification 2022.

2.106

At the magistrates' court and the Crown Court it is necessary to make an application for legal aid. This is currently on a Crim 14 form that is available online (although this will be arranged by the criminal solicitor).

2.107

The merits test will be deemed to have been met in all cases in the Crown Court, apart from an appeal against conviction, where full details will need to be given. In cases where there has to be substantive consideration to the merits of a case there are a number of different criteria to take into account[52].

2.108

In relation to the means test, the exact calculation is complex and depends on a number of factors including whether the applicant has a partner and children (and their ages). In certain cases, there will need to be a 'full means testing' procedure to confirm eligibility. However, people on some benefits will be passported.

2.109

Where the case is in the Crown Court, even if eligible for legal aid, the person may need to make a contribution as the case goes along (although this will be refundable if they are acquitted). The Crown Court does not have power itself to grant legal aid, except in a small number of stand alone cases[53].

2.110

The legal aid order in the Crown Court covers an advice on appeal by the trial advocate and, if applicable, the drafting and lodging of grounds of appeal. Legal aid will be granted by the Court of Appeal if permission is granted. Where a case has finished (including with an appeal), there is provision for legal aid for a review of the case by another provider. Generally, there must be a reason for seeking a second opinion. Advice and assistance can be applied for using the CRM2 form.

List of acronyms/shorthands

2.111

CPS	Crown Prosecution Service
CRIS	Crime Report (Crime Reporting Information System)

52 These are set out in Legal Aid, Sentencing and Punishment of Offenders Act 2012, s 17(2) and repeated as a checkbox list, in the legal aid form that is completed.

53 Contempt of Court proceedings, breach of a Crown Court Order (where there is not sufficient time to arrange a solicitor) and bench warrants (where legal aid is not already in place). In these cases there is no means test.

FCMH	Further Case Management Hearing – a review between the PTPH and trial
FNO	Foreign National Offender
FNP	Foreign National Prisoner
OIC	Officer in the Case – police officer in charge of overseeing a police investigation
PNC	Police National Computer – it will always be used as a shorthand for the printout provided that contains someone's criminal record history
PDH	Plea and Directions Hearing – the 'old' name for a PTPH
PSR	Pre-Sentence Report
PTPH	Plea and Trial Preparation Hearing – first appearance in the Crown Court
S 51	the method by which most cases will be sent from the magistrates' court to the Crown Court (a reference to the legislative provisions in the Crime and Disorder Act 1998, s 51)
SOPC	Sentence of Particular Concern

3 Document offences

Introduction

3.1

This chapter provides an overview of the main serious (ie, imprisonable) document offences that are likely to be found in practice. Other document offences (some of which are imprisonable, but less likely to be prosecuted) are considered in Chapter 7. Some are only capable of being committed by non-British nationals, whilst others can be committed by anybody, although the focus here will be on offences committed in an immigration context.

False passport offences

Historical Note

3.2

The offence of using a false passport will be charged under the following Acts, depending on the date of commission:

- 21 January 2011 onwards – the Identity Documents Act 2010, s 4
- 7 June 2006 to 20 January 2011 – the Identity Cards Act 2006, s 25
- Prior to 7 June 2006[1] – the Forgery and Counterfeiting Act 1981, s 3

3.3

Especially as offences may come to light many years after the date of commission, care must be taken to ensure that the correct offence is charged as otherwise any conviction will be bound to be unsafe[2].

1 The Forgery & Counterfeiting Act (at least as it related to identity documents) was repealed by Identity Cards Act 2006, s 44 when the 2006 Act received Royal Assent on 30 March 2006. This appeared to leave a lacuna whereby it was not a criminal offence to have or use a false passport. This was filled by the Divisional Court in *R (CPS v Bow Street Magistrates' Court)* [2006] EWHC 1763 (Admin), [2007] 1 WLR 291, where it was held that this was an obvious drafting error, that the Court could fill. Subsequently, s 25 was formally brought into force on 7 June 2006 by The Identity Cards Act 2006 (Commencement No 1) Order 2006.

2 *R v Boateng* [2016] EWCA Crim 57, [2016] 4 WLR 70, following on from *R v Abdul* [2012] EWCA Crim 1788. Note that in *Idhoiaissine* [2015] EWCA Crim 1872 this view was doubted, or at least left open for another day. This was not referred to in the judgment in *Boateng*, and it may be that the Court of Appeal would revisit this in a suitable case.

3.4

The 2006 Act was introduced to pave the way for a national identity register for all people (British citizens or otherwise) in the United Kingdom. However, repeal of this was included in the Conservative-Liberal Democrat Coalition Agreement following the Hung Parliament in the 2010 General Election and it was, in fact, the first Government Bill introduced to the new Parliament.

Definitions

3.5

It is, unsurprisingly, a criminal offence to have a false passport, whether or not it is used. The offence, as currently drafted under the Identity Documents Act 2010, is created by s 4:

> **'Possession of false identity documents etc with improper intention**
>
> (1) It is an offence for a person ("P") with an improper intention to have in P's possession or under P's control—
>
> (a) an identity document that is false and that P knows or believes to be false,
>
> (b) an identity document that was improperly obtained and that P knows or believes to have been improperly obtained, or
>
> (c) an identity document that relates to someone else.
>
> (2) Each of the following is an improper intention—
>
> (a) the intention of using the document for establishing personal information about P;
>
> (b) the intention of allowing or inducing another to use it for establishing, ascertaining or verifying personal information about P or anyone else.
>
> (3) In subsection (2)(b) the reference to P or anyone else does not include, in the case of a document within subsection (1)(c), the individual to whom it relates.'

An 'Identity Document' is defined in s 7(1) as:

> '(a) an immigration document,
>
> (b) a United Kingdom passport (within the meaning of the Immigration Act 1971),
>
> (c) a passport issued by or on behalf of the authorities of a country or territory outside the United Kingdom or by or on behalf of an international organisation,

(d) a document that can be used (in some or all circumstances) instead of a passport,

(e) a licence to drive a motor vehicle granted under Part 3 of the Road Traffic 1988 or under Part 2 of the Road Traffic (Northern Ireland) Order 1981, or

(f) a driving licence issued by or on behalf of the authorities of a country or territory outside the United Kingdom.'

With 'immigration document' defined further in s 7(2) as:

'(a) a document used for confirming,

(i) the right of a person at a time before IP completion day under the EU Treaties[3] in respect of entry or residence in the United Kingdom, or

(ii) the right of a person under the Immigration (European Economic Area) Regulations 2016 (as they continue to have effect by virtue of the Citizens' Rights (Application Deadline and Temporary Protection) (EU Exit) Regulations 2020) in respect of entry or residence in the United Kingdom[4],

(b) a document that is given in exercise of immigration functions and records information about leave granted to a person to enter or to remain in the United Kingdom, or

(c) a registration card (within the meaning of section 26A of the Immigration Act 1971).

'Personal Information' is defined in s8:

(1) (a) A's full name,

(b) other names by which A is or has previously been known,

(c) A's gender,

(d) A's date and place of birth,

(e) external characteristics of A that are capable of being used for identifying A,

(f) the address of A's principal place of residence in the United Kingdom,

(g) the address of every other place in the United Kingdom or elsewhere where A has a place of residence,

---

3 Further defined in s 7(2A) as '(2A) In subsections 2(a)(i) 'EU Treaties' includes a reference to those Treaties so far as applicable to and in the United Kingdom by virtue of Part 4 of the EU withdrawal agreement.'

4 Prior to 31 December 2020, s 7(a) read 'a document used for confirming, the right of a person under the EU Treaties in respect of entry or residence in the United Kingdom'.

(h) where in the United Kingdom and elsewhere A has previously been resident,

(I) the times at which A was resident at different places in the United Kingdom or elsewhere,

(j) A's current residential status,

(k) residential statuses previously held by A, and

(l) information about numbers allocated to A for identification purposes and about the documents (including stamps or labels) to which they relate.

(2) In subsection (1) "residential status" means—

(a) A's nationality,

(b) A's entitlement to remain in the United Kingdom, and

(c) if that entitlement derives from a grant of leave to enter or remain in the United Kingdom, the terms and conditions of that leave.'

Meaning of Identity Document

3.6

The definition covers almost every document that could be used as a passport, or in lieu of a passport (and a few more besides). As well as passports, it includes any 'document that can be used (in some or all circumstances) instead of a passport'. This appears extremely wide, and must be read with some sort of restriction as to the reasonableness of whether a passport would truly by required.

3.7

A passport issued by an authority that is not recognised by the UK would likely be covered by 'territory' in the Identity Documents Act 2010, s 7(1)(c). In any event, it would come with the 'catch all' subsection (d).

3.8

It has not been determined whether a National Insurance Card was an Identity Document as it contains no means of identifying the bearer[5], although it is arguably 'information about numbers allocated to A for identification purposes and about the documents (including stamps or labels) to which they relate'[6]. The intention of the Identity Documents Act 2010 was to 'simply re-enact [the offences]' as they were under the 2006 Act, but recognising the abolition of ID Cards[7].

5 A National Insurance Number was a registerable fact under the 2006 Act – Sch 1, para 4(1)(c)..
6 Documents Act 2010, s 8(l).
7 Lynne Featherstone (Parliamentary Under Secretary of State), Public Bill Committee, 06 July 2010.

3.9

In *R v Osunderu*[8] there had been guilty pleas to three Counts, Count 3 being possession of a false National Insurance Card (under the 2006 Act, with a near identical definition). Nothing was said about this in the Court of Appeal, although the conviction was quashed as the date of the offence meant that that offence was charged under the wrong section. Further it seems to have been initiated as an appeal against sentence only. This can be contrasted with *R v Oniya*[9] where the false card was charged as being an article for use in fraud.

3.10

The last plastic National Insurance Cards were issued in 2011, and so this will likely be less of an issue as time passes. If it arises, it may be that a charge under the Fraud Act 2007, s 6 would be more appropriate. Although there is a lower maximum sentence (five years instead of ten), it is likely that this would be more than sufficient for most cases.

Meaning of 'false'

3.11

Under the legislation, a document can be 'false' in three ways (Identity Documents Act 2010, s 4(1)):

(a) an identity document that is false and that P knows or believes to be false,

(b) an identity document that was improperly obtained and that P knows or believes to have been improperly obtained, or

(c) an identity document that relates to someone else.

3.12

For the purposes of Identity Documents Act 2010, s 4(1)(b), a document is 'improperly obtained' if (s 9(3)):

(a) false information was provided in, or in connection with, the application for its issue to the person who issued it, or

(b) false information was provided in, or in connection with, an application for its modification to a person entitled to modify it.

3.13

A genuine passport with a forged stamp in it will be a false document by virtue of s 9(5) – 'References to the making of a false identity document include the modification of an identity document so that it becomes false', this being a s 4(1)(a) offence.

8 [2011] EWCA Crim 3122.
9 [2012 EWCA Crim 2883.

3.14

A passport, or stamp that is obtained by deception, but is contained within a genuine passport will also be false, but under the Identity Documents Act 2010, s 4(1)(b).

3.15

By virtue of subsection (c), the document need not be 'false' in any normal sense of the word. The statute covers a genuine document that is being used by a person other than the one who it belongs to. The position of a person who holds a genuine document on behalf of another for them to use themselves is specifically exempted from liability (Identity Documents Act 2010, s 4(1)(3)).

Intention

3.16

'Intention' is a plain English word. In *R v YY*[10], YY 'presented himself to an immigration desk … together with an Israeli passport … When the immigration officer challenged him as to whether that passport was genuine, he admitted that it was false' and claimed asylum. The CPS accepted that there was no 'improper intent', on the basis that he had handed the passport over and not tried to pretend that it was his.

3.17

This was noted without comment by the Court of Appeal, although it may be that, especially where the passport is handed to Immigration Officer, that would be sufficient to prove the requisite intention.

Sentencing

3.18

The offence is indictable only, with a maximum sentence of ten years. There are no Guidelines from the Sentencing Council. For use of a false passport at the UK border, 'the appropriate sentence, even on a guilty plea, by a person of good character, should now usually be within the range of 12 to 18 months', even on a plea of guilty, and has been since at least *Kolawole*[11].

3.19

In reality, the lower end of that tariff is generally the starting point taken by most judges. In Court centres near to international airports (and other international ports) where many of these cases are seen, the sentences are frequently lower

10 [2016] EWCA Crim 18, [2016] 1 Cr App R 28.
11 [2004] EWCA Crim 3047.

(with 8–10 months being commonplace). However, if a sentence is passed in the above 12–18 months range, then it is unlikely to be successfully appealed.

3.20

A critical distinction is drawn between where the passport was used to enter the country (and thereby to evade immigration controls), and for ancillary purposes (such as someone with no status to obtain work illegally).

3.21

After different constitutions of the Court of Appeal came to differing conclusions on this point, the distinction was confirmed in the case of *Ovieriakhi*[12]. Ms Ovieriakhi pleaded guilty to an offence under the 2006 Act. She was a Zimbabwean national who had arrived in the UK legally and overstayed. She obtained employment at a nursing home.

3.22

The court concluded (paras 15 and 16):

> '15. At one end of the scale is the use or possession for use of false passports for the purpose of evading, or enabling others to evade, the controls on entry into the United Kingdom. Such evasion may at worst be for terrorist or other malign purposes, or at least for the purpose of securing the entry of someone into the United Kingdom which would otherwise be forbidden. The documents may be possessed by those whose business it is to help others to circumvent the rules on entry. At the other end of the scale is the use by someone who is lawfully in the United Kingdom of a document other than a passport for the purpose of obtaining employment or a bank account.
>
> 16. Where, however, a false passport is used to obtain work or a bank account, its use does not enable the offender to obtain entry to the United Kingdom and for that reason it may properly be treated less severely than the use of a passport which does, or may, have that effect. What the use of a passport to obtain work does, however, do is to facilitate the offender remaining in the United Kingdom in breach of immigration controls. For that reason a custodial sentence is usually required. But it can justifiably be less, particularly if the offender is of good character and has done no more than use or try to use it to seek employment in order to maintain himself/herself or his/her family.'

3.23

Drawing that together, the court said that 'there is a valid distinction to be made between use of a false passport to gain entry and its use to gain work', and

12 [2009] EWCA Crim 452.

substituted a sentence of six months. This (with full credit for a plea of guilty) has now become the standard starting point, for in-country use of a passport.

3.24

It is not fixed (*Overieriakhi* establishes a continuum from 6 to 12 months rather than a fixed tariff), and it still leave a number of cases that are grey areas. A paradigm example being where the charge relates to in-country use, and it is clear that there has been an illegal entry, but there is no Count on the indictment in relation to that. For example, in *Owolabi*[13] the appellant received a 12-month sentence for two counts of possession of a false ID document with intent. This related to possession of a counterfeit Nigerian Passport with a counterfeit Indefinite Leave to Remain stamp (which she used to try to open a bank account) and a counterfeit British passport that she had on her on arrest. She had not entered the UK lawfully.

3.25

The sentence was upheld (on a plea of guilty), it was said:

(1) The appellant had two false passports and she pleaded guilty to both counts of having them with intent.

(2) It seems clear, at least so far as concerns the entry into this country in 2009, she had entered illegally.

(3) The matter could no doubt have been clarified by the appellant but she has wholly resisted doing so. We accept that there was legal advice not to answer the questions, but, in consequence, we have nothing from her in evidential form which could assist in clarifying how she obtained the passports and when she did so.

3.26

On that basis, 'although the evidence does not establish that the two passports were used to gain entry illegally into this country, the inference is irresistible that they have nonetheless been used to circumvent immigration control in enabling her to live and work here'. Whilst this makes sense, it is a fine line between inflating the sentence because of the surrounding circumstances, to move to sentencing for offences not indicted[14]. In *Owolabi*, the passports were indicted as being used in relation to a bank account, with the argument being that this is part and parcel of living an 'illegal' life, but not related to the illegal entry, and therefore the 12-month sentence was excessive.

---

13 [2012] EWCA Crim 1853, [2013] 1 Cr App R(S) 99.

14 As to the importance in the general criminal law to sentence only on what is proved or admitted see, *inter alia*, *Nottingham Crown Court, ex p DPP* [1996] 1 Cr App R(S) 283 and *Chadderton* (1980) 2 Cr App R(S) 272.

3.27

In *Acheampong*[15] it was held that there was a further distinction to be drawn between those who had never been in the UK legally (who could expect a sentence somewhere between *Overieriakhi* and *Kolawole*) and those who had at some point been lawfully present (with presumably a further distinction for those who entered lawfully) at some time, which were 'true' *Overieriakhi* cases.

'Sham' marriages

3.28

In cases of individuals who enter into 'sham marriages' in-country for the purpose of evading immigration control, they will be sentenced on the same basis as *Kolawole*[16] with a guideline of 12–18 months on a guilty plea. This would be the case for both parties whether they are the one with status in the United Kingdom or the one seeking it.

Driving licences

3.29

For offences that involve driving licences, a significantly shorter sentence is appropriate, even though many will attract an immediate custodial sentence (four months for using a false driving licence in *Hoxha*[17], being a typical example).

3.30

The offences under the 2006 and 2010 Acts are both indictable only, whilst the FCA offences are either way. It is unclear why this was changed, but it would appear that this was as a result of a greater level of concern about immigration.

Possession of a false passport

3.31

On the face of it, what distinguishes the offences of simple possession is the ulterior intent. However, it is slightly more complicated than this. Although on the face of it, it is hard to see why someone would have a false passport *without* the relevant intention, there are a number of reasons why it would be proper to charge this offence. The offence includes false documents that are passed their expiry date so they cannot be used. In addition, there might be reasons for having a false identity document to prove something other than 'personal information' as defined in the Act.

15 [2015] EWCA Crim 1894.
16 Examples include *Kuku* [2010] EWCA Crim 2533 and *Gambo* [2011] EWCA Crim 491.
17 [2012] EWCA Crim 1765.

Legislation

3.32

The offence is defined under the Identity Documents Act 2010, s 6(1):

> It is an offence for a person ("P"), without reasonable excuse, to have in P's possession or under P's control—
>
> (a) an identity document that is false,
>
> (b) an identity document that was improperly obtained,
>
> (c) an identity document that relates to someone else,
>
> (d) any apparatus which, to P's knowledge, is or has been specially designed or adapted for the making of false identity documents, or
>
> (e) any article or material which, to P's knowledge, is or has been specially designed or adapted to be used in the making of such documents.

Intention

3.33

In *Jamalov*[18], when asked for identification by the police after a road traffic accident, the appellant had produced a fake Czech driving licence, but with his correct name. He pleaded guilty to the s 25(1) offence under the Identity Cards Act 2006. On appeal against conviction it was argued that the licence did not come within the Act as it contained his correct details, and it was not therefore being used to establish any false 'registrable facts'. The appeal was dismissed as:

> 'When asked whether he had any identification, he produced the false driving licence. By his plea of guilty, he was admitting his intention to use the false driving licence for the purposes of establishing who he was.'

3.34

Therefore, whilst the question of whether someone is lawfully allowed to drive is *not* a registerable fact, where someone has a false driving licence that he intends to use to establish something that *is* a registerable fact (such as his identity) then he will be guilty of the s 4 offence. On that basis then presumably had J produced his genuine passport in response to the police officer's request for identification, and had only then produced the fake driving licence in response to a further question as to whether he could drive, it would appear that he would be guilty only of the s 6 offence.

18 [2010] EWCA Crim 309, [2010] 2 Cr App R 4.

Defences

3.35

Although knowledge or belief in falsity is required for s 4 and not for s 6, this does not create an entirely strict liability offence as there is a 'reasonable excuse' defence in s 6. Belief that the false document is a genuine one is not sufficient, of itself, to be a complete defence. However, it is a relevant factor in deciding whether a reasonable excuse is established:

> 'although the fact that the defendant does not know or believe that the document is false is not of itself and without more a reasonable excuse, a defendant is entitled to ask the jury to consider objectively whether he has a reasonable excuse for possessing the material and for not having destroyed it or handed it in to the authorities, and the fact that he does not know or believe that it is a false document, because of the circumstances in which it has been obtained, may well have a bearing on that question[19].'

3.36

The reasoning of the Court of Appeal appears to reveal a concern that someone who had an unreasonable (but genuine) belief in the genuineness of a document may escape liability altogether[20].

3.37

Whilst it may not be clear why a belief in the genuineness of the document that someone has is not an entire defence, especially given the seriousness of the offence (it is imprisonable rather than being a regulatory, or quasi-criminal one, that would likely lead to a fine), the Court of Appeal concluded that this followed from the House of Lord's judgment in *R v G*[21].

3.38

As was said in *Perrin v The Commissioners for Her Majesty's Revenue and Customs*[22]:

> 'in the criminal sphere there is a long line of the highest authority to the effect that the concept of "reasonable excuse" includes a requirement that the excuse in question should be objectively reasonable.'

---

19 *Unah* [2011] EWCA Crim 1837, [2012] 1 WLR 545, decided under the 2006 Act, but would be applicable to the 2010 Act.

20 For example someone who states that he obtained his passport from someone he met in a pub without passing any of the expected checks.

21 [2009] UKHL 13, [2010] 1 AC 43. The ECtHR considered this in relation to one of the appellants in the House of Lords in *Jobe v United Kingdom* (2011) 53 EHRR SE17 where the application was made in relation to alleged breaches of Arts 7 and 10, but not Art 6.
Further, recent support for this is found (in the context of the offensive weapon legislation) in *Garry v CPS* [2019] EWHC 636 (Admin), [2019] 2 Cr App R 4.

22 [2018] UKUT 0156 (TCC).

3.39

See also *Garry v CPS*[23], where it was said:

> '16. A tribunal of fact has a wide discretion in determining whether reasonable excuse is made out. An innocent purpose for having an offensive weapon in a public place does not equate to a reasonable excuse, rather the court is entitled to consider necessity or immediate temporal connection between possession and purpose for which it is carried. In this case the evidence did not lead to a finding of fact that for the quotidian tasks of opening access panels and stripping aluminium sheathing no other implement would suffice.'

3.40

In any trial, the fact that a defendant's explanation is implausible would no doubt go to the likelihood of his account being accepted by the jury, although it would be a rare case where this should be withdrawn from the jury[24].

Sentence

3.41

Simple possession is an either way offence, with a maximum sentence of two years. There are no Sentencing Guidelines or guideline case, but clearly the lower maximum sentence means that a lower sentence can be expected than for the offence of possession with intent. Further, there tends to be a greater range of sentences that are passed for this offence.

3.42

Sentences as high as eight months have been passed (reduced from 12 in *Vargas*[25]), although this should probably be seen as an outlier. It is hard to see how, absent some very unusual circumstances, a sentence higher that the six months in *Overieriakhi* could be justified (see *Marques*[26] as one such example – 12 months for possession of six blank, forged Italian passport covers). In general, these cases can be dealt with in the magistrates' court (*Jamalov*) and a suspended sentence or Community Order is appropriate in many cases (*Li* [2012] EWCA Crim 1052).

3.43

Cases where a defendant has an expired passport should not be sentenced on the basis that they had previously been used without a count on the indictment

23 [2019] EWHC 636 (Admin), [2019] 2 Cr App R 4.
24 *Unah*, at [6].
25 [2011] EWCA Crim 2482.
26 [2014] EWCA Crim 1078.

to reflect this. Care must be taken that there is no suggestion that a defendant is being sentenced for possession with intent, and be true to the indictment. It also follows from this that the prosecution must be careful before accepting a plea to the lesser offence (*Goodings*[27]).

3.44

Should a false driving licence, that has less value as an immigration document for international travel, attract a lower sentence? On the basis of the purpose of the legislation, and the sentence typically passed for the s 4 offence, this would appear to be a proper distinction to be drawn.

Possessing equipment to make false documents

3.45

Under the Identity Documents Act 2010, s 5:

> '(1) It is an offence for a person ("P") with the prohibited intention to make or to have in P's possession or under P's control—
>
> > (a) any apparatus which, to P's knowledge, is or has been specially designed or adapted for the making of false identity documents, or
> >
> > (b) any article or material which, to P's knowledge, is or has been specially designed or adapted to be used in the making of such documents.
>
> (2) The prohibited intention is the intention—
>
> > (a) that P or another will make a false identity document, and
> >
> > (b) that the document will be used by somebody for establishing, ascertaining or verifying personal information about a person.'

Sentence

3.46

The maximum sentence is ten years' imprisonment. The offence is triable only. There are no guidelines from the Sentencing Council, or from the Court of Appeal. It is a little charged offence and does not appear to have been considered by the Court of Appeal. Some guidance can be drawn from cases where people have been sentenced for similar activity, but charged under other legislation.

27 [2012] EWCA Crim 2586.

3.47

In *Mihaylov*[28] it was said[29]:

> It is clear that cases of this sort are highly fact-sensitive, but in cases of very large-scale production of false identity cards and passports, organisers can expect sentences near the 10 year maximum after a trial. Workers and lieutenants should receive sentences in the order of six-and-a-half years.

3.48

In passing sentence a judge should consider:

> the role of the offender in the operation, its scale and the sophistication of its products, the type of false documents being manufactured, the damage caused in terms of the distribution of false documents and the income generated[30].

3.49

Historically this offence would typically be committed by someone who was part of an organised crime group or similar. However, as technology has moved on it is now more likely that an individual is able to use modern computers to produce high-quality false documents. Although the references to 'apparatus' and 'article or material' would not appear to be designed with a computer and printer in mind, it is likely that it would cover such a scenario. However, in that case it is likely that there would be other offences committed.

Entering without a passport (AI(TC)A 2004, s 2)

Legislation

3.50

Around the turn of the century there were increasing concerns that asylum seekers were boarding international flights to come to the United Kingdom using forged documents and disposing of these mid-journey[31]. This would sometimes be by ripping them up or otherwise throwing them away, but more often it would be that an agent (the people smuggler engaged by the asylum seeker) would accompany them and retrieve the document, both to make it harder for the authorities to track their activities, but also because such documents were valuable in their own right.

28 [2014] EWCA Crim 624.

29 At [10]. Adopting the words of Silber J in *Velvev* [2009] 1 Cr App R(S) 96.

30 *Mussa* [2012] EWCA Crim 693 at [11].

31 It was concerns over undocumented passengers that had previously led to the Carriers Liability Scheme, which led to the increase in the use of false passports.

3.51

These concerns led to an attempt to dissuade such behaviour by criminalising it. The offence is under AI(TC)A 2004, s 2[32]:

'(1) A person commits an offence if at a leave or asylum interview he does not have with him an immigration document which –

(a) is in force, and

(b) satisfactorily establishes his identity and nationality or citizenship.

...

(3) But a person does not commit an offence under subsection (1) or (2) if—

(a) the interview referred to in that subsection takes place after the person has entered the United Kingdom, and

(b) within the period of three days beginning with the date of the interview the person provides to an immigration officer or to the Secretary of State a document of the kind referred to in that subsection.

(4) It is a defence for a person charged with an offence under subsection (1)—

(a) to prove that he is[33] —

(i) an Irish citizen,

(ii) has leave to enter or remain in the United Kingdom which was granted by virtue of residence scheme immigration rules, or

(iii) is a frontier worker within the meaning of regulation 3 of the Citizens' Rights (Frontier Workers) (EU Exit) Regulations 2020,

(c) To prove that he has a reasonable excuse for not being in possession of a document of the kind specified in subsection (1),

(d) To produce a false immigration document and to prove that he used that document as an immigration document for all purposes in connection with his journey to the United Kingdom, or

32 The Home Office provides guidance as to their interpretation of the offence in 'Prosecution under section 2: failure to produce immigration document' v.4 (20 May 2020).

33 This used to provide a defence to an EEA national or, in certain circumstance, a family member of an EEA national.

(e) To prove that he travelled to the United Kingdom without, at any stage since he set out on the journey, having possession of an immigration document.

(6) Where the charge for an offence under subsection (1) or (2) relates to an interview which takes place after the defendant has entered the United Kingdom –

(a) subsection (4)(c) and (5)(c) shall not apply, but

(b) it is a defence for the defendant to prove that he has a reasonable excuse for not providing a document in accordance with subsection (3).

(7) For the purposes of subsections (4) to (6) –

(a) the fact that a document was deliberately destroyed or disposed of is not a reasonable excuse for not being in possession of it or for not providing it in accordance with subsection (3), unless it is shown that the destruction or disposal was –

(i) for a reasonable cause, or

(ii) beyond the control of the person charged with the offence, and

(b) in paragraph (a)(i) "reasonable cause" does not include the purpose of –

(i) delaying the handling or resolution of a claim or application or the taking of a decision,

(ii) increasing the chances of success of a claim or application, or

(iii) complying with instructions or advice given by a person who offers advice about, or facilitates, immigration into the United Kingdom, unless in the circumstances of the case it is unreasonable to expect non-compliance with the instructions or advice.'

3.52

As was noted by the then Lord Chief Justice in *Thet v DPP* [2006] EWHC 2701 (Admin), the 'draftsmanship of the section leaves much to be desired'. This is, if anything, an understatement, as anyone who has grappled with the section can vouch.

3.53

In recent years, there appears to have been a sharp drop in prosecutions for this offence. It is not known whether this will be permanent or not, but the introduction of IA 1971, s 24(D1) (and, when it is in force, s 24(E1)) would appear to cover the purpose of the s 2 offence in much simpler form. In addition, it is also either way and has a higher maximum sentence, as well as a less complex legal structure. For that reason, it may be that the CPS would charge that offence instead.

Definitions

3.54

The offence is set out in s 2(1) – not having a passport at a 'leave or asylum' interview. A 'leave or asylum interview' means (s 12) an interview with an immigration officer or an official of the Secretary of State at which a person—

> '(a) seeks leave to enter or remain in the United Kingdom, or
>
> (b) claims that to remove him from or require him to leave the United Kingdom would breach the United Kingdom's obligations under the Refugee Convention or would be unlawful under section 6 of the Human Rights Act 1998 (c. 42) as being incompatible with his Convention rights.'

3.55

The term 'immigration document' for the purposes of subsection 1 is defined in subsection 12. An 'immigration document' means—

> '(a) a passport, and
>
> (b) a document which relates to a national of a State other than the United Kingdom and which is designed to serve the same purpose as a passport.'

3.56

This should be contrasted with the concept of a 'false immigration document' in s 2(13):

> '(a) a document which purports to be, or is designed to look like, an immigration document, is a false immigration document, and
>
> (b) an immigration document is a false immigration document if and in so far as it is used
>
> (i) outside the period for which it is expressed to be valid,
>
> (ii) contrary to provision for its use made by the person issuing it, or
>
> (iii) by or in respect of a person other than the person to or for whom it was issued.'

3.57

The reference in s 2(1) to a 'passport' therefore means a genuine passport. This follows from *Thet* and *Mohammed & Osman*[34]. The latter being a judgment

34 [2007] EWCA Crim 2332, [2008] 1 Cr App R 20.

that considered *Thet* and, to one extent, determined that the interpretation of 'immigration document' in s 2(4)(e) should not be followed.

3.58

The offence can be committed in two different circumstances, as reflected in subsections (4) and (6). This depends on whether the defendant has 'entered' the United Kingdom (with 'enter' given its legal meaning) at the point of the interview.

3.59

In practice, someone who claims asylum at a port of entry will come under s 2(4), someone who comes in on false papers, or clandestinely, and claims asylum at a later stage, will have to rely on the defence under s 2(6). There is also a parallel offence for someone who attends an interview without a document for a dependent child.

General defences

3.60

The s 31 defence does *not* apply to this offence. In *Embaye*[35], the Crown accepted that 'the offence created by section 2 of the 2004 Act falls within the ambit of' Article 31. However, this concession was not investigated, as the court concluded that it was up to Parliament how to incorporate (or not incorporate) Art 31, and therefore this would not assist the Appellant in any event. What the position would be following the House of Lord's judgment in *Asfaw* is unclear.

Defences – interview at point of entry (under s 2(4))

3.61

There are three separate defences contained in s 2(4)(c)–(e). The defence under (d) is straightforward; anyone who travels on a false document to the UK, and then produces it, will have a defence.

3.62

They would then *prima facie* be committing an offence under the Identity Documents Act 2010 (which is more serious in terms of maximum sentence). However, as they will almost inevitably be claiming asylum, then they may well have the s 31 defence to the passport charge.

35 [2005] EWCA Crim 2865.

3.63

In relation to (e), notwithstanding that the defence refers to 'immigration document' this was held to not be an 'immigration document' as defined in s 2(12), as this would defeat the purpose of the legislation (as it would), but rather 'an immigration document, *or false immigration document*' should be read in to it.

3.64

As stated by the former Lord Chief Justice, the drafting of this offence is not happy. It can be assumed that Parliament's intention was clear – s 2 should have read '"an immigration document, *or false immigration document*", but in *Thet* he felt unable to ignore the plain words of the statute. As to (c), see below for 'reasonable excuse'.

Defences – interview after entry (s 2(6))

3.65

Someone who claims asylum in-country has a three-day 'grace period' within which to submit their genuine document (s 2(3)). Section 2(6) disapplies the reasonable excuse defence under s 2(4)(c), but it is then re-enacted in the same terms, but to cover the situation where somebody has a reasonable excuse to not provide their genuine document within the grace period.

Reasonable excuse

3.66

This defence of reasonable excuse places a legal, rather than an evidential, one on the defendant (*Embaye*).

3.67

Following *Thet* and *Mohammed*, the position is that if someone is unable to produce their own document because they do not have it in the UK to be produced, then this is capable of constituting a reasonable excuse.

3.68

In *Thet*, the appellant was a Burmese dissident who could not obtain a passport from his home country due to his political activity. In *Mohammed*, the appellants were Somalis where there was no functioning state who could have issued either of them a passport. These were both held to be capable of being reasonable excuses.

3.69

El Hudarey[36], concerned a Libyan who had his own passport, but left it behind because, due to persecution in Libya, he 'felt unable to travel to the UK with

36 [2008] EWCA Crim 1761.

his own genuine passport'. This was held (on the agreed facts) to be a reasonable excuse.

3.70

It is unclear to what extent there must be an element of reasonableness in the reasonable excuse. Someone who has never had a passport for the above reasons relating to persecution clearly has a reasonable excuse. Similar would be someone who had their own passport but could not take it with them due to a fear of persecution if it were to be discovered.

3.71

But what about somebody from, say, the USA who does not have a passport because they never applied for one. Or someone who leaves it at home due to an irrational fear of persecution, or simply to avoid committing this offence? Are these of itself reasonable excuses, or do those individuals have to show that there is a reasonable reason for their actions? This is not clear, although *Mohammed* would tend towards the latter interpretation.

3.72

The defence of 'reasonable excuse' is further refined in s 2(7) which has a complicated 'double reasonableness' clause – a reasonable excuse is needed, but deliberately disposing of a document is not reasonable, unless this was for a reasonable cause, and complying with the directions of an agent is not a reasonable cause, unless it is unreasonable to expect non-compliance. This is a difficult direction to give to the jury.

3.73

A judge should not withdraw the defence or reasonable excuse until the evidence has been completed. Even in those circumstances, the fact that a defence appears 'hopeless' is not reason to withdraw a defence – it is a matter for the jury (*Asmeron*[37]).

Sentence

3.74

The offence is either way, with a maximum sentence of two years. There are no sentencing guidelines. The first case in the Court of Appeal was *Wang*[38] where the sentence was reduced to two months due to the exceptional features of the case (the fact that the appellant was just 18, had an extant asylum claim and had only had possession of the false passport for a matter of minutes). This would normally be the lowest sentence that would be passed on an adult.

---

37 [2013] EWCA Crim 435.
38 [2005] EWCA Crim 293.

3.75

A sentence of nine months was reduced to five months in *Ai*[39], for a similar case (but involving someone aged 26), and one that can be considered a 'standard' case on the facts. The Court of Appeal noted that co-operation with an agent can be mitigation, but caution had to be taken to not elevate its significance, and so undermine the specific exclusion from the defence.

3.76

The court reconsidered sentence levels in *Jeyarasa*[40]. A sentence of 12 months for a Sri Lankan who left his passport in Sri Lanka and flew to the UK to claim asylum (which he did immediately at the airport) was reduced to six months. Although it was noted that higher sentences could be expected now as opposed to 2005 due to greater public concern, and that the asylum claim had been refused, it does not seem that this sentence was that out of line with *Ai*.

3.77

It would appear that, unless there are some unusual features, a sentence of more than nine months may well be manifestly excessive (at least on a guilty plea).

Failing to co-operate with removal (s 35)

3.78

It is an offence under the AI(TC)A 2004, s 35 to fail to co-operate with a direction given by the Secretary of State. This was introduced to tackle the perceived problem of people without a right to be in the United Kingdom (typically asylum seekers who have exhausted their appeal rights) but who refused to co-operate with attempts to get them re-documented.

Legislation

3.79

If a person, without reasonable excuse, fails to comply with a direction from the Secretary of State, then that is an offence under s 35.

3.80

The direction is made under subsection (1):

> '(1) The Secretary of State may require a person to take specified action if the Secretary of State thinks that–

39 [2005] EWCA Crim 936.
40 [2014] EWCA Crim 2545.

(a) the action will or may enable a travel document to be obtained by or for the person, and

(b) possession of the travel document will facilitate the person's deportation or removal from the United Kingdom.'

3.81

Examples of the directions include (but are not limited to):

'(2) In particular, the Secretary of State may require a person to–

(a) provide information or documents to the Secretary of State or to any other person;

(b) obtain information or documents;

(c) provide biometric information (within the meaning of section 15 of the UK Borders Act 2007), or submit to a process by means of which such information is obtained or recorded;

(d) make, or consent to or cooperate with the making of, an application to a person acting for the government of a State other than the United Kingdom;

(e) cooperate with a process designed to enable determination of an application;

(f) complete a form accurately and completely;

(g) attend an interview and answer questions accurately and completely;

(h) make an appointment.'

Definitions

3.82

The CPS have provided guidance[41] that sets out the procedure that will be followed before a prosecution is brought, although a failure to follow this will not preclude a prosecution or provide a defence. However, it can (and should) be raised in representations to the CPS as to whether to proceed, and a failure to follow the procedure may be a factor in determining the admissibility of any

41 "Amended instructions for documenting removals and the implementation of AI(TC)A 2004, s 35 in non-compliant cases" https://assets.publishing.service.gov.uk/government/uploads/system/uploads/attachment_data/file/274935/section-35.pdf

evidence provided. There have been very few prosecutions for this offence, it being seen generally as an action of last resort[42].

3.83

An issue under (g), and potentially (f), may arise as to the privilege against self-incrimination, although this has not been considered as yet[43].

3.84

The CPS guidance recognises this, stating that[44]:

> 'It is very important that if it becomes apparent that the individual will not comply, the interviewing officer should not question the individual about the offence of failing to comply with the documentation process other than to confirm that the individual will not comply and establish the reason for non compliance on the Annex B form.'

Defences

3.85

Unlike the offence in s 2, 'reasonable excuse' is not limited or defined in the statute. It must however be a reason why the person is unable to comply, rather than merely being unwilling to do so:

> 'As a matter of law, reasons why a defendant is unwilling to comply with a s.35 requirement with which he is perfectly able to comply cannot constitute a reasonable excuse for non-compliance[45].'

3.86

The cases on s35 subsequent to that have all been in the context of challenges to immigration detention, which have refined the decision in *Tabnak*[46].

3.87

R (Babbage) v Home Secretary[47] concerned a Judicial Review of decision to detain. There is a discussion of the s 35 offence at paras [71]–[75]. Mr Babbage was a

42 See discussion at paras 6.14-6.47 'An Inspection of the Emergency Travel Document Process' (May-September 2013, Report of the Independent Chief Inspector of Borders and Immigration. This records (at [6.15]) that there were 40 people charged with the s 35 offence between 2009 and 2012, with 30 being in 2009-2010. Just over half led to a conviction.

43 The s 35 offence is not included in Youth Justice and Criminal Evidence Act 1999, Sch 3 which gives a statutory restriction on the use of 'answers and statements given under compulsion' in criminal proceedings. However, it is arguable that a court would hold that such answers would be inadmissible in a prosecution.

44 Guidance, para 6.

45 *Tabnak* [2007] EWCA Crim 380.

46 [2007] EWCA Crim 380, [2007] 2 Cr App R 4.

47 [2016] EWHC 148 (Admin), at [74].

Zimbabwean national who did not want to return, and had not co-operated. The court held that it was not a proper use of immigration detention powers to detain someone with a view to prosecuting them for a breach of s 35. In the High Court judgment of *R (JM (Zimbabwe)) v SSHD*[48] Jay J stated:

> '127. Putting to one side the difficult facts of the instant case, and the obvious complication introduced by the attitude of the Zimbabwean authorities, may section 35 be legitimately used by the Secretary of State both to secure compliance and to justify detention? Its purpose is to secure the obtaining of necessary travel documents to facilitate the deportation of individuals from the UK who do not have them. Such individuals may be detained under immigration powers, although many will not be. In relation to those who are detained, who are refusing to comply voluntarily, and who then commit a criminal offence under section 35 by disobeying the Secretary of State's requirement to take specified action, it may properly be said that it is the policy of the law that they are now to be treated as deliberately obstructive, assuming that they did not already merit that label. In principle, this is a factor which must be relevant to Hardial Singh (ii) – (iv), to be weighed in the balance.
>
> 128. In most cases, there will be a realistic prospect of removal within a reasonable time, and the sole or principal impediment to removal is the detainee's wilful obstructiveness. In such cases, the detention is being maintained for a legitimate purpose, and it would be incorrect to characterise what is happening as being detention for the purpose of prosecuting under section 35. Of course, Garnham J's dicta were not being directed to this state of affairs at all. In my judgment, the Secretary of State would be entitled to deploy section 35 in these circumstances. She is doing so not for the purpose of maintaining or legitimating detention, but for the purpose of facilitating the detainee's deportation from the UK. I abstain from deciding in this context whether the Secretary of State can use section 35 serially, "for as many times as it takes". However, I do have serious doubts about whether she may do so in relation to a person subject to immigration detention, having regard in particular to Hardial Singh (ii), if not (iii).'

3.88

In relation to whether there could be a prosecution for failing to 'complete the disclaimer form accurately and completely' and 'to attend an interview at the Zimbabwean High Commission', Garnham J said:

> 'I have the gravest doubt whether a breach of Section 35 could be made out against the Claimant. The Claimant was being asked to sign

48 [2016] EWHC 1773 (Admin), [2017] 1 WLR 268.

a document indicating that he intended to leave the United Kingdom. If, in truth, he did not intend to leave the United Kingdom he could not properly be required to sign the voluntary disclaimer; or to put it another way, he would have a reasonable excuse for not doing so.'

3.89

R (JM (Zimbabwe)) v SSHD[49], was another case of a Zimbabwean national who did not wish to return. He was served with a s 35 notice requiring him to attend the Zimbabwean Embassy to apply for an Emergency Travel Document (EDT), his passport having expired. This also required him to give consent to return if asked. JM attended the interview, but refused to say that he was willing to return. As a result he was charged with the s 35 offence and pleaded guilty. After he was released from that, he was re-detained under the Immigration Acts and a further s 35 notice was served in similar terms as to the first one.

3.90

The Court of Appeal held that the list in s 35(2) was not an exhaustive list of what could be required. However, s 35 has to be read as a whole, and it was not permissible to have a requirement under one subsection of s 35(2) that conflicted with a different one. Therefore, as requiring JM to state (untruthfully) that he was willing to return would be inconsistent with the requirement in s 35(2)(g) to 'answer questions accurately and completely', the notice was not a lawful one[50].

3.91

Whilst these are immigration cases, and therefore not technically binding on the criminal courts, it is extremely likely that they will be followed as to the proper interpretation of s 35.

3.92

The only case from the Court of Appeal (Criminal Division) after *Tabnak* was AAI in the case of *AAD & Others*[51], although this related to a conviction from 2008. In that case AAI was prosecuted for refusing failing to comply with a s 35 notice requiring him 'to attend an interview and answer accurately and fully questions put to him at the Sierra Leonean High Commission, with a view to obtaining an ETD'. The grounds of appeal were that subsequent evidence showed that he was a victim of trafficking and should not have been prosecuted for that reason and, alternatively, that new medical evidence showed that he had a reasonable excuse. The appeal failed on the facts[52].

---

49 [2017] EWCA Civ 1669, [2018] 1 WLR 2329.
50 *R (JM (Zimbabwe)) v SSHD* [2017] EWCA Civ 1669, [2018] 1 WLR 2329, at [77].
51 [2022] EWCA Crim 106, [2022] 1 Cr App R 19.
52 *AAD & Othrs* at [158] – [167].

Burden of proof

3.93

In terms of the burden of proof, the CPS guidance[53] suggests that once it is raised by the defence, the burden to disprove it is on the Crown, which is consistent with authorities[54]. However, this has not yet been determined by the courts.

Specific defences

3.94

The s 31 defence does not apply to the offence. As the offence would be committed after the entry to the UK, it would seems that that is consistent with Art 31. Further, a fear of persecution is not capable of amounting to a reasonable excuse (*Tabnak*).

Sentence

3.95

The offence is an either way one, with a maximum sentence of two years. There are no sentencing guidelines.

3.96

It seems likely that similar sentences to the s 2 offence will be passed, albeit perhaps slightly higher given that a conviction implies that there is a deliberate and considered breach of the law[55]. As the defendant is likely to be in detention, anything other than an immediate custodial sentence would be surprising.

Making an untrue statement to obtain a passport

Legislation

3.97

Under the Criminal Justice Act 1925, s 36 'the making by any person of a statement which is to his knowledge untrue for the purpose of procuring a passport, whether for himself or any other person', is an offence. There is no requirement for dishonesty (*McCrea* (2013) unreported), although the person has to know that the statement was false.

---

53 Guidance, para 8.2.

54 See, as an example, *Charles* [2010] 1 Cr App R 2, [2009] EWCA Crim 1570.

55 The appellant in *AAD & Othrs* received a sentence of 18 months, which was reduced to 12 months on appeal due to the fresh psychiatric evidence. However, the appeal was more than a decade after the sentence had been served in full, and the focus of the appeal was on the conviction.

Procedure

3.98

Where an application for a passport is successful, it is appropriate to charge the offence under the Fraud Act 2006, and there is no need to be constrained by the maximum sentence of two years (*Ashbee*[56]).

3.99

Where it is unsuccessful, this offence is the correct charge, although it would not be an abuse to charge an offence under the Fraud Act 2006 (which requires only a false statement, not that anything is obtained (*Bunche*[57]). On general principles, in those circumstances a sentencer should consider themselves bound by the two-year maximum (*Hardy*[58]) for this offence.

Sentence

3.100

The offence is either way, with a maximum sentence of two years. There are no sentencing guidelines.

3.101

The case of *Walker*[59] has been suggested as a guideline case of sorts. This suggested a sentence of nine months following a guilty plea for a Zimbabwean overstayer who pretended to have been born in the UK in an application form.

3.102

In *Crossdale*[60] it was noted that a higher sentence would now be applicable following *Kolawole*. Allowance must presumably be made for the fact that the maximum sentence is two years instead of ten. However, this does not leave much room between the two as this offence is less serious that the '*Kolawole*' ones.

Offences under the British Nationality Act 1981

3.103

Two summary only offences are created by the BNA 1981, s 46. These relate to the operation of that Act. In practice, these are rarely used, and there are no reported cases dealing with them. They are included here for completeness.

56 (1989) 88 Cr App R 357.
57 (1993) 96 Cr App R 274.
58 [2013] EWCA Crim 2125.
59 [1999] 1 Cr App R(S) 42.
60 [2006] EWCA Crim 2541.

Legislation

3.104

The offences are:

> '(1) Any person who for the purpose of procuring anything to be done or not to be done under this Act—
>
> (a) makes any statement which he knows to be false in a material particular; or
>
> (b) recklessly makes any statement which is false in a material particular, shall be liable on summary conviction in the United Kingdom to imprisonment for a term not exceeding three months or [a level 5 fine].'

3.105

There is a less serious offence:

> '(2) Any person who without reasonable excuse fails to comply with any requirement imposed on him by regulations made under this Act with respect to the delivering up of certificates of naturalisation shall be liable on summary conviction [to a level 4 fine].'

Procedure

3.106

For the offence under subsection (1), the information must be laid either within six months of commission or within three years and 'not more than two months after the date certified by a chief officer of police to be the date on which evidence sufficient to justify proceedings came to the notice of an officer of his police force'.

Jurisdiction

3.107

Section 46(5) provides:

> '(5) For the purposes of the trial of a person for an offence under subsection (1) or (2), the offence shall be deemed to have been committed either at the place at which it actually was committed or at any place at which he may be.'

4 Deception and leave offences

Introduction

4.1

This chapter provides details of the main offences related to illegal arrival or entry, or remaining unlawfully after a lawful entry, whether clandestinely or by deception.

Illegal entry (IA 1971, s 24)

The meaning of 'entry' in the Immigration Acts

4.2

One matter that has historically caused a large number of difficulties is that the meaning of 'enter' in the context of immigration offences (and immigration law generally) has a technical meaning as defined in the IA 1971, s 11:

> **'11 Construction of references to entry, and other phrases relating to travel.**
>
> A person arriving in the United Kingdom by ship or aircraft shall for purposes of this Act be deemed not to enter the United Kingdom unless and until he disembarks, and on disembarkation at a port shall further be deemed not to enter the United Kingdom so long as he remains in such area (if any) at the port as may be approved for this purpose by an immigration officer; and a person who has not otherwise entered the United Kingdom shall be deemed not to do so as long as he is detained … under the powers conferred by Schedule 2 to this Act or section 62 of the Nationality, Immigration and Asylum Act 2002 or on immigration bail within the meaning of Schedule 10 to the Immigration Act 2016.'

4.3

There is a long line of authority going back to *Naillie*[1], and culminating recently in *Kakaei*[2] (subsequently confirmed in *Bani*[3]) that the effect of the IA 1971,

1 [1993] AC 674.
2 [2021] EWCA Crim 503, [2021] Crim LR 1079.
3 [2021] EWCA Crim 1958, [2022] Crim LR 507.

s 11 is that someone who arrives at the United Kingdom at a designated port (air or sea) and claims asylum does not 'enter' the country (and may never do so, despite living here for a number of years) whilst they are detained or on immigration bail.

4.4

The practical effect is that someone who comes to the United Kingdom in an irregular fashion and lands on a beach or similar will have 'entered' at that point, as will someone who uses false documents to come through passport control at a designated port. The only people that will not be is those small number who present to Immigration Officers on arrival at a designated port.

4.5

A further consequence is for those who are intercepted at sea. This could be either on board a RHIB or similar 'small boat'[4], or someone who has boarded a regular boat that is then intercepted by Immigration Officers. If they are brought to shore by Immigration Officers then they are likely detained (for the purposes of the IA 1971, Sch 2) at the point that they encounter the Immigration Officers, and will remain so when they are brought to shore. They therefore will not 'enter' the UK at the point of arrival and, if they claim asylum, may not enter at all[5].

4.6

The potential problem for criminal cases was encountered almost immediately on the passing of the IA 1971[6], but the difficulties that arose persisted long after. This is perhaps understandable as, on the face of it, it would appear 'obvious' that someone who lands in the UK and, after speaking to Immigration Officers, is released into the UK, should be considered to have 'entered'.

---

4 This mode of transport is not new to the 21st Century. See, as an example, all three of the appellants in *R v Governor of Pentonville Prison, ex parte Azam* [1974] AC 18. At least one came to the UK 'on a small motorboat' with three other passengers and two people smugglers acting as pilots. It can be noted that even at that time, 'although the agents who arranged and conducted the illegal landings were sometimes prosecuted and convicted, I believe that the illegal entrants were not often prosecuted' (29C – from Lord Denning's judgment in the Court of Appeal).

Further back than that, there are other examples of such journeys being made. For example, on 9 December 1938 Ludwig Schlesinger, a German Dentist, came to the UK on a motorboat. He had been detained in Germany for 9 months for a political crime and, having been released, was directed to report to the police. Fearing the worst, he fled to France and paid someone to bring him to England on a motorboat. He pleaded guilty to a precursor offence to the IA 1971, s24 (landing without permission, seeming contrary to Art 1 Aliens Order 1920 and s13 Aliens Restriction (Amendment) Act 1919, but the prosecution (seemingly accepting him to be a refugee) did not ask for any punishment (see also Taylor, *Refugees in Twentieth-Century Britain: a history* (1st edn, Cambridge, 2021) 50 for further examples.

5 The Home Office draw a distinction between two sorts of irregular arrival; 'uncontrolled arrival' and 'controlled arrival' with the latter being where the person is brought ashore following a lawful interception or rescue by a body such as the UKBA, RNLI or Navy. See 'Irregular or unlawful entry and arrival' v.2 (08 July 2022) at pages 6-7.

6 *Singh* [1972] 1 WLR 1600.

Meaning of Port/Approved area

4.7

'Port' is not defined for the purposes of the IA 1971, Part III (the criminal offences), other than to say that 'port' includes an airport[7]. It is also distinct (perhaps counter-intuitively) from a 'port of entry', which is one of the major ports and airports that receive large numbers of passengers[8].

4.8

This should not matter in a criminal case as the critical part of the IA 1971, s 11 is that for someone to have not entered they must remain in an area that 'may be approved for this purpose by an immigration officer'. In the case of a small port or harbour there may well be no such designation in place. In larger ports it will often be clear on the facts whether someone has entered or not.

4.9

However, the question of where the approved areas are is not straightforward. It does not appear to be defined anywhere in primary or secondary legislation. In response to a Freedom of Information request[9] referring to Home Office Guidance on the Common Travel Area and asking:

> '[in relation to] the terms: "zone approved under section 11 of the Immigration Act 1971", "s.11 approved area", "s.11 authorised area", "s.11 approved area", and "s.11 approved zone".
>
> Please provide me with the recorded information that already exists (such as staff guidance, memoranda, directives, etc) available touching on these questions:
>
> a) the number of such designated areas,
>
> b) their locations and boundaries,
>
> c) the dates of designation of each,
>
> d) the areas previously but no longer designated and the date of designation and removal, and
>
> e) the process for designation.'

4.10

The answer given was that:

7 IA 1971, s 33(1).

8 A full list is contained in The Immigration (Ports of Entry) Order 1987, made under IA 1971, s 33(3). The distinction is drawn there, and can also be seen in the criminal offence created in IA 1971, s 27(1)(b) which criminalises the owner or agent of a ship which is carrying passengers for reward arranging for it to go to a 'port other than a port of entry'.

9 FOI 15 April 2022. See – https://www.whatdotheyknow.com/request/immigration_act_1971_section_11.

> 'After careful consideration we have decided that this information is exempt from disclosure under section 31 (1) of the FOIA. This provides that information can be withheld where disclosure would or would be likely to, prejudice law enforcement and the public interest falls in favour of maintaining the exemption.'

4.11

The burden of proof as to whether someone has entered has not been determined, but would likely be on the Crown on the basis that whilst this is an exception, it is something that is part of the offence and the Crown are in a much better position to prove.

4.12

For cases after 28 June 2022 it will likely be possible to charge the 'arrive' version of the relevant offence, rather than the 'enter' one, where there is any doubt. Where the offending is prior to then, and there is real doubt as to whether there was an entry, it is unlikely that it could be considered to be fair for there to be a prosecution.

Channel Tunnel

4.13

Where someone comes to the United Kingdom on a train through the Channel Tunnel then they will 'enter' the UK when they 'leave any control area designated under para 26, Sch 2' or remains on the train after it has ceased to be in a control area[10].

Illegal entry offences

4.14

The IA 1971, s 24 created an offence of entering the United Kingdom without leave (or in breach of a Deportation Order). This was summary only, which had a number of consequences. One was that it was not possible to attempt to commit the offence[11]. That meant that if someone was stopped in a relevant port area prior to coming into the United Kingdom, or at sea, then they would not be committing an offence even if their intention was to enter the country without leave. In certain circumstances a conspiracy charge could be brought[12], although in practice this was not a course that was followed, even if there was more than one person involved in the alleged offending.

10 Channel Tunnel (International Arrangements) Order 1993, SI 1993/1813, Sch 4, para 5.

11 Criminal Attempts Act 1981 only applies to indictable (meaning either way or indictable only) offences (s 1(4)).

12 Criminal Law Act 1977, s 1which creates the statutory offence of conspiracy, applies to summary offences if the consent of the DPP is given (s 4(1)).

4.15

This summary only offence was amended as of 28 June 2022[13] by the Nationality and Border Act 2022 ('NABA 2022'). This creates a set of five either way offences that relate to persons who are not British Citizens. These are set out in s 24 as follows:

> '(A1) A person who knowingly enters the United Kingdom in breach of a deportation order commits an offence.
>
> (B1) A person who—
>
> (a) requires leave to enter the United Kingdom under this Act, and
>
> (b) knowingly enters the United Kingdom without such leave,
>
> commits an offence.
>
> (C1) A person who—
>
> (a) has only a limited leave to enter or remain in the United Kingdom, and
>
> (b) knowingly remains beyond the time limited by the leave,
>
> commits an offence.
>
> (D1) A person who—
>
> (a) requires entry clearance under the immigration rules, and
>
> (b) knowingly arrives in the United Kingdom without a valid entry clearance,
>
> commits an offence.'

4.16

The fifth offence relates to travelling without an ETA[14] for those that require it.

> '(E1) A person who—
>
> (a) is required under immigration rules not to travel to the United Kingdom without an ETA that is valid for the person's journey to the United Kingdom, and
>
> (b) knowingly arrives in the United Kingdom without such an ETA,
>
> commits an offence.'

---

13 NABA 2022, s 40, as brought into force by Nationality and Borders Act 2022 (Commencement No 1, Transitional and Saving Provisions) Regulations 2022, SI 2022/590, reg 2.

14 An ETA is an 'Electronic Travel Authorisation' that will apply to all people (other than British or Irish Citizens) who are not visa-nationals (and will therefore require entry clearance before travelling) and require them to obtain the equivalent of an 'ESTA' in the USA. See Chapter 1 for further information.

Transitional provisions

4.17

As would be expected:

> 'The amendments made by section 40 (to the extent brought into force by regulation 2) and section 41 of the 2022 Act apply only in relation to an offence committed on or after the appointed day[15].'

4.18

As time passes, it will be more likely that it will not be possible to say exactly when someone arrived. Given that prior to 28 June 2022 the offence was summary only and cannot be prosecuted more than three years after commission, the question of jurisdiction may have to be addressed.

A1 – entering in breach of a deportation order

4.19

This requires an 'entry' as defined in the IA 1971, s11, which means that the issues set out above in relation to s 11 will arise. For further details of the process related to deportation see Chapter 9. The existence of the deportation order will need to be proved, although there is a presumption that a document purporting to be a copy of the deportation order is admissible and is deemed to have been made by the Secretary of State, unless the defence show otherwise[16].

4.20

Whilst the background of offending is not relevant to the commission of the offence, it would be good practice to obtain the full details of the offence that led to the deportation order being made, as this may have a bearing on the culpability of the defendant.

4.21

In some cases the defendant will not have challenged the deportation order, and there will be limited Home Office papers. However, where there was a previous appeal, the judgment of the Tribunal Judge will likely assist in setting out the immigration history.

---

15 Nationality and Borders Act 2022 (Commencement No 1, Transitional and Saving Provisions) Regulations 2022, SI 2022/590, Sch 2, para 7.

16 IA 1971, s 32(2).

B1 – entering without leave

4.22

This is the successor offence to the 'old' s 24 offence, although it is now either way. The requirement to prove an 'entry' raises the same issues in relation to s 11 that arose previously.

4.23

Someone cannot enter the UK without arriving. Generally, when someone is arrested in-country after having entered, then there is no issue, and the B1 offence would be the proper charge. Where someone is intercepted at sea or at a port prior to the point of entry, and there is doubt as to their intention, then it is likely that the appropriate charge would be an arrival or attempted arrival under D1 rather than B1[17].

4.24

Evidential provisions are made in s 24(4) that mean that the burden on showing that someone had leave to enter is on the defence. Where a defendant produces a document showing what purports to be a valid entry clearance, then it is presumed to be duly issued unless the contrary is shown. For that reason, it is likely to be sufficient for the prosecution to state the suspect's nationality and point to the relevant part of the Immigration Rules[18], although given the nature of electronic records an Immigration Officer will generally give a statement confirming that there is no record of an entry clearance being granted (whether because none has been applied for, or because an application has been refused).

C1 – overstaying a period of leave

4.25

By making this offence either way, the aim was to 'ensure that the police, prosecutors and the courts consider the offence as serious enough to take through the Criminal Justice System. If individuals are given a sentence of 12 months or more it will make them subject to auto-deportation unless an exception applies'[19].

---

17 Where they have not yet arrived in the UK, the appropriate charge would be an attempted entry or arrival under the Criminal Attempts Act 1981, charged with reference to either B1 or D1.

18 Immigration Rules, Appendix V.

19 Explanatory Notes 409, Nationality and Borders Act 2022,

4.26

Subject to the question of time limits, this now being an either way offence means that it can be prosecuted at any time. Unlike arriving or entering, which is a one-off event, specific provision is made in s 24(1A) that:

> 'A person commits an offence under subsection (C1) above on the day when he first knows that the time limited by his leave has expired and continues to commit it throughout any period during which he is in the United Kingdom thereafter; but a person shall not be prosecuted under that provision more than once in respect of the same limited leave.'

4.27

Where someone has been granted leave to enter that expired prior to 28 June 2022, can they be prosecuted for this offence? This has not been resolved, but it would appear to be the case as it is now defined as a continuous offence. On that basis it appears that someone who had leave that expired prior to 28 June 2019, and could not be prosecuted as of 27 June 2022 (as being, on any view, beyond the three year extended time limit), would then become liable again to be prosecuted, but this time for the more serious C1 offence.

4.28

There are no equivalent evidential provisions to those for the B1 and D1 offences. In reality, given that grants of leave will now be recorded electronically, this is unlikely to be an issue in most cases.

D1 – arriving without an entry clearance

4.29

Chapter 1 sets out the visa regime in more detail but, in essence, for non-nationals there are two different regimes for those nationalities that require entry clearance and those that do not[20].

4.30

Arrive is not defined in the Act. At a first instance preparatory hearing in a number of 'small boat' cases, Cavanagh J held[21] that:

> '(1) "arrival" for the purposes of sections 24(D1) means arrival on land in the United Kingdom, whether in the approved area of a port or elsewhere;

20 The full list is at VN 1.1 Immigration Rules – 'Immigration Rules Appendix Visitor: Visa national list'.

21 *Mohamed & Others*, 21 December 2022 (para 104) – available online at https://www.judiciary.uk/wp-content/uploads/2022/12/Preparatory-hearing-Small-Boats-cases-rulings-21Dec22-final-v.pdf. There was an appeal (*Mohamed & Othrs* [2023] EWCA Crim 211) against some of the points of law, but not this one (see [11]).

(2) A Defendant "arrives" in the United Kingdom if he or she is rescued at sea and is transported to land by the maritime authorities or other rescuers;'

4.31

It is likely that this will be adopted if the issue is considered in future. This offence applies to all people who require an entry clearance, whether or not they an asylum seeker[22].

4.32

Similar evidential provision as to those relating to B1 are made in the IA 1971, s 24(5) that mean that the burden on showing that someone had valid entry clearance is on the defence. Where they produce a document showing what purports to be a valid entry clearance, then it is presumed to be duly issued, unless the contrary is shown.

E1 – arriving without an ETA (Electronic Travel Authorisation)[23] *– not yet in force*

4.33

NABA introduced a requirement[24] for those passengers who do not require an entry clearance prior to coming to the United Kingdom, to nonetheless obtain an 'Electronic Travel Authorisation' ('ETA') – 'an authorisation in electronic form to travel to the United Kingdom'. This is a similar idea to the ESTA[25] that operates in the USA that readers may be familiar with (as well as ETIAS[26] – the EU equivalent – that is being put in place to start at the end of 2023). The mechanics of how this operates will be set out in the Immigration Rules when it is implemented.

4.34

There is currently no fixed date for implementation, but it is anticipated that it will be by the end of 2023. When it is, the regime as it operates to the criminal offence is likely to be similar to the D1 offence.

22 *Mohamed* at [49]-[68].

23 The above changes (apart from s 24(E1) came into force on 28 June 2022 (Nationality and Borders Act 2022 (Commencement No 1, Transitional and Saving Provisions) Regulations 2022, SI 2022/590).

24 NABA 2022, s 75 introduces a new IA 1971, s 11C.

25 Electronic System for Travel Authorization.

26 European Travel Information and Authorization System, which will run alongside the Entry-Exit System that will collect details of the identities of those coming to the EEA, as well as their time and place of entry and exit, as well as any refusals of entry.

General considerations

'Knowingly'

4.35

'Knowingly' is not defined in the Act. It is an open question whether, where there is a requirement not to do an action X without satisfying a condition Y, the 'knowingly' in the offence of 'knowingly do X without Y' applies solely to the first condition. In other words, where someone is charged with knowingly arriving without an entry clearance, is it a defence if the defendant does not know that they need an entry clearance?

4.36

The general principle is that ignorance of the law is no excuse. This is a long-standing rule from at least 1231 where a man who was fined for entering land that was not his, the fact that he believed that it was his, and that this belief arose on the advice of a lawyer, did not provide an answer[27]. This rule applies as much to foreign nationals as to British ones, and so a French national who takes part in a dual 'ignorant of the fact that by the law of England killing an adversary in a fair duel, amounted to murder' is not a defence to murder if one of the parties dies[28].

4.37

In *Grant v Borg*[29], Lord Bridge said (in the context of the IA 1971, s 24(1)(b) offence[30]):

> 'First, the principle that ignorance of the law is no defence in crime is so fundamental that to construe the word "knowingly" in a criminal statute as requiring not merely knowledge of the facts material to the offender's guilt, but also knowledge of the relevant law, would be revolutionary and, to my mind, wholly unacceptable. I reserve my opinion as to whether the courts might nevertheless be driven to that extremity if a statutory offence embodying a requirement of knowledge in the definition of the offence were of such a nature that it was impossible to envisage circumstances in which the facts necessary to establish the offender's guilt would not be known to him. But that is certainly not this case. It would be unusual, but by no means impossible, for an immigrant (as, for example, one who was wholly illiterate) to remain beyond the time in fact limited by his leave, but nevertheless to be honestly mistaken in believing that his leave had not expired.'

27 *Robert Waggehastr's Case*, cited in Bracton's Note Book, Maitland's Ed. 496.
28 *Barronett's Case* 1 El & &Bl. 1 (1852).
29 [1982] 2 All ER 257.
30 Remaining beyond a grant of leave, the summary only equivalent of what is now the C1 offence.

4.38

This was summarised, more pithily, in *Christian & Others*[31], as follows – 'if information is accessible, a defendant is deemed to know of it' ([42]). In this case it would be readily ascertainable, at least on a broad basis (or 'at a broad level'?), what nationalities require permission to come to the United Kingdom and what do not, as well as the fact that foreign nationals require permission before being admitted to the UK. This has long been the case, what changed on 28 June 2022 was that it became a criminal offence to arrive without the necessary clearance, rather than a breach of the Immigration Rules.

4.39

Therefore, it is likely that a court would conclude that once someone without entry clearance (who requires it) arrives in the UK, the fact that they did not know that they needed an entry clearance would appear not be a defence (the same would apply to the ETA offence).

4.40

On that basis, someone who embarks on a boat journey from France to Ireland but is simply bad at navigation and lands in Dover rather than Dublin would have a defence to the D1 offence in that he did not knowingly arrive in the UK (whether or not he knew that he would have required entry clearance). However, it would not be a defence to say that he believed that he did not need entry clearance (whether in general or because, for example, he believed that as a refugee he did not need it), however honest and reasonable (or unreasonable) that belief may be.

4.41

Whilst the structure of the A1 offence is different to the B1-E1 offences in that the offence is set out in one sentence, rather than split into different parts, this does not appear to make any difference.

Mistake of fact

4.42

What of the person who genuinely, but mistakenly, believes that they have an entry clearance or, more likely (when it comes into force), an ETA? It is not hard to envisage this arising in a number of circumstances. One example might be a family where the paperwork is dealt with by one family member and the others rely on their assurances that everything is in order. Another might by the American who has an ETA that expires on 5 April 2024 and takes a last minute trip to the United Kingdom on 20 April 2024, but reads the expiration date of 05/04/2023 as being 4 May 2024 and thinks that he is covered.

31 [2006] UKPC 47, [2007] 2 AC 400.

4.43

In both cases there may be a degree of carelessness which may mean it is not unfair to refuse them entry. However, many may consider it unjust for them to be convicted of a criminal offence.

4.44

The general rule in the criminal law is that when a mistake of fact is made by a defendant, then they will fall to be judged on the facts as they believed them to be[32]. In the above examples, it would appear that such people would have a defence, although it may not be clear what the actual difference in culpability is between the family member who believed that they had a valid ETA as against one who believed that they did not need one.

4.45

Most people coming to the United Kingdom do so on commercial travel, where the 'carrier's liability' scheme is well established. This places an onus on the transport company to carry out checks on people seeking to come to the United Kingdom to check that they have valid documentation. It is likely that a similar scheme will apply to the ETA. However, there are a number of people who do come to the United Kingdom by private boat or plane, where the situation is more complicated. For example, a pilot (or owner or operator) of a private plane flying to the United Kingdom must submit a 'GAR' (General Aviation Report) that sets out a number of things that must be reported including who will be flying so that an Immigration Officer can consider whether permission needs to be (and if so, should) granted to anyone on board[33]. There are similar, but less onerous, requirements for people coming by boat[34]. In theory this will ensure that people are aware of their obligations and are not accidentally criminalised for arriving unlawfully under the IA 1971, s 24(D1) or (E1).

Knowingly versus intentionally

4.46

The Act requires that the defendant knows that they arrive, which is more passive that intentionally arriving.

4.47

So, the person who embarks on a boat journey from France to Ireland but is blown off course and lands in England and Wales would knowingly (albeit unwillingly) arrive, and would likely have to rely on a defence of duress of

32 *B v DPP* [2000] UKHL 13, [2000] 2 AC 428.
33 See General Aviation Report Guidance, updated 23 March 2023.
34 Pleasure Craft Report Service – see 'Sailing pleasure craft to and from the UK' (22 August 2022).

circumstances and/or on the basis that the act of arrival was not sufficiently voluntary as to amount to the *actus reus*, as would someone travelling on a flight from Paris to Dublin that was directed to London (although it is clearly unlikely that such a person would be prosecuted)[35].

Decision to prosecute

4.48

Whilst it is not clear exactly how many people coming to the United Kingdom would fall foul of these provisions, it is many tens of thousands a year[36]. For instance, in 2022 more than 47,500 people arrived in the UK on a 'small boat'[37]. Almost all are likely to be visa nationals who do not have an entry clearance (as otherwise they would choose a safer, and cheaper, route). As such they are, *prima facie*, guilty of the IA 1971, s 24(D1) offence. Added to that are the many more people who were lawfully in the United Kingdom, but have overstayed, and are therefore potentially committing the s 24(C1) offence.

4.49

The CPS have issued guidance[38] as to how they will approach the decision to prosecute in s 24 cases:

> '**Section 24 illegal/arrival entry and arrival offences**
>
> **Factors tending in favour of prosecution (aggravating factors)**
>
> - The level of culpability involved in securing illegal entry (this might include other relevant offences committed alongside immigration offences). When an individual pilots a small boat, but there is insufficient evidence to prove a facilitation offence, culpability is likely to be higher as their actions will have made at least some contribution to the passage of others, in addition to directly contributing to their own illegal arrival or attempt.
> - Offenders who are in breach of a Deportation Order and those who are repeat offenders who have previously been removed
> - Offenders who are in breach of a decision or order to exclude them from the UK or to ban them from re-entry for a specified period

35 It is unlikely that that it would be a case of non-insane automatism by analogy with the driver who is attacked by a swarm of bees – *Kay v Butterworth* (1945) 61 TLR 452, or has a sneezing fit – *Woolley v DPP* [1998] CLY 914, as that would only apply where the person's involuntary act causes the offence as opposed to external factors that the person cannot control.

36 For example, in 2021 there were approximately 48,500 asylum applications made (National Statistics – Summary of latest statistics (3 March 2022)). Some of these would be children and some would be made by people lawfully present in the United Kingdom. That still leaves a large number of people who would have arrived in the United Kingdom without valid entry clearance.

37 Illegal Migration Bill (2023) Explanatory Notes, at [11].

38 CPS 'Immigration' legal guidance, available at https://www.cps.gov.uk/legal-guidance/immigration (06 December 2022).

- Where the suspect has previous convictions or has committed other offences in addition to the immigration offending
- A potentially substantial confiscation order and the likelihood of timely enforcement
- Evidence of violence / harm or risk to life to others
- Evidence of money flows or financial advantage / gain or benefit.
- Evidence of repeated attempts to enter the UK illegally
- Evidence of document destruction (where not charged as a separate offence)
- Evidence that the suspect could have sought asylum in a safe country before beginning the final leg of their journey
- Evidence that the suspect was previously refused entry clearance or a prior application for an Electronic Travel Authorisation (ETA) to the UK.
- The offending compromised the genuine identity of another person, causing them loss, distress, or inconvenience (obtaining leave by deception / entering without leave through fraud)
- of provable involvement with an organised crime group behind the criminality.

In relation to the s 24 illegal arrival/entry and arrival offences, it may be that those refugees, or presumptive refugees, who commit criminal offences as a necessary part of their journey to the UK are not prosecuted, provided the conditions in s 31(1) (as interpreted in *Asfaw*[39]) are met.

Where a claim for asylum has been made, factors in support of prosecution may be:

- non-meritorious claims
- additional factual elements providing the context of the offence or particular circumstances of the unlawful arrival in the UK, indicative of higher culpability or higher seriousness of the offending
- factors relating to the suspect, whether relating to the suspect's circumstances in their country of origin or to their journey, indicative of higher culpability

Examples may include asylum seekers with a particular organisational role, such as the facilitation of the buying of the boat in *Bani and others*[40], or the different seriousness in conduct in a case like *Mirahessari* [41].'

39 See Chapter 8 for more detail, and for discussion as to the potential impact of the changes made by NABA 2022, s 31 defence.
40 [2021] EWCA Crim 1958.
41 [2016] EWCA Crim 1733.

4.50

Whilst these are geared more towards 'small boat' crossings, they are applicable to all s 24(D1) cases. It is likely that a similar approach would be taken to the other s 24 offences (with the above checklist suitably amended).

Sentences

4.51

The above offences are all either way. They have a maximum penalty of four years, apart from the A1 offence, where the maximum is five years.

4.52

There are no sentencing guidelines for these offences, nor have the Court of Appeal yet given consideration to these. The Resident Judge at Canterbury Crown Court (where many of the 'small boat' cases have been heard) gave considered and detailed sentencing remarks in relation to the s 24(D1) offence that have been widely shared[42], albeit that this is not a formal guideline[43]. These suggest that in a typical case of someone arriving in a RHIB, a sentence of 12 months after trial is likely to be appropriate if there are no aggravating features.

4.53

It is likely that a court will consider that the A1 offence, involving the deliberate breach of a formal order, to be more serious (as can be seen in the higher maximum sentence). It is less clear whether there should be any distinctions between the sentences for the B1–E1 offences. The argument in favour of this would be that 'entering' involves a breach of immigration law (evading the immigration controls that exist in one way or another) in a way that merely 'arriving' does not. Further, overstaying existing leave could be less serious than the entry offence (in part by analogy with *Overieriakhi*[44]).

Defences

4.54

The IAA 1999, s 31 defence does not apply to any of the offences. An attempt to argue in *Mohamed* that it did by virtue of the NABA 2022 was unsuccessful[45].

---

42 *R v M* (28 September 2022).

43 See *Blackshaw* [2011] EWCA Crim 2312, at [20] for a discussion about the propriety of Crown Court judges issuing ('or appearing to' be issuing) sentencing guidelines.

44 See Chapter 3.

45 At [64]-[68].

Time limits

4.55

As the offences are either way, no time limit would normally apply. However, the IA 1971, s 24(3) states that:

> '(3) The extended time limit for prosecutions which is provided for by section 28(1) below shall apply to offences under subsections (A1), (B1), (D1), (E1) and (1)(c) above.'

4.56

It is not clear why Parliament has done so, but it would appear that the effect of this is to introduce a time limit (at least in relations to prosecutions in the magistrates' court) for four of the five either way offences[46]. For that reason, practitioners will need to consider the question where a prosecution is started more than six months after the commission of the offence and remains in the magistrates' court.

Deception (IA 1971, s 24A)

4.57

The IA 1971, s 24A creates two offences of entering or remaining in the United Kingdom by deception. Care must be taken not to confuse the offence under s 24(A1) above with the s 24A(1) offence.

Definitions

4.58

The offence is as follows:

> **'Deception**
>
> (1) A person who is not a British citizen is guilty of an offence if, by means which include deception by him
>
> (a) he obtains or seeks to obtain –
>
> (i) leave to enter or remain in the United Kingdom, or
>
> (ii) an ETA; or
>
> (b) he secures or seeks to secure the avoidance, postponement or revocation of enforcement action against him

46 See Chapter 10 for more details as to how these time limits operate.

(2) "Enforcement action", in relation to a person, means

(a) the giving of directions for his removal from the United Kingdom ("directions") under Schedule 2 to this Act or section 10 of the Immigration and Asylum Act 1999

(b) the making of a deportation order against him under section 5 of this Act; or

(c) his removal from the United Kingdom in consequence of directions or a deportation order

Separate Offences/Leave

4.59

The offence cannot be committed by a British Citizen (who would not require leave to enter). Enforcement action is defined in the IA 1971, s 24A(2) as being: (a) giving of Removal Directions; (b) making a Deportation Order; and (c) removal in accordance with either of the other two.

4.60

It is not clear whether there needs to actually be enforcement action in progress, or merely that the defendant contemplates them, and the dishonest act is done 'in case'. It is presumably the latter.

4.61

There was historically a distinction between EEA nationals and Non-EEA nationals as to how the law applies. Under EU law, an EEA national did not require leave to enter[47], and so somebody who obtained a residence permit by deception does not commit the offence under subsection (a)[48].

4.62

Although this no longer applies post-Brexit, the nature of these offences are that they often come to light a number of years after event, so consideration will still need to be given to this issue in some case. It is arguable that they would have committed the offence under subsection (b) by virtue of the Immigration (European Economic Area) Regulations 2006, SI 2006/1003, reg 24 (prior to 1 February 2017), or reg 32 (prior to 1 January 2021) as they would then be 'treated as if he were a person to whom the IAA 1999, s 10(1)(a) applied'.

47 IA 1988, s 7: 'A person shall not under the principal Act require leave to enter or remain in the United Kingdom in any case in which he is entitled to do so by virtue of an enforceable EU right or of any provision made under section 2(2) of the European Communities Act 1972.'

48 *Boateng* [2016] EWCA Crim 57, [2016] 4 WLR 70.

4.63

This would depend on whether 'as if he were a person' is sufficient to bring him in (b), and whether the contemplated removal would not be sufficiently remote. Somebody in this position who obtained a Residence Permit could be charged with a document offence in relation to that.

4.64

The deception has to be committed by the defendant, and it must be a material (albeit not a sole) cause of the grant of leave or deferral of enforcement action.

ETA

4.65

See above in relation to the nature of an ETA.

Defences

4.66

The defence under the IAA 1999, s 31 ('s 31 defence') does apply to this offence, as does the defence under the Modern Slavery Act (MSA), s 45.

Sentence

4.67

The offence is either way, with a maximum sentence of two years. This has not changed since the introduction of the offence on 14 February 2000[49], which may be surprising given the overall trend in increasing sentences. At the time it was created, it was an aggravated version of the offence of entering without leave. However, now that that offence is either way with a maximum sentence double that for the s 24A offence, it appears to be an anomaly.

4.68

Although the maximum sentence is a fifth of that for using a false passport, it has been seen by the courts as being equivalent to the *Kolawole* offences, so the same tariff will apply: 12–18 months even on a guilty plea (*Ali*[50] and *Ding*[51]).

49 As inserted by IAA 1999, s 28. See *R (Badur) v Birmingham Crown Court* [2006] EWHC 539 (Admin) for the interplay with s 24A and the summary only offence of obtaining leave to enter or remain by deception under IA 1971, s 24(1)(aa).

50 [2001] EWCA Crim 2874.

51 [2011] 1 Cr App R(S) 91, [2010] EWCA Crim 1979.

4.69

There is no distinction in culpability between the s 24A(1)(a) and (b) offences[52].

4.70

When sentencing youths then, in accordance with general principles, different considerations apply. Special attention should be paid to the role of agents in such cases, and a custodial sentence is not inevitable[53].

False statement for marriage

Definition

4.71

This is an offence contrary to the Perjury Act 1911, s 3 which is defined as follows:

> '**3.— False statements, &c. with reference to marriage.**
>
> (1) If any person—
>
> (a) for the purpose of procuring a marriage, or a certificate or licence for marriage, [or a marriage document or a marriage schedule,]1knowingly and wilfully makes a false oath, or makes or signs a false declaration, notice or certificate required under any Act of Parliament for the time being in force relating to marriage; or
>
> (b) knowingly and wilfully makes, or knowingly and wilfully causes to be made, for the purposes of being inserted in any register of marriage or register of conversions, a false statement as to any particular required by law to be known and registered relating to any marriage or any civil partnership which is to be converted into a marriage; or
>
> (c) forbids the issue of any certificate or licence for marriage [or marriage schedule by falsely representing himself to be a person whose consent to the marriage is required by law knowing such representation to be false, or
>
> (d) with respect to a declaration made under section 16(1A) or 27B(2) of the Marriage Act 1949—
>
> (i) enters a caveat under subsection (2) of the said section 16, or
>
> (ii) makes a statement mentioned in subsection (4) of the said section 27B,
>
> which he knows to be false in a material particular.

52 *Ding* [2010] EWCA Crim 1979, at [9].
53 *K v Croydon Crown Court* [2005] EWHC 478 (Admin).

(2) No prosecution for knowingly and wilfully making a false declaration for the purpose of procuring any marriage out of the district in which the parties or one of them dwell shall take place after the expiration of eighteen months from the solemnization of the marriage to which the declaration refers.

(3) In subsection (1)(b), *"register of conversions"* means the register of conversions of civil partnerships into marriages kept by the Registrar General in accordance with section 9 of the Marriage (Same Sex Couples) Act 2013 and regulations made under that section.'

4.72

The false statement must be in relation to something that the law requires should be stated correctly. In *Frickey*[54] a false declaration on a form purporting to give parental consent that was for the convenience of the Superintendent Registrar, but not mandatory, was not an offence contrary to the Perjury Act 1911, s 3. The offence is the *making* of the false statement, and it does not matter whether the statement was acted on.

4.73

As with other offences of perjury, by virtue of the Perjury Act 1911, s 13:

> 'A person shall not be liable to be convicted of any offence against this Act, or of any offence declared by any other Act to be perjury or subornation of perjury, or to be punishable as perjury or subornation of perjury, solely upon the evidence of one witness as to the falsity of any statement alleged to be false.'

4.74

This means that before there can be a conviction, there needs to be two sources of evidence of the falsity of the statement. This can be two witnesses, or one witness and another source independent of that witness.

4.75

The only exception is if the case is put not on the basis that the statement was false, but that whether or not it was, the defendant did not believe it to be true.

4.76

This can also be satisfied by two people who hear a confession by a defendant.

54 [1956] Crim LR 421.

Defences

4.77

The Perjury Act 1911, s 3(2) reads:

> 'No prosecution for knowingly and wilfully making a false declaration for the purpose of procuring any marriage out of the district in which the parties or one of them dwell shall take place after the expiration of eighteen months from the solemnization of the marriage to which the declaration refers.'

4.78

This should be interpreted so that it will only apply if the false declaration is made for the purpose of procuring the marriage out of the relevant district, rather than procuring a marriage that happens to be outside the relevant district. Ie, it will not be a defence if the relevant false declaration is nothing to do with the location of the marriage[55]. This might be thought to be a not entirely uncontroversial interpretation.

4.79

This has the consequence of severely limiting the impact of the defence. It dates from 1836 which, amongst other matters, created provision for civil marriages and to recognise those from religions and denominations other than the Church of England, Quakers, and Jews.

4.80

There were not many places for people who were not members of the Church of England to get married and so provision was made to allow people to marry out of their district provided they declared their reasons, their place of intended marriage, and that there was no location in their home district. The Perjury Act 1911, s 3(2) re-enacts the defence that such a false declaration could only be prosecuted if started within 18 months.

Impact on civil partnerships

4.81

Marriages includes the conversion of a civil partnership to marriage. An analogous offence for civil partnerships was created by the Civil Partnership Act 2004, s 80. This has the same maximum penalty. The rules contained in the Perjury Act 1911, s 13 apply (s 80(4)).

---

55 *Garvin* [2005] EWCA Crim 2088 at [13].

Sentence

4.82

The maximum sentence is seven years. There are no Sentencing Guidelines or guidance from the Court of Appeal

4.83

Assuming that the offence is committed for the purposes of evading immigration control, then the appropriate sentence is the same as for the *Kolawole* type of offences; 12–18 months imprisonment[56].

Historical note – entry offences

4.84

As noted above, the consequences of the IA 1971, s 11 were brought into renewed focus by the decision in *Kakaei*[57] . This led to the passing of the NABA 2022[58], which made radical changes to the entry offences. However, it is still necessary to give some consideration to the previous version.

4.85

Prior to then, s 24 contained a set of summary only offences[59]:

'(a) entering without leave/in breach of a Deportation Order

(b) (i) remaining beyond a grant of leave

(ii) failing to observe a condition of leave that has been granted

(c) overstaying following a period of valid leave granted under s8 (an exemption for crew members)

(d) failing to comply with directions relating to health checks

(e) failing to comply with employment or reporting conditions

(f) leaving a boat or aircraft that he was put on to be removed (either administratively or by virtue of a deportation order)

56 *Kuku* [2010] EWCA Crim 2533 and *Biloum* [2004] EWCA Crim 3462.

57 [2021] EWCA Crim 503.

58 From the explanatory notes NABA 2022:

399. The offence of knowingly entering the UK without leave dates back to the original version of the 1971 Act. Entering the UK without leave is no longer considered entirely apt given the changes in ways in which people have sought to come to the UK through irregular routes.

415 ... As noted regarding the offence of entry without leave, migrants who are intercepted at sea and are brought into an immigration control area may not have "entered" the UK unlawfully and so a person facilitating their journey may not be charged with assisting a breach of immigration law for that offence. This amendment will ensure that the offence of facilitation also applies to those assisting persons to arrive in the UK without a valid entry clearance.

59 These survive in a modified form as considered in Chapter 7.

(g) embarking contrary to an Order in Council made under s3(7) Immigration Act 1971 (there are currently no such orders).'

4.86

In practice, these were rarely, if ever, charged. Where they were charged (certainly in the last twenty years or so) it is normally where another, more serious, charge has been laid[60] with these being 'added on'.

Procedure/time limits

4.87

Although the offences are all summary only, under the IA 1971, s28 the extended time limit for the bringing of a prosecution applies (see Chapter 10). For that reason, someone is at risk of prosecution for more than six months for some of the offences. This risk (at least the risk of prosecution under the pre-NABA offences) will expire in June 2025.

4.88

The other area where practitioners may need to be aware of the offence is in the context of an IA 1971, s 25 facilitation offence. Whilst, following *Kakei*, such an offence would now not form the basis of the underlying breach, in reviewing a historic conviction it may be that this would have been pleaded as the underlying breach of immigration law.

Defences

4.89

Offences (a) and (b) can only be committed 'knowingly': (d) and (e) have a defence of 'reasonable excuse'. There is no guidance as to what can or cannot amount to a reasonable excuse.

Sentence

4.90

The maximum penalty for all these offences was six months or a Level 5 (unlimited) fine. There are no guidelines and, as noted above, where there has been any remotely recent case it has come alongside a more serious charge and attracted a concurrent sentence which does not assist in establishing any guidance. Absent more serious offending, it is unlikely that a prosecution for these offences would be pursued.

---

60 See, as examples; *Bucpapa* [2005] EWCA Crim 521 – forged passport / entering without leave, *Gabier* [2008] EWCA Crim 985 – false ID docs / remaining beyond a period of leave granted).

5 Facilitation and trafficking offences

Introduction

5.1

In this Chapter, 'entry' is used in the technical, legal sense contained in the IA 1971, s 11. See Chapter 4 for further details of this.

Facilitation offences

Overview and background

5.2

In 1972 it was an either way offence (with a maximum sentence of seven years) for a person to knowingly make or carry out arrangements to secure or facilitate the entry of someone they knew or had reasonable cause to believe was an illegal entrant. Further, it was a summary only offence to knowingly harbour such a person inside the United Kingdom. Moving forward just over 50 years, the law has becoming increasingly more complex, and breaches more serious.

5.3

Substantial changes were made to the IA 1971, s 25 offence on 10 February 2003 by virtue of the NIAA 2002, s 143. As well as introducing the concept of the facilitation of a breach of 'immigration law', it also brought in the IA 1971, s 25A and s 25B[1] offences.

5.4

As was stated in the Explanatory Notes to the NIAA 2002:

> 'This is a measure required to enable the United Kingdom to comply with Article 27 of the Schengen Convention, and will also assist compliance with a European Directive defining the facilitation of unauthorised entry, transit and residence and its associated Framework Decision, which will replace that Article[2].'

1 This made it an offence to facilitate the entry of someone in breach of a Deportation Order,

2 These are Council Directive 2002/90/EC (the Facilitation Directive) and Council Framework Decision 2002/946/JHA.

5.5

Articles 1 and 2 of Council Directive 2002/90/EC read as follows:

> '**Article 1 – General infringement**
>
> 1. Each Member State shall adopt appropriate sanctions on:
>
>   (a) any person who intentionally assists a person who is not a national of a Member State to enter, or transit across, the territory of a Member State in breach of the laws of the State concerned on the entry or transit of aliens;
>
>   (b) any person who, for financial gain, intentionally assists a person who is not a national of a Member State to reside within the territory of a Member State in breach of the laws of the State concerned on the residence of aliens.
>
> 2. Any Member State may decide not to impose sanctions with regard to the behaviour defined in paragraph 1(a) by applying its national law and practice for cases where the aim of the behaviour is to provide humanitarian assistance to the person concerned.
>
> **Article 2 – Instigation, participation and attempt**
>
> Each Member State shall take the measures necessary to ensure that the sanctions referred to in Article 1 are also applicable to any person who:
>
> (a) is the instigator of,
>
> (b) is an accomplice in, or
>
> (c) attempts to commit
>
> an infringement as referred to in Article 1(1)(a) or (b).'

5.6

Reading this, the origin of the modern law is clear. The Directive refers to 'enter, or transit across'. These do not appear to have an autonomous meaning across the EU akin to its meaning in the UK (although the IA 1971, s 25 offence did use the word 'enter' prior to the implementation of the NIAA 2002, s 143[3]).

5.7

In those circumstances, it is not clear whether Parliament at the time intended the facilitation offence to be restricted to those who 'enter' in its legal meaning. It would not appear that that the Directive would require that conclusion either, notwithstanding the reference to 'in breach of the laws of the State concerned on the entry or transit of aliens'. In fact, the s 25 offence as it is currently drafted,

3 Section 25 originally read 'Any person knowingly concerned in making or carrying out arrangements for securing or facilitating the entry into the United Kingdom of anyone whom he knows or has reasonable cause for believing to be an illegal entrant shall be guilty of an offence …'.

is more aligned to the principles of the Directive than the pre-Nationality and Borders Act 2022 (NABA 2022)[4]. However, given the terms of the IA 1971, s 11, and the number of times that the s 25 offence has been considered, it is unlikely that a court would be persuaded that 'enter' in the IA 1971, Part III should be given a different meaning to that given in Part I.

The IA 1971, s 25 – assisting unlawful immigration

Offence

5.8

The offence is set out in the IA 1971, s 25:

> **25 Assisting unlawful immigration to member State or the United Kingdom**
>
> (1) A person commits an offence if he—
>
> (a) does an act which facilitates the commission of a breach or attempted breach of immigration law by an individual who is not a national of the United Kingdom,
>
> (b) knows or has reasonable cause for believing that the act facilitates the commission of a breach or attempted breach of immigration law by the individual, and
>
> (c) knows or has reasonable cause for believing that the individual is not a national of the United Kingdom.

4 See, as a comparison the Criminal Justice (Smuggling of Persons) Act 2021 passed by the Republic of Ireland explicitly to fully implement the Directive. This includes the following:

> '"immigration law", in relation to a designated state, means a law which has effect in the designated state and which controls the entry into, transit across or presence in the designated state of a person who is not a national of that state;
>
> **Assisting unlawful entry into, transit across or presence in State**
>
> 6. (1) A person is guilty of an offence if he or she intentionally assists the entry into, transit across or presence in the State of another person, where—
>
> (a) such entry into, transit across or presence in the State is in breach of a specified provision, and
>
> (b) the first-mentioned person knows or has reasonable cause to believe that such entry into, transit across or presence in the State is in breach of a specified provision.
>
> (2) A person who, in a place outside the State, engages in conduct that would, if the conduct occurred in the State, constitute an offence under subsection (1), is guilty of an offence.
>
> (3) A person who, in a place outside the State, aids, abets, counsels, procures or attempts the commission of an offence under subsection (1) or subsection (2) is guilty of an offence.
>
> With similar provision for the offence to be committed in another state.
>
> **Assisting unlawful entry into, transit across or presence in designated state**
>
> 7. (1) A person is guilty of an offence if he or she intentionally assists the entry into, transit across or presence in a designated state of another person, where—
>
> (a) such entry into, transit across or presence in the designated state is in breach of an immigration law in the designated state, and
>
> (b) the first-mentioned person knows or has reasonable cause to believe that such entry into, transit across or presence in the designated state is in breach of an immigration law in the designated state.'

(2) In subsection (1) "immigration law" means a law which has effect in a member State or the United Kingdom and which controls, in respect of some or all persons who are not nationals of the State or, as the case may be, of the United Kingdom, entitlement to—

(a) enter or arrive in the State or the United Kingdom ,

(b) transit across the State or the United Kingdom, or

(c) be in the State or the United Kingdom.

(2A) In subsections (1) and (2), "national of the United Kingdom" means—

(a) a British citizen;

(b) a person who is a British subject by virtue of Part 4 of the British Nationality Act 1981 and who has the right of abode in the United Kingdom; or

(b) a person who is a British overseas territories citizen by virtue of a connection with Gibraltar.

(3) A document issued by the government of a member State certifying a matter of law in that State—

(a) shall be admissible in proceedings for an offence under this section, and

(b) shall be conclusive as to the matter certified.

(4) Subsection (1) applies to things done whether inside or outside the United Kingdom.

...

(7) In this section–

(a) a reference to a member State includes a reference to Norway or Iceland.'

Facilitation

What is facilitation?

5.9

The act of facilitation is at the heart of the offence (the IA 1971, s 25 offence is often referred to, along with s 25A, as the 'facilitation offences'). Whilst the typical means of facilitating would be a people smuggler bringing another person to the United Kingdom in a clandestine manner, there are a multitude of different ways in that it can be committed. Examples given by the Home Office are[5]:

---

5 'Dealing with potential criminality (ICE teams)', v2.0 (February 2023).

- people smuggling across the border
- cheating on the knowledge of life test
- cheating on the long residency rule
- corrupt Home Office staff members involved in this abuse

5.10

Facilitation is not defined in the Act, and the judge need not elaborate on its meaning[6].

De minimis

5.11

In *Kakaei*[7], in relation to what is meant by facilitation in the context of pilots of small boat crossing the English Channel, it was said:

> '[22]. The *de minimis* point the judge refers to is the submission on behalf of the appellant that his actions in piloting the boat, and doing nothing more, could not amount to facilitation of the unlawful entry of the other migrants in the boat. The content of the Defence Statement, see [9] above, was designed to set out the facts on which this is based. That submission was abandoned before us by Mr. Brewer as being completely hopeless. It was, however, treated by the judge as a matter which would be determined by the jury if the appellant did not plead guilty.
>
> [55]. The effect of the ruling in fact was that the appellant was advised to plead guilty to counts 1 and 3 because he was advised that the judge had withdrawn his defence to those counts, leaving only the *de minimis* issue open. As we have said, the appellant was advised that this was hopeless. This appeal is not based on the suggestion that this last piece of advice was incompetent, and it clearly was not. Steering the boat is a pretty clear case of facilitation, many people would think.'

5.12

The actions that could amount to facilitation will therefore be wide. It would be capable of including crew members of a boat that is smuggling illegal immigrants (who have knowledge of the operation) as well as, potentially, people on a small boat who were navigating or otherwise assisting in a cross-Channel crossing. If there is an issue then, provided the act or acts relied on are capable of being sufficient to amount to facilitation (defined widely), it would be for the jury to determine whether it did.

6 *Ali* [2015] EWCA Crim 43, [2015] 1 Cr App R 32 at [52].
7 [2021] EWCA Crim 503.

Attempt

5.13

As the IA 1971, s 25 is defined as facilitating the commission of a 'breach or attempted breach' what scope is there for an attempt?

5.14

It was confirmed in *Ali* that it is not necessary that a breach actually occurred, provided that that the acts committed by a defendant make it easier for a future breach of immigration law to occur[8]. Further, in *Bani* it was said[9]:

> 'The offence is complete when the act of facilitation ("the act") is done with the necessary knowledge or reasonable cause for belief. The words "or attempted breach" in section 25(1) of the 1971 Act mean that it is an offence to facilitate a breach of immigration law at any stage in the plan which may result in such a breach. It does not matter whether the plan results in a breach of immigration law or not. It is an offence to facilitate any step in the journey which is more than merely preparatory to the breach.'

5.15

In those circumstances where an attempt to bring migrants to the United Kingdom is thwarted mid-Channel, there would be an attempted breach of immigration law so the full offence will have been committed.

5.16

For those reasons, the scope for an attempt is limited. It would perhaps cover instances where someone tried to facilitate the arrival of someone in circumstances where they believed that there would be a breach of immigration law, but that would not, in fact, be the case. An example would be the situation where a people smuggler transports a British journalist, or undercover agent, who was pretending to be a visa national.

Immigration law

Definition

5.17

There has to be a breach of 'immigration law'. This is defined in the IA 1971, s 25(2) as:

8 *Ali* at [41]–[51].
9 *Bani* at [105].

'(2) In subsection (1) *"immigration law"* means a law which has effect in a member State or the United Kingdom and which controls, in respect of some or all persons who are not nationals of the State or, as the case may be, of the United Kingdom, entitlement to—

(a) enter or arrive in the State or the United Kingdom,

(b) transit across the State or the United Kingdom, or

(c) be in the State or the United Kingdom.'

5.18

'In breach of immigration laws' (in the plural) is defined elsewhere in the IA 1971[10], as well as in other Acts[11], but the definition in s 25 has been considered to be a standalone one.

5.19

In relation to the IA 1971, s 25, it is clear that an immigration law need not be a criminal offence[12], although it may be[13]. However, where a criminal offence is alleged to be the underlying breach, it must be proved that that offence occurred (or would have occurred)[14]. This creates an extra hurdle for the Crown and would create particular difficulties where the person facilitated could not commit the offence (for example, because they are a child and under the age of criminal responsibility). In those circumstances it would generally be preferable to charge the breach as being contrary to the civil law where possible.

5.20

Immigration law must be a substantive provision of the law relating to the person's entitlement to enter (or arrive, transit, or be in, as the case may be) the United Kingdom rather than a procedural one such as the AI(TC)A 2004, s 2[15].

5.21

Historically, the immigration law that is alleged to have been breached has been the IA 1971, ss 1(2) and 3(1)(b)[16]:

---

10 Section 33:
'"immigration laws" means this Act and any law for purposes similar to this Act which is for the time being or has (before or after the passing of this Act) been in force in any part of the United Kingdom and Islands;'

11 For example, British Citizenship Act 1981, ss 50 and 50A have a definition of 'immigration laws (with a plural 's') and 'being in breach of immigration laws' for the purpose of the acquisition of British Citizenship. See also NIAA 2002, s11 (now repealed) had a comprehensive definition that related to the availability of rights of appeal.

12 *Javaherifad* [2005] EWCA Crim 3231, [2006] Imm AR 185 at [44].

13 *Kakaei* [2021] EWCA Crim 503, [2022] CLR 507 at [28]–-36]. See also *Mohamed* [2023] EWCA Crim 211 at [78] where it was said that 'a person is not entitled to do something which is illegal by virtue of being a criminal offence'.

14 *Kaile* [2009] EWCA Crim 2868 at [14]–[15].

15 *Kapoor* [2012] EWCA Crim 435, [2012] 2 Cr App R 11 at [34]–[40].

16 *Boateng* [2016] EWCA Crim 57, [2016] 2 Cr App 5 at [27].

'1 General Principles

...

(2) Those not having that right may live, work and settle in the United Kingdom by permission and subject to such regulation and control of their entry into, stay in and departure from the United Kingdom as is imposed by this Act; and indefinite leave to enter or remain in the United Kingdom shall, by virtue of this provision, be treated as having been given under this Act to those in the United Kingdom at its coming into force, if they are then settled there (and not exempt under this Act from the provisions relating to leave to enter or remain).

3 General provisions for regulation and control.

(1) Except as otherwise provided by or under this Act, where a person is not [a British citizen—

...

(b) he may be given leave to enter the United Kingdom (or, when already there, leave to remain in the United Kingdom) either for a limited or for an indefinite period;

...'

5.22

In *Mohamed*[17] it was said that[18]:

> 'Since 2000 section 3A (together with the definition of "entry clearance" in section 33(1)) has enabled Immigration Rules to be made requiring entry clearance to be obtained before a person arrives in the UK. To adapt the language of *Kapoor* at [36], the regime created by section 3A of the 1971 Act falls within section 25(2) because it determines whether a person lawfully or unlawfully arrives in and then enters the UK.'

5.23

It is likely that almost all cases would fall within the above parts of immigration law.

Enter

5.24

As noted above, 'enter' has the specialised meaning in s 11.

---

17 [2023] EWCA Crim 211.
18 Ibid at [75].

Arrive

5.25

'Arrive' in the IA 1971, s 25 is likely to be read in accordance with s 24(D1), even if the criminal offence is not pleaded as the underlying immigration law.

Transit

5.26

This is not generally pleaded as the underlying alleged breach of immigration law, mainly as any cases where someone is genuinely transiting is unlikely to be identified in advance, and anyone who is found in the United Kingdom in transit will have arrived (and possibly entered). Following the inclusion of arrival in the s 25 definition, it would appear that there is very little scope for 'transit' to add anything.

Be in

5.27

Although many people who are 'in' the United Kingdom in breach of immigration law will have arrived in breach of immigration law previously, this will not always be the case. Someone who arrived with leave, but who overstayed it, would be the primary example, although someone who was born in the United Kingdom to someone not lawfully present would 'be in' the United Kingdom without leave, even though they never arrived or entered in the legal sense, nor had they overstayed.

5.28

Someone who assisted an overstayer obtain further leave to remain by fraudulent means, or who provided them with false papers, would be facilitating them being in the United Kingdom in breach. It is not as clear whether someone who knowingly employs someone without leave would commit the offence[19].

Illegal employment and renting as facilitating

5.29

There is a potential overlap between facilitation and both the IANA 2006, s 21 offence (employing someone illegally) and the IA 2014, ss 33A and 33B (landlord and agent) offences in that someone who employs another who is not lawfully allowed to work, or rents accommodation to them, may be 'facilitating

19 See Chapter 6 for further discussion.

the commission of a breach of immigration law', namely one which controls the 'entitlement to … be … in the United Kingdom'.

5.30

By analogy with *Kapoor*[20], it could be argued that those offences are not 'immigration law' for the purposes of the 1971 Act. Someone who employs another person who does not have the right to work is facilitating their ability to stay in the country in the sense that their wages would allow them to live here[21]. However, whilst illegal working facilitates somebody's *ability* to remain in the UK it does not appear to be related to their entitlement to *be* here[22]. Likewise with the housing offences[23]. Further support for that would be that there would be no need to introduce these specific offences if the person could simply be charged with facilitation.

5.31

In addition, see below as to the question of *mens rea* which would be a live issue in any prosecution based on these offences.

5.32

In accordance with cases such as *Hardy*[24], it is arguable that even if the conduct that constituted either offence did amount to facilitation, then it is not appropriate to charge the s 25 offence where the alleged criminality is solely that of employing someone illegally, although it would not be an abuse of process to do so. However, it is likely that the sentencer should then consider themselves bound by a maximum sentence of five years.

5.33

A prosecutor may wish to give consideration to the above before pursuing a s 25 charge based on either offence. A practitioner representing a client who is charged with the s 25 offence in such circumstances should make representations as to why the case should proceed (if it should proceed at all) on the NAIA, ss 21 or 33A 33B offence[25]. This would be separate to any argument on the law or facts raised.

---

20 [2012] EWCA Crim 435, [2012] 2 Cr App R 11.

21 Even prior to NABA 2022, it was said in *Javaherifard* [2005] EWCA Crim 3231, [2006] Imm AR185 to be 'absurd if unlawful presence did not constitute a breach of immigration law' whether or not it was a criminal offence.

22 In *Nevin v HM Advocate* (2006) SCCR 460 (a Scottish case) there was no issue raised in relation to someone who provided employment and accommodation to illegal entrants.

23 *R(JCWI) v SSHD* [2020] EWCA Civ 542, [2021] 1 WLR 1151 proceeded on the basis that the facilitation offence would cover the illegal housing case, but it appears that this was set out more by way of background and the decision did not turn on it [2]–[3] and [7].

24 [2013] EWCA Crim 2125.

25 The CPS Guidance on Immigration reads, in relation to illegal employment, 'An offence of Assisting unlawful immigration to a member state or to the UK (see section above on Facilitation offences) can be considered in serious cases, such as organised criminal activity to evade immigration rules'.

Procedure

5.34

The immigration law that is alleged to have been breached should be named in the indictment and, in many cases, it is appropriate for the prosecution to give further details in an opening note or other document[26].

Mens rea

5.35

The *mens rea* is set out in the Act (at s 25(1)(b) and (c)), and there is no further gloss needed to be put on that[27].

5.36

There is no requirement for the person facilitated to be called (and it may often be impossible, such as when they are a child or cannot be traced) and the necessary inferences can be drawn. For example, in a 'small boat' case it is likely that a court will readily accept that none of the passengers on a boat had permission to come, and that this would have been clear to anyone piloting it, as for obvious reasons, 'no one enters a country by night in a small boat if he is coming in lawfully'[28].

5.37

However, the position in relation to people who fall into the category of those who could be said to have 'good intentions' is complex. In *Javaherifard* it was said that the critical points are whether that person is seeking to facilitate a further breach, and whether they are seeking to aid the person as someone who is in breach of immigration law or on the basis of common humanity[29]:

> 'The s 25 offence is only committed if, with the requisite guilty knowledge, the acts facilitate the commission of a breach of immigration law controlling, in this instance, "being in the State": that is, being unlawfully in the UK. If the provision of legal advice is about how lawfully and honestly to regularise the stay of someone known to be an illegal entrant, no offence arises: those acts do not facilitate the commission of a breach of immigration law through continued illegal presence; they do the opposite. If someone provides food, money or accommodation to an illegal entrant, knowing or having reasonable cause for believing that such acts facilitate him being in the country *as an illegal entrant*, he would be guilty of an offence and we see no

26 *Bani* at [99].
27 *Mohamed* at [81].
28 *R v Governor of Pentonville Prison, ex parte Azam* [1974] AC 18 at [33G].
29 *Javaherifard* at [50].

> reason why that should not be so. If food, money or accommodation is supplied to someone known to the provider to be an illegal immigrant, but is not supplied with the knowledge that it will assist his presence *as an illegal entrant* but instead is supplied knowing that it will assist him simply as a human being eg to avoid degradation or destitution, there would be no offence. The provision of NASS support and other statutory benefits is made under the protection of statutory provision if no other defence is available, but it is difficult to see how that would assist someone to remain as an illegal entrant, as opposed to remain while seeking to regularise his stay.'

5.38

So, the solicitor or charity that provides advice as to somebody's status and seeks to help them regularise it would not commit the offence. That is relatively straightforward, but the other example given in *Javaherifard*, that of the person who provides 'food, money or accommodation' is more complicated. The distinction between the two examples given in *Javaherifard* in relation to that example is an extremely fine one.

5.39

What of the person who is the passenger on a small boat who takes over the steering in order to protect others? They are probably facilitating the arrival or the others (as well as themselves) in the United Kingdom and are thereby committing the offence (even though their intention was not to facilitate that breach), although this aspect of the *mens rea* has not yet been resolved. One point of distinction may be that such a person is already engaged in a criminal enterprise (attempting to arrive), and so would not be the impartial third person envisaged in *Javaherifard*. This would be reinforced by the fact that they are specifically excluded from the 'Rescuer' defence.

Conspiracies

5.40

Although the *mens rea* for the substantive offence is knowledge or reasonable cause to believe, where a conspiracy is alleged, then it will be necessary to prove actual knowledge[30].

Defence for rescuers

5.41

The defence is as set out in the IA 1971, s 25BA:

30 *Saik* [2006] UKHL 18, [2006] 1 AC 18.

'25BA Facilitation offences: application to rescuers

(1) A person does not commit a facilitation offence if the act of facilitation was an act done by or on behalf of, or co-ordinated by—

(a) Her Majesty's Coastguard, or

(b) an overseas maritime search and rescue authority exercising similar functions to those of Her Majesty's Coastguard.

(2) In proceedings for a facilitation offence, it is a defence for the person charged with the offence to show that—

(a) the assisted individual had been in danger or distress at sea, and

(b) the act of facilitation was an act of providing assistance to the individual at any time between—

(i) the time when the assisted individual was first in danger or distress at sea, and

(ii) the time when the assisted individual was delivered to a place of safety on land.

(3) For the purposes of subsection (2), the following are not to be treated as an act of providing assistance—

(a) the act of delivering the assisted individual to the United Kingdom in circumstances where—

(i) the United Kingdom was not the nearest place of safety on land to which the assisted individual could have been delivered, and

(ii) the person charged with the offence did not have a good reason for delivering the assisted individual to the United Kingdom instead of to a nearer place of safety on land;

(b) the act of steering a ship in circumstances where the person charged with the offence was on the same ship as the assisted individual at the time when the individual was first in danger or distress at sea.

(4) A person is taken to have shown a fact mentioned in subsection (2) if—

(a) sufficient evidence of the fact is adduced to raise an issue with respect to it, and

(b) the contrary is not proved beyond reasonable doubt.

(5) In this section—

"act of facilitation" —

(a) in relation to an offence under section 25 (assisting unlawful immigration), means the act mentioned in subsection (1)(a) of that section;

(b) in relation to an offence under section 25A (helping asylum-seeker to enter the UK), means the act of facilitating the arrival (or attempted arrival) in, or entry (or attempted entry) into, the United Kingdom of an individual, as mentioned in subsection (1)(a) of that section;

(c) in relation to an offence under section 25B(1) (facilitating breach of deportation order), means the act mentioned in subsection (1)(a) of that section;

(d) in relation to an offence under section 25B(3) (assisting entry to UK in breach of an exclusion order), means the act mentioned in subsection (3)(a) of that section;

"assisted individual"—

(a) in relation to an offence under section 25, means the individual whose breach (or attempted breach) of immigration law is facilitated by the act of facilitation;

(b) in relation to an offence under section 25A, means the individual whose arrival (or attempted arrival) in, or entry (or attempted entry) into, the United Kingdom is facilitated by the act of facilitation;

(c) in relation to an offence under section 25B(1), means the individual whose breach (or attempted breach) of a deportation order is facilitated by the act of facilitation;

(d) in relation to an offence under section 25B(3), means the individual who is assisted to arrive in, enter or remain (or to attempt to arrive in, enter or remain) in the United Kingdom by the act of facilitation;

"facilitation offence" means—

(a) an offence under section 25 (assisting unlawful immigration),

(b) an offence under section 25A (helping asylum-seeker to enter the United Kingdom), or

(c) an offence under section 25B (assisting entry to the United Kingdom in breach of deportation or exclusion order) to the extent that the section continues to apply by virtue of regulation 5(7) of the Immigration and Social Security Co-ordination (EU Withdrawal) Act 2020 (Consequential, Saving, Transitional and Transitory Provisions) (EU Exit) Regulations 2020 (S.I. 2020/1309);

"ship" includes—

(a) every description of vessel (including a hovercraft), and

(b) any other structure (whether with or without means of propulsion) constructed or used to carry persons, goods, plant or machinery by water.'

5.42

This creates two separate defences. Firstly is where HM Coastguard or other body is co-ordinating a rescue and seeks the assistance of others. There will then be a defence regardless of whether there was a risk of life and regardless of the intention of the defendant.

5.43

The other defence will cover private citizens who act to prevent 'danger or distress'[31] at sea, provided that they satisfy the conditions in the IA 1971, s 25BA(3). This requires that they deliver the people that they are rescuing to the nearest place of safety on land or, if they do not do so, they had a 'good reason' to take them to the United Kingdom.

5.44

Examples of what may constitute a 'good reason' in the Explanatory Notes[32] are weather conditions and the fact that the rescuer is operating a commercial ferry service heading to the United Kingdom.

5.45

Where raised, the defence in the IA 1971, s 25BA(2) creates an evidential burden on the defendant only. Despite the absence of subsection (1) from the evidential burden provisions, the same would presumably apply to the defence in s 25BA(1), although it is unlikely to be in dispute.

5.46

There is an important exclusion for those on the same boat, who cannot benefit from the defence, although if two 'small boats' are heading to the United Kingdom then there would not appear to be any reason why someone who moves from one to the other to help steer it would not have this defence, even if the motives were mixed (to help the passengers on board, as well as to get to the United Kingdom).

31 This is not defined in the Act, but comes from the general, and long standing, 'duty to render assistance' to those in distress as encapsulated by Art 98 United Nations Convention on the Law of the Sea (1982).

32 NABA 2022, Explanatory Notes, [425]-[427].

Defences relating to stowaways

5.47

The defence is set out in the IA 1971, s25BB:

'25BB Facilitation offences: defences relating to stowaways

(1) In proceedings for a facilitation offence brought against a master of a ship, it is a defence for the master to show—

(a) that the assisted individual was a stowaway when the act of facilitation took place, and

(b) that the master, or a person acting on the master's behalf, reported the presence of the assisted individual on the ship to the Secretary of State or an immigration officer—

(i) in a case where the ship was scheduled to go to the United Kingdom, as soon as reasonably practicable after the time when the ship's next scheduled port of call became a port in the United Kingdom, or

(ii) in a case where the ship was not scheduled to go to the United Kingdom but the master of the ship decided that the ship needed to go to the United Kingdom (whether for reasons relating to the presence of the assisted individual on board or for other reasons), as soon as reasonably practicable after the master made that decision.

(2) In proceedings for a facilitation offence, it is a defence for the person charged with the offence to show—

(a) that the assisted individual was a stowaway when the act of facilitation took place,

(b) that they were acting to ensure the security, general health, welfare or safety of the assisted individual, and

(c) that they had reported the presence of the assisted individual to the master of the ship as soon as reasonably practicable.

(3) A person is taken to have shown a fact mentioned in subsection (1) or (2) if—

(a) sufficient evidence of the fact is adduced to raise an issue with respect to it, and

(b) the contrary is not proved beyond reasonable doubt.

(4) For the purposes of this section, an individual is a stowaway on a ship if—

(a) they boarded the ship without the knowledge of the master of the ship, and

(b) the master was not aware of their presence on the ship when the ship departed from the port where the individual boarded.

(5) But an individual ceases to be a stowaway if, after the master of the ship has become aware of their presence on the ship, the individual is given permission to leave the ship by the immigration authorities of a country that the ship arrives at (whether or not they do in fact leave the ship there).

(6) In this section, "act of facilitation", "assisted individual", "facilitation offence" and "ship" have the same meanings as in section 25BA.'

5.48

This again provides two separate defences to a facilitation offence. Firstly, there is a specific defence for the Master of a ship who is charged with bringing a facilitated migrant to the United Kingdom. This will apply where the person facilitated comes on board without the knowledge of the Master, provided that the ship has left the port where the stowaway came on board by the time of their discovery.

5.49

The defence requires that the Master reports the presence of the migrant to the Home Office or an Immigration Officer as soon as reasonably practicable after the stowaway was discovered or, if the next intended stop was not in the United Kingdom, then as soon as reasonably practicable after it was decided that it was necessary to go to the United Kingdom. This defence arises even if other members of the crew were aware of (or arranged for) the stowaway being on board.

5.50

Secondly, there is a general defence for anyone charged with a s 25 or 25A offence who provides assistance to a stowaway to ensure their health and welfare, provided that they reported the presence of the stowaway to the Master of the ship as soon as reasonably practicable. This would cover both passengers and crew members who discover a stowaway on board.

5.51

Again, there is an evidential burden on the defendant in relation to both defences.

The IA 1971, s 25A – helping an asylum seeker to enter the United Kingdom

Introduction

5.52

The offence is defined in the IA 1971, s 25A as:

'25A Helping asylum-seeker to enter United Kingdom

(1) A person commits an offence if—

(a) he knowingly facilitates the arrival or attempted arrival in, or the entry or attempted entry into, the United Kingdom of an individual, and

(b) he knows or has reasonable cause to believe that the individual is an asylum-seeker.

(2) In this section "asylum-seeker" means a person who intends to claim that to remove him from or require him to leave the United Kingdom would be contrary to the United Kingdom's obligations under—

(a) the Refugee Convention (within the meaning given by section 167(1) of the Immigration and Asylum Act 1999 (c. 33) (interpretation)), or

(b) the Human Rights Convention (within the meaning given by that section).

(3) Subsection (1) does not apply to anything done by a person acting on behalf of an organisation which—

(a) aims to assist asylum-seekers, and

(b) does not charge for its services.

(4) subsections (4) and (6) of section 25 apply for the purpose of the offence in subsection (1) of this section as they apply for the purpose of the offence in subsection (1) of that section.'

Definitions

5.53

'Facilitates' for the purposes of the IA 1971, s 25A(1)(a) will have the same meaning as it does under s 25.

5.54

The person must presumably be an 'asylum seeker' at the time of the facilitation, so someone who arrives in the United Kingdom and, by the time of the trial has married a British citizen and has made a claim to remain in the UK under Art 8 of the ECHR, would not be an 'asylum seeker'. Although that may seem obvious, there will be other cases where it may not be as clear. For example, where the facilitator is bringing in the person facilitated in order to exploit them, then they would not be an asylum seeker even if they subsequently made a claim.

5.55

A person who is already recognised as a refugee, and is coming to the United Kingdom on that basis, would presumably not be an 'asylum seeker' for the purposes of the legislation as otherwise any airline that carried him would be committing the offence.

5.56

The defence in the IA 1971, s 25A(3) only applies to an organisation. It is also not a general 'humanitarian defence'. For that reason, somebody who buys a ticket for a relative to come to the UK to claim asylum does not have a defence to the s 25A offence (nor the s 25 offence for that matter). That does not mean that a prosecution must follow, and a representative should make representations to the CPS as to why it is not in the public interest to proceed. However, given the changes brought by the NABA 2022 it is unclear whether s 25A(3) has any purpose.

Defences

5.57

The rescuer and stowaway defences apply to the IA 1971, s 25A as they do to s 25.

Mens rea

5.58

Again, it would appear that the *mens rea* would be the same as for the s 25 offence.

Difference between the two offences

5.59

The difference between the s 25 and s 25A offence is now extremely limited. In most cases (at least of the person being facilitated is an asylum seeker) a person who is guilty of one will be guilty of the other.

5.60

The main distinctions are that (even when indicted with reference to 'arrive' rather than 'enter'), there is still a requirement under s 25 to prove a breach of immigration law which does not apply in s 25A.

5.61

Against that, in relation to the s 25A offence, this will only apply where the people facilitated are asylum seekers, and the defendant knew (or had reasonable cause to believe) that that was the case, whereas the s 25 offence would apply to anyone.

5.62

For a prosecutor, subject to the question of sentence (see below) the decision of which charge to pursue may not matter.

5.63

The only caveat would be that where there is an indication that the person facilitated is *not* an asylum seeker then the s 25 offence should be chosen. Examples would be where the facilitator is related to the person facilitated and is well aware that they are not an asylum seeker, or where the facilitation is part of a wider plan to exploit the person facilitated and it is known that the person is not an asylum seeker.

Sentencing for the facilitation offence

Introduction

5.64

The offences are either way with the maximum sentence for both the s 25 and 25A offences being life imprisonment[33]. There are no Sentencing Guidelines for either offence and, whilst there are a number of guideline cases for the s 25 offence, there are none for the s 25A offence.

5.65

When having regard to any previous authorities, the date (and therefore maximum sentence) must be checked. Further, the s 25 sentencing cases considered here are all based around the offence as it was prior to 28 June 2022. In those circumstances, the Crown will have proved that there was an illegal entry (none of these cases related to transiting or 'being in' the United Kingdom).

5.66

It remains to be seen whether the courts will consider that a lower sentence is appropriate when the case is indicted on the basis of 'arrival' rather than enter. See below for further discussion on the likely different approaches.

Guidelines

5.67

The authorities all make clear that the IA 1971, s 25 offence is a serious one, which will generally carry a deterrent sentence. Further, it is an area where the courts have said that public concern has risen and higher sentences have been required to reflect this.

33 Increased from 14 years from 28 June 2022.

5.68

The two main cases are *Le & Stark*[34] and *AG Ref (Nos 49 & 50 of 2015)*[35] 4 which sets out the following, non-exhaustive, list of matters to take into account:

- Whether the offence is isolated or repeated
- The duration of offending
- Whether the offender had previous similar convictions
- Whether the offender's motivation was commercial or humanitarian
- The number of individuals involved in the breach of immigration law
- Whether they were strangers or family
- The degree of organisation involved
- Whether the offender recruited others
- The offender's role
- Whether the offender's conduct involved exploitation of or pressure put upon others

5.69

Not all of these factors will be present in all cases. However, as was said in *Le & Stark*, at a time when the maximum sentence was seven years' imprisonment:

> 'It is plain from the authorities to which we have been referred and to which we shall return that in the ordinary way the appropriate penalty for all but the most minor offences against section 25(1)(a) is one of immediate custody. The offence is one which calls very often for deterrent sentences and, as the statistics make plain, the problem of illegal entry is on the increase.'

5.70

It is clear that sentences in double figures will be appropriate, especially in cases where the smuggling of people is a commercial enterprise[36] and/or where there is exploitation.

---

34 [1999] 1 Cr App R 422.

35 [2015] EWCA Crim 1402, [2016] 1 Cr App R(S).

36 See, as a recent example, *Mohamad* [2022] EWCA Crim 875, where permission to appeal a starting point of 11½ years after trial for a sophisticated operation where a number of migrants were brought into the United Kingdom on different occasions for gain. In *Ali & Othrs* [2018] EWCA Crim 405 there was a people smuggling operation where the participants benefitted to approximately £1.2 million relating to twenty trips. The Court of Appeal said that sentences for the 'real organisers' would start around 10 years with the drivers starting at 2½ years. Those with an organisational role would be in between, but towards the higher end. These are just two examples, and neither purport to set any formal guidance, but are an indication of seriousness of which the offences are taken.

5.71

However, especially in the absence of formal guidelines from the Sentencing Council, each case is fact specific and the fact that a particular sentence was passed in one case, does not mean that another Judge should follow that. With that caveat, some consideration of particular cases that are different to the paradigm example of the person smuggling in a number of foreign nationals is set out below.

Family members/humanitarian motives

5.72

Where someone is involved in a one-off incident to bring in a family member much shorter sentences will be appropriate.

5.73

In *Walid*[37] a sentence of 15 months (after a trial) was appropriate for someone who smuggled in the partner of his son in an 'unsophisticated' manner in order for her to claim asylum. Against that, in *Mohammed*[38] where a refugee from Iraq went to the 'Jungle' in Calais and gave his genuine British passport to his brother to use to come to the UK, 30 months (after a trial) was appropriate due to the use of the document and the pressure put on his partner. Other cases have tended to fall in between these examples.

5.74

It follows that in some cases of this nature, whilst a custodial sentence is likely, it will sometimes be appropriate to suspend it.

Sham marriages

5.75

In *Olivieria*[39] against a maximum sentence of 14 years it was said that a bracket of 18 months to 3 years is appropriate for the people involved in a 'sham marriage' where one person lawfully present marries another who is not. This would not apply in cases where there is a wider or professional conspiracy to arrange a number of sham marriages.

---

37 [2016] EWCA Crim 1120.
38 [2016] EWCA Crim 2272.
39 [2012] EWCA Crim 2279, [2013] 2 Cr App R(S) 4.

Small Boat crossings

5.76

The sentence appeal of *Bani*[40] sets out guidance for the sentencing of pilots of small boats. A sentence of five years was substituted for a pilot of a small boat that he had purchased along with others on board. In practice, people in that position will receive a shorter sentence, although a sentence of that length is unlikely to be appealable.

The resident judge at Canterbury Crown Court has also given considered sentencing remarks (not guidelines[41]) in relation to 'small boat' cases under the NABA 2022. This draws what may be thought to be a sensible parallel with the Drugs Guidelines in terms of role, and suggested a lower starting point than *Bani* in cases after trial for someone who's role was to pilot the boat, but who had no wider organisational role.

Effect of increase in maximum sentence to life imprisonment

5.77

The above Court of Appeal cases were all before the increase in the maximum sentence to life imprisonment. Whilst the Court of Appeal have not considered the new powers in relation to the facilitation offences, it has considered the consequences for the purposes of sentencing of the increase in maximum sentence for causing death by dangerous driving from 14 years to life imprisonment[42]. In *AG Ref (Soto)*[43] it was said that there is a distinction between offences where there are no Sentencing Council guidelines and those where they are. The approach in *Richardson*[44] was endorsed:

> 'Statutory changes in sentencing levels are constant. In recent years, maximum sentences have been increased (for example, drug related offences) or reduced (for example, theft). In general, changes like these provide clear indications to sentencing courts of the seriousness with which the criminal conduct addressed by the changes is viewed by contemporary society. In our parliamentary democracy, sentencing courts should not and do not ignore the results of the legislative process, and as a matter of constitutional principle, reflecting the careful balance between the separation of powers and judicial independence, and an appropriate interface between the judiciary and the legislature, judges are required to take such legislative changes into account when deciding the appropriate sentence in each individual case, or where guidance is being offered to sentencing courts, in the formulation of the guidance.'

40 [2020] EWCA Crim 233. The conviction was subsequently successfully appealed (see above).

41 *R v M* (28 June 2023). Again, see *Blackshaw* [2011] EWCA Crim 2312, at [20] for a discussion about the propriety of Crown Court judges issuing ('or appearing to' be issuing) sentencing guidelines.

42 That offence had also seen a number of increases in the maximum sentence from five years in 1992.

43 [2023] EWCA Crim 55.

44 [2006] EWCA Crim 3186, [2007] 2 Cr App R(S) 36.

5.78

The Court of Appeal went on to say:

> 'That core principle was expounded when there was no guideline in relation to the offence with which the court was concerned. There were in reality very few guidelines at all in 2006. However, the core principle is not affected by the fact that now there are guidelines for almost every offence. A change of the kind introduced by Section 86(2) of the 2022 Act must be taken into account by the sentencing court.'

5.79

In that case (causing death by dangerous driving) the Explanatory Notes indicated that the intention of the increase in maximum sentence to life imprisonment was to 'provide the courts with enhanced powers to sentence appropriately for the most serious cases'. However, the Explanatory Notes for the NABA 2022 state:

> '417. Section 25 offences currently attract a prison sentence of up to 14 years. This section increases the penalty to life imprisonment in order to discourage unlawful facilitation of migrants to the UK.
>
> 422. Subsection 2 amends subsection (6)(a) of section 25, increasing the maximum custodial penalty for assisting unlawful immigration from 14 years to life imprisonment. By virtue of section 25A(4), the maximum penalty set out here also applies to the other offence of facilitating the arrival or entry of an asylum seeker to the UK.'

5.80

In those circumstances it may be that the Court of Appeal would approve of an increase in sentences to all categories of offences, although this is likely to be more profound the more serious the offending. However, unless and until the Sentencing Council provide guidelines it will remain an inexact science.

Difference between the two offences – implications for sentence

5.81

It has not yet been determined whether the IA 1971, s 25A offence is less serious that the s 25 offence. They both have the same maximum sentence, although there are a number of other indicators that the s 25 offence is more serious[45]:

45 In *Ulaj* [2015] EWCA Crim 2456 an attempt to argue that the s 25A offence was less serious than the s 25 offence was unsuccessful, albeit that this was a permission application, and so has no value as a precedent.

- The Modern Slavery Act 2015 (MSA 2015), s 45 defence applies to the s 25A offence, but not the s 25 offence.
- The s 25 offence is a 'Priority Offence' for the purposes of the Online Safety Bill[46], while the s 25A offence is not[47].
- Someone convicted of a s 25 offence is automatically barred from registering as an OISC adviser, where someone convicted of a s 25A offence is not.

5.82

Against that, there is the following:

- Both are 'lifestyle offences' under the POCA 2002.
- Both are 'particularly serious crime(s)', as set out in NIAA 2002, Schs 1–6 (Specification of Particularly Serious Crimes) Order 2004).

5.83

It is arguable that as the IA 1971, s 25 offence contains within it the fact that immigration law was breached means that it is inherently more serious, although it is hard to see how (post-NABA 2022) anyone committing the s 25A offence is not also committing the s 25 one. This would have been offset previously by the fact that the s 25A offence requires proof of gain which is not inherent in the s 25 (although it would be an aggravating feature).

5.84

Post-NABA 2022, the breach for the s 25 offence can be related to the arrival of the person facilitated which, it is suggested, is less serious than facilitating their entering.

5.85

On balance it is suggested that when the immigration law that is breached is pleaded as relating to 'entering', the court will treat the s 25 offence as more serious (albeit not to a great extent). When the underlying law is 'arriving', which often carries with it the implication that the people facilitated will not try to enter in a clandestine manner, there is a less significant breach, and the distinction between that and the s 25A offence is such that it is unlikely to make a great deal of difference.

46 Meaning that service providers will have to have in place measures to ensure that they are tackling and removing content relating to this in internet sites.

47 The Government announced on 17 January 2023 that the s 24 offences will be added, which would make the omission of the s 25A offence all the more surprising (Written statement of the Secretary of State for Digital, Culture, Media and Sport, Statement UIN HCWS500). This has now been included in the Draft Bill for the s 24(A1)-(D1) offences from 6 July 2023, but not the s 24(E1) offence. The reason would appear to be that s 24(E1) is not in force, although this will require a further amendment as and when the ETA Scheme is up and running. The offence under MSA 2015, s 2 will also be added.

Historical note and timeline

5.86

As noted above, these offences have changed considerably over time. Given that offences can often come to light years (if not decades) later, it is important to identify the exact provisions that were in force at the time of the allegation.

5.87

The offence of s 25B – assisting someone to enter the United Kingdom in breach of a Deportation Order, was repealed by the Immigration and Social Security Co-ordination (EU Withdrawal) Act 2020.

Date	Impact on s 25	Impact on s 25A
14/02/2000	Maximum penalty increased to 10 years (from 7)	
10/02/2003	Maximum penalty increased to 14 years Widening of definition of immigration law to EU	Offence created – maximum 14 years
31/05/2016	Disapplication of Territorial Waters Jurisdiction Act 1878	Disapplication of Territorial Waters Jurisdiction Act 1878
28/06/2022	Maximum penalty increased to life Inclusion of 'arrival'	Maximum penalty increased to life Removal of requirement to show a 'gain'

Change in offence details during the indictment period

5.88

Where the offence spans 28 June 2022 care will need to be taken to ensure that the indictment reflects the offence as it was at the time (splitting it into two counts if needed).

Trafficking Offences

Overview and background

5.89

The MSA 2015 repealed the previous trafficking offences and replaced them with two substantive and one inchoate offence as of 31 July 2015. This is not retrospective, and so for offences committed prior to then, reference will need to be made to the previous legislation[48].

Slavery, servitude and forced or compulsory labour

The offence

5.90

The offence is at the MSA 2015, s 1:

'1 Slavery, servitude and forced or compulsory labour

(1) A person commits an offence if—

(a) the person holds another person in slavery or servitude and the circumstances are such that the person knows or ought to know that the other person is held in slavery or servitude, or

(b) the person requires another person to perform forced or compulsory labour and the circumstances are such that the person knows or ought to know that the other person is being required to perform forced or compulsory labour.

(2) In subsection (1) the references to holding a person in slavery or servitude or requiring a person to perform forced or compulsory labour are to be construed in accordance with Article 4 of the Human Rights Convention.

(3) In determining whether a person is being held in slavery or servitude or required to perform forced or compulsory labour, regard may be had to all the circumstances.

(4) For example, regard may be had—

(a) to any of the person's personal circumstances (such as the person being a child, the person's family relationships, and any mental or physical illness) which may make the person more vulnerable than other persons;

(b) to any work or services provided by the person, including work or services provided in circumstances which constitute exploitation within section 3(3) to (6).

(5) The consent of a person (whether an adult or a child) to any of the acts alleged to constitute holding the person in slavery or servitude, or requiring the person to perform forced or

48 For offences spanning, or potentially spanning, 31 July 2015 the Modern Slavery Act 2015 (Commencement No 1, Saving and Transitional Provisions) Regulations 2015, SI 2015/1476 provide that where there is reasonable doubt about the timings then 'it shall be conclusively presumed that the offence was committed wholly or partly before 31st July 2015'.

compulsory labour, does not preclude a determination that the person is being held in slavery or servitude, or required to perform forced or compulsory labour.'

Definitions

5.91

As noted, the definition in the MSA 2015, s 1(1) is defined in relation to Art 4 and, in cases of ambiguity, reference should be had to the Art 4 case law. In *K(S)*[49] the Court of Appeal adopted the following analysis[50]:

> '9.17. … 'Slavery' involves being in the legal ownership of another – a concept which is sometimes referred to as 'chattel slavery'. It has been suggested that this concept has evolved to encompass various other forms of slavery which are also based on the 'exercise of any or all of the powers attaching to the right of ownership.' In practice, issues concerning slavery have not arisen under the Convention because legally sanctioned slavery does not exist in any of the states which are parties to it.
>
> 9.18. 'Servitude' also embraces the totality of the status or condition of a person. However, it is distinguishable from slavery in that servitude does not involve ownership, but concerns less extensive forms of restraint. For Convention purposes 'servitude' means an obligation to provide one's services that is imposed by the use of coercion.
>
> 9.19. Servitude can be differentiated from forced labour. In the *Van Droogenbroeck* case, the Commission stated that:
>
>> "In addition to the obligation to provide another with certain services the concept of servitude includes the obligation on the part of the "serf" to live on another's property and the impossibility of changing his condition."

5.92

The court adopted the formulation in *Rantsev*[51] that 'for 'forced or compulsory labour' to arise, the court has held that there must be some physical or mental constraint, as well as some overriding of the person's will'[52]. This was determined under a predecessor offence to the one contained in the MSA 2015 (contained in the Asylum and Immigration (Treatment of Claimants, etc) Act 2004), but is still good law[53].

49 [2011] EWCA Crim 1691, [2011] 2 Cr App R 34.
50 At [24] adopting the analysis of Clayton and Tomlinson, *The Law of Human Rights* (2nd edn, OUP, 2009).
51 (2010) 51 EHRR 1.
52 Rantsev at [276].
53 Confirmed in *Nguyen & Othrs* [2019] EWCA Crim 670 (albeit that this was a permission application).

5.93

This was confirmed and elaborated in *Rooney & Othrs*[54] where the court adopted the guide published by the ECtHR[55]. It was said:

> '46. It is common ground between the parties that the word "labour" must be given a broad meaning and is not confined to manual labour. The European Court of Human Rights has published a guide to Article 4 which notes that reference to forced labour brings to mind the idea of physical or mental constraint whilst compulsory does not extend to every form of legal compulsion or obligation. It is clear from the case law that the penalty which is threatened may go as far as physical violence or restraint but it can also take subtler forms of a psychological nature, such as threats to denounce to the authorities a worker whose employment status is illegal. The assessment of whether a service required to be performed falls within the definition of FCL must take into account all the circumstances of the case in the light of the underlying objectives of Article 4.'

Human trafficking

Offence

5.94

The offence is at the MSA 2015, s 2:

> **'2 Human trafficking**
>
> (1) A person commits an offence if the person arranges or facilitates the travel of another person ("V") with a view to V being exploited.
>
> (2) It is irrelevant whether V consents to the travel (whether V is an adult or a child).
>
> (3) A person may in particular arrange or facilitate V's travel by recruiting V, transporting or transferring V, harbouring or receiving V, or transferring or exchanging control over V.
>
> (4) A person arranges or facilitates V's travel with a view to V being exploited only if—
>
> (a) the person intends to exploit V (in any part of the world) during or after the travel, or
>
> (b) the person knows or ought to know that another person is likely to exploit V (in any part of the world) during or after the travel.

54 [2019] EWCA Crim 681, [2019] 4 WLR 89.

55 The ECtHR provides a number of helpful guides to the Convention.

(5) *"Travel"* means—

(a) arriving in, or entering, any country,

(b) departing from any country,

(c) travelling within any country.

(6) A person who is a UK national commits an offence under this section regardless of—

(a) where the arranging or facilitating takes place, or

(b) where the travel takes place.

(7) A person who is not a UK national commits an offence under this section if—

(a) any part of the arranging or facilitating takes place in the United Kingdom, or

(b) the travel consists of arrival in or entry into, departure from, or travel within, the United Kingdom.'

Definitions

Travel

5.95

This is a domestic statute but, as it comes from the Trafficking Convention, it should be interpreted in light of that. This is also necessary to give effect to the UK's obligations under Art 4 ECHR. To the extent that there is a difference between the MSA 2015, s 2 and the international definition then (subject to the question of a declaration of incompatibility) it would have to be the domestic legislation that prevails.

5.96

The MSA 2015, s 2 has a requirement of 'travel' which implies movement. 'Travel' is specifically defined as arriving in, entering or leaving a country, or travelling within a country. However, it also appears to be defined as *including* the 'actions' for the first part of the Trafficking Convention. Someone who (in particular) harbours another would likely not be involved in their 'travel' in common language.

5.97

In *Ali and Ahsraf*[56] it was said (at [80]):

> 'In our view the key factor in the present context is that travel – a journey – is contemplated and the fact that it may be short does not

56 [2015] EWCA Crim 1279, [2015] 2 Cr App R 33.

affect whether or not the offence is committed. The judge correctly observed that the appellant was the driver of the car on each occasion, and in that sense there was clear evidence that he intentionally arranged or facilitated travel. It is self-evident that walking, for instance, between adjacent rooms, or other journeys involving truly minimal distances (for instance of a few feet or yards) may well be outside the ambit of this provision because there is a clear geographical element to this offence; but in the present case, substantive journeys took place involving a number of miles. The legislation does not specify a minimum distance or duration for the travel or journey, no doubt because victims can be "*trafficked*" within or across a small area or locality. The cases before our courts indicate that victims are exploited in this way within small, tight-knit communities, and it would unjustifiably undermine the reach of this statutory provision to introduce a requirement that journeys over a specified distance or time need to be contemplated or covered before a person is "*trafficked*" for the purposes of sexual exploitation. It would lead to absurdity to try to stipulate, for instance, a minimum number of miles, or that the journey must be planned with a clear destination, before the provision is engaged. On the evidence, this count was properly left to the jury.'

5.98

This was decided under the predecessor offence of trafficking within the United Kingdom for sexual exploitation. It is not clear whether someone who harbours another, but plays no part in their movement, would be guilty under the MSA 2015, s 2[57]. *Ali and Ashraf* appears clear, although it could be argued that, as s2 should be interpreted in line with the Trafficking Convention, 'may' in s 2(3) would include within the offence someone who is not responsible for arranging or facilitating the travel as defined under s 2(5)[58]. One difficulty with that argument is that as s 2 is a penal statute it would not be warranted to extend liability in those circumstances.

5.99

This also has potentially implications for the s 45 defence, although where a defendant has been trafficked for the purpose of the Convention, but has not been moved (in the meaning of s 2(5)), they would still be able to argue that it is an abuse of process to prosecute.

---

57 If not then it would be arguable that this would be a breach of the Trafficking Convention, and the victim would be able to claim a breach of Art 4.

58 This was recognised in the 'Independent Review of the Modern Slavery Act 2015: Final Report' (May, 2019):

> '2.3.3 Some stakeholders reported their concern that the emphasis on 'travel' in the Act could mean that offenders not directly involved in the transportation or transfer of the victim could escape prosecution. The notion of travel can also prove problematic when the victim arranges their own travel into and around the United Kingdom, and to the site of exploitation. This often occurs for victims from European Union countries who are currently free to enter the UK and travel around the country, and for victims who are deceived as to the conditions of work, or when those conditions deteriorate over time.'

Exploitation

5.100

The MSA 2015, s 3 sets out the meaning of 'exploitation' for the purposes of s 2:

> **'3 Meaning of exploitation**
>
> (1) For the purposes of section 2 a person is exploited only if one or more of the following subsections apply in relation to the person.
>
> *Slavery, servitude and forced or compulsory labour*
>
> (2) The person is the victim of behaviour—
>
> (a) which involves the commission of an offence under section 1, or
>
> (b) which would involve the commission of an offence under that section if it took place in England and Wales.
>
> *Sexual exploitation*
>
> (3) Something is done to or in respect of the person—
>
> (a) which involves the commission of an offence under—
>
> (i) section 1(1)(a) of the Protection of Children Act 1978 (indecent photographs of children), or
>
> (ii) Part 1 of the Sexual Offences Act 2003 (sexual offences), as it has effect in England and Wales, or
>
> (b) which would involve the commission of such an offence if it were done in England and Wales.
>
> *Removal of organs etc*
>
> (4) The person is encouraged, required or expected to do anything—
>
> (a) which involves the commission, by him or her or another person, of an offence under section 32 or 33 of the Human Tissue Act 2004 (prohibition of commercial dealings in organs and restrictions on use of live donors) as it has effect in England and Wales, or
>
> (b) which would involve the commission of such an offence, by him or her or another person, if it were done in England and Wales.
>
> *Securing services etc by force, threats or deception*
>
> (5) The person is subjected to force, threats or deception designed to induce him or her—
>
> (a) to provide services of any kind,
>
> (b) to provide another person with benefits of any kind, or

(c) to enable another person to acquire benefits of any kind.

Securing services etc from children and vulnerable persons

(6) Another person uses or attempts to use the person for a purpose within paragraph (a), (b) or (c) of subsection (5), having chosen him or her for that purpose on the grounds that—

(a) he or she is a child, is mentally or physically ill or disabled, or has a family relationship with a particular person, and

(b) an adult, or a person without the illness, disability, or family relationship, would be likely to refuse to be used for that purpose.'

5.101

This is an exclusive definition – someone will be exploited for the purposes of the s 2 offence if, and only if, they fall into one of the above categories (it may be that they fall into more than one). The fact that the victim has consented (whether or not they are an adult) is not a defence to a charge under s 2.

Jurisdiction

5.102

The MSA 2015, s 2(6) and (7) differentiate between UK and non-UK nationals, but both provide for a form of extra-territorial effect. Where any part of the arranging or facilitating is carried out in the UK, or the travel is into, out of, or within the UK, then there will be jurisdiction in all cases.

5.103

In other cases, the English and Welsh courts will only have jurisdiction over defendants who are UK nationals.

Inchoate offence

5.104

It is an offence under MSA 2015, s 4 to commit an offence with the intent to commit an offence under s 2:

'4 Committing offence with intent to commit offence under section 2

A person commits an offence under this section if the person commits any offence with the intention of committing an offence under section 2 (including an offence committed by aiding, abetting, counselling or procuring an offence under that section).'

5.105

It should be noted that this only applies to the s 2 offence, and not the s 1 one. The stated intention was to increase penalties to those who commit lesser offences preparatory to the substantive offence[59].

Sentencing

Maximum penalties

5.106

The offences under ss 1 and 2 are either way, with a maximum sentence of life imprisonment.

5.107

In relation to the s 4 offence, whilst it is either way the maximum sentence depends on the offence that is intended to be committed. Where it is kidnapping or false imprisonment then the maximum is life. Otherwise, the maximum is ten years' imprisonment[60].

5.108

The Sentencing Council has issued Sentencing Guidelines[61] for the above three offences (as well as for breaching a Slavery and Trafficking Risk Order ('STRO') or a Slavery and Trafficking Prevention Order ('STPO')[62]). For that reason, authorities prior to that should not generally be relied upon.

5.109

These provide a wide range from a Community Order up to 18 years' imprisonment, as well as a number of aggravating and mitigating factors.

Ancillary Orders

5.110

The offences under the MSA 2015, ss 1 and 2 are 'lifestyle offences' for the purposes of POCA. In addition, there is the power of forfeiture of a vehicle

---

59 Para 36, Explanatory Notes. The example given there is someone who steals a car with the intention of using it to transport a victim.

60 MSA 2015, s 5.

61 Available online at https://www.sentencingcouncil.org.uk/offences/magistrates-court/item/slavery-servitude-and-forced-or-compulsory-labour-human-trafficking/.

62 These are preventative orders under MSA 2015, Part 2 (ss 14–34). A STOP can be made on conviction for a slavery or trafficking offence (or on application against someone who has such a conviction), whilst an STRO can be applied for where there is a risk that someone will commit such an offence and it is necessary to make an order to prevent them from doing so. These can be applied for by Immigration Officers. The Order can have a number of conditions, including conditions relating to foreign travel. As well as the full Order, an Interim one can be made pending the resolution of the full application.

of vessel used in the commission of a s 2 offence[63] and the ability to make a 'Slavery and Trafficking Reparation Order' ('STRO')[64]. This provides that where someone has been committed an offence under s 1, 2 or 4 and a Confiscation Order is made, then an STRO can be made requiring the defendant to pay compensation to the victim in any sum less than the Confiscation Order. If this is done, then no Compensation Order under the Sentencing Act 2020, s 134 can be made.

Forced marriage

5.111

The Anti-social Behaviour, Crime and Policing Act 2014 introduced two offences relating to forced marriage[65]:

> **'121 Offence of forced marriage: England and Wales**
>
> (1) A person commits an offence under the law of England and Wales if he or she—
>
> (a) uses violence, threats or any other form of coercion[66] for the purpose of causing another person to enter into a marriage, and
>
> (b) believes, or ought reasonably to believe, that the conduct may cause the other person to enter into the marriage without free and full consent.
>
> (3) A person commits an offence under the law of England and Wales if he or she—
>
> (a) practises any form of deception with the intention of causing another person to leave the United Kingdom, and
>
> (b) intends the other person to be subjected to conduct outside the United Kingdom that is an offence under subsection (1) or would be an offence under that subsection if the victim were in England or Wales.'

5.112

Where the victim lacks capacity[67] then:

---

63 MSA 2015, s 11.

64 MSA 2015, s 8.

65 'Marriage is defined in s 121(4) as 'any religious or civil ceremony of marriage (whether or not legally binding).'

66 By virtue of s 121(6) 'It is irrelevant whether the conduct mentioned in paragraph (a) of subsection (1) is directed at the victim of the offence under that subsection or another person.'

67 As defined in the Mental Capacity Act 2005 (s 121(5)).

> 'the offence under subsection (1) is capable of being committed by any conduct carried out for the purpose of causing the victim to enter into a marriage (whether or not the conduct amounts to violence, threats or any other form coercion).'

Jurisdiction

5.113

In relation to jurisdiction:

> '(7) A person commits an offence under subsection (1) or (3) only if, at the time of the conduct or deception—
>
> (a) the person or the victim or both of them are in England or Wales,
>
> (b) neither the person nor the victim is in England or Wales but at least one of them is habitually resident in England and Wales, or
>
> (c) neither the person nor the victim is in the United Kingdom but at least one of them is a UK national[68].'

5.114

In reality, this gives a wide level of jurisdiction to the English Court.

Sentence

5.115

The offence is either way, with a maximum sentence of seven years' imprisonment. There are no sentencing guidelines.

Forced Marriage Protection Order

5.116

A Family Court has the power under the Family Law Act 1996[69] to make a 'Forced Marriage Protection Order', which is a civil order to protect someone who has either been forced into marriage, or is at risk of being forced into marriage. Potential terms of the order are wide[70], containing[71]:

---

68 This is defined in s 121(8) as:
(a) a British citizen, a British overseas territories citizen, a British National (Overseas) or a British Overseas citizen;
(b) a person who under the British Nationality Act 1981 is a British subject; or
(c) a British protected person within the meaning of that Act.

69 The power is set out in Family Law Act 1996, s 63A, which contains the definition, with the procedure set out at s 63C.

70 See *In re K(CA)* [2020] EWCA Civ 190, [2020] 2 WLR 1279 at [56–67] for a discussion of possible terms relating to passports and travel bans.

71 FLA 1996, s 63B(2)(a).

'63B Contents of orders

(1) A forced marriage protection order may contain—

(a) such prohibitions, restrictions or requirements; and

(b) such other terms;

as the court considers appropriate for the purposes of the order.

(2) The terms of such orders may, in particular, relate to—

(a) conduct outside England and Wales as well as (or instead of) conduct within England and Wales;

(b) respondents who are, or may become, involved in other respects as well as (or instead of) respondents who force or attempt to force, or may force or attempt to force, a person to enter into a marriage;

(c) other persons who are, or may become, involved in other respects as well as respondents of any kind.

(3) For the purposes of subsection (2) examples of involvement in other respects are—

(a) aiding, abetting, counselling, procuring, encouraging or assisting another person to force, or to attempt to force, a person to enter into a marriage; or

(b) conspiring to force, or to attempt to force, a person to enter into a marriage.'

Offence

5.117

It is an offence under the Family Law Act 1996, s 63CA someone who 'without reasonable excuse does anything that the person is prohibited from doing by a forced marriage protection order'. Any such behaviour would also be punishable by the family court as a contempt of court (which is, in practice, the usual method of enforcement).

Procedure

5.118

Where the Order has been obtained on an *ex parte* basis, the offence can only be committed when the person has been made aware of the existence of the Order.

5.119

Whilst the statute is silent on it, the burden of proof is presumably on the prosecution to prove that he was aware of the order. Further it is likely that the prosecution must prove not only that the defendant was aware of the Order, but that it contained the particular term in issue.

5.120

As would be expected, s 63C contains a provision (at (3) and (4)) prohibiting prosecution where he has punished for contempt for the same breach, or *vice versa*.

Sentence

5.121

The offence is either way, with a maximum sentence of five years in the Crown Court.

5.122

There are no specific sentencing guidelines, but it is likely that guidance would be taken from the Sentencing Council guidance 'Breach of a protective order (restraining and non-molestation order)', which has the same maximum sentence.

6 Employment offences

Introduction

6.1

This chapter provides details of the main offences related to illegal working. There is separate legislation dealing with the criminal offence of employing someone who does not have permission to work, that is different to the offence relating to an individual working when they are not entitled to.

Legal framework of the 2006 act

6.2

In order to stop people working when they do not have permission to do so, Parliament has created parallel schemes for criminal and civil penalties for employers that are set out in the IANA 2006, ss 15–26. Whilst the focus will be on the criminal sanctions, practitioners will need to be aware of the existence of the civil regime which provides not just for financial penalties, but also other consequences (such as loss of a sponsor's licence) for employers who employ people who do not have the right to work.

6.3

This is part of the 'hostile environment'; a set of measures that 'aim to create … a really hostile environment for illegal immigrants'[1] by setting up a number of legal and administrative measures to prevent those without status accessing services and accommodation, as well as working. The intention is that people without status, when faced with this, will decide to voluntarily leave the United Kingdom.

6.4

The exact mechanics of the regime depends on when the employment started[2], but where it is discovered that someone is employing an 'illegal worker' they are liable for a penalty of up to £20,000 per worker[3]. This can be challenged on a

1 From an interview with then Home Secretary to the *Telegraph* (25 May 2012).
2 Useful guidance is in the Home Office document 'An employer's guide to right to work checks: 6 April 2022' and 'Code of practice on preventing illegal working: 6 April 2022'.
3 IANA 2006, s 15.

number of grounds[4] (most notably because the necessary 'right to work' checks had been carried out) and, if the penalty is maintained, then there is a right of appeal to the county court[5].

Right to work checks

6.5

Someone who 'complied with any prescribed requirements in relation to the employment' is excused from paying a penalty[6] (unless they actually knew that the person had no right to work[7]). These must be carried before an employee starts working. There are currently three ways of carrying these checks out:

1 a manual right to work check;

2 a right to work check using Identity Document Validation Technology (IDVT) via the services of an Identity Service Provider (IDSP);

3 a Home Office online right to work check.

6.6.

Full details of how these operate are set out in 'Code of practice on preventing illegal working: 6 April 2022'. This is a document that is made pursuant to the IANA 2006, s 19.

6.7

The regulatory regime can place employers in particular difficulties in that faced with the possibility of large civil penalties and criminal sanctions, it is understandable that employer would take a cautious approach. However, a too cautious approach, such as dismissing an employee where there is a concern as to his legal status, may also put them in difficulties[8].

6.8

It is important that an adviser who is representing a client facing a criminal allegation is alive to the mechanics of the civil penalties regime and (if they are not also representing them in the civil penalty case) liaises with any lawyer instructed on that.

4 IANA 2006, s 16.
5 IANA 2006, s 17.
6 IANA 2006, s 15(3).
7 IANA 2006, s 15(4).
8 See the Code of Practice for employers: avoiding unlawful discrimination while preventing illegal working: 6 April 2022 and *Afzal v East London Pizza Ltd, t/a Dominos* Pizza (2018) UKEAT/0265/17.

Employee offences

Offences

6.9

The offence for employees is set out in the IANA 2006, s 21:

> '(1) A person commits an offence if he employs another ("the employee") knowing that the employee is disqualified from employment by reason of the employee's immigration status.
>
> (1A) A person commits an offence if the person—
>
> (a) employs another person ("the employee") who is disqualified from employment by reason of the employee's immigration status, and
>
> (b) has reasonable cause to believe that the employee is disqualified from employment by reason of the employee's immigration status.'

Definitions

6.10

The offence therefore prohibits the employment of a 'disqualified person', as defined in the IANA 2006, s 21(1B):

> '… a person is disqualified from employment by reason of the person's immigration status if the person is an adult[9] subject to immigration control and—
>
> (a) the person has not been granted leave to enter or remain in the United Kingdom, or
>
> (b) the person's leave to enter or remain in the United Kingdom—
>
> (i) is invalid,
>
> (ii) has ceased to have effect (whether by reason of curtailment, revocation, cancellation, passage of time or otherwise), or
>
> (iii) is subject to a condition preventing the person from accepting the employment.'

6.11

A person is 'subject to immigration control' if they require leave to enter or remain in the United Kingdom[10]. This will now include EEA citizens.

9 Note that 'adult' in this offence means someone aged over 16 (not 18) – IANA 2006, s 25(a).
10 IANA 2006, s 25(c).

Historical Note/Mens Rea

6.12

This offence as originally drafted came into force on 29 February 2008[11] and replaced the previous offence under the AIA 1996, s 8. However, there were transitional provisions that meant that for employment commenced before 29 February 2008 any prosecution would be under the old s 8[12]. Whilst that is now a considerable period of time ago, practitioners must be aware of this, as there may be people who this applies to (especially given that the increased nature of checks since then may mean that people are more reluctant to move jobs). This would appear to be the case for someone whose employment was lawful prior to that date, but became unlawful after then, although that is an open question.

6.13

The offence was substantially redrafted by the IA 2016, s 35, with the new provision coming into force on 12 July 2016[13]. Importantly, this included expanding the *mens rea* from knowledge to include 'reasonable cause to believe' and increasing the maximum penalty from two to five years. No transitional provisions were needed as the legislation creating the offence remained the same. However, where the employment spans 12 July 2016 it will necessary to give consideration to how the case should be presented, and whether the Prosecution consider that they have sufficient evidence to prove knowledge prior to the relevant date. This may include splitting the indictment at that date to allow for the differing *mens rea.*

6.14

'Reasonable cause to believe' would appear to be an objective test[14]. The majority decision in *Liversidge v Anderson*[15][16] that those words were purely subjective is unlikely now to be followed in any context. The Court of Appeal in *Bani*[17] appeared to think it would be an objective test in the IA 1971, s 25 facilitation

---

11 The Immigration, Asylum and Nationality Act 2006 (Commencement No 8 and Transitional and Saving Provisions) Order 2008.

12 IANA 2006, para 5 (Commencement No 8 and Transitional and Saving Provisions) Order 2008. This offence was summary only until 1 October 2004 (AI(TC)A 2004, s 6) and even then was, in fact, non-imprisonable. Any case where there is a prosecution will need careful consideration of the transitional provisions and the question of whether 'employ' is a continuing act, to determine whether there is actually jurisdiction.

13 Immigration Act 2016 (Commencement No 1) Regulations 2016/603.

14 The CPS Guidance states 'The mens rea of "reasonable cause to believe" ... is intended to capture employers who deliberately fail to check if a worker has the right to work in the UK', although it is not clear if that accurately summarises the effect of the change.

15 [1941] UKHL 1, [1942] AC 206.

16 This related to Defence (General) Regulations 1939, reg 18B(1A) which reads '(1A.) If the Secretary of State has reasonable cause to believe any person to have been or to be a member of, or to have been or to be active in the furtherance of the objects of, any such organization as is hereinafter mentioned, and that it is necessary to exercise control over him, he may make an order against that person directing that he be detained'. The case is well-known for Lord Acton's famous (and now widely accepted) dissent holding that there must be an objective element to this.

17 [2021] EWCA Crim 1958.

offence which has a similar *mens rea*[18]. An objective test would appear to follow from the legislation, otherwise 'reasonable cause to' would be superfluous.

6.15

Further, analysing the phrase 'reasonable cause to suspect' in the context of the Terrorism Act 2000, s 17[19], the Supreme Court stated[20] that:

> 'The question which arises on this appeal concerns the correct meaning of the expression "has reasonable cause to suspect" in section 17(b). Does it mean that the accused must actually suspect, and for reasonable cause, that the money may be used for the purposes of terrorism? Or is it sufficient that on the information known to him there exists, assessed objectively, reasonable cause to suspect that that may be the use to which it is put?'

6.16

The answer was clear[21]:

> 'In that section, or any other similarly constructed, it is plain beyond argument that the expression "has reasonable grounds for suspicion" cannot mean "actually suspects".'

6.17

Although that was due in part to the fact that other offences in the Terrorism Act required 'knowledge or [actual] suspicion', it would appear likely that the same conclusion would have been reached in any event.

6.18

Belief is a different, and higher, state of mind to suspicion, in that one may suspect something without believing it. A jury can be told that[22]:

> 'Suspicion … even coupled with the fact that he shut his eyes to the circumstances, is not enough, although those matters may be taken into account by a jury when deciding whether or not the necessary knowledge or belief existed.'

---

18 At [36] the Recorder's direction that the prosecution had to prove that 'at the time he either knew, or objectively had reasonable cause to believe' was noted without comment.

19 This reads:

17 Funding arrangements.

A person commits an offence if –

(a) he enters into or becomes concerned in an arrangement as a result of which money or other property is made available or is to be made available to another, and

(b) he knows or has reasonable cause to suspect that it will or may be used for the purposes of terrorism."

20 *Lane* [2018] UKSC 36, [2018] 2 Cr App R 35 at [4].

21 Lane at [22].

22 *Moys* (1984) 79 Cr App R 72. See also *Augunas* [2013] EWCA Crim 2046, [2014] 1 Cr App R 17.

6.19

An alternative formulation (in the context of knowledge of belief that goods were stolen) is[23]:

> 'We think that a jury should be directed along these lines. A man may be said to know that goods are stolen when he is told by someone with first hand knowledge (someone such as the thief or the burglar) that such is the case. Belief, of course, is something short of knowledge. It may be said to be the state of mind of a person who says to himself: "I cannot say I know for certain that these goods are stolen, but there can be no other reasonable conclusion in the light of all the circumstances, in the light of all that I have heard and seen." Either of those two states of mind is enough to satisfy the words of the statute. The second is enough (that is, belief) even if the defendant says to himself: "Despite all that I have seen and all that I have heard, I refuse to believe what my brain tells me is obvious". What is not enough, of course, is mere suspicion. "I suspect that these goods may be stolen, but it may be on the other hand that they are not." That state of mind, of course, does not fall within the words "knowing or believing".'

6.20

Although the *mens rea* for the substantive offence is knowledge or reasonable cause to believe, where a conspiracy is alleged, then it will be necessary to prove actual knowledge[24].

Corporate liability

6.21

The offences can be committed by a 'body', whether corporate or not[25]. This includes a partnership. In relation to knowledge, 'a body (whether corporate or not) shall be treated as knowing a fact about an employee if a person who has responsibility within the body for an aspect of the employment knows the fact'. This is not further defined, and there is no guidance on this.

6.22

Presumably this will mean that the fact that a disqualified person's colleagues knows of his lack of immigration status will not, of itself, mean that the body will. However, the number of people that are capable of 'infecting' the corporate body with the requisite knowledge, is wider than just the officers. For example,

---

23 *Hall* (1985) 81 Cr App R 260.
24 *Saik* [2006] UKHL 18, [2006] 2 AC 18.
25 IANA 2006, s 22.

someone working in the HR department may be responsible for the 'right to work' checks[26], even if they are not an officer.

Who is an employee?

6.23

By virtue of the IANA 2006, s 25(b), 'a reference to employment is to employment under a contract of service or apprenticeship, whether express or implied and whether oral or written'.

6.24

'Employment' is not further defined. Whilst it is not the role of the criminal courts to resolve complex questions of employment law, it is likely that in cases of ambiguity the courts will have regard to the case law relating to the Employment Rights 1996, s 230[27]. This is a complex area of law which has occupied Employment Tribunal, the EAT and the higher courts in relation to employment cases on a large number of occasions given the significance of the status of employee on the employment rights that a person has. The distinction also arises in other areas (such as tax law[28]). There are a number of tests devised to consider whether someone is employed or whether they are self-employed which include the 'Control Test'[29], the 'Integration Test'[30], or the 'Multiple Test'[31].

6.25

Under health and safety legislation[32], there are the following definitions:

> '*"employee"* means an individual who works under a contract of employment, or is treated by section 51A as being an employee[33], and related expressions shall be construed accordingly'.
>
> *"contract of employment"* means a contract of employment or apprenticeship (whether express or implied and, if express, whether oral or in writing)
>
> *"self-employed person"* means an individual who works for gain or reward otherwise than under a contract of employment, whether or not he himself employs others.'

26 See the Government guidance at https://www.gov.uk/government/collections/right-to-work-checks-employer-guidance. The explanatory notes state 'a body will be treated as having 'reasonable cause to believe' a fact for the purposes of the amended offence, if an individual within that body with responsibility for an aspect of the employment has reasonable cause to believe that fact'.

27 The definition in s 25(b) is effectively identical to the definition in ERA 1996, s 230(2).

28 *HMRC v Atholl House Productions Ltd* [2022] EWCA Civ 501, [2022] 4 All ER 461.

29 See *Denham v Midland Employers Mutual Assurance Ltd* [1955] 2 QB 437.

30 See *Cassidy v Ministry of Health* [1951] 2 KB 343.

31 See *Ready Mixed Concrete (South East) Ltd v Minister of Pensions and National Insurance* [1968] 2 QB 497.

32 Health and Safety at Work Act 1974, s 53.

33 Health and Safety at Work Act 1974, s 51A extends the definition to police officers.

6.26

It can be seen that the language is similar to that in the IANA 2006, s 21 offence. In *Pola*[34][35], the Court of Appeal gave consideration to the question of whether the appellant was the 'employer' of one or more of a number of 'unqualified Slovakian nationals' who were paid at a low rate, one of whom suffered a serious brain injury during the course of the demolition of a wall.

6.27

This was considered at paras [4]–[25], where the Court of Appeal gave an analysis consistent with employment law, saying:

> '5. The scrupulous accuracy of submissions advanced by Mr Robert Smith QC, who did not appear at trial, enables us to avoid any lengthy exegesis as to the principles by which employment can be identified for the purposes of the 1974 Act. Mr Smith submitted that before the jury could be sure that the defendant was an employer there first had to be evidence of a contract. This required evidence of what has been described as "mutual obligations", in other words, evidence that both the defendant and a worker owed each other obligations. That would be sufficient only to establish a contract. Secondly, the prosecution had to prove that the nature of the contract was one of employment, in other words, that in return for payment the worker placed himself under an obligation to work. It is on that issue that the appeal is focussed. Thirdly, if the worker was under an obligation to the defendant to work, it was necessary to prove that the contract was one of employment and not for services. For that purpose the prosecution would have to prove that the worker was under the control of the defendant. In the instant case, Mr Smith submitted, there was no evidence that any Slovakian worker was under any obligation to the defendant. True, some of them, in fluctuating numbers, turned up daily to work on the site and when they worked for a day they were paid. But it was not possible to infer from that fact alone that during the day any worker was under any obligation; there was no evidence to establish other than that he was free to leave at any time he chose.
>
> 6. Framed carefully as those submissions were, they accurately represent the relevant legal principles. Indeed, we did not understand the prosecution to dispute them.'

6.28

It is likely that the court will follow the above and treat 'employer' and 'employee' as being a question of employment law. It would be a matter for the judge to

---

34 [2009] EWCA Crim 655, [2010] 1 Cr App R(S) 6.

35 The case is reported in the Criminal Appeal Reports, but only on the point of compensation orders that were made after conviction. The report omits paras 4-25, which addresses the question of whether the appellant was an employer. It would therefore be necessary to obtain the full transcript of the judgment if this is to be relied upon.

determine whether the relationship is capable of being one of employment, but whether the defendant actually is an 'employer' would then be a question for the jury.

6.29

The reality is that (especially given the seriousness of the offence), the courts would likely seek to avoid lengthy and technical arguments about employment law, and it may be that it is unlikely that a prosecution will be brought if there is a clear and genuine ambiguity about the employment status of the relevant people. However, the courts will want to ensure that people do not escape liability by the creation of particular forms of disguised employment.

6.30

Someone representing a person being investigated for, or charged with, this offence should ensure that they have full access to all the records relating to the claimed relationship of employment. This would obviously include any contract, but also letters of 'employment' or engagement, pay slips, etc. In a suitable case, it may be that a representative should speak to other people who worked with their client to find the true 'situation on the ground'. In appropriate cases representations should be made on the question of employment.

Can an employer be charged with facilitating?

6.31

There is a potential overlap between the s 21 offence and the IA 1971, s 25 (which is more serious, now carrying a sentence of life imprisonment) offence in that someone who employs someone who is not lawfully allowed to work may be 'facilitating the commission of a breach of immigration law'. The definition of 'immigration law' for s 25 is one which controls the 'entitlement to … be … in the United Kingdom'[36]. It is suggested that this offence is not (without anything more) an offence that controls someone's entitlement to be in the United Kingdom, rather it controls their entitlement to work (and therefore sustain themselves) whilst here. However, it is an open question.

Procedure

6.32

In practice the CPS will not generally go straight to a prosecution, even where the evidential test is met. In any representations, it is worth considering the CPS guidance and addressing the reasons why the case could properly be dealt with by the civil penalty regime which states:

36 See Chapter 5 for further consideration.

'In some cases a civil penalty procedure is considered inadequate and the Civil Penalties Department may refer cases to the CPS for possible criminal proceedings.

This is likely to occur when it is apparent that the employer has deliberately and knowingly breached the law, shown a pattern of exploitative behaviour or evaded payment of penalties by closing and re-opening businesses in another identity.'

6.33

Where someone is facing a civil penalty, there is a 'defence' for someone who complies 'with any prescribed requirements in relation to the employment'[37], although this does not apply if the person knew that the person did not have the right to work[38]. In theory that may mean that someone who was employing a person that they did not know had no right to work, although it would appear clear that they did not, will have a defence to a civil penalty, but not a criminal one.

6.34

'Employs' is presumably a continuing act, and so where somebody loses the right to work during the course of the employment then the offence will be committed from that point. This would follow from the IANA 2006, s 21(1B)(b)(ii) which caters for the situation where someone's leave is curtailed.

6.35

A criminal investigation can be conducted at the same time as an investigation for a possible civil penalty. As stated, if there are different lawyers for the different strands of the allegation, then it is necessary for them to liaise closely with each other and ensure that there is a co-ordinated approach. Someone instructed in the civil case will also need to ensure that their client is aware of the potential eligibility for legal aid in relation to any criminal proceedings.

Consequences of Brexit

6.36

Following the United Kingdom's withdrawal from the European Union, EEA nationals require leave to enter and remain as would any other non-national. However, those that came into the UK prior to the ending of free movement are in a different position in the sense that they did not require leave to enter at that point. Arguably, they may still be lawfully present, even if they failed to apply under the EU Settlement Scheme[39]. However, it is likely that a court

37 IANA 2006, s 15(3).
38 IANA 2006, s 15(4).
39 See *CIO v Wolke* [1997] 1 WLR 1640, at p1656.

would hold that someone in that position does 'require leave'[40], even if they are lawfully present, and therefore the employment offences would 'bite' on them.

Sentence

6.37

The offence is either way, with a maximum sentence in the Crown Court of five years' imprisonment or an unlimited fine. There are no sentencing guidelines or Court of Appeal guideline cases. Any sentencing would be very fact specific.

6.38

Sentences of immediate imprisonment towards the maximum would likely be appropriate in case of organised criminality where there is exploitation of a number of illegal immigrants for gain. At the other end would be where someone employs a person with leave which subsequently expires with no ulterior motive. In those circumstances, it may be that a non-custodial sentence (including a suspended sentence of imprisonment) would be appropriate.

6.39

In *Wahiduzzama*[41] the appellant was the part-owner of a restaurant. A Borders Agency visit in July 2010 found an overstayer who was acting as a chef (and had been employed as such for seven years). The chef was released pending removal from the UK with a condition to stay in the flat above the restaurant, but provided that he did not continue to work there. The appellant received a civil penalty. Eight months later (in March 2011) a return visit from the Borders Agency found the chef was again working in the kitchen. When they returned 11 days after that, they found two other people without leave working there. The appellant was charged with three counts of facilitation under the IA 1971, s 25 (relating to the March 2011 visits) pleaded guilty after the jury was sworn and was sentenced to 23 months. The Court of Appeal concluded that this was a proper sentence (although it was reduced to 18 months as an act of mercy based on further mitigation). Although he was charged under the facilitation offence, it would appear that the sentence passed would have been equally appropriate if he had been charged under the IANA 2006, s 21 offence (and, given the upward trend in sentences and the flagrant breach, it may well be higher).

6.40

A similar sentence was passed in *Rahman*[42]. The appellant was the owner of several restaurants. A UKBA enforcement visit in 2009 found nine people working illegally and the appellant received penalty notices in relation to these. A different restaurant was visited in September 2009 and again in January 2010

40 *Barnet LBC v Ismail* [2006] EWCA Civ 383, [2006] 1 WLR 2771.
41 [2012] EWCA Crim 584, [2012] 2 Cr App R(S) 91.
42 [2011] EWCA Crim 1985, [2012] 1 Cr App R(S) 51.

found three and five people respectively working illegally (again, penalty notices were served on both occasions). When both restaurants were raided in March 2010, four people working illegally were found in one and three in the other. In addition, the conditions that they were living in were 'basic and cramped'. The appellant was sentenced to two years (reduced from a starting point of three years). That sentence was upheld. Again, he was charged under the facilitation offence, but given the facts a similar (if not longer) sentence would now likely be upheld for the NAIA 2006, s 21.

6.41

The appellant in *Ansari*[43] employed (without any exploitation) seven illegal immigrants (including his brother and partner) over a number of years in different businesses. A sentence of 12 months for facilitation (reduced from 18 months) for a guilty plea was upheld.

6.42

None of these are guideline cases, but give some idea of the approach that the courts will take. It should be noted that in the last decade the courts have treated immigration offences as being more serious, and therefore likely to attract higher sentences.

Financial orders on sentence

6.43

It is a case where the court is likely to give consideration to the financial means of a convicted defendant, both in terms of a financial penalty, as well as making orders for costs. For that reason, a practitioner will need to ensure that they have all the financial records for the individual (and, if applicable, the company) to ensure that any financial penalty is proportionate to the defendant's means and realistic.

6.44

An offence under s 21 is not a lifestyle offence for the Proceeds of Crime Act 2002, although a confiscation order can still be made.

Offences by individuals

6.45

Whilst someone without status who worked illegally may have committed a number of offences (such as document offences if they used false identification to secure employment), it was not illegal to work *per se*[44] until relatively

43 [2011] EWCA Crim 1640, [2012] 1 Cr App R(S) 37.
44 *Nuro v Home Office* [2014] EWHC 462 (Admin) at [10].

recently[45]. In order to fill what was considered to be a lacuna, the offence of illegal working was introduced by the IA 2016, as an amendment to the IA 1971:

> **'24B Illegal working**
>
> (1) A person ("P") who is subject to immigration control commits an offence if—
>
> (a) P works at a time when P is disqualified from working by reason of P's immigration status, and
>
> (b) at that time P knows or has reasonable cause to believe that P is disqualified from working by reason of P's immigration status.
>
> (2) For the purposes of subsection (1) a person is disqualified from working by reason of the person's immigration status if—
>
> (a) the person has not been granted leave to enter or remain in the United Kingdom, or
>
> (b) the person's leave to enter or remain in the United Kingdom—
>
> (i) is invalid,
>
> (ii) has ceased to have effect (whether by reason of curtailment, revocation, cancellation, passage of time or otherwise), or
>
> (iii) is subject to a condition preventing the person from doing work of that kind.
>
> …
>
> (5) If a person is convicted of an offence under subsection (1) in England and Wales, the prosecutor must consider whether to ask the court to commit the person to the Crown Court under section 70 of the Proceeds of Crime Act 2002 (committal with view to confiscation order being considered).
>
> …
>
> (8) The reference in subsection (1) to a person who is subject to immigration control is to a person who under this Act requires leave to enter or remain in the United Kingdom.
>
> (9) Where a person is on immigration bail within the meaning of Part 1 of Schedule 10 to the Immigration Act 2016[46]—

45 As of 12 July 2016.

46 See Chapter 1 for further consideration of bail under the Immigration Act 2016. The effect of IA 1971, s 24B(9) and IA 2016, Sch 10, para 2(1)(b) is that someone who is released on Immigration Bail can have a condition ' restricting the[ir] work, occupation or studies in the United Kingdom', which puts them in the same position as someone granted leave to enter, but with a restriction on work.

(a) the person is to be treated for the purposes of subsection (2) as if the person had been granted leave to enter the United Kingdom, but

(b) any condition as to the person's work in the United Kingdom to which the person's immigration bail is subject is to be treated for those purposes as a condition of leave.

(10) The reference in subsection (1) to a person working is to that person working—

(a) under a contract of employment,

(b) under a contract of apprenticeship,

(c) under a contract personally to do work,

(d) under or for the purposes of a contract for services,

(e) for a purpose related to a contract to sell goods,

(f) as a constable,

(g) in the course of Crown employment,

(h) as a relevant member of the House of Commons staff, or

(i) as a relevant member of the House of Lords staff.

(11) In subsection (10)—

- "contract to sell goods" means a contract by which a person acting in the course of a trade, business, craft or profession transfers or agrees to transfer the property in goods to another person (and for this purpose "goods" means any tangible moveable items);
- "Crown employment"—

  (a) in relation to England and Wales and Scotland, has the meaning given by section 191(3) of the Employment Rights Act 1996;

...

- "relevant member of the House of Commons staff" has the meaning given by section 195(5) of the Employment Rights Act 1996;
- "relevant member of the House of Lords staff" has the meaning given by section 194(6) of the Employment Rights Act 1996.

(12) Subsection (1) does not apply to—

(a) service as a member of the naval, military or air forces of the Crown, or

(b) employment by an association established for the purposes of Part 11 of the Reserve Forces Act 1996.

(13) In this section "contract" means a contract whether express or implied and, if express, whether oral or in writing.'

Definitions

6.46

The offence mirrors the offence for employers in that there is the broadly same definition of a disqualified person. Specifically, the definition in (i) and (ii) are the same. However, there is an important difference in subsection (iii) which, instead of 'subject to a condition preventing the person from *accepting the employment*' the employee offence reads 'subject to a condition preventing the person from *doing work of that kind*.'

6.47

The definition of 'work' is wider than 'employment'. It follows that the fact that someone is working illegally does not mean that the person 'employing' them will be guilty of the employer offence.

6.48

For example, an Uber driver would not be an employee of Uber (or anyone else)[47]. However, he would be a worker for the purposes of the Employment Rights Act 1996 and, if he did not have status, would appear to be committing an offence under s 24B:

> 'A "contract of employment" is defined in section 230(2) of the Act to mean "a contract of service or apprenticeship, whether express or implied, and (if it is express) whether oral or in writing." An "employee" means an individual who has entered into or works under a contract of employment: see section 230(1). However, the terms "employer" and "employed" are defined more broadly to refer to the person by whom an employee or worker is (or was) employed under a worker's contract: see section 230(4) and (5)[48].'

6.49

Again, it is likely that the criminal court would not want to get involved in complicated questions of employment law, and it is likely that it will only be prosecuted in a clear-cut case. However, there is no guarantee of this, and both prosecution and defence may need to be prepared to argue the point. As a trial would be in front of a lay bench of magistrates or a District Judge, rather than (potentially) a jury, it may be that there will be a greater willingness to delve into arguments about employment law.

47 *Uber BV v Aslam & Othrs* [2021] UKSC 5, [2021] 4 All ER 209.

48 *Uber BV v Aslam*, at [36]

Disqualified person v working in breach of conditions

6.50

There is a difference between working illegally and working in breach of conditions. For example, a student will likely have a condition prohibiting them from working more than 20 hours a week. If they exceed this then whilst they will be in breach of their leave, they will not be committing an offence under s 24B.

Age

6.51

A further difference is that whilst the employer offence only applies to adults, a youth can be convicted of the employee offence, although it is perhaps unlikely that a youth would be prosecuted.

Mens rea

6.52

The *mens rea* for this offence is effectively the same as for the employer's offence – see above for a discussion as to what this would amount to. As a practical matter, a defendant employee will generally have actual knowledge of the matters that will constitute the offence, so the scope for a belief (reasonable or otherwise) is limited. However, given the complexity of immigration law, it can be anticipated that there may be arguments about this.

6.53

Practitioners (both defence and prosecutors) will need to be aware of the risk that someone who is arrested for this offence may well be vulnerable. Consideration will often have to be given to whether there is a Modern Slavery Act defence[49].

Sentence

6.54

The offence is summary only, with the maximum sentence being the general limit in the magistrates' court. Because of that, there are no Sentencing Council guidelines or guideline cases. On the few occasions that the cases have been considered by the higher courts, it has been in the context of people who have been prosecuted for document offences (which attract a higher penalty). For

---

49 See Chapter 8, and *BXR* [2022] EWCA Crim 1483 for an example.

that reason, they should be approached with caution as guidance for the illegal working offence.

6.55

In *Aderemi*[50] the appellant's valid leave had expired and he used a fake Dutch ID card to register with an employment agency, although this was unsuccessful due to suspicions about the validity of the documents. A second agency took him on, and he then secured work for ten weeks, earning £2,875. In the Crown Court, he pleaded guilty to a document offence as well as the employee's offence. The judge took a starting point of 24 months before credit. The Court of Appeal held that the judge should have been steered by *Ovierakhi* and taken a starting point of 12 months (with a starting point of four months for the s 24B offence)[51].

6.56

In *Tjakuwa*[52] the appellant had previously been convicted of obtaining leave to enter by deception and three ID Documents offences for which he was sentenced to 16 months. He subsequently used a false Dutch passport to work in a care home. With credit of 15% he received 16 months for the ID Documents offence and three months concurrent for the s 24B. The 16 months was reduced to 12 months. The three months was not altered[53], although as it was concurrent that was academic.

6.57

Where the s 24B offence is charged on its own, it would appear appropriate to approach sentencing on the basis that it is a form of *Ovierakhi* case, but less serious due to the lack of a false ID document being produced (as is reflected by the lower sentence). Given the current approach to sentencing on immigration offences, it is still likely that there will generally be a sentence of imprisonment passed in many cases, although a court may be more willing to suspend this in appropriate cases.

6.58

It may be that the four different categories of people who are disqualified under s 24B(2) will have a differing level of culpability in descending order of seriousness from sub-s 2(a) down to sub-s 2(b)(iii) where each 'step' is someone who is closer to have existing leave. However, the maximum sentence would mean that this is, in reality, not much room for any distinction to be made.

---

50 [2018] EWCA Crim 1502.

51 There is power for the Crown Court to deal with a summary only offence such as s 24B under Crime and Disorder Act 1998, Sch 3, para 6 in this case as it is clearly related to the documents offence. Likewise, the Court of Appeal has jurisdiction to deal with an appeal by virtue of Criminal Appeal Act 1968, s 9(2).

52 [2020] EWCA Crim 1869.

53 The judgment refers to the s 24B offence as being 'Count 2', although it is not clear what power there would be for the s 24B offence to appear on the indictment, so this may be an error.

Confiscation orders

6.59

A magistrates' court does not have power to make a confiscation order. Although this offence is summary only, there is power for the magistrates' court to commit for sentence for the purpose of making a confiscation order, if the prosecution request this[54]. If that happens then the Crown Court can pass any sentence that the magistrates' court could have passed.

6.60

If the defendant has been convicted on a summary trial of another offence that is either way (such as, for example, a fraud offence relating to the illegal working), then the magistrates' court should state whether or not they would have committed for sentence were it not for the purpose of confiscation. If so, then the Crown Court can pass any sentence as if it has just convicted the defendant[55]. If not, then they will be bound by the sentencing powers of the magistrates' court (other than in relation to confiscation)[56].

6.61

The purpose of the Proceeds of Crime Act 2002 is, in part, 'to provide for confiscation orders in relation to persons who benefit from criminal conduct and … to allow the recovery of property which is or represents property obtained through unlawful conduct'.

6.62

In relation to a case of theft where someone steals a ten pound note, it is straightforward (in the sense that the law is ever straightforward) in that that person has gained the ten pound note, and a confiscation order can be made in that sum. With illegal working, it is more complicated. Take someone who secures employment when they are not permitted to do so, and then works for a year earning £24,000. Whilst they would not have been able to earn that money had they not committed the Proceeds of Crime Act 2002, s 24B offence, is it right to say that the whole £24,000 is the proceeds of crime?

6.63

In *Carter*[57], this issued was raised in relation to one appellant L who had earned £50,000 over three years using a false identity. The Court of Appeal said:

> '38 The case of Lewis, as it will be apparent, cannot be taken as having decided any principle of law. It is a case which stands obviously upon its own facts, with its own limitations. It seems to us to be

54 POCA 2002, s 70, preserved by Sentencing Act 2020, s 24(1)(b). It may be that the ability to make a confiscation order was one of the drivers of the introduction of the employee offence.
55 POCA 2002, s 71(2).
56 POCA 2002, s 71(3).
57 [2006] EWCA Crim 416.

obvious that where you obtain an opportunity to work from an offer of employment being made to you, and the offer has been induced by a false representation that you are entitled to work, then the false representation continues thereafter for the benefit of the offender who, permitting the representation to continue is able to retain employment.

39 Once made, it continues to have effect throughout the employment which has been taken up. At any stage, had the representation been corrected, it is plain the employment would have ceased. Although the question as formulated by Neill LJ in the case of King was directed towards a different statutory provision from the one which we are considering, namely whether or not the benefit was obtained within the meaning of section 71(4), namely, obtained as a result of or in connection with its commission, the formulation of the question, in our judgment, is nevertheless apt. Substituting "benefit" for "property" the question is: was the deception an operative cause of obtaining? In our judgment, the answer to that question is plainly, yes.'

6.64

Following that there were a number of similar cases, including *Paulet*[58] where the appellant had no right to work in the UK, but secured employment by using false documents. During the relevant period he earned just under £22,000. The Court of Appeal adjourned that appeal pending the publication of DPP guidance on when it is proper to pursue confiscation proceedings, but subsequently made the order[59]. On appeal to the ECtHR[60] he was successful in the sense that he won on the grounds that the review conducted by the Court of Appeal (by considering it through the lens of abuse of process rather than proportionality) was too narrow and there was therefore a violation of Art 1, Protocol 1.

6.65

In *Andrewes*[61] the Supreme Court considered the case of someone who had secured employment, and then maintained it for ten years, earning nearly £650,000 (net of tax and NI), but who had lied about his academic qualifications in the initial application. A confiscation order was made (in the lesser sum of nearly £97,000, which was the available amount) by the Crown Court but overturned by the Court of Appeal as being disproportionate.

6.66

The Supreme Court allowed the CPS appeal, saying:

58 [2009] EWCA Crim 288.

59 *Nelson* [2009] EWCA Crim 1573, [2010] QB 678.

60 *Paulet v UK* (2015) 61 EHRR 39.

61 [2022] UKSC 24, [2022] 1 WLR 3878.

> '56. Although we are not attempting to deal with all possible circumstances, the answer to the question certified (see para 2) is that in cv fraud cases, where, focusing solely on the performance of services, the fraudster has given full value for the earnings received—***and putting to one side where the performance of the services constitutes a criminal offence***—it will normally be disproportionate under the proviso in section 6(5)[62] to confiscate all the net earnings made. But it will be proportionate to confiscate the difference between the higher earnings made as a result of the cv fraud and the lower earnings that the defendant would have made had he or she not committed the cv fraud. In many situations of cv fraud, it will be appropriate, as a pragmatic approximation of that profit, simply to base it on the percentage difference between the fraudster's initial salary in the new job obtained by fraud and the fraudster's salary in his or her prior job. Moreover, there is no need for much time and effort to be expended in assessing, even in a broad-brush way, the difference between the earnings with and without the cv fraud if it is clear that, in any event, that difference will exceed the recoverable amount. (*emphasis added*)'

6.67

This is expanded on at para [42]:

> '42. It is very important to add that we put to one side cases where the performance of the services is illegal. Say, for example, a person is appointed to a job as a surgeon or airline pilot or HGV driver because he or she has lied in the job application about having the necessary qualifications or licence to be appointed to that job. In that situation, the performance of the services by that person would constitute a criminal offence and it would not be disproportionate to confiscate the full net earnings because the performance of those services has no value that the law should recognise as valid. There is no lawful market for the performance of those services by that person. Confiscation of the full net earnings would not therefore constitute double disgorgement. Indeed, this can be regarded as the equivalent to the confiscation of the turnover from the illegal sale of goods such as criminal drug dealing or arms dealing. Confiscation of the turnover from the illicit drugs or arms dealing is proportionate without making any deduction for the (illicit) value of the drugs or arms supplied. Further, as was said in *Waya [2013] 1 AC 294* (see para 28(iii) above), the costs of acquiring or manufacturing the drugs or arms are the non-deductible costs of carrying on an unlawful business. The same applies analogously to the value of services that it is illegal for the defendant to perform.'

62 Following the judgment in *Waya* [2012] UKSC 51, [2013] 2 Cr App R(S) 20 this 'proviso' was added to the mandatory requirement under POCA 2002, s 6(5) to make a confiscation order. It reads 'only if, or to the extent that, it would not be disproportionate to require the defendant to pay the recoverable amount'.

6.68

This case also establishes that the burden of proof is on the prosecution to show that it would not be a disproportionate response to require the defendant to pay the amount.

6.69

For a s 24B case it is likely that the benefit would be the salary net of tax (and national insurance)[63].

6.70

Two points arise. Firstly, where the defendant is charged with more serious offences (such as false ID documents or fraud) does there need to be an offence under s 24B charged in order for a court to conclude that the performance of the service is illegal? It would appear unlikely as the facts speak for themselves generally, and the defendant's criminal conduct that constituted the other offence would likely mean that he would, of necessity, be committing the s 24B offence. However, prosecutors may wish to avoid any potential difficulty by charging the s 24B offence as well. Being summary only will mean that it cannot appear on an indictment, but can be sent to the Crown Court with the main charge[64].

6.71

Secondly, what is the scope for an argument about proportionality in cases where the performance of the service is illegal? This would include a s 24B offence, but there are other cases. It is clear that the proviso does not provide a general discretion[65] to sentencers to act to correct perceived unfairness. Further, the exception flagged up in *Andrewes* was foreshadowed in *Waya*[66].

6.72

The principle underpinning *Andrewes* is that the provision of illegal labour does not constitute 'restoration of value' however well done the job was. However, it could be argued that the situation of a defendant in a s 24B case is different to someone who is engaged in a fully criminal enterprise, where the argument that it is not appropriate to carry out a profit and loss exercise can more easily be seen. Further, it may be that the rationale for the surgeon, pilot and HGV driver is different as there the defendant would be lying about their ability to satisfy a regulatory regime that is in place for the protection of the public.

---

63 *Asplin* [2021] EWCA Crim 1313 at [55], confirmed at *Asplin (No 2)* [2022] EWCA Crim 9 at [5].

64 Given the general trend for higher penalties in immigration offences, it is perhaps surprising that this has remained a summary only one.

65 *Andrewes* at [38].

66 See [26] and [34].

6.73

The resolution of this may require a case where it is arises. It is suggested that whilst a confiscation order for the full amount earned may well be unappealable in most cases, it is unlikely to be the case that a confiscation order will *never* be disproportionate in a s 24B (or similar) cases as there is no such limitation in Art 1, Protocol 1.

6.74

It may be that the answer in most cases is what is said at [56]:

> 'Moreover, there is no need for much time and effort to be expended in assessing, even in a broad-brush way, the difference between the earnings with and without the cv fraud if it is clear that, in any event, that difference will exceed the recoverable amount.'

6.75

The reality in most cases will be that the defendant has little, if anything, by way of realisable assets, although an adviser will have to advise a client that if a broad brush approach is adopted (including when arguments about proportionality are not litigated) then if their client buys a lottery ticket on their way home from court which happens to win the jackpot, then the CPS can come after them for the full benefit figure[67].

Application to territorial waters

6.76

As of 12 April 2023[68], the NABA 2022[69] introduced new IA 1971, ss 11A and 11B. Section 11A reads:

> **'11A Working in United Kingdom waters**
>
> (1) An *"offshore worker"* is a person who arrives in United Kingdom waters—
>
> (a) for the purpose of undertaking work in those waters, and
>
> (b) without first entering the United Kingdom (see, in particular, section 11(1)).
>
> But see subsection (6).

67 POCA 2002, s 22.

68 NABA 2022 (Commencement No. 5 and Transitional Provisions) Regulations 2023), reg 5. See Immigration (Offshore Worker Notification and Exemption from Control (Amendment)) Regulations 2023 for the procedure relating to Offshore Workers.

69 NABA 2022, s 43(1) and Sch 6.

(2) An offshore worker arrives in the United Kingdom for the purposes of this Act when they arrive in United Kingdom waters as mentioned in subsection (1)(a).

(3) An offshore worker enters the United Kingdom for the purposes of this Act when they commence working in United Kingdom waters.

(4) Any reference in, or in a provision made under, the Immigration Acts to a person arriving in or entering the United Kingdom, however expressed, is to be read as including a reference to an offshore worker arriving in or entering the United Kingdom as provided for in subsection (2) or (3).

(5) References in this section to work, or to a person working, are to be read in accordance with section 24B(10).

(6) A person is not an offshore worker if they arrive in United Kingdom waters while working as a member of the crew of a ship that is—

(a) exercising the right of innocent passage through the territorial sea or the right of transit passage through straits used for international navigation, or

(b) passing through United Kingdom waters from non-UK waters to a place in the United Kingdom or vice versa.

(7) For the purposes of any provision of, or made under, the Immigration Acts, a person working in United Kingdom waters who, in connection with that work, temporarily enters non-UK waters is not to be treated by virtue of doing so as leaving, or being outside, the United Kingdom.

(8) In this section—

"non-UK waters" means the sea beyond the seaward limits of the territorial sea;

"right of innocent passage", *"right of transit passage"* and *"straits used for international navigation"* are to be read in accordance with the United Nations Convention on the Law of the Sea 1982 and any modifications of that Convention agreed after the passing of the Nationality and Borders Act 2022 that have entered into force in relation to the United Kingdom;

"the territorial sea" means the territorial sea adjacent to the United Kingdom;

"United Kingdom waters" means the sea and other waters within the seaward limits of the territorial sea.'

6.77

This gives the Secretary of State power to make regulations relating to registration and other ancillary matters. The effect is that someone working in

UK territorial waters will be treated as if they are on-shore for the purposes of the Immigration Acts. This will include the requirement to obtain leave to enter before starting to work and, if they are a visa national, to obtain entry clearance before arriving in UK waters (not just prior to when they start work).

6.78

The NABA 2022, Sch 6, para 4(b) came into force on 24 August 2022[70]. This amends the IA 1971, s 28(2A) to read:

> 'Section 3 of the Territorial Waters Jurisdiction Act 1878 (consent of Secretary of State for certain prosecutions) does not apply to proceedings for an offence under this Part.'

6.79

For the purposes of the employee offence, NABA 2022, Sch 6, para 4(a) added a new IA 1971, s 28(A1) from 12 April 2023:

> 'Proceedings for an offence under this Part that is committed in the territorial sea adjacent to the United Kingdom may be taken, and the offence may for all incidental purposes be treated as having been committed, in any place in the United Kingdom.'

6.80

The effect of these together is that there is no longer any jurisdictional bar on prosecuting the s 24B as a summary only offence[71]. However, the disapplication of the Territorial Waters Jurisdiction Act 1878, s 3 (which is procedural, rather than substantive, in nature), of itself, still leaves ss 4 and 7, and the likely prohibition on prosecuting summary only offences[72], where committed prior to 12 April 2023.

6.81

In relation to the employer's offence, as this is either way there are likely no jurisdictional issues. However, as that offence is not contrary to the IA 1971, then Sch 6, para 4(b) will not impact the requirement (in suitable circumstances) for consent under the 1878 Act. However, Sch 6, para 11 contains similar provisions as para 4 that also came into force on 12 April 2023:

> '(3A) Proceedings for an offence under this section that is committed in the territorial sea adjacent to the United Kingdom may be taken, and the offence may for all incidental purposes be treated as having been committed, in any place in the United Kingdom.
>
> (3B) Section 3 of the Territorial Waters Jurisdiction Act 1878 (consent of Secretary of State for certain prosecutions) does not apply to proceedings for an offence under this section.'

---

70 NABA 2022, (Commencement No 2) Regulations 2022, reg 2.

71 Consequential amendments are made to IA 1971, Sch 2, para 2 to extend the power to examine anyone arriving in the United Kingdom.

72 Sec Chapter 10 for more details of the 1878 Act.

Labour market offences

Gangmasters offences

Gangmasters and Labour Abuse Authority

6.82

In the evening of 5 February 2004 at least 21 trafficked illegal immigrants from China drowned in Morecombe Bay whilst picking cockles. As a result of this, and general concerns over exploitation of workers in the agriculture/fisheries sector, what is now called the Gangmasters and Labour Abuse Authority (GLAA) was formed in 2005 by virtue of the Gangmasters (Licensing) Act 2004.

Gangmasters (Licensing) Act 2004

6.83

This Act creates a licensing regime applicable to people in the following sectors[73]:

> '(a) agricultural work,
>
> (b) gathering shellfish, and
>
> (c) processing or packaging—
>
> > (i) any produce derived from agricultural work, or
> >
> > (ii) shellfish, fish or products derived from shellfish or fish.
>
> This is subject to any provision made by regulations under subsection (5) below and to section 5 (territorial scope of application)[74].'

6.84

The definition of "gangmaster' is in s 4:

> **'Acting as a gangmaster**
>
> (1) This section defines what is meant in this Act by a person acting as a gangmaster.
>
> (2) A person ("A") acts as a gangmaster if he supplies a worker to do work to which this Act applies for another person ("B").
>
> (3) For the purposes of subsection (2) it does not matter—
>
> > (a) whether the worker works under a contract with A or is supplied to him by another person,

73 G(L)A 2004, s 3. The terms are further defined in s 3(2)(4), including that '"agricultural work" means work in agriculture', although that is further defined in s 3(3).

74 The definition is provided in s 5 and, broadly speaking, covers the UK, the shoreline and coastal waters (meaning 6 nautical miles from the shoreline).

(b) whether the worker is supplied directly under arrangements between A and B or indirectly under arrangements involving one or more intermediaries,

(c) whether A supplies the worker himself or procures that the worker is supplied,

(d) whether the work is done under the control of A, B or an intermediary,

(e) whether the work done for B is for the purposes of a business carried on by him or in connection with services provided by him to another person.

(4) A person ("A") acts as a gangmaster if he uses a worker to do work to which this Act applies in connection with services provided by him to another person.

(5) A person ("A") acts as a gangmaster if he uses a worker to do any of the following work to which this Act applies for the purposes of a business carried on by him—

(a) harvesting or otherwise gathering agricultural produce following—

(i) a sale, assignment or lease of produce to A, or

(ii) the making of any other agreement with A,

where the sale, assignment, lease or other agreement was entered into for the purpose of enabling the harvesting or gathering to take place;

(b) gathering shellfish;

(c) processing or packaging agricultural produce harvested or gathered as mentioned in paragraph (a).

In this subsection "agricultural produce" means any produce derived from agriculture.

(6) For the purposes of subsection (4) or (5) A shall be treated as using a worker to do work to which this Act applies if he makes arrangements under which the worker does the work—

(a) whether the worker works for A (or for another) or on his own account, and

(b) whether or not he works under a contract (with A or another).'

6.85

It is not unlawful to be a gangmaster as defined in the Act, but anyone in such a position must comply with the licensing regime overseen by the GLAA. The procedure (including appeals) is set out in the Gangmasters (Licensing) Act 2004, ss 7–11.

6.86

There are a number of offences created as follows:

- Acting as an unlicensed gangmaster[75] – either way, maximum 10 years
- Possessing a false or improperly obtained Gangmaster's Licence, or one relating to a different person [76] – either way, maximum ten years
- Entering into an arrangement for services where the person providing the services breaches s 6[77] – summary only, maximum six months
- Obstructing an Enforcement Officer or Compliance Officer , failure to comply with a requirement made by such an officer, or making a false statement to such an officer[78] – summary only, maximum six months

Procedure

6.87

A 'worker' is defined as 'an individual who does work to which this Act applies'. This includes anyone who is not legally entitled to work in the United Kingdom[79].

6.88

The GLAA operates an 'Enforcement Policy Statement' that includes guidance as to when a prosecution will follow[80]. The GLAA website contains a list of the number of cases prosecuted to conviction by the GLAA[81] ('working either independently or in partnership with other law enforcement agencies'). As at the end of 2022, there were a total of 183 people convicted for a variety of offences, 102 of these related to convictions under the Gangmasters Licencing Act 2004 (three quarters of these being for the s 12 offence).

6.89

The Act applies to individuals as well as to corporate bodies[82], unincorporated bodies[83] and partnerships[84]. There is provision for the liability of officers and partners where it is shown that the legal body committed the offence

---

75 G(L)A 2004, s 12(1).

76 G(L)A 2004, s 12(2).

77 G(L)A 2004, s 13. It is a defence to show that:
 (a) took all reasonable steps to satisfy himself that the gangmaster was acting under the authority of a valid licence, and
 (b) did not know, and had no reasonable grounds for suspecting that the gangmaster was not the holder of a valid licence.

78 G(L)A 2004, s 18(1)-(2).

79 G(L)A 2004, s 26.

80 The latest version is dated 08 May 2019 and is available online – https://www.gla.gov.uk/media/5955/enforcement-policy-statement-v40-080519.pdf

81 https://www.gla.gov.uk/our-impact/conviction-totals/

82 G(L)A 2004, s 20.

83 G(L)A 2004, s 21.

84 G(L)A 2004, s 22.

with their 'consent or connivance' or (perhaps more controversially) if it attributable to their 'neglect'. As with other employment cases, it is important that if the same solicitor is not acting (or competent to act) in both the criminal and employment strands, then the criminal lawyer is brought in early (and ideally before any prosecution is started) and there is good links between the two.

Sentence

6.90

There are no Sentencing Guidelines, or guideline cases. In *Morkunas*[85] (at [51]) the court set out the following factors as being relevant:

(1) The scale of the gangmaster's activities in the supply of labour;

(2) The role played by the gangmaster in the operation as a whole, whether leading or significant, for example;

(3) The level of organisation and planning behind these activities;

(4) The number of workers involved;

(5) The nature and scale of any associated methods of organisation and control, including the supply of accommodation and transport;

(6) The amount of money made by these combined activities;

(7) The use of false documents and other breaches of the law regulating these activities;

(8) The level of exploitation evinced by these activities;

(9) The level of vulnerability of the workers because of age or background, for example;

(10) The use of violence to enforce debts and other requirements;

(11) The use of coercion and threats, short of violence;

(12) The degree of harm suffered by the workers; and

(13) Any previous convictions for similar offences.

6.91

For the s 12 offences then it is likely that where the above questions are answered adversely to the defendant, lengthy custodial sentences of up to ten years may be imposed after a trial.

---

85 [2014] EWCA Crim 2750.

Labour market enforcement

Labour market offences

6.92

The full list of labour market offences are set out in IA 2016, s 3(3):

(a) an offence under the Employment Agencies Act 1973 other than one under section 9(4)(b) of that Act;

(b) an offence under the National Minimum Wage Act 1998;

(c) an offence under the Gangmasters (Licensing) Act 2004;

(d) an offence under section 1 of the Modern Slavery Act 2015;

(e) an offence under section 2 or 4 of that Act—

  (i) which is committed in relation to a worker or a person seeking work, or

  (ii) which is otherwise committed in circumstances where subsection (2) of section 3 of that Act applies;

(f) an offence under section 30(1) or (2) of that Act which is committed in relation to—

  (i) an order which was made on the application of the Gangmasters and Labour Abuse Authority, or

  (ii) an order which was made under section 14 of that Act and which falls within subsection (4) below;

(g) an offence under section 27;

(h) any other offence prescribed by regulations made by the Secretary of State;

(i) an offence of attempting or conspiring to commit an offence mentioned in paragraphs (a) to (h);

(j) an offence under Part 2 of the Serious Crime Act 2007 in relation to an offence so mentioned;

(k) an offence of inciting a person to commit an offence so mentioned;

(l) an offence of aiding, abetting, counselling or procuring the commission of an offence so mentioned.

Labour market enforcement undertaking and orders

6.93

The IA 2016 created the post[86] of 'Director of Labour Market Enforcement' who has oversight of the enforcing authorities[87] who have responsibility for tackling

---

86 IA 2016, s 1.

87 Currently the Gangmasters and Labour Abuse Authority, the Employment Agency Standards Inspectorate and HMRC's National Minimum Wage Team.

'non-compliance in the labour market'. This is not, of itself, an immigration offence and many of the people affected would be British citizens. However, there is a clear overlap given the vulnerability of many people without status, or with precarious immigration status.

6.94

As part of the enforcement regime, when one of the enforcing authorities[88] believes that someone has created a 'trigger offence'[89], they can, in certain circumstances[90] invite them to give a 'Labour Market Enforcement Undertaking'. This can last up to two years 'may include a[ny] prohibition, restriction or requirement' that is 'just and reasonable' in the circumstances (provided that at least one of the measures is necessary to prevent or reduce the risk of the person continuing to commit the trigger offence, or committing a further trigger offence). If the person refuses to do so, or does but then breaches the undertaking, then an application for a Labour Market Enforcement Order can be made to the magistrates' court who will determine the matter on the balance of probabilities[91]. An appeal lies to the Crown Court and an application to vary can be made to the magistrates' court by either side. An order can also be made as part of a sentence for a 'trigger offence'.

Offence of breaching an Order

6.95

It is a criminal offence[92] to fail to comply with an order without reasonable excuse. This is either way, with a maximum penalty of two years' imprisonment.

6.96

As with the Gangmasters (Licensing) Act 2004 provisions, an unincorporated association is a legal person for this (and other) purposes[93]. There is similar provision for the liability of officers and partners where it is shown that the legal body committed the offence with their 'consent or connivance' or) if it attributable to their 'neglect'[94]. Again, it is important that if the same solicitor is not acting (or competent to act) in both the criminal and employment strands, then the criminal lawyer is brought in early (and ideally before any prosecution is started) and there is good links between the two.

---

88 As defined in IA 2016, s 14(5).
89 As defined in IA 2016, s 14(4).
90 See IA 2016, ss 14 and 15.
91 See IA 2016, ss 18–24.
92 IA 2016, s 27.
93 IA 2016, s 29.
94 IA 2016, ss 28–30.

7 Miscellaneous criminal offences

Introduction

7.1

This chapter provides an overview of the regulatory offences that apply to advisers, as well as a number of other immigration offences that are on the statute books that are mainly summary only and tend to be rarely charged.

Offences relating to housing

7.2

As part of the 'hostile environment' the government's stated intention was to 'deny illegal migrants access to public and other services and benefits to which they were not entitled by virtue of their immigration status, in the expectation that this would persuade large numbers to depart the UK voluntarily and would reduce the 'pull factor' for anyone thinking to come to the UK to settle illegally'[1].

7.3

As part of this, there are several offences relating to landlords and agents who let premises to people without status. The reason for this is said to be that '[h]ousing illegal migrants in the private rented sector allows such people to establish a settled life in the UK and frustrate the necessary process of returning them to their home country'[2]. The framework is similar to the illegal employment employer offences[3], not just in terms of who is a 'disqualified person', the question of corporate liability and the *mens rea*, as well as the existence of a parallel civil enforcement regime.

7.4

As of 1 February 2016 the whole of England is subject to the 'right to rent scheme'[4]. This creates an obligation on a landlord to undertake checks on a

---

1 'An inspection of the 'hostile environment' measures relating to driving licences and bank accounts', report by Independent Chief Inspector of Borders and Immigration (2016).

2 Immigration (Residential Accommodation) (Prescribed Requirements and Codes of Practice) (Amendment) Order 2016, SI 2016/9, art 7.2.

3 IANA 2006, s 21. See also Chapter 6.

4 IA 2014, s 22 and the Immigration Act 2014 (Commencement No 6) Order 2016.

prospective tenant that they have the legal right to occupy the premises under a tenancy agreement. If the tenant has a limited leave to remain then the checks must be repeated prior to expiry, or (if longer) annually. An occupier who has 'a limited right to rent at the time when the occupier was first granted a right to occupy the premises under the agreement' is a 'limited right occupier'[5]. It is not a criminal offence to fail to conduct the right to rent checks, but failing to do so puts the landlord and agent at a higher risk of prosecution.

7.5

The offence is set out in the IA 2014, s 33A:

> **'33A Offences: landlords**
>
> (1) The landlord under a residential tenancy agreement which relates to premises in England commits an offence if the first and second conditions are met.
>
> (2) The first condition is that the premises are occupied by an adult who is disqualified as a result of their immigration status from occupying premises under a residential tenancy agreement.
>
> (3) The second condition is that the landlord knows or has reasonable cause to believe that the premises are occupied by an adult who is disqualified as a result of their immigration status from occupying premises under a residential tenancy agreement.
>
> (4) But unless subsection (5) applies the landlord does not commit an offence under subsection (1) if—
>
> (a) the premises are located in an area in relation to which section 22 is in force,
>
> (b) the adult mentioned in subsections (2) and (3) is a limited right occupier, and
>
> (c) the eligibility period in relation to that occupier has not expired.
>
> (5) This subsection applies if the Secretary of State has given a notice in writing to the landlord which—
>
> (a) identifies the adult mentioned in subsections (2) and (3), and
>
> (b) states that the adult is disqualified as a result of their immigration status from occupying premises under a residential tenancy agreement.
>
> (6) It is a defence for a person charged with an offence under subsection (1) to prove that—

5 IA 2014, s 24(9).

(a) the person has taken reasonable steps to terminate the residential tenancy agreement, and

(b) the person has taken such steps within a reasonable period beginning with the time when the person first knew or had reasonable cause to believe that the premises were occupied by the adult mentioned in subsections (2) and (3).

(7) In determining whether subsection (6)(a) or (b) applies to a person, the court must have regard to any guidance which, at the time in question, had been issued by the Secretary of State for the purposes of that subsection and was in force at that time.

(8) Guidance issued for the purposes of subsection (6)—

(a) must be laid before Parliament in draft before being issued, and

(b) comes into force in accordance with regulations made by the Secretary of State.

(9) Section 22(9) applies for the purposes of subsection (1) as it applies for the purposes of that section[6].

(10) A person commits an offence if—

(a) there has been a post-grant contravention in relation to a residential tenancy agreement which relates to premises in England,

(b) the person is the responsible landlord in relation to the postgrant contravention,

(c) the person knows or has reasonable cause to believe that there has been a post-grant contravention in relation to the agreement, and

(d) none of paragraphs (a), (b) and (c) of section 24(6) applies in relation to the post-grant contravention.

(11) Subsection (10) applies whether or not the landlord is given a notice under section 23 in respect of the contravention.

33B Offences: agents

(1) Subsection (2) applies to an agent who is responsible for a landlord's contravention of section 22 in relation to premises in England.

(2) The agent commits an offence if the agent—

6 This states: 'A contravention of this section does not affect the validity or enforceability of any provision of a residential tenancy agreement by virtue of any rule of law relating to the validity or enforceability of contracts in circumstances involving illegality'.

(a) knew or had reasonable cause to believe that the landlord would contravene section 22 by entering into the residential tenancy agreement in question,

(b) had sufficient opportunity to notify the landlord of that fact before the landlord entered into the agreement, but

(c) did not do so.

(3) Subsection (4) applies where—

(a) a landlord contravenes section 22 in relation to a residential tenancy agreement relating to premises in England,

(b) the contravention is a post-grant contravention, and

(c) a person acting as the landlord's agent ("the agent") is responsible for the post-grant contravention.

(4) The agent commits an offence if—

(a) the agent knows or has reasonable cause to believe that there has been a post-grant contravention in relation to the agreement, and

(b) neither of paragraphs (a) and (b) of section 26(6) applies in relation to the post-grant contravention.

(5) Subsection (4) applies whether or not the agent is given a notice under section 25 in respect of the contravention.

37 Interpretation

(1) In this Chapter—

"adult" means a person who has attained the age of 18;

"agreement" includes an agreement in any form (whether or not in writing);

"eligibility period", in relation to a limited right occupier, is to be read in accordance with section 27;

"limited right occupier" has the meaning given in section 24(9);

"occupy" means occupy as an only or main residence;

"penalty notice" means a penalty notice given under this Chapter;

"person with a limited right to rent" has the meaning given in section 21(4);

"post-grant contravention" has the meaning given in section 22(10)[7];

7 This refers back to s 22(5):
(a) a residential tenancy agreement is entered into that grants a right to occupy premises on an adult with a limited right to rent,
(b) the adult later becomes a person disqualified as a result of their immigration status, and
(c) the adult continues to occupy the premises after becoming disqualified.

"pre-grant contravention" has the meaning given in section 22(10);

"premises" includes land, buildings, moveable structures, vehicles and vessels;

"prescribed" means prescribed in an order made by the Secretary of State;

"recipient" means the recipient of a penalty notice;

"relevant occupier" has the meaning given in section 22(10);

"residential tenancy agreement" has the meaning given in section 20(2).

(2) For the purposes of this Chapter a residential tenancy agreement grants a person a right to occupy premises if—

(a) the agreement expressly grants that person the right (whether or not by naming the person), or

(b) the person is permitted to occupy the premises by virtue of an express grant given to another person,

and references to a person occupying premises under an agreement are to be read accordingly.

(3) A reference in this Chapter to the "prescribed requirements", in connection with compliance with the requirements at a particular time, is a reference only to such of the requirements as are capable of being complied with at that time.

(4) Where two or more persons jointly constitute the landlord in relation to a residential tenancy agreement—

(a) the references to the landlord in—

(i) section 22(7)(a),

(ii) section 24(5), (6)(a) and (7) ,

(iii) section 26(6)(a) and (7)(b),

(iv) section 33A,

(v) section 33D, and

(vi) section 33E,

are to be taken as references to any of those persons;

(b) any other references to the landlord in this Chapter are to be taken as references to all of those persons.

(5) Where two or more persons jointly constitute the agent in relation to a residential tenancy agreement—

(a) the references to the agent in section 26(5), (6)(a) and (7) are to be taken as references to any of those persons;

(b) any other references to the agent in this Chapter are to be taken as references to all of those persons.

(6) The Secretary of State may by order prescribe cases in which—

(a) a residential tenancy agreement is, or is not, to be treated as being entered into for the purposes of this Chapter;

(b) a person is, or is not, to be treated as occupying premises as an only or main residence for the purposes of this Chapter.

(7) An order under subsection (6) prescribing a case may modify the application of this Chapter in relation to that case.

(8) The cases mentioned in subsection (6)(a) include, in particular, cases where—

(a) an option to renew an agreement is exercised;

(b) rights of occupation under an agreement are varied;

(c) an agreement is assigned (whether by the landlord or the tenant);

(d) a periodic tenancy arises at the end of a fixed term;

(e) an agreement grants a right of occupation on satisfaction of a condition;

(f) there is a change in the persons in occupation of the premises leased under an agreement or in the circumstances of any such person.'

Overview of the offence

7.6

The offence criminalises the situation where someone who is not permitted to rent occupies a premises under a residential tenancy agreement. This is not limited to people who are named on the tenancy agreement[8].

7.7

A landlord will commit the offence where a premises is occupied by an adult who is disqualified from doing so by virtue of their immigration status, and the landlord knew or had reasonable cause to suspect that. An agent will commit the offence if they knew or had reasonable cause to believe that someone is a disqualified person and had sufficient opportunity to warn the landlord of this, but did not do so.

8 See *R (Stewart) v Birmingham City Council* [2018] EWHC 61 (Admin), [2018] PTSR 1204 at [88].

7.8

There is a 'reasonable excuse' defence for someone who takes 'reasonable steps' in a reasonable time to terminate the tenancy once they know or had reasonable cause to believe that a disqualified person was occupying it. In determining that, the court 'must have regard to' the relevant guidance[9].

7.9

Where someone becomes a disqualified person during the course of the tenancy then the offence is committed if the landlord knows or has reasonable cause to believe that that is the case unless certain exceptions apply[10]. The agent will commit an offence where they know or have reasonable cause to believe that that is the case unless certain exceptions apply[11].

7.10

A further exception is where someone is a limited right occupier and their eligibility period has not expired[12].

Procedure

7.11

As with the illegal working offence (and many other of the immigration offences) the offence can be committed by a corporate body and, where it is done so with the 'consent or connivance of an officer of the body[13]' then the officer will be guilty as well.

9 See 'Guidance on taking reasonable steps to end a residential tenancy agreement within a reasonable time' (December 2016) and, generally, 'Landlord's guide to right to rent checks' (28 February 2023).

10 These are set out in IA 2014, s 24(6):
(a) the landlord has notified the Secretary of State of the contravention as soon as reasonably practicable;
(b) a person acting as the landlord's agent is responsible for the contravention;
(c) the eligibility period in relation to the limited right occupier whose occupation caused the contravention has not expired.

11 This are similar to, but not the same as, the exceptions for landlords and are set out at 26(6):
(a) the agent has notified the Secretary of State and the landlord of the contravention as soon as reasonably practicable;
(b) the eligibility period in relation to the limited right occupier whose occupation caused the contravention has not expired.

12 IA 2014, s 33A(4).

13 IA 2014, s 33C(3). By virtue of s 33C(4): 'an officer of a body includes a reference to—
(a) a director, manager or secretary,
(b) a person purporting to act as a director, manager or secretary, and
(c) if the affairs of the body are managed by its members, a member.'
There is a similar provision in relation to partnerships in s 33C(5).

Interaction with the facilitation offence

7.12

See Chapter 5 for comment as to whether someone who is guilty of this offence would be guilty of the facilitation offence.

Sentence

7.13

Both the offences are either way, with a maximum sentence of five years' imprisonment[14]. There are no Sentencing Guidelines or guideline cases. It is likely that consideration will be given to making a confiscation order.

7.14

In addition, a Banning Order under the Housing and Planning Act 2016 can be made[15].

Regulation of legal services

Background

7.15

Whilst the First-tier Tribunal (Immigration and Appeal Chamber) has had a number of iterations over the years[16], it has sat outside the court structure where the regulation of legal professionals is typically stronger. As a result, it was historically the case that no right of audience was needed in order to appear at an immigration appeal.

14 IA 2014, s 33C(1).

15 Housing and Planning Act 2016, ss 13–17 and The Housing and Planning Act 2016 (Banning Order Offences) Regulations 2018. See 'Banning Order Offences under the Housing and Planning Act 2016 – Guidance for Local Housing Authorities' (2018). It is a criminal offence to breach this.

16 The first provision for an appeals structure, albeit one with very limited powers, was in the Immigration Appeals Act 1969 which created Adjudicators. Their decisions could be appealed to the Immigration Appeal Tribunal.

7.16

Due to a number of concerns about the poor quality of immigration advisors in the 1990s, it was felt necessary to introduce a regulatory framework for those advisers who were not already otherwise regulated[17].

Regulatory framework

7.17

The 1999 Act created the Office of the Immigration Services Commissioner ('OISC'). The Commissioner is a 'Corporation Sole' with the OISC being an arms-length body of the Home Office. The Commissioner's role is to oversee the regulation of anybody giving legal advice in relation to immigration matters who is not regulated by another professional body (the Bar Standard's Board, the Law Society of ILEX for barristers, solicitors and legal executives as the case may be). Whilst the Commissioner has responsibility over the whole of the United Kingdom, this will focus on the position in England and Wales.

7.18

As part of the enforcement regime the Act created a number of criminal offences. The offences only applies to those who provide 'immigration advice' or 'immigration services', as defined in the IAA 1999, s 82:

> '"immigration advice" means advice which—
>
> (a) relates to a particular individual;
>
> (b) is given in connection with one or more relevant matters;

---

17 Introducing the Bill in the House of Commons Jack Straw, the then Home Secretary, stated the intention as being (*Hansard*, HC (Series 6) Vol 326, cols 37-129 (22 February 1999):

> 'Part V of the Bill deals with immigration advisers and immigration service providers, and fulfils a further manifesto commitment to regulate immigration advisers. It was my hon. Friend the Member for Tottenham (Mr. Grant) who first exposed the scandalous behaviour of some of these people, and I pay tribute to him for his work. Like my hon. Friend and me, many colleagues in the House have received endless complaints from their constituents about the activities of unscrupulous immigration advisers. They cheat their clients and manipulate the system for their own profit. We intend to put them out of business.
>
> The Bill will create a statutory scheme for regulating both unqualified and—to a degree—legally qualified advisers. It will be a criminal offence—punishable on indictment by up to two years' imprisonment or a fine, or both—to provide advice in breach of the scheme.
>
> Part V also makes provision for the appointment of an immigration services commissioner, who will be responsible for administering the regulation of advisers. Only those who are registered with the commissioner, who are members of designated professional bodies, or who are otherwise exempt, will be permitted to give immigration advice and services.
>
> The commissioner will investigate complaints against registered immigration advisers, in the light of which he may withdraw registration or, in certain cases, lay a disciplinary charge. There will be an immigration services tribunal to hear any disciplinary charges laid by the commissioner, and to which any person aggrieved at a decision by the commissioner may appeal.'

(c) is given by a person who knows that he is giving it in relation to a particular individual and in connection with one or more relevant matters; and

(d) is not given in connection with representing an individual before a court in criminal proceedings or matters ancillary to criminal proceedings;

"immigration services" means the making of representations on behalf of a particular individual—

(a) in civil proceedings before[18] a court, tribunal or adjudicator in the United Kingdom, or

(b) in correspondence with a Minister of the Crown or government department,

in connection with one or more relevant matters;

with 'relevant matter' then being defined:

"relevant matters" means any of the following—

(a) a claim for asylum[19];

(aa) an application for an ETA (within the meaning of section 11C of the Immigration Act 1971 (electronic travel authorisations));

(b) an application for, or for the variation of, entry clearance or leave to enter or remain in the United Kingdom;

(ba) an application for an immigration employment document[20];

(c) unlawful entry into the United Kingdom;

(d) nationality and citizenship under the law of the United Kingdom;

(h) removal or deportation from the United Kingdom;

(i) an application for bail under the Immigration Acts or under the Special Immigration Appeals Commission Act 1997;

(j) an appeal against, or an application for judicial review in relation to, any decision taken in connection with a matter referred to in paragraphs (a) to (i).'

18 'Before' here means in relation to proceedings that are in train. It is not limited to oral advocacy before the Court or Tribunal, and so will apply to correspondence to the Court or Tribunal; *Akhtar (Designated Qualified Regulator: s 84(3A)(b) restrictions) Pakistan* [2022] UKUT 00038 (IAC) at [30].

19 Which includes a claim for protection under Art 3 ECHR.

20 This is further defined in s 82(3) as:
'(a) a work permit (within the meaning of IA 1971, s 33(1) (interpretation)), and
(b) any other document which relates to employment and is issued for a purpose of immigration rules or in connection with leave to enter or remain in the United Kingdom.'

7.19

This only applies to advice or services given by someone who is in the United Kingdom at the time (regardless of where the recipient is)[21]. Difficulties can arise in practice in some cases given that the jurisdiction of the Tribunal is UK-wide, but barristers, solicitors and legal executives are regulated in England and Wales[22].

7.20

A further important restriction is that the Act does not bite on someone unless they are acting 'in the course of a business carried on (whether or not for profit) by him or by another person'[23]. This was considered in *RK (entitlement to represent: s 84) Bangladesh*[24] where the headnote provides a clear summary:

> '(1) Section 84(1) of the Immigration and Asylum Act 1999 provides that no person may provide immigration advice or immigration services unless he is a qualified person.
>
> (2) Section 82(2) provides that references to the provision of immigration advice or immigration services are to the provision of such advice or services by a person in the United Kingdom "in the course of a business carried on (whether or not for profit) by him or by another person".
>
> (3) Rule 48(1) of the Asylum and Immigration Tribunal (Procedure) Rules 2005 provides that "an appellant … may … be represented by any person not prohibited from representing him by section 84 … ".
>
> (4) Accordingly, where a family friend was seeking (otherwise than in the course of a business) to represent the appellant at a hearing, the Immigration Judge had no right to restrict the friend's involvement to that of a Mackenzie Friend on the basis that he was not legally qualified (see also HH (Sponsor as representative) Serbia [2006] UKAIT 00063).'

7.21

Subject to the above, nobody can give immigration advice, or provide immigration services, unless they are a 'qualified person' as provided by the

21 IAA 1999, s 82(2)(a)

22 See *Akhtar (Designated Qualified Regulator: s 84(3A)(b) restrictions) Pakistan* [2022] UKUT 00038 (IAC). The consequence of this is that barristers, solicitors and legal executives can only give legal advice and provide legal services whilst they are located in their 'home' jurisdiction of England and Wales, wherever the advice or representation is 'consumed'. So, an English barrister can represent a client before the Tribunal in Scotland if they appear by video-link from England. If they attend in person however, they would appear to be committing a criminal offence. Even if this is unlikely to ever be prosecuted, it is likely to have knock-on effects on matters such as the ability to recover costs and, potentially, insurance.

23 IAA 1999, s 82(2)(b).

24 [2011] UKUT 00409 (IAC).

IAA 1999, s 84[25]. As well as those who are regulated by a designated professional body or authorised by a qualifying regulator (barristers, solicitors or legal executives)[26], there are those who are registered by the OISC[27].

7.22

The OISC maintains a list of advisers who are duly authorised on their website. They operate three tiers of accreditation for individual advisers, with only those accredited to Level 3 being authorised to provide representation at appeals. On application the OISC will assess an application. This process includes a competency assessment as well as an assessment as to whether that the person is a 'fit and proper person'. An application fee is payable. If the application is granted, the OISC can apply restrictions on a registrant's entitlement to act[28].

7.23

An appeal against certain decisions (essentially, to refuse an application for initial or continuing registration, or to the imposition of a restriction or a failure to vary or lift a restriction, or to cancel a registration) lies to the General Regulatory Chamber (GRC) of the First-tier Tribunal (not the IAC (Immigration and Asylum Chamber)). Again, onward appeals are to the Administrative Appeals Chamber of the Upper Tribunal.

7.24

On an appeal the Tribunal will not conduct a review of the Commissioner's decision, but will make a decision for itself, which includes taking account of any new evidence not before the Commissioner[29].

7.25

Particular issues can arise with someone who is not a 'qualified person' in their own right, but is acting under the supervision of someone who is. Under the IAA 1999, s 84(2)(e) this covers someone 'acting on behalf of, and under the supervision of, a person within any of paragraphs (a) [*registered by the OISC*], (b) [*authorised by a designated professional body to practice as a member of that body*] to (ba) [*authorised by a designated regulator to provide immigration advice or services*] (whether or not under a contract of employment)'.

7.26

The requirement for the individual to both be acting on behalf of *and* under the supervision of, is important. The BSB and SRA have restrictions on who can

25 The Tribunal has what is known as a 's 84 form' which should be completed by a representative before they can appear. This contains a number of boxes, one of which should be ticked to confirm the authority of the person representing.

26 In practice, these bodies impose restrictions under their own professional rules as to who can give immigration advice or services.

27 IAA 1999, s 84(2)(a).

28 IAA 1999, Sch 6, para 2.

29 *Visa Joy Ltd v The Immigration Commissioner* [2017] EWCA Civ 1473, [2018] 1 WLR 2273.

supervise, as do the OISC. It is not clear whether a supervision arrangement that is in breach of the person's professional rules would mean that the individual then falls outside of s 84(2)(e), thereby potentially committing a criminal offence (although a prosecution would be unlikely). On the basis of *R v K* [2008][30] it would appear likely that the court would approach the case on the basis that the provisions of the Act be interpreted in light of the relevant regulator's internal rules.

Restraining orders and injunctions

7.27

The Commissioner has various powers of enforcement, including the power to lay a disciplinary charge against a registered person before the First-tier Tribunal.

7.28

If proved, restrictions on the provision or advice or services can be placed on the registration of the person concerned, or they can be prohibited from providing advice or services[31]:

> 'The First-tier Tribunal may direct that the person charged or any person [acting on his behalf or under his supervision is to be—
>
> (a) subject to such restrictions on the provision of immigration advice or immigration services as the First-tier Tribunal considers appropriate;
>
> (b) suspended from providing immigration advice or immigration services for such period as the First-tier Tribunal may determine; or
>
> (c) prohibited from providing immigration advice or immigration services indefinitely.'

7.29

There is also power to impose restrictions, or prohibit advice or services, on an interim basis whilst a charge is being determined[32]. Any such order under s 89(8), interim order, or equivalent order made by a different disciplinary body[33], is defined as being a 'restraining order'.

30 EWCA Crim 1900, [2009] 1 Cr App R 9. In *R v K* The Court of Appeal determined that under the Barristers previous Code of Conduct someone who had been called to the bar, but not obtained a practicing certificate, was not 'authorised' to give immigration advice or services under s 84.

31 IAA 1999, s 89(8).

32 IAA 1999, Sch 5, para 9(3).

33 As defined in IAA 1999, s 86A which is currently the Law Society, the Bar Council and ILEX.

7.30

The Commissioner also has power to apply to the county court for an injunction preventing someone from providing immigration advice or immigration services if he is satisfied that the person is currently doing so, and will continue to do so unless restrained[34].

Unauthorised legal advice or services – criminal offence

7.31

The offence is set out in the IAA 1999, s 91:

(1) A person who provides immigration advice or immigration services in contravention of section 84 or of a restraining order is guilty of an offence and liable—

(a) on summary conviction, to imprisonment for a term not exceeding six months or to a fine not exceeding the statutory maximum, or to both; or

(b) on conviction on indictment, to imprisonment for a term not exceeding two years or to a fine, or to both.

(2) "*Restraining order*" means —

(a) a direction given by the First-tier Tribunal under section 89(8) or paragraph 9(3) of Schedule 5; or

(b) an order made by a disciplinary body under section 90(1).

(3) If an offence under this section committed by a body corporate is proved[35]—

(a) to have been committed with the consent or connivance of an officer, or

(b) to be attributable to neglect on his part,

the officer as well as the body corporate is guilty of the offence and liable to be proceeded against and punished accordingly.

(4) "*Officer*", in relation to a body corporate, means a director, manager, secretary or other similar officer of the body, or a person purporting to act in such a capacity.

(5) If the affairs of a body corporate are managed by its members, subsection (3) applies in relation to the acts and defaults of a member in connection with his functions of management as if he were a director of the body corporate.'

34 IAA 1999, s 92.
35 A similar provision is contained in s91(6)-(7) relating to corporate bodies in Scotland.

7.32

The offence can be committed in one of two ways. Common to both is the provision or 'immigration advice' or 'immigration services' (as defined above) in an unlawful way. That can either be either in contravention of the IAA 1999, s 84 or in breach of a restraining order.

Burden of proof

7.33

The prosecution must prove to the criminal standard that the defendant has provided a relevant immigration service. At that point the burden is on the defendant (on the usual civil standard) to prove that he was qualified to do so[36].

Procedure

7.34

The offence is either way. Whilst it can be prosecuted by the CPS (especially where other offences, such as fraud, are alleged) it can also be prosecuted by the OISC.

7.35

The OISC publishes a 'Criminal Prosecution Policy' that is available online[37] which sets out the framework that the OISC will apply in beginning and continuing with a prosecution. This relates both to the main s 91 offence, but also the s 92B and s 92A offences and any offences prosecuted under the criminal law. The OISC can administer a simple caution as an alternative to prosecution.

Sentence

7.36

The offence is either way, with a maximum sentence of two years in the Crown Court. There are no sentencing guidelines. In cases that have reached the Court of Appeal, there are often other, and more serious, offences indicted[38] which means those cases have not got great value as precedent.

---

36 *Clarke* [2008] EWCA Crim 893.

37 The latest version is dated 24 May 2017 – https://www.gov.uk/government/publications/criminal-prosecution-policy/oisc-criminal-prosecution-policy.

38 For example in *Ahmed* [2020] EWCA Crim 1561 a sentence of 21 months for ten instances of providing immigration services (presumably after trial) was upheld. However, the focus of the appeal was on the concurrent sentences of 7 years for facilitation (falsification of documents for applicants seeking a visa to bring a spouse into the UK).

7.37

Any sentencing exercise is intensely fact specific and sentences will range from a fine or other non-custodial penalty, up to imprisonment close to the maximum in cases where there are relevant previous convictions, or widespread or cynical exploitation of others[39]. It is hard to discern any clear sentencing bands. The relatively low maximum sentence however, does not leave much room for big distinctions between cases for this offence (which is one of the reasons why fraud or other offences are often charged).

Offering to provide immigration advice when not qualified

7.38

There is a further, and less serious, offence under the IAA 1999, s 92B of offering to provide immigration advice or services where not qualified to do so:

> '(1) A person commits an offence if—
>
> > (a) he offers to provide immigration advice or immigration services, and
> >
> > (b) provision by him of the advice or services would constitute an offence under section 91.
>
> (2) For the purpose of subsection (1) a person offers to provide advice or services if he—
>
> > (a) makes an offer to a particular person or class of person,
> >
> > (b) makes arrangements for an advertisement in which he offers to provide advice or services, or
> >
> > (c) makes arrangements for an advertisement in which he is described or presented as competent to provide advice or services.
>
> (4) Subsections (3) to (7) of section 91 shall have effect for the purposes of this section as they have effect for the purposes of that section.'

Sentence

7.39

The offence is summary only, with a maximum sentence of a Level 4 fine[40].

39 A further example is 12 months on a plea on the day of trial for provision on a 'large scale' by someone with relevant previous convictions (*Malik* [2019] EWCA Crim 1079).

40 IAA 1999, s 92(3).

Procedure

7.40

An extended time limit for prosecution applies (IAA 1999, s 92B(5)):

> '(5) An information relating to an offence under this section may in England and Wales be tried by a magistrates' court if—
>
> (a) it is laid within the period of six months beginning with the date (or first date) on which the offence is alleged to have been committed, or
>
> (b) it is laid—
>
> (i) within the period of two years beginning with that date, and
>
> (ii) within the period of six months beginning with a date certified by the Immigration Services Commissioner as the date on which the commission of the offence came to his notice.'

7.41

Whilst this is similar to the time limit under the IA 1971, s 28 the extension is only for two years (rather than the three years in s 28) and the certificate must be signed by the Immigration Services Commissioner rather than a police officer[41].

7.42

It does not appear that this offence has been charged much (if at all). This is presumably as those who go on to commit the IAA 1999, s 91 offence will be charged with that. For those that do not, the OISC may often provide a warning based on the above[42], rather than proceed straight to enforcement action, although there would be no legal bar on doing so.

Search powers

7.43

The Commissioner can apply for a warrant to enter and search premises (domestic or commercial) (IAA 1999, s 92A(1)–(4), (7)):

---

41 See Chapter 10 – Criminal Procedure – for the authorities under s 28. It is likely that similar principles will apply.

42 See *Ali v Office of the Immigration Services Commissioner* [2021] ICR 452 at [18], a judgment of the Employment Appeal Tribunal.

'(1) On an application made by the Commissioner a justice of the peace may issue a warrant authorising the Commissioner to enter and search premises.

(2) A justice of the peace may issue a warrant in respect of premises only if satisfied that there are reasonable grounds for believing that–

(a) an offence under section 91 has been committed,

(b) there is material on the premises which is likely to be of substantial value (whether by itself or together with other material) to the investigation of the offence, and

(c) any of the conditions specified in subsection (3) is satisfied.

(3) Those conditions are–

(a) that it is not practicable to communicate with a person entitled to grant entry to the premises,

(b) that it is not practicable to communicate with a person entitled to grant access to the evidence,

(c) that entry to the premises will be prevented unless a warrant is produced, and

(d) that the purpose of a search may be frustrated or seriously prejudiced unless the Commissioner can secure immediate entry on arrival at the premises.

(4) The Commissioner may seize and retain anything for which a search is authorised under this section.

...

(7) In this section–

(a) a reference to the Commissioner includes a reference to a member of his staff authorised in writing by him,

(b) a reference to premises includes a reference to premises used wholly or partly as a dwelling, and

(c) a reference to material–

(i) includes material subject to legal privilege within the meaning of the Police and Criminal Evidence Act 1984,

(ii) does not include excluded material or special procedure material within the meaning of that Act, and

(iii) includes material whether or not it would be admissible in evidence at a trial.'

7.44

Related to this there is a criminal offence of obstructing a search. This is summary only, but it is imprisonable (IAA 1999, s 92A(5), (6)):

(5) A person commits an offence if without reasonable excuse he obstructs the Commissioner in the exercise of a power by virtue of this section.

(6) A person guilty of an offence under subsection (5) shall be liable on summary conviction to–

(a) imprisonment for a term not exceeding six months,

(b) a fine not exceeding level 5 on the standard scale, or

(c) both.

7.45

There are no reported cases relating to this offence.

Offences under legal professional regulation

7.46

Where someone pretends to be a regulated legal professional, or carries out work (such as litigation) that is a reserved legal activity, then they can be prosecuted under the offences under the Legal Services Act 2007, ss 14–17. In addition, the standard criminal law can be applied (for example, offences under the Fraud Act 2006)[43].

Non-compliance offences under the IA 1971

7.47

The IA 1971, s 26 contains eight separate offences that, broadly speaking, prosecute certain behaviours towards Immigration Officers (IOs) by immigrants or would-be immigrants to the United Kingdom[44].

43 See, as an example form a non-immigration context, *R v Di Stefano* [2017] EWCA Crim 601 the notorious case of Giovanni di Stefano.

44 It was said in *Clarke* [1985] AC 1037, HL that 'The offences, apart from that under (*c*), created by section 26(1) are all, with the exception of that under (*g*) (obstructing an immigration officer or other person lawfully acting in the execution of the Act), primarily concerned with failure to give information required or with giving false information under or in connection with the various procedures of the Act'.

Offences

7.48

These are defined as follows:

26.— General offences in connection with administration of Act.

(1) A person shall be guilty of an offence punishable on summary conviction with a fine of not more than level 5 on the standard scale or with imprisonment for not more than six months, or with both, in any of the following cases—

(a) if, without reasonable excuse, he refuses or fails to submit to examination under Schedule 2 to this Act;

(b) if, without reasonable excuse, he refuses or fails to furnish or produce any information in his possession, or any documents in his possession or control, which he is on an examination under that Schedule required to furnish or produce;

(c) if on any such examination or otherwise he makes or causes to be made to an immigration officer or other person lawfully acting in the execution of a relevant enactment a return, statement or representation which he knows to be false or does not believe to be true;

(d) if, without lawful authority, he alters any certificate of entitlement, entry clearance, work permit or other document issued or made under or for the purposes of this Act, or uses for the purposes of this Act, or has in his possession for such use, any passport, certificate of entitlement, entry clearance, work permit or other document which he knows or has reasonable cause to believe to be false;

(e) if, without reasonable excuse, he fails to complete and produce a landing or embarkation card in accordance with any order under Schedule 2 to this Act;

(f) if, without reasonable excuse, he fails to comply with any requirement of regulations under section 4(3) or of an order under section 4(4) above;

(g) if, without reasonable excuse, he obstructs an immigration officer or other person lawfully acting in the execution of this Act;

(h) if, without reasonable excuse, the person fails to comply with a direction under paragraph 1(6) of Schedule 2 (direction to move a container for purposes of a search)[45]

---

45 Section 26(1)(h) was introduced by NABA 2022, s 44 as of 28 June 2022. This relates to a new power contained in the 2022 Act to search a container under the Immigration Acts.

(3) "*Relevant enactment*" means—

(a) this Act;

(b) the Immigration Act 1988;

(c) the Asylum and Immigration Appeals Act 1993 (apart from section 4 or 5);

(d) the Immigration and Asylum Act 1999 (apart from Part VI); or]

(e) the Nationality, Immigration and Asylum Act 2002 (apart from Part 5)

7.49

These three offences can be taken together. They criminalise the refusal of a would-be immigrant to comply with the provisions of the IA 1971, Sch 2. See the chapter on powers of arrest for more detail.

(c) False representation

7.50

The offence under (c) is one of dishonesty as it requires a defendant to make a false statement (knowingly or recklessly) to an Immigration Officer (or similar person) when being examined under the IA 1971, Sch 2[46].

7.51

There must be a positive false statement of a material fact. Non-disclosure of a relevant factor is not sufficient[47]:

> 'I reject the view that there is a duty of positive candour imposed by the immigration laws and that mere non-disclosure by an entrant of material facts in the absence of fraud is a breach of the immigration laws.'

7.52

However[48]:

> 'It is clear on general principles of law that deception may arise from conduct, and from conduct accompanied by silence as to a material fact.'

46 *Kaile* [2009] EWCA Crim 2868 at [15].

47 *R v SSHD, ex parte Khawaja* [1983] 1 All ER 765, at p 779.

48 *Zamir v SSHD* [1980] 2 All ER 768. See also *R v SSHD, ex parte Patel* [1986] Imm AR 515 where 'the silent' handing over of a passport containing false information was sufficient..

7.53

The offence does not apply to a false statement made to a police officer investigating an offence under the Immigration Acts[49] (as defined in s 26(3)), but will likely apply to police officers when they exercise other powers under the Immigration Acts, as well as to Immigration Officers and other Home Office officials.

7.54

In many cases, someone committing this offence would also be committing the offence under the IA 1971, s 24A[50]. The s 24A offence does not require that the person receiving the information is acting in the course of his duty, and is therefore generally easier to prove. Because of that, and the higher maximum sentence, it is likely that the CPS would charge the s 24A offence instead in those circumstances.

(d) Altering an official document

7.55

This creates a wide-ranging offence that would apply to official documents, but would not appear to cover something such a false bank statement that someone may intend to present to an Immigration Officer. In many cases such behaviour would be covered by more serious document offences, or offences under the Forgery Act 1981.

7.56

The IAA 1999, s 31 defence applies to this offence.

(f) Failing to register with police as directed / failing to provide information as to accommodation

7.57

This contains, in effect, two separate offences. The first is in relation to the requirements contained in Regulations made under the IA 1971, s 4(3) for certain foreign nationals to register with police.

7.58

As of 9 November 2022, the Regulations that have been in place since 1972[51] requiring this have been repealed[52]. This has retrospective effect[53], but it would

49 *Clarke* [1985] AC 1037, HL.
50 See Chapter 4.
51 Immigration (Registration with Police) Regulations 1972.
52 Immigration (Registration with Police) Revocation Regulations 2022.
53 Reg 3 Immigration (Registration with Police) Revocation Regulations 2022.

still be possible (although very unlikely) for there to be a prosecution for a past breach. It is unlikely that the scheme will be replaced.

7.59

The other part of the offence is in relation to the IA 1971, s 4(4) which makes provision to require 'hotels and other premises where lodging of sleeping accommodation is provided' to compile a Register of all people (including British citizens) over the age of 16 who stay at least one night there. Further, a non-British citizen is required to provide details of his passport of identity document, as well as his next destination when he leaves[54]. It is an offence to fail to do so.

(g) Obstructing an Immigration Officer

7.60

There is no definition of 'obstructing'[55], but similar principles to the offence of obstructing a police officer will likely apply. This would require an act of the defendant that makes it more difficult for the Immigration Officer to carry out his job (provided the Officer was acting in the course of his duty)[56]. An Immigration Officer can arrest without warrant someone they reasonably believe is, or has, committed or attempted to commit, the offence.

7.61

One difference is that obstructing a police officer must be committed 'wilfully'[57] which requires that there is an intention to obstruct, rather than a mere intention to do an act that does, in fact, obstruct[58]. This is not the case with the s 26(1)(g) offence.

Sentence

7.62

All offences are summary only, with a maximum sentence of six months' imprisonment or a Level 5 fine.

54 The Immigration (Hotel Records) Order 1972.

55 The Home Office produce a document simply called 'Obstruction', as guidance for Immigration Enforcement Officers – https://assets.publishing.service.gov.uk/government/uploads/system/uploads/attachment_data/file/1039501/Obstruction.pdf (v1.0, 08 December 2021). This also considers the offences relating to assaulting an Immigration Officer.

56 *Hinchliffe v Sheldon* [1955] 1 WLR 1207.

57 Police Act 1996, s 89(2).

58 *Wilmott v Atack* [1977] QB 498.

Procedure

7.63

The extended time limit for prosecution applies to offences under s 26(c) and (d) only[59].

7.64

These offences are rarely charged. As noted, this is not least because someone guilty of these offences are very likely to have also committed a more serious offence. For example, as well as the relationship between the offences under s 26(c) and the attempted or full offence of obtaining leave to enter or remain by deception, many offences under s 26(d) will constitute an offence under the Identity Documents Act 2010.

Reasonable excuse

7.65

Several of the offences makes it a defence for there to be a reasonable excuse for any failure. This has been examined by the courts on a number of different occasions in relation to different offences.

7.66

It is essentially a fact specific question in all cases. In assessing any particular reason, some guidance can be found in *R v Jones*[60]:

> 'where there is an honest, but mistaken, belief of facts which, if true, would have constituted lawful authority, it is capable of being a reasonable excuse within the section, and the judge should so direct the jury, leaving them to determine whether the defendant has proved his belief of the requisite facts and whether in the circumstances that belief amounts to a reasonable excuse.'

7.67

For example, someone who has lost their landing card would likely have a reasonable excuse to a prosecution under the IA 1971, s 26(1)(e), whereas someone being prosecuted under s 26(1)(a) who believed that they did not have to be examined under Sch 2 would not.

---

59 IA 1971, s 26(2).
60 [1995] 2 WLR 64.

7.68

A refusal to comply with a request would not be an offence unless it relates to a duty under the Act (such as providing a passport or other document under Sch 2, para 2.

Offences under the IA 1971 having entered the United Kingdom

7.69

There are a number of similar, summary only offences, contained in the IA 1971, s 24(1). These criminalise various behaviours relating to someone who has been granted leave to enter, or otherwise given permission to be in the United Kingdom, but acts in breach of the permission granted.

Offences

7.70

These are defined as follows (IA 1971, s 24(1)):

> '(1) A person who is not a British citizen shall be guilty of an offence punishable on summary conviction with a fine of not more than level 5 on the standard scale or with imprisonment for not more than six months, or with both, in any of the following cases –
>
> (b) if, having only a limited leave to enter or remain in the United Kingdom, he knowingly fails to observe a condition of the leave;
>
> (c) if, having lawfully entered the United Kingdom without leave by virtue of section 8(1) above, he remains without leave beyond the time allowed by section 8(1);
>
> (d) if, without reasonable excuse, he fails to comply with any requirement imposed on him under Schedule 2 to this Act to report to a medical officer of health, or to attend, or submit to a test or examination, as required by such an officer;
>
> (f) if he disembarks in the United Kingdom from a ship or aircraft after being placed on board under Schedule 2 or 3 to this Act with a view to his removal from the United Kingdom;
>
> (g) if he embarks in contravention of a restriction imposed by or under an Order in Council under section 3(7) of this Act[61];
>
> (h) if the person is on immigration bail within the meaning of Schedule 10 to the Immigration Act 2016 and, without reasonable excuse, the person breaches a bail condition within the meaning of that Schedule.'

61 There are currently no such orders in place.

7.71

These can be seen as 'companion' offences to the offences under the IA 1971, s 24(A1)-(F1) relating to unlawful arrival or entry, although these arise in-country.

7.72

The offence under (b) requires that a written notice under the IA 1971, s 4 has been given of the relevant limitation[62]. Where the condition restricts employment, it is likely that a breach would be charged under the illegal working legislation[63], rather than s 24. Where a person's leave is extended under IA 1971, s 3C then their existing conditions will apply. However, where their leave expires they will no longer be subject to these conditions (but will be liable for the more serious offence of overstaying contrary to s 24(C1)).

7.73

In relation to s 26(c), s 8(1) makes provision for, amongst other categories of people, ship and airline crew (who have not previously been subject to a Deportation Order, been refused leave to enter or required to submit for an examination under Sch 2) to be permitted to enter the United Kingdom without leave and remain until the ship or aircraft leaves.

The Illegal Migration Act 2023

7.74

The Illegal Migration Act 2023, s 10(2) creates a new offence under the IA 1971, s 24(1):

> '(fa) if the person disembarks in the United Kingdom from a ship, aircraft, train or vehicle after being placed on board under section 8(11) of the Illegal Migration Act 2023 with a view to the person's removal from the United Kingdom;'

It is not known when this will be brought into force. When it is the same maximum sentence and procedure will apply.

Sentence

7.75

The offences are summary only, with a maximum sentence of six months' imprisonment or a Level 5 fine.

---

62 *Lamptey v Owen* [1982] Crim LR 42 – the fact that the defendant's passport had been incorrectly stamped and did not contain notice of the limited leave to remain meant that there was not sufficient notice of the terms of the grant of leave.

63 IA 1971, s 24B – see Chapter 6.

Procedure

7.76

An extended time limit for prosecution under the IA 1971, s 28(1) applies to the offence under s 24(1)(c) [64]. There is a separate, but similar, extended time limit for the s 24(1)(h) offence that applies in relation to other offences[65].

7.77

The IA, s 24(1A) which is still in force in an amended format, made provision for the offence under s 24(1)(b) as follows:

> 'A person commits an offence under subsection (1)(b)(i) on the day when he first knows that the time limited by his leave has expired and continues to commit it throughout any period during which he is in the United Kingdom thereafter; but a person shall not be prosecuted under that provision more than once in respect of the same limited leave.'

7.78

Thereafter it is a continuing offence[66]. The reference to '1(b)(i)' was repealed by the NABA 2022, s 40 and replaced with the new offence under s 24(C1). As that offence is either way, many of the issues with time limits that arose may not be relevant (but see Chapter 4 for further discussion)[67]. What is now the 1(b) offence can be committed by someone with valid leave. It would make sense for it to be applied to the s 24(1)(c) offence, although there would not appear to be any way of interpreting s 24(1A) that way, and the application of the extended time limit to prosecution of those offences would suggest that that is not the case.

7.79

Given that they appear to refer to single acts, and by implication of not being included in the exception under the IA 1971, s 24(1A) the other offences would appear not to be continuing ones[68].

---

64 See Chapter 10. It also applies to the offences under s 24(A1)–(E1) despite the fact that they are either way.

65 This is provided for in IA 1971, s 28(1A). The difference between the two extended time limits is that the extension for the s 24(1)(c) offence is only to three months after the time that the defendant was arrested for this offence or for breach of Immigration Bail.

66 This reversed the conclusion of the House of Lords in *Grant v Borg* [1982] 2 All ER 257 that the offence was a 'once and for all' one committed on the after his leave to remain expired.

67 Subject to the caveat of whether Parliament has, in fact, introduced time limits – see Chapter 4.

68 Most of the cases dealing with this are prior to the Immigration Act 1988, and are of some age. It was confirmed in *Nuro v Home Office* [2014] EWHC 462 (Admin) that the offence under the (now-repealed) s 24(1)(a) – entering without leave or in breach of a deportation order, was committed on the day of entry and not thereafter, see [21]-[22]

Defences

7.80

The s 31 defence applies to the offence under s 26(1)(d), but not under the other sections.

Application to EU citizens

7.81

An EEA national who arrived prior to Brexit (at least, prior to the ending of free movement) would not require leave to enter[69]. However, following 31 December 2020 (the date of the implementation period of the Withdrawal Agreement) they would require leave under the EU Settlement Scheme.

7.82

In those circumstances, any such person who had not obtained the requisite leave (either under the EUSS or the Immigration Rules) would not be someone who is an 'overstayer' for the purposes of s 24(1)(b) as they would not have entered with leave.

Reasonable excuse

7.83

See above for consideration of reasonable excuse. A mistake as to when leave expired would appear to be a mistake of fact that can provide a defence.

Registration card

7.84

When someone claims asylum, they will be given an Application Registration Card (an 'ARC'). This is a physical, plastic, card that contains the applicant's name, nationality, age (which will be marked as disputed if that is the case) and right to work[70]. This is a 'registration card', and is an important document for someone to have. The person will only be eligible for an ARC whilst their claim (or any appeal) is pending. The submission of a fresh claim will not revive a person's eligibility for an ARC, unless it is accepted as such by the Home Secretary[71].

---

69 IA 1988, s 7(1).

70 Home Office Guidance is produced 'Application Registration Card' (28 November 2022). The Guidance specifically states that an ARC is not to be used as proof of identity.

71 Home Office Guidance. See also *In the matter of an application by Abdual Said for Judicial Review* [2023] NIKB 1.

7.85

A 'registration card' is defined in the IA 1971, s 26A(1):

> '(1) In this section "registration card" means a document which—
>
> (a) carries information about a person (whether or not wholly or partly electronically), and
>
> (b) is issued by the Secretary of State to the person wholly or partly in connection with—
>
> (i) a claim for asylum (whether or not made by that person), or
>
> (ii) a claim for support under IAA1999, s 4 (whether or not made by that person).
>
> The difference between s4 and s95 is that s95 support is for people (or their dependents) who have made a claim for asylum, but which is either yet to be determined, or that an appeal is still pending, whilst s4 support is for those asylum seekers who's claim (including any appeal) has been finally determined and (broadly speaking) either there is a barrier on their ability to leave the UK, or they are liable to be destitute.'

7.86

The definition in s 26A(1)(b)(ii) relates to documents that relate to a claim for support under the IAA 1999, s 4 (relating to accommodation and subsistence) for certain people subject to immigration control. This is mostly people who have had an asylum claim rejected, but remain in the United Kingdom.

7.87

The IA 1971, s 26A creates an offence (which can be committed in a number of different ways) relating to a 'registration card'.

> '(3) A person commits an offence if he—
>
> (a) makes a false registration card,
>
> (b) alters a registration card with intent to deceive or to enable another to deceive,
>
> (c) has a false or altered registration card in his possession without reasonable excuse,
>
> (d) uses or attempts to use a false registration card for a purpose for which a registration card is issued,
>
> (e) uses or attempts to use an altered registration card with intent to deceive,

(f) makes an article designed to be used in making a false registration card,

(g) makes an article designed to be used in altering a registration card with intent to deceive or to enable another to deceive, or

(h) has an article within paragraph (f) or (g) in his possession without reasonable excuse.'

Sentence

7.88

The offences are all either way, although the maximum sentence depends on which subsection is alleged:

'(5) A person who is guilty of an offence under subsection (3)(a), (b), (d), (e), (f) or (g) shall be liable—

(a) on conviction on indictment, to imprisonment for a term not exceeding ten years, to a fine or to both, or

(b) on summary conviction, to imprisonment for a term not exceeding six months, to a fine not exceeding the statutory maximum or to both.

(6) A person who is guilty of an offence under subsection (3)(c) or (h) shall be liable—

(a) on conviction on indictment, to imprisonment for a term not exceeding two years, to a fine or to both, or

(b) on summary conviction, to imprisonment for a term not exceeding six months, to a fine not exceeding the statutory maximum or to both.'

7.89

The offences under s 26A(3)(c) and (h) are both less serious as they relate to 'passive' offending of possession without an ulterior intent.

7.90

In *Mohammed*[72] a Somali national used a false registration card to try and obtain work. He was later arrested at his home address where the false card was in a suitcase and charged with an offence under s 26(3)(c), presumably in relation to having it on arrest, and s 26(3)(b) in relation to the attempt to secure employment. He was of good character.

72 [2006] EWCA Crim 2172.

7.91

He pleaded guilty at the earliest opportunity and was sentenced to 18 months for the (b) offence and six months consecutive for (c). This was reduced nine 9 months with three months concurrent.

7.92

This was prior to *Overieriakhi*[73]. Whilst the sentence in *Mohammed* is broadly consistent with that case, it could be said that Mr Mohammed was lawfully present in the United Kingdom (in the sense that his asylum claim was still under consideration) and his case would now likely attract a sentence more towards the six-month mark.

Possessing an immigration stamp

7.93

An immigration stamp is defined in the IA 1971, s 26B(3) as:

> '(a) "immigration stamp" means a device which is designed for the purpose of stamping documents in the exercise of an immigration function,
>
> (b) "replica immigration stamp" means a device which is designed for the purpose of stamping a document so that it appears to have been stamped in the exercise of an immigration function, and
>
> (c) "immigration function" means a function of an immigration officer or the Secretary of State under the Immigration Acts.'

7.94

It is an offence to have an 'immigration stamp'[74], or a 'replica immigration stamp'[75] without a reasonable excuse. Reasonable excuse is not defined, and it is unlikely that there will be many reasons that would constitute this.

7.95

'Immigration function' is defined at the IA 1971, s 26B(3)(c). The courts have not yet considered this in the context of this offence but it is likely to include all the day to day functions of an Immigration Officer[76].

---

73 [2009] EWCA Crim 452.

74 IA 1971, s 26B(1).

75 IA 1971, s 26B(2).

76 IA 2016, ss 46–58 sets out a useful summary of the main functions of an Immigration Officer or someone exercising the powers of the Secretary of State.

Sentence

7.96

The offence is either way, with a maximum sentence of two years' imprisonment, or a fine (or both).

Offences relating to passengers and ports

7.97

There are a number of summary only offences that impose liability on ship and airplane captains and agents, and port managers for failure to comply with other requirements of the Immigration Acts – the IA 1971, s 27:

> **'27 Offences by persons connected with ships or aircraft or with ports**
>
> (1) A person shall be guilty of an offence punishable on summary conviction with a fine of not more than level 5 on the standard scale or with imprisonment for not more than six months, or with both, in any of the following cases—
>
> (a) if, being the captain of a ship or aircraft,—
>
> > (i) he knowingly permits a person to disembark in the United Kingdom when required under Schedule 2 or 3 to this Act to prevent it, or fails without reasonable excuse to take any steps he is required by or under Schedule 2 to take in connection with the disembarkation or examination of passengers or for furnishing a passenger list or particulars of members of the crew; or
> >
> > (ii) he fails, without reasonable excuse, to comply with any directions given him under Schedule 2 or 3 or under the Immigration and Asylum Act 1999 with respect to the removal of a person from the United Kingdom;
>
> (b) if, as owner or agent of a ship or aircraft,—
>
> > (i) he arranges, or is knowingly concerned in any arrangements, for the ship or aircraft to call at a port other than a port of entry contrary to any provision of Schedule 2 to this Act; or
> >
> > (ii) he fails, without reasonable excuse, to take any steps required by an order under Schedule 2 for the supply to passengers of landing or embarkation cards; or
> >
> > (iii) he fails, without reasonable excuse, to make arrangements for or in connection with the removal of a person from the United Kingdom when required to do so by directions given under Schedule 2 or 3 to this Act or under the Immigration and Asylum Act 1999; or

(iiia) he fails, without reasonable excuse, to comply with a direction under paragraph 5B of Schedule 2; or

(iv) he fails, without reasonable excuse, to comply with any other requirement imposed by or under Schedule 2;

(c) if, as a person concerned in the management of a port, he fails, without reasonable excuse to take any steps required by Schedule 2 in relation to the embarkation or disembarkation of passengers where a control area is designated.

(ca) if as a person concerned in the management of a port he fails, without reasonable excuse,

to comply with a direction under paragraph 5B of Schedule 2.'

7.98

In practice, these offences are rarely (if ever) charged. There is an overlap between many of the offences and the Carriers Liability Scheme which is likely to be the initial (if not sole) means of enforcement[77].

The Illegal Migration Act 2023

7.99

The Illegal Migration Act 2023, s 10(3) creates two new offences under the IA 1971, s 27:

'(aa) if, being the captain of a ship or aircraft, the train manager of a train or the driver of a vehicle, the person knowingly permits a person to disembark in the United Kingdom when required under section 8(12)(a) of the Illegal Migration Act 2023 to prevent it;'

...

'(ba) if, as owner or agent of a ship, aircraft, train or vehicle, the person fails, without reasonable excuse, to make arrangements for or in connection with the removal of a person from the United Kingdom when required to do so by directions given under section 8(8) or (9) of the Illegal Migration Act 2023;'

It is not known when this will be brought into force. When it is, the same maximum sentence and procedure will apply.

77 Proceedings under s 27 (1)(a)(i) or (1)(b)((iv) cannot be brought for actions for which a civil penalty has been brought, see s 27(2).

Assaults on immigration officers and other staff

Introduction

7.100

As would be expected there is a specific offence of assaulting an Immigration Officer in the execution of his duty.

7.101

However, there are other charges that could be brought, that will also be briefly considered here.

7.102

More serious assaults (typically those that leave more than a minor injury) would likely be charged under the Offences Against the Person Act 1861[78]. The fact that an offence is against an Immigration Officer who was carrying out a public duty is an aggravating feature[79].

Assaulting an immigration officer

7.103

This offence is created under the UKBA 2007, s 22:

> **'22 Assaulting an immigration officer: offence**
>
> (1) A person who assaults an immigration officer commits an offence.
>
> (2) A person guilty of an offence under this section shall be liable on summary conviction to—
>
> (a) imprisonment for a period not exceeding 51 weeks,
>
> (b) a fine not exceeding level 5 on the standard scale, or
>
> (c) both.'

78 Typically wounding or causing Grievous Bodily Harm with (s 18) or without (s 20) intent to do so, and causing Actual Bodily Harm (s 47).

79 Whilst an Immigration Officer is not an emergency worker for the purpose of Assaults on Emergency Workers Act 2018, s 3 or Sentencing Act 2020, s 67, they would be likely be 'providing a public service, performing a public duty or providing services to the public', which is a statutory aggravating factor under Sentencing Act 2020, s 68A, which came into force for anyone who was sentenced on or after 28 June 2022.

Powers of detention

7.104

A designated Immigration Officer at a port has the power to detain individuals in certain circumstances (generally speaking, where they are suspected of offending) for up to three hours whilst a police officer attends[80].

7.105

As well as it being an offence to abscond from such detention[81], it is also an offence to assault[82] or obstruct[83] the Immigration Officer exercising those powers.

7.106

These offences are summary only and punishable by imprisonment of 51 weeks and a Level 5 fine (for absconding or assaulting) or a Level 3 fine (for obstruction)[84].

Assaulting an 'emergency worker'

7.107

The Assaults on Emergency Workers (Offences) Act 2018 created an aggravated version of common assault or battery.

7.108

Once the basic offence of assault or battery is proven, the person will be guilty of the aggravated offence if it is 'committed against an emergency worker acting in the exercise of functions as such a worker'[85]. This is further defined in the Assaults on Emergency Workers (Offences) Act 2018, s 1(3) as:

> 'For the purposes of subsection (1), the circumstances in which an offence is to be taken as committed against a person acting in the exercise of functions as an emergency worker include circumstances where the offence takes place at a time when the person is not at work but is carrying out functions which, if done in work time, would have been in the exercise of functions as an emergency worker.'

80 UKBA 2007, s 2.
81 UKBA 2007, s 2(1)(a).
82 UKBA 2007, s 2(1)(b).
83 UKBA 2007, s 2(1)(c).
84 UKBA 2007, s 2(2)–s 2(3).
85 Assaults on Emergency Workers (Offences) Act 2018, s 1.

7.109

An Immigration Officer is not an emergency worker (as defined in s 3(1)). However, under s 3(1)(e) 'a person (other than a prison officer) employed or engaged to carry out functions in a custodial institution of a corresponding kind to those carried out by a prison officer' will be. A 'custodial institution' includes 'a removal centre, a short-term holding facility or pre-departure accommodation, as defined by section 147 of the Immigration and Asylum Act 1999'.

Sentence

7.110

The offence is either way, with a maximum sentence of two years' imprisonment.

Assaulting a detainee custody officer

7.111

There is also an offence of assaulting[86] or obstructing[87] a detainee custody officer who is performing certain functions under the Immigration Act[88]. The maximum penalty is six months imprisonment or a Level 5 fine for the assault offence and a Level 3 find for the obstructing charge.

7.112

This extends to a prison officer or prisoner custody officer performing an official function under the IA 2016, s 51[89], including searching someone to find nationality documents. Where the relevant person is acting in accordance with escort arrangements, he must be 'readily identifiable' as such, 'whether by means of a uniform or badge which he is wearing or otherwise)[90].

7.113

In relation to Detainee Custody Officers, there is an offence of (knowingly or recklessly) making a false statement to obtain a certificate of authorisation[91]. Despite this appearing to be an offence akin to one of dishonesty, the offence is summary only, with the maximum sentence being a Level 4 fine.

86 IAA 1999, Sch 11, para 4.
87 IAA 1999, Sch 11, para 5.
88 As set out at para 4(a)-(d) of Sch 11. A Detainee Custody Officer is someone who is authorised under IAA 1999, s 154.
89 IAA 1999, Sch 11, para 9.
90 IAA 1999, Sch 11, para 6.
91 IAA 1999, Sch 11, para 1.

Asylum support offences

7.114

The IAA 1999, Part 6 sets out the support available for asylum seekers who have not yet had their claim determined, or who still have an outstanding appeal.

7.115

Two offences are created:

'106— Dishonest representations.

(1) A person is guilty of an offence if, with a view to obtaining any benefit or other payment or advantage under this Part for himself or any other person, he dishonestly—

(a) makes a statement or representation which is false in a material particular;

(b) produces or gives to a person exercising functions under this Part, or causes or allows to be produced or given to such a person, any document or information which is false in a material particular;

(c) fails to notify a change of circumstances when required to do so in accordance with any provision made by or under this Part; or

(d) causes another person to fail to notify a change of circumstances which that other person was required to notify in accordance with any provision made by or under this Part.

(2) A person guilty of an offence under this section is liable—

(a) on summary conviction, to imprisonment for a term not exceeding six months or to a fine not exceeding the statutory maximum, or to both; or

(b) on conviction on indictment, to imprisonment for a term not exceeding seven years or to a fine, or to both.

105— False representations.

(1) A person is guilty of an offence if, with a view to obtaining support for himself or any other person under any provision made by or under this Part, he—

(a) makes a statement or representation which he knows is false in a material particular,

(b) produces or gives to a person exercising functions under this Part, or knowingly causes or allows to be produced or given to such a person, any document or information which he knows is false in a material particular;

(c) fails, without reasonable excuse, to notify a change of circumstances when required to do so in accordance with any provision made by or under this Part; or

(d) without reasonable excuse, knowingly causes another person to fail to notify a change of circumstances which that other person was required to notify in accordance with any provision made by or under this Part.

(2) A person guilty of an offence under this section is liable on summary conviction to imprisonment for a term not exceeding three months or to a fine not exceeding level 5 on the standard scale, or to both.

7.116

The distinction between the two offences is the requirement for dishonesty, although conceptually it is not necessarily easy to distinguish the two offences, and identify a representation that is knowingly false, but not dishonest.

Sentence

7.117

The dishonesty offence is far more serious, being either way and carrying a sentence of seven years, as opposed to the false representations which is summary only with a maximum sentence of three months.

7.118

The framework would appear to follow the legislative framework of the 'benefit fraud' legislation, where the Social Security Administration Act 1992, s 111 has an either way offence (with the same sentence of seven years) of making a dishonest representation to obtain benefits

7.119

There are no sentencing guidelines for either offence, although in *Abaker*[92], the fraud guidelines appear to have been applied. It is likely that the benefit fraud guidelines would be used for both offences. In *Abaker* the appellant claimed asylum on a fraudulent basis and received £1,064.50 in asylum support and received two months (with credit for a plea of guilty) for the s 105 offence. This was reduced to six weeks by the Court of Appeal, although this is in the context of other, more serious, offending for which concurrent and consecutive sentences were passed. For that reason, this is unlikely to be of assistance (even above the difficulty in relying on unreported sentencing decisions).

92 [2014] EWCA Crim 2966.

Other matters

7.120

Powers or arrest, and of search and seizure, are set out in the Social Security Administration Act 1992, ss 109A and 109B. An Immigration Officer can arrest without warrant someone he reasonably suspects of committing an offence under s 105 or 106.

> **'109B Entry, search and seizure**
>
> (1) An offence under section 105 or 106 shall be treated as–
>
> (a) a relevant offence for the purposes of IA 1971, ss 28B and 28D and
>
> (b) an offence under Part 3 of that Act (criminal proceedings) for the purposes of sections 28(4), 28E, 28G and 28H (search after arrest, &c.) of that Act.
>
> (2) The following provisions of the Immigration Act 1971 shall have effect in connection with an offence under section 105 or 106 of this Act as they have effect in connection with an offence under that Act–
>
> (a) section 28I (seized material: access and copying),
>
> (b) section 28J (search warrants: safeguards),
>
> (c) section 28K (execution of warrants), and
>
> (d) section 28L(1) (interpretation).'

7.121

There is provision in s 109 for the prosecution of a corporate body if it is committed with the 'consent or connivance' of an officer, or if it is attributable to his neglect. It is a separate offence under s 107 to 'intentionally delay or obstruct' a person exercising functions under. The maximum sentence is a Level 3 fine.

7.122

There is power under the Immigration Rules, require that someone sponsoring a would-be immigrant to give an undertaking:

7.123

Where this is not honoured and money is necessarily expended to support that person then, as well as a civil power to recoup, the person giving an undertaking may commit a criminal offence (Social Security Administration Act 1992, s 108):

'108— Failure of sponsor to maintain.

(1) A person is guilty of an offence if, during any period in respect of which he has given a written undertaking in pursuance of the immigration rules to be responsible for the maintenance and accommodation of another person—

(a) he persistently refuses or neglects, without reasonable excuse, to maintain that person in accordance with the undertaking; and

(b) in consequence of his refusal or neglect, support under any provision made by or under this Part is provided for or in respect of that person.

(2) A person guilty of an offence under this section is liable on summary conviction to imprisonment for a term not exceeding 3 months or to a fine not exceeding level 4 on the standard scale, or to both.

(3) For the purposes of this section, a person is not to be taken to have refused or neglected to maintain another person by reason only of anything done or omitted in furtherance of a trade dispute.'

7.124

In cases where it could arise, the civil recovery route would have to be tried first, but this gives an extra sanction in a suitable case.

8 Specific defences to immigration offences

Introduction

8.1

Whilst all the usual defences (duress, necessity, etc) will apply to an immigration offence, there are two specific defences that fall for consideration, and that all practitioners will need to be familiar with. These are the 'section 31 defence' (IAA 1999, s 31) and the modern slavery/victim of trafficking defence. The former will apply only to certain immigration offences (although the wider principles of Art 31 will apply generally), whilst the latter is a defence to a wide number of offences and, in fact, is now more likely to be raised in related to British citizens.

8.2

The specific defences (of 'rescuer' and 'stowaway') to the facilitation offences are dealt with in Chapter 5.

The s 31 defence

Overview

8.3

The Refugee Convention[1] was signed in 1951 in the aftermath of, and as a response to the atrocities of, the Second World War. At its heart is the protection against *non-refoulment*, the principle that states should not return a refugee (as defined in Art 1) to another country where their life or freedom would be threatened for a Convention reason[2]. The Convention also sets out a number of other social and political rights.

1 The Convention Relating to the Status of Refugees, Geneva, 28 July 1951, along with the Protocol Relating to the Status of Refugees, New York, 4 October 1967, universally known as the 'Refugee Convention'. The Convention, as originally signed, only applied to people who became refugees due to 'events occurring … before 1 January 1951', but this temporal limit was removed by the Protocol.

2 There is an exception for someone about 'whom there are reasonable grounds for regarding as a danger to the security of the country in which he is, or who, having been convicted by a final judgment of a particularly serious crime, constitutes a danger to the community of that country'. Alongside this, Art 32 provides a protection against expulsion for a refugee lawfully in the country, again 'save on grounds of national security or public order'.

8.4

At the time that the Convention was drafted, although there had been a huge amount of mass migration from displaced people at the end of the Second World War, commercial air travel was still in its infancy. Nowadays, whilst most refugees still travel by land to neighbouring countries[3], someone who is seeking to go further afield, or is forced to do so, will be often forced to take an irregular route to safety.

8.5

With a small number of exceptions (UNHCR resettlement and some country-specific schemes such as was set up following the Russian invasion of Ukraine), there is no provision in UK law for a 'refugee visa', and somebody who applies for leave to enter on the basis that they are at risk of persecution in their home country is liable to be refused[4]. For that reason, people wishing to come to the UK to seek protection will often entail using people smugglers (euphemistically called 'agents') to get them across international borders.

8.6

This presents difficulties for states, particularly at times of mass migration during a conflict. Governments have to balance their legitimate concern about, and interest in, checking the identities of those who enter their country, against the broad aims of common humanity and offering sanctuary to those at risk of persecution.

8.7

As border controls have got tighter, the role of agents has increased and the only realistic option for many asylum seekers is to travel on false documents, or to enter the destination country in a clandestine manner. This has increased the tension between the interests of the authorities in controlling their borders, whilst not penalising those refugees who are effectively forced into committing criminal offences in their quest for safety.

8.8

The Refugee Convention tried to balance these competing interests in Article 31 which reads:

> '1. The Contracting States shall not impose penalties, on account of their illegal entry or presence, on refugees who, coming directly from a territory where their life or freedom was threatened in the sense of Article 1, enter or are present in their territory without authorization, provided they present themselves without delay to the authorities and show good cause for their illegal entry or presence.

3 As of June 2022 the UNHCR estimates that 69% of the world's 32½ million refugees and other people in need of international protection live in neighbouring countries (Mid-year trends, 2022).

4 See, inter alia, *R v (European Roma Rights Centre) v Immigration Officer at Prague Airport* [2004] UKHL 55, [2005] 1 All ER 527.

2. The Contracting States shall not apply to the movements of such refugees restrictions other than those which are necessary and such restrictions shall only be applied until their status in the country is regularized or they obtain admission into another country. The Contracting States shall allow such refugees a reasonable period and all the necessary facilities to obtain admission into another country.'

8.9

Although the United Kingdom signed the Refugee Convention in 1951, this has not been formally incorporated into English law[5].

8.10

The issue of whether this would provide an immunity to asylum seekers in the UK had seemingly never arisen until *R v Uxbridge Magistrates' Court, ex parte Adimi*[6] ('*Adimi*') when an attempt was made to challenge the prosecution of asylum seekers for using a false passport. The Divisional Court gave guidance on the meaning of Art 31, essentially giving it the wide meaning that the s 31 defence now has (see below)[7].

The Convention definition of who is a refugee

8.11

The question of 'who is a refugee' is, at the margin, an incredibly complex one. Whilst it will sometimes need to be considered, the criminal courts are understandably reluctant to get too involved with questions of immigration law.

8.12

The definition of a refugee is set out in Art 1(1) Refugee Convention as being:

> 'A person who owing to a well-founded fear of being persecuted for reasons of race, religion, nationality, membership of a particular social group or political opinion, is outside the country of his nationality and is unable or, owing to such fear, is unwilling to avail himself of the protection of that country; or who, not having a nationality and being outside the country of his former habitual residence as a result of such events, is unable or, owing to such fear, is unwilling to return to it.'

---

5 By virtue of AIAA 1993, s 2:

> **Primacy of Convention.**
>
> Nothing in the immigration rules (within the meaning of the 1971 Act) shall lay down any practice which would be contrary to the Convention.

However, this does not apply to criminal offences and, in any event, it would not prevent Parliament legislating in contravention of the Convention in subsequent legislation.

6 [2001] QB 667.

7 Practitioners should note that the Home Office provide guidance on s 31 in 'IAA 1999, s 31: defence against prosecution', v4.0 (21 May 2015).

Guidance on interpretation of the Refugee Convention

8.13

Guidance can be found in the UNHCR publication 'Handbook on Procedures and Criteria for Determining Refugee Status under the 1951 Convention and the 1967 Protocol relating to the Status of Refugees', as well as a number of other publications available on the UNHCR website.

Immigration Rules

8.14

The Immigration Rules now contain the test for refugee status, as well as the test for protection claims under Art 3[8] and Art 15[9].

Persecution

8.15

Ill treatment must reach a certain level before it can be considered to be persecution. As the UNHCR Handbook notes, this is easy to state, but difficult to put into practice:

> '51. There is no universally accepted definition of "persecution", and various attempts to formulate such a definition have met with little success. From Article 33 of the 1951 Convention, it may be inferred that a threat to life or freedom on account of race, religion, nationality, political opinion or membership of a particular social group is always persecution. Other serious violations of human rights – for the same reasons – would also constitute persecution.

---

8 Art 3 European Convention on Human Rights.

9 Para 326A-352 Immigration Rules. Art 15 refers to Art 15 Council Directive 2004/83/EC of 29 April 2004 on minimum standards for the qualification and status of third country nationals or stateless persons as refugees or as persons who otherwise need international protection and the content of the protection granted (the 'Qualification Directive'):

> **QUALIFICATION FOR SUBSIDIARY PROTECTION**
> **Article 15**
> *Serious harm*
> Serious harm consists of:
> (a) death penalty or execution; or
> (b) torture or inhuman or degrading treatment or punishment of an applicant in the country of origin; or
> (c) serious and individual threat to a civilian's life or person by reason of indiscriminate violence in situations of international or internal armed conflict.
>
> Art 15(a) and (b) mirror the ECHR rights, but Art 15(c) is wider and concerned with generalised, rather than individual risk, with the test being 'Is there in [country] or a material part of it such a high level of indiscriminate violence that substantial grounds exist for believing that an applicant would, solely by being present there, face a real risk which threatens their life or person?' (*QD (Iraq) v SSHD* [2009] EWCA Civ 620, [2011] 1 WLR 689. This also includes harm that would not constitute a breach of Art 3.

52. Whether other prejudicial actions or threats would amount to persecution will depend on the circumstances of each case, including the subjective element to which reference has been made in the preceding paragraphs. The subjective character of fear of persecution requires an evaluation of the opinions and feelings of the person concerned. It is also in the light of such opinions and feelings that any actual or anticipated measures against him must necessarily be viewed. Due to variations in the psychological make-up of individuals and in the circumstances of each case, interpretations of what amounts to persecution are bound to vary.

53. In addition, an applicant may have been subjected to various measures not in themselves amounting to persecution (e.g. discrimination in different forms), in some cases combined with other adverse factors (e.g. general atmosphere of insecurity in the country of origin). In such situations, the various elements involved may, if taken together, produce an effect on the mind of the applicant that can reasonably justify a claim to well-founded fear of persecution on "cumulative grounds". Needless to say, it is not possible to lay down a general rule as to what cumulative reasons can give rise to a valid claim to refugee status. This will necessarily depend on all the circumstances, including the particular geographical, historical and ethnological context.'

8.16

Clearly matters such as execution, imprisonment, or torture satisfies this threshold. As a rough rule of thumb, if there is treatment that would amount to a breach of Arts 2, 3 or 4(1) ECHR, or to a 'flagrant denial' of the other ECHR rights, then there is likely to be persecution. It will be a question of fact for the jury whether any mistreatment would amount to persecution.

8.17

Although persecution is usually at the hands of the state, treatment from non-state actors can amount to persecution if the state is unwilling or unable to provide protection (the failure of state protection being the important part). This could be from groups that are quasi-state like (such as ISIS), or other groups (such as skinhead gangs).

8.18

Persecution is distinct from prosecution, although it is possible that a prosecution for a 'normal' crime can amount to persecution in certain circumstances. For example, a prosecution for fraud that was politically motivated could be persecution. Likewise, a prosecution for behaviour that is covered by the Convention (for example for homosexuality) may also be persecutory.

Well-founded

8.19

There must be an objective risk of persecution. The burden of proof has been variously expressed as 'a real and substantial risk', 'a reasonable degree of likelihood', 'a reasonable chance'. This is a lower threshold than a balance of probabilities[10].

8.20

In relation to claims made after 28 June 2022, the NABA 2022, s 32(2) makes a change to the burden of proof:

> 'The decision-maker must first determine, on the balance of probabilities—
>
> (a) whether the asylum seeker has a characteristic which could cause them to fear persecution for reasons of race, religion, nationality, membership of a particular social group or political opinion (or has such a characteristic attributed to them by an actor of persecution), and
>
> (b) whether the asylum seeker does in fact fear such persecution in their country of nationality (or in a case where they do not have a nationality, the country of their former habitual residence) as a result of that characteristic.'

8.21

At that point they carry on to consider the remainder of the definition. This will apply to a criminal court[11], as well as to the police and CPS in making charging decisions. However, this is unlikely to have a real impact on the conduct of a criminal prosecution.

8.22

Whilst practitioners should have regard to these definitions, it is unlikely that any criminal prosecution will turn on any differences that exist.

Convention reason

8.23

It is not sufficient that there is persecution, it needs to be persecution that has occurred for a 'convention reason'. There are five reasons that will engage the Refugee Convention:

---

10 *R v Home Secretary, ep Sivakumuran* [1987] UKHL 1. Whilst it is not quite the reverse of the criminal standard, that may be useful as a guide.

11 NABA 2022, s 30(1).

- Race
- Religion
- Nationality
- Political belief
- Membership of a particular social group

8.24

The first four are fairly uncontentious, and will tend to mean what is commonly understood by the terms. If there is doubt, then it should be remembered firstly that they should be interpreted widely, and secondly that the criminal court is not generally the right forum to resolve potentially complex questions of immigration law.

8.25

The fifth is more complicated, and there have been a multitude of cases as to what is – and what is not – a social group.

8.26

What is important is what the agents of persecution perceive to be the case, rather than the actual state of affairs. Whether somebody is a member of a particular social group is a very fact specific question that depends on the situation in the defendant's home country. The following is taken from the UNHCR Guidelines[12]:

> 'A particular social group is a group of persons who share a common characteristic other than their risk of being persecuted, or who are perceived as a group by society. The characteristic will often be one which is innate, unchangeable, or which is otherwise fundamental to identity, conscience or the exercise of one's human rights.'

8.27

In *Evans*[13], the Court of Appeal upheld the trial Judge's decision to withdraw a s 31 defence from the jury. The grounds for the asylum claim were that the appellant was targeted on his return to Jamaica by a gang on the belief that as someone returning from the UK, he had money. The Court of Appeal upheld the judge's ruling that as there was no persecution independent of the group, there could be no persecution for a Convention reason[14].

---

12 See UNHCR (United Nations High Commissioner for Refugees) 'Guideline on International Protection – "Membership of a particular social group" within the context of Article 1A(2) of the 1951 Convention and/or its 1967 Protocol relating to the Status of Refugees' at page 3.

13 [2013] EWCA Crim 125.

14 Another example is *YY* [2016] EWCA Crim 18, where the defendant was an Iranian man accused of adultery.

8.28

In *Elmi*[15] the Court of Appeal confirmed that the question of who is a refugee must be determined by reference to the Convention[16]. This confirms that those who are not refugees, but who would be entitled to protection from a risk of Art 3 or Art 15 mistreatment, will not be covered by the defence (although such a finding should factor into the public interest decision as to whether to prosecute).

8.29

On general principles, a judge would not be entitled to withdraw a defence when the issue over refugee status was one of credibility.

Convention definition – impact of the NABA 2022

8.30

Sections 30, taken with the NABA 2022, ss 31–38 set out a variety of tools to interpret the various terms of the Refugee Convention. It is likely that these will be interpreted (if at all possible) to be consistent with previous caselaw.

8.31

Other than the change to the burden of proof mentioned above, there is also a potentially significant change to the definition of 'particular social group'[17] where there is a requirement for both there to be a common, immutable characteristic and (rather than or) perceived distinct identity.

Incorporation of the defence

8.32

As a consequence of the *Adimi* judgment, the IAA 1999, s 31 was enacted to provide a statutory defence for a refugee:

> (1) It is a defence for a refugee charged with an offence to which this section applies to show that, having come to the United Kingdom directly from a country where his life or freedom was threatened (within the meaning of the Refugee Convention), he –
>
> (a) presented himself to the authorities in the United Kingdom without delay;
>
> (b) showed good cause for his illegal entry or presence; and
>
> (c) made a claim for asylum as soon as was reasonably practicable after his arrival in the United Kingdom.

15 [2022] EWCA Crim 1428, [2023] 1 Cr App R 7.
16 *Elmi* at [49].
17 NABA 2022, s 33(2)–(5).

(2) If, in coming from the country where his life or freedom was threatened, the refugee stopped in another country outside the United Kingdom, subsection (1) applies only if he shows that he could not reasonably [be expected to have sought] protection under the Refugee Convention in that other country[18].

...

(4A) But this section does not apply to an offence committed by a refugee in the course of an attempt to leave the United Kingdom.

...

(5) A refugee who has made a claim for asylum is not entitled to the defence provided by subsection (1) in relation to any offence committed by him after making that claim.

(6) *"Refugee"* has the same meaning as it has for the purposes of the Refugee Convention.

(7) If the Secretary of State has refused to grant a claim for asylum made by a person who claims that he has a defence under subsection (1), that person is to be taken not to be a refugee unless he shows that he is.'

The elements of the s 31 defence

8.33

The defence can be broken down in to the following six elements. It will apply to a defendant who is a:

- refugee; who
- came 'directly' from their home country; and
- did not stop in any country along the way; and
- presented themselves to the authorities in the UK 'without delay'; and
- claimed asylum as soon as was reasonably practicable after arrival; and
- had good cause for their illegal entry or presence in the UK

Come directly/did not stop

8.34

These two elements are inter-linked. They have also historically caused the most problems of application and have featured in many of the appeals to the Court of Appeal.

18 The words in square brackets were inserted as of 28 June 2022 by NABA 2022, s 37(5)(a) to replace 'have expected to be given'.

8.35

The courts have not always made a clear distinction between the two elements of the defence, and have frequently approached them together. It will be looked at here through the prism of 'coming directly' before considering whether there is, in fact, anything added by s 31(2).

Historical note – impact of the NABA 2022

8.36

For offences allegedly committed on or after 28 June 2022, the NABA 2022, s 37(5)(a) made the following amendment to s 31(2)[19]:

> 'for "have expected to be given" substitute "be expected to have sought"'

8.37

The Explanatory Notes state (at 372):

> 'Subsection 1 provides an interpretation of the term "coming directly" as found in Article 31(1). It stipulates that a person will not be deemed to have come directly if they have stopped in another country between leaving the country where they faced persecution and arriving in the UK. An exception would apply if the individual can demonstrate that it was not reasonable for them to have sought protection under the Refugee Convention in the country they stopped in, for example, where a person was under the control of people smugglers and therefore unable to present themselves to the authorities in that country. Individuals who are deemed not to have come directly, as defined by this section, may not be immune to penalties imposed on them on grounds of their illegal presence or illegal entry into the UK.'

8.38

It is unclear what difference (if any) this makes in practice, especially as s 31(2) has been left unamended. It could be that it is a more liberal interpretation, in that someone who may well have expected to be given protection (had it been sought) may be adjudged not to have been expected to have sought it. It is likely that the previous authorities will apply to the new formulation, although practitioners will need to be alive to the change in definition.

---

19 If, in coming from the country where his life or freedom was threatened, the refugee stopped in another country outside the United Kingdom, subsection (1) applies only if he shows that he could not reasonably *be expected to have sought* protection under the Refugee Convention in that other country.

Come directly

8.39

The classic formulation was set out by Simon Brown LJ in *Adimi*:

> 'I conclude that any merely short term stopover *en route* to such intended sanctuary cannot forfeit the protection of the Article, and that the main touchstones by which exclusion from protection should be judged are the length of stay in the intermediate country, the reasons for delaying there (even a substantial delay in an unsafe third country would be reasonable were the time spent trying to acquire the means of travelling on), and whether or not the refugee sought or found there protection de jure or de facto from the persecution they were fleeing.'

8.40

This interpretation has been followed in both England and Wales, as well as a number of other countries.

Test

8.41

What is the test as to whether someone has 'come directly' and not 'stopped'? There is no simple answer to this question, and no one factor that will be determinative. One question to ask (quoting Lord Williams, the then Attorney General) is whether the defendant is 'still running away' from persecution (per Lord Bingham in *Asfaw)* or whether that journey is at an end.

8.42

An alternative formulation[20] from 2010 is:

> 'The real question is, looking at all the circumstances: is the person in the course of a flight? Is he making a short-term stop over? Is he in transit? Whichever phrase is used, one has to see whether at the material time the person was here, not having come to this country either temporarily or permanently seeking to stop here, but was going on. That is a question of fact.'

8.43

This means that even long periods of time in a third country will not, of itself, preclude reliance on the defence. A quest for asylum is often an irregular journey which can take place over many months (and even years). Although people born and brought up in the UK may be aware of which countries are safe, and which are not, it may not be as clear to an asylum seeker brought

---

20 *SK* [2010] EWCA Crim 1335, at [5].

up with a less free media and who, in any event, may not even know which country they are in).

8.44

Finally, and significantly, a refugee has an element of choice as to which country they wish to settle in. Therefore, a period of time in transit is not sufficient, in itself, to lose the protection of the defence. As was said by Simon Brown J 'some element of choice is indeed open to refugees as to where they may properly claim asylum'. There are many reasons, good and bad, why someone would pass through other safe (including safe EU) countries in order to get to the UK – knowledge of English and family members already present here being two obvious ones. A failure to claim asylum elsewhere may provide ammunition for a prosecutor when cross-examining a defendant, but does not mean that the defence is excluded.

8.45

Any case must turn on its own facts and, to that extent, it is not necessarily helpful to consider previous authorities. However, it is worth considering some cases to see how the courts have interpreted the requirement:

AM & Others [2010] EWCA Crim 2400, [2011] 1 Cr App R 35:

- MV – Iranian who went by land to Turkey, then by plane to Syria (one week) before flying to Spain (three hours spent in the airport).
- RM – Somali. Left Somalia by lorry through 'various African countries' before flying to the Netherlands (three days) and on to the UK.
- MN – Iranian. Left Iran on a lorry for 25 days, ending up in Greece (two weeks locked in a flat) before flying to the UK.

Jaddi [2012] EWCA Crim 2565:

Iranian who had previously unsuccessfully claimed asylum in the UK and returned. Came to UK with the help of an agent through Turkey (one month), Greece (two–three days), Italy (three–four days) before flying to Gatwick. There he produced two false documents before being arrested (although there was some factual dispute as to exactly what happened).

Mateta [2013] EWCA Crim 1372, [2013] 2 Cr App R 35:

- Bashir – Somali. Travelled via Kenya (one month), Dubai and Greece (length of stay unknown). Claimed asylum after arrest.
- Amir Ghavami and Saeideh Afshar – Iranian husband and wife. Came to UK via Thailand (two months, flying there on their own passports with a valid visa), Tanzania (20 days), Kenya (seven days) and Spain (20 days). Flew to Gatwick, before getting a bus to Heathrow to fly to Canada where they intended to claim asylum. Arrested whilst trying to board the plane to leave the UK.

Hussein [2014] EWCA Crim 1978:

Somali, left Somalia and spent two years in Kenya. Didn't claim asylum there as 'he did not wish to be held in a refugee camp where he could not earn a living in order to support his family'. Came to UK via Tanzania (with a stop of about three weeks), not stopping there as he 'did not come across any refugee camps, and in any event did not know how to apply for asylum'.

Sadeghi [2014] EWCA Crim 2933:

Iranian. Left via Turkey, before flying to Tanzania, then going to Zambia by train, before flying to the UK (length of time in those countries unknown). Intending to go on to Canada to claim asylum. Spent seven–eight days in UK before being arrested trying to board a flight to Canada. Claimed asylum 23 days after arrival in the UK.

It is worth noting some comments from the Court of Appeal:

> 'He could not reasonably have been expected to claim asylum in Turkey, Tanzania or Zambia. Indeed it is clear that in any event he was under the control of an agent at that time who was conducting his intended transit to Canada, which provides a perfectly sensible explanation, on his part, as to why he did not seek asylum in any of those places.'

Mulugeta and others [2015] EWCA Crim 6:

- Issa – Somali, came to the UK via Dubai (some weeks), then transiting through Holland.
- Firouzi – Iranian, came via Thailand and Uganda (total of six weeks). Spent 14 days in the UK before being arrested trying to board a flight to Canada where he was intending to claim asylum.

Shabani [2015] EWCA Crim 1924:

Iranian. Left via Turkey, before flying to Spain (for 11 days), then to the UK.

8.46

Whether a defence is available will depend on a number of factors, including the nature of the countries passed through (generally speaking, EU countries are safer than non-EU countries). Additionally, the longer the stay in a third country the weaker the defence is. However, it will also depend on the personal characteristics of the individual. What the authorities do show is that someone reading s 31 as if it were a domestic criminal statute runs a real risk of having their advice scrutinised, and criticised, at a later date.

8.47

It would be an exceptional case where a judge would be entitled to withdraw the defence from the jury as this limb would inevitably fail.

Did not stop

8.48

The existence of s 31(2) shows that '*coming directly*' for the purposes of s 31(1) does not literally mean directly without stopping. Any country that is not a signatory to the Refugee Convention can be discounted for the purposes of s 31(2). A list of all signatories is available online[21].

8.49

Whilst it appears that s 31(2) contained an additional requirement, over and above what was required by Art 31, it was confirmed in *MMH*[22] that s 31(2) must be read in the spirit of Art 31, so that somebody who was in transit for a short period of time can be considered to have not 'stopped' for the purpose of the legislation (rather than saying that he could not reasonably have been given protection). In essence, it is likely that there is no longer any real difference between these two definitions.

Passengers in transit

Background

8.50

Many people (including the appellant in *Asfaw*), were arrested at an airport trying to leave the United Kingdom having previously entered on a false passport. Do they have the protection of the Convention in that case?

8.51

The House of Lords (in a 3-2 decision) concluded that they did. In doing so, the majority drew on a large expanse of international law material to ascertain the true meaning of Art 31.

8.52

Since then, a number of the cases that have gone to the Court of Appeal have been people who were in such a position. The test is again fact-specific, with the issue being whether someone was still in the course of their journey fleeing persecution, or whether they had stopped. So, someone who was simply changing planes would likely fall within the defence. Where they had spent time landside, then it may be harder to say that they did. That did not stop a

---

21 https://www.unhcr.org/protection/convention/5d9ed32b4/states-parties-including-reservations-declarations-1951-refugee-convention.html

22 [2008] EWCA Crim 3117.

number a number of people who had spent days (and sometimes weeks) in the United Kingdom from succeeding[23].

8.53

However, NABA 2022 introduces a new s 31(4A) into the IAA 1999 that appears to reverse the conclusion in *Afsaw*. The explanatory notes state that the purpose of this is[24]:

> 'Subsection 4 provides an exemption to imposing penalties on individuals where they have broken these rules in the course of leaving the UK.
>
> Subsection 5 substitutes wording used in subsection 2 of section 31 of the Immigration and Asylum Act 1999 to align it to wording used in Section 36, and also inserts new subsection 4A into section 31 relating to the defences based on Article 31(1) that an individual may rely upon if charged of an offence. 4A provides an exception, whereby an individual may not use the section 31 defence if they committed an offence in their attempt to leave the UK.

8.54

This should be read with the NABA 2022, s 30(3):

> 'Section 37 applies for the purposes of the determination by any person, court or tribunal whether Article 31(1) of the Refugee Convention (immunity from certain penalties) applies in relation to a person who is a refugee within the meaning of Article 1(A)(2) of the Refugee Convention.'

8.55

The effect of s 31(4A) in domestic law would appear to be clear and, going forward, someone who is arrested trying to leave the United Kingdom would not be able to claim the benefit of s 31.

8.56

However, that may not be the end of the matter. The ruling in *Afsaw* was not as to the meaning of s 31 in domestic law, but rather as to the interpretation of Art 31. Whilst Parliament undoubtedly has the power to enact the new s 31(4A), and to say how the Refugee Convention will be given effect in domestic law, it is not clear that it can legislate as to the actual meaning of the Convention itself, especially when relating to a restriction in a penal statute.

---

23 See, as an example, *Idahosa* [2019] EWCA Crim 1953 where the appellant came to the United Kingdom on a tourist visa and was arrested 54 days later trying to board a plane to Canada on a false passport where he had always intended to claim asylum. Notwithstanding the length of time and the fact that he was lawfully in the UK, the appeal was allowed.

24 Explanatory notes at [378] and [379].

8.57

Historically it was held that s 31 was the way that Parliament had incorporated Art 31 and there was no scope for separate argument based on Art 31 (at least where the s 31 defence applies)[25]. However, it is doubtful that such a conclusion has survived the developments in the Modern Slavery Act 2015, s 45 defence and the fact that someone can still rely on the non-prosecution principle.

8.58

It would appear that the CPS will also be bound (as a 'person' determining whether Art 31 applies) by s 30(3). However, until the question of interpretation is resolved, practitioners will need to consider whether representations should be made to the CPS and, depending on the outcome, an abuse of process application made, where they have a client who is covered by Art 31, but not s 31. The Code for Crown Prosecutors at para 2.10 concerning public interest, also says "Prosecutors must apply the principles of the European Convention on Human Rights, in accordance with the Human Rights Act 1998, at each stage of a case. They must comply with any guidelines issued by the Attorney General and with the policies and guidance of the CPS issued on behalf of the DPP, unless it is determined that there are exceptional circumstances. CPS guidance contains further evidential and public interest factors for specific offences and offenders and is available for the public to view on the CPS website. Prosecutors must also comply with the Criminal Procedure Rules and Criminal Practice Directions, and have regard to the Sentencing Council Guidelines and the obligations arising from international conventions.

Retrospectivity

8.59

The new s 31(4A) is not retrospective[26], and therefore anyone advising a client for a historic conviction for leaving the UK prior to 28 June 2022 should have regard to the law as it was pre-NABA 2022.

Present without delay

8.60

The rationale for this aspect of the defence is that a genuine refugee who comes to a safe country should co-operate with the host country and not hide their presence. 'Present' does not mean 'present and claim asylum'. Given that, it is likely that it will be only be an issue in cases where there is a clandestine, rather than an irregular, entry.

25 *R (Pepushi) v CPS* [2004] EWHC 798 (Admin), [2004] Imm AR 549.

26 Nationality and Borders Act 2022 (Commencement No 1, Transitional and Saving Provisions) Regulations 2022, Sch 2, para 6.

8.61

Somebody who enters the UK and presents a false passport intending to claim asylum as a later stage will be able to avail themselves of the defence[27]:

> 'The appellant did present himself to the authorities as soon as he arrived in the United Kingdom on 11 May 2009 and proceeded through immigration control, albeit that at that time he did not claim asylum. This appellant entered the United Kingdom with false documentation. His physical entry was not concealed from the authorities.'

8.62

This interpretation would appear to undermine the purpose of the legislation to some extent – everyone who enters the UK on a false passport would then be covered. However, even if that is incorrect, whether someone has presented themselves without delay will still be a question of fact. Even under the law post-NABA 2022, there is an element of latitude to an asylum seeker who is arriving in an unfamiliar country. Many may have a history that means that they have an understandable mistrust of uniformed border guards, or they would have proper reasons to wish to consult with members of the diaspora community and/or legal advisers before claiming asylum.

8.63

Further, it is common for asylum seekers to be told (erroneously) that if they are intercepted at the airport they will be deported straightaway. Although this is incorrect, it seems to have gained currency. One explanation for this may be that people smugglers encourage this narrative so that they can retrieve the false passports after the defendant leaves the airport and re-use them. Even if that is not possible, there is less likelihood of any document being traced back to them.

8.64

Someone who is in transit in the UK, and who does not state that he is travelling on a false passport on arrival, will not be deprived of the defence[28]:

> 'it was explicable that he did not present himself to the authorities in the UK. As will be evident from the facts which we have set out above, he was, at the time of being in the UK, in transit to Canada having been told he was not able to claim asylum in the United Kingdom … having accepted that the appellant had good reason not to claim asylum in the United Kingdom prior to his arrest and whilst still in transit, he did in fact claim asylum, on 3 February 2012, not long after the criminal proceedings in his case had been concluded.'

27 *Mulugeta* [2015] EWCA Crim 6, at [21].
28 *Sadeghi* [2014] EWCA Crim 2933.

Present without delay – changes brought in by the NABA 2022

8.65

The NABA 2022, s 37 states the following:

> '(2) A refugee is not to be taken to have presented themselves without delay to the authorities unless—
>
> (a) in the case of a person who became a refugee while they were outside the United Kingdom, they made a claim for asylum as soon as reasonably practicable after their arrival in the United Kingdom;
>
> (b) in the case of a person who became a refugee while they were in the United Kingdom—
>
> (i) if their presence in the United Kingdom was lawful at that time, they made a claim for asylum before the time when their presence in the United Kingdom became unlawful;
>
> (ii) if their presence in the United Kingdom was unlawful at that time, they made a claim for asylum as soon as reasonably practicable after they became aware of their need for protection under the Refugee Convention.
>
> (3) For the purposes of subsection (2)(b), a person's presence in the United Kingdom is unlawful if they require leave to enter or remain and do not have it.'

8.66

Unlike the changes to 'come directly' in the NABA 2022, s 37(1) there is no amendment to the drafting of s 31. The stated aim is[29]:

> 'Subsection 2 specifies what it means for a refugee to "present themselves without delay" in making a claim for asylum. In cases where an individual has fled persecution and arrives in the UK, they would be expected to make a claim for asylum as soon as it was reasonably practicable to do so after their arrival in the UK. In cases where an individual was present in the UK with permission (for example on a visa) and experienced a change in their circumstances meaning they have a well-founded fear of persecution preventing them from returning to their country of nationality, they would be expected to make their claim for asylum before their permission to stay in the UK expires. In cases where an individual was present in the UK without permission (for example a visa overstayer) and experienced a change in their circumstances preventing them from returning to their country of nationality, they would also be expected to make their claim for asylum

29 NABA 2022, Explanatory Notes, [377].

as soon as it was reasonably practicable after their need for protection arose. Such individuals who require permission to be present in the UK and do not have it will be considered to be present in the UK illegally (subsection 3). Therefore, such individuals even if they present themselves without delay, as defined by this section, would not be immune to penalties imposed on them on grounds of not having good cause for their illegal presence or illegal entry into the UK.'

8.67

When considering the phrasing of s 31, in particular the requirement in s 31(1)(c) to make a claim for asylum as soon as was reasonably practicable, it appears that this will not make any real difference to the operation of the defence. Again, however, practitioners will need to be aware of the difference in wording.

Claimed asylum as soon as reasonably practicable

8.68

There is an overlap with 'presenting without delay' and this aspect of the defence. It is common for asylum seekers to hand over their false documents to Immigration Officers, and then only claim asylum after these have been discovered as being forged. Whether this precludes the defence from being relied on will again be a question of fact in every case.

8.69

In *Jaddi*[30], the appellant had claimed asylum in the UK in 2006, having been a student here for several years. This claim was rejected and he left the UK in 2008 (before being removed). In 2012 he returned to claim asylum, armed with a false French passport and ID document. He undoubtedly handed over his false passport to an immigration officer rather than claim asylum, but there was an element of uncertainty as to the exact sequence of events. However, the appeal was allowed. The court held that:

> '26 … In the great majority of cases there will simply be no excuse for a genuine refugee not to make himself known immediately he arrives in the safe place — that is to say the arrivals immigration hall at a United Kingdom airport …
>
> 29 As it seems to us, the question of whether section 31(1(c) is satisfied or not must be a question of fact in every case … The question of whether it was reasonably practicable to make a claim for asylum sooner than was done is an objective one for the jury to decide but, in deciding it, the jury will certainly have to take account of the defendant's state of knowledge, intention and mind …

30 [2012] EWCA Crim 2565.

> 30 … it is certainly open to a tribunal of fact to conclude and in many cases it may be the right conclusion, that there is simply no reason for such a traveller not to identify himself the moment he is in friendly official hands.'

8.70

The jury will be directed to look at all the surrounding factors; age of the defendant, whether an agent was used and present, and so forth.

8.71

The defence can only apply to actions taken before the claim of asylum (s 31(5) and *Mulugeta*).

Show good cause

8.72

This is likely to be relatively uncontentious and has not featured in any of the Court of Appeal cases to date. A genuine claim for asylum is a good reason to be illegally present in the UK.

Burden and standard of proof

8.73

It is for the prosecution to first prove that a defendant was in possession of the false passport, or practised a deception as the case may be.

8.74

The Court of Appeal determined in *Makuwa*[31] that apart form the question of whether someone is a refugee, for the remaining elements of the defence, the burden is on the defendant with the standard being the usual one of the balance of probabilities.

8.75

In relation to the question of whether the defendant is a refugee, the position is more complicated and will depend on whether there has been a decision on the defendant's claim for asylum. If there has not been, then there is an evidential burden only on the defendant to raise the issue that he is a refugee. When this has been done, the burden is then on the prosecution to disprove this, to the usual criminal standard.

---

31 [2006] EWCA Crim 175, [2006] 2 Cr App R 11.

8.76

If the Home Secretary has refused an asylum claim, then by virtue of s 31(7), the burden will be on the defendant, again to the usual 'balance of probabilities' standard[32].

8.77

The statute is silent on what the situation would be if the Home Secretary either grants asylum to a defendant, or the defendant successfully appeals to the First-Tier Tribunal before the criminal trial. Although as a matter of law this would not be binding on the CPS, it is likely that they would accept that that element of s 31(1) would be satisfied (and, in many cases, would not continue with the prosecution in any event).

8.78

Despite the aim being a period of six months, decisions on asylum claims by the Home Office are currently a lot slower than that. If a decision is adverse to the defendant, then it may well take a long time before an appeal is heard, certainly longer that the average wait for a Crown Court trial (if the defendant is in custody at least), although it is more likely that there will be a clear timeframe. Whether or not to adjourn a trial pending an initial decision or an appeal is a matter for the trial Judge's discretion in all the circumstances, but it is unlikely to be desirable to do so (unless, perhaps, there is an appeal hearing scheduled very shortly).

Interplay with duress/necessity

8.79

In theory both the common law defences of 'duress' and 'necessity' are available. In practice, these are very difficult defences to run. They are both wider than the s 31 defence, and could therefore apply in cases where that defence is not available (for example for someone who would otherwise be a refugee but for the fact that there was no Convention reason). In practice however, it is very unlikely that it could succeed given the range of other options likely available to a defendant.

Which offences the s 31 defence applies to

8.80

The s 31 defence applies to the following false documentation offences (depending on when they were committed):

32 *Sadighpour* [2012] EWCA Crim 2669, [2013] 1 Cr App R 20.

- Identity Cards Act 2006, s 25 – 21 January 2011 onwards
- Identity Documents Act 2010, s 4 – between 7 June 2006 and 20 January 2011
- Forgery and Counterfeiting Act 1981, Part 1 – before 7 June 2006

as well as the following offences:

- IA 1971, s 24A (leave to enter by deception)
- IA 1971, s 26(1)(d) (alteration or falsification of an entry clearance document, work permit, or similar)

8.81

The IA 1971, s 26(1)(d) is summary only, with a maximum sentence of 6 months. It is very rarely charged, not least because wherever it is committed it is very likely that a more serious offence will also have been committed.

Offences not covered by s 31

8.82

The s 31 defence only applies to the offences set out above. There are a number of omissions, most notably the illegal entry/arrival offences under s 24 (the s 31 defence does *not* apply of any of the s 24 offences). In *Asfaw*, Lord Roger (who was in the minority) stated:

> the offence of entering the United Kingdom unlawfully, contained in section 24 of the Immigration Act 1971, is not listed in section 31(3). Nor is the offence of attempting to obtain services by deception, contrary to section 1(1) of the Criminal Attempts Act 1981. While, for the reasons I shall give, the omission of the second provision is entirely understandable and correct, as presently advised, I am at a loss to understand why the first of these provisions has been omitted from the lists in section 31(3) and (4), since section 24, like section 24A, falls four-square within the terms of article 31. Article 31 is designed indeed for precisely that kind of offence[33]

8.83

In *Asfaw*, Ms Asfaw was an Ethiopian woman arrested whilst trying to leave the UK on a flight to the USA with a false passport, having been in transit in the United Kingdom. She was charged with an offence under the Forgery and Counterfeiting Act 1981 for using the false passport, and also an offence of Attempting to Obtain Services by Deception, this being the flight. She was later recognised as a refugee.

33 *Asfaw* at [77].

8.84

At trial she was acquitted of the passport offence having relied on the s 31 defence. As there was no defence to the deception offence, she had pleaded guilty after an application to stay the proceedings as an abuse of process had failed before the jury was sworn. The House of Lords allowed the appeal as, once Ms Asfaw was acquitted of the first charge, it was wrong to proceed with the second.

8.85

What *Asfaw* does not resolve and what, despite it now being 15 years since *Asfaw* was decided, has not yet been definitively resolved, is what the court should do when faced with a defendant who is someone who potentially would have the benefit of the Art 31 defence, but is charged with an offence to which the s 31 defence does not apply. This may be thrown into sharper focus following the changes to the s 24 entry offences, specifically to s 24(D1), which widens the offence to include those who 'arrive' rather than just 'enter' and makes the offence either way.

8.86

In considering the scope of Art 31, it will not cover everyone charged with an offence relating to their entry, so in *Mirahessari*[34] the Court of Appeal considered the prosecution of two people who were among a group of asylum seekers who 'broke down fences and barriers' on the French side of the Channel Tunnel and forced their way through to the English side. The court concluded that Art 31 would not cover them[35]:

> 'We do not find it possible to equate the present case with a situation such as obtained in Asfaw. The applicants' criminality here was very different in character from that of an asylum seeker who resorts to committing an identity documents offence in seeking to enter or pass through this country. The applicants were not only trying to enter the United Kingdom either with false documents or with no documents, they went substantially further than that: they were trying to enter the United Kingdom in a dangerous manner which obstructed railway traffic through the Channel Tunnel.'

8.87

This should not be read too widely given the humanitarian purpose of Art 31.

Multi-count indictment

8.88

If there are several counts on the indictment covering the same conduct, only some of which attract the s 31 defence, then *Asfaw* would suggest that

34 [2016] EWCA Crim 1733.
35 *Mirahessari* at [23].

the procedure is relatively straightforward – a trial should proceed on those offences where there is a defence, with the defence being run. If there is an acquittal, then the other count(s) should not be proceeded with (and it being likely that the CPS will offer no evidence at that point). If the defendant is convicted then, whilst he cannot be forced to enter a plea of guilty, his position would likely be preserved on appeal if he did. In any event, the CPS will likely invite the count to lie on file as a further trial would not be in the public interest

Single count indictment

8.89

If an individual is charged with only an offence or offences where Art 31 would apply, but the s 31 defence does not, then the situation is more complicated. *Asfaw* makes it clear that a court cannot 'read in' the s 31 defence to the general law. It may be that if there is an alternative charge that could be indicted on the facts, to which the s 31 defence applies, then the CPS could be invited to add that count, and the case proceed to trial. However, that will often not be the case and it would not be an abuse of process for the CPS to charge an offence that is properly made out on the facts[36].

8.90

If there is no such charge that is possible on the facts, then the only remedy open to a defendant is an application to stay the proceedings an abuse of process. There is no authority as to how the courts should approach this in relation to the Art 31 question, but it is likely that the same approach that is currently taken in relation to an argument under the Modern Slavery Act 2015, s 45 defence will be followed[37] (see below for further consideration of that).

8.91

The sequencing would likely be as follows:

- The defendant should make written representations to the CPS setting out why the case should not be prosecuted.
- The CPS then review the case in light of these, having regard to the relevant CPS policy and Art 31.
- The defendant can apply to the court to stay the indictment as an abuse of process.

36 *Mirahessari* [2016] EWCA Crim 1733 at [20]-[23].

37 It could be argued that the review in relation to a modern slavery case should be at a higher threshold that a s 31 case due to the heightened obligations to victims of trafficking under Art 4 ECHR. However, especially given the significance of the subject matter it is likely that the same approach would be taken in a refugee case.

8.92

This will not be followed in every case, and the court would not routinely stay proceedings. In addition, there will be a number of cases where there may be good reasons to seek a review of the decision to prosecute which do not engage Art 31[38]. In relation to this, it must be remembered that Art 31 does not prohibit the prosecution (technically, the imposition of penalties) of refugees generally, or in relation to immigration offences specifically, but only the prosecution in certain circumstances. For that reason, the CPS are entitled to prosecute someone who is a refugee if they are not coming directly (as defined widely).

Representations to the CPS

8.93

Once a representative has instructions to make disclosure of their case to the CPS (at either a pre or post-charge stage) a representative should take care to make the submissions as detailed as possible.

8.94

These should set out the background of their client's difficulties in their home country and their journey to the United Kingdom. It should address the question of why their client is a refugee and why they would fall within Art 31. As well as considering this through the lens of s 31 and Art 31, it should also address the wider CPS Immigration policy, and the Code generally.

8.95

It should not be assumed that the CPS lawyer will have full (or any) details of the immigration claim, or any of the Home Office papers. For that reason, practitioners will need to consider whether to serve the Screening Interview and other documents on the CPS.

CPS Review

8.96

The CPS will then review the case in light of all the information and their policy and reach a fresh conclusion. This review will generally be undertaken by a specially trained prosecutor.

---

38 There are a number of factors that the CPS have to take account, both generally under the Code, but also under the specific policy on Immigration Offences.

Abuse of process

8.97

Rule 3.28 Criminal Procedure Rules covers applications to stay the proceedings as an abuse of process.

8.98

For there to be an abuse of process there has to be something more than a disagreement by the defence (or the Judge) with the decision to prosecute. Further, where there are relevant matters of fact that are in dispute, this would be for a jury to decide[39].

Application to the facilitation offences

8.99

The s 31 defence does not apply to the facilitation offences (IA 1971, ss 25 and 25A). In most cases that conclusion is straightforward. Where someone is smuggled to the United Kingdom, there would be no question that the facilitators would have the benefit of Art 31.

8.100

However, there may be scenarios where it could be argued that the letter, or the spirit, of Art 31 applies. For example, someone who helps a family member to come to the United Kingdom by buying a plane ticket or arranging their journey would be guilty of the substantive offence of facilitation. If so, then could the defendant object to an indictment containing the facilitation offence on the basis that a prosecution is a breach of Art 31?

8.101

In *R v Appulonappa*[40] the Canadian Supreme Court considered the case of a boat that was intercepted in Canadian waters with 76 Sri Lankan Tamils on board who were coming to Canada intending to claim asylum. The Captain and three crew members (who were also Tamil and intending to claim asylum) were prosecuted for an offence of 'people smuggling'[41].

8.102

The Canadian Supreme Court concluded that the facilitation law that they were prosecuted under was overbroad, and therefore unconstitutional, insofar as is permitted 'prosecution for humanitarian aid to undocumented entrants,

39 *AAD* [2022] EWCA Crim 106, [2022] 1 Cr App R 19 at [118]–[119].

40 (2015) 41 BHRC 31.

41 Immigration and Refugee Protection Act, SC 2001, s 117(1) which read (at the time):
No person shall knowingly organize, induce, aid or abet the coming into Canada of one or more persons who are not in possession of a visa, passport or other document required by this Act.

mutual assistance amongst asylum-seekers or assistance to family members'[42]. Art 31 must be given a wide reading, and[43]:

> 'As I explain in B010[44], art. 31(1) of the Refugee Convention seeks to provide immunity for genuine refugees who enter illegally in order to seek refuge. For that protection to be effective, the law must recognize that persons often seek refuge in groups and work together to enter a country illegally. To comply with art. 31(1), a state cannot impose a criminal sanction on refugees solely because they have aided others to enter illegally in their collective flight to safety.'

8.103

Whilst it would not be possible for the same argument to succeed in England and Wales given the different constitutional set-up, the English and Welsh courts have yet to rule on whether Art 31 would apply to someone who facilitates another's journey either for purely humanitarian reasons, or as part of their own journey to sanctuary[45].

Procedure at court

Case management

8.104

In a case which is to be contested, early discussions should be held as to what the issues at trial will be. It is not unusual for defence representative to obtain expert evidence of country conditions or the operations of people smugglers, although it may be undesirable for an expert to be called in most cases to do so, with admissions by the prosecution covering most situations[46].

8.105

Whilst the prosecution is generally free[47] to challenge the defendant's account in any respect, or put in issue any part of the s 31 defence,

---

42 *Appulonappa* at [5] and [70].

43 *Appulonappa* at [43].

44 *B010 v. Canada* (Citizenship and Immigration), 2015 SCC 58.

45 The appellant in *Makuwa* was also convicted of two counts of facilitation relating to her children. However, the appeal against conviction was solely in relation to her own use of a false passport rather than the facilitation offences.

46 Expert evidence that has been obtained can be used to assist in representations to the CPS, even if not utilisted at trial. It may also be used in applications (including an abuse application) to the court. The requirements in relation to expert reports are set out in CPR r19.

47 Where there is a judicial finding on an issue, on a similar or higher standard of proof, in the defendant's favour (such as a FtT determination that his account may well be true, or that he is a refugee) whilst the Crown would not be bound by it, it would be unlikely for the Crown to seek to go behind it unless there was a very good reason.

> 'It may well be that, in many cases where the defendant claims to be a refugee, the Crown, while not accepting the claim, will not seek to establish that he is not. In such cases there will be no issue for the jury to decide and no need to explain the term[48].'

8.106

Practitioners should be alive to this, and it may be that the CPS would be assisted by early disclosure of a summary of the asylum claim with reasons why the issue of whether the person is a refugee need not be an issue for trial.

Guilty pleas

8.107

Many defendants will plead guilty for a number of reasons, good and bad (and often for a multitude of different reasons). There is no reason why somebody should not plead guilty, provided that they have had sufficient advice. However, given the number of cases that have gone to the Court of Appeal on guilty pleas, an advisor would be well advised to ensure that a full note is taken of discussions relating to the availability of the s 31 defence.

8.108

Further, solicitors would be advised to have a full account of the instructions received and advice given, and an advocate should similarly obtain a full endorsement before a plea is entered.

Impact of refugee status on sentence

False passport/leave to enter by deception

8.109

The case of *Kolawole*[49] still sets the 'tariff' for people entering the UK on a false passport[50]. For someone of good character on a plea of guilty, the guidance is a sentence in the range of 12–18 months (although in practice Crown Courts that are in the catchment area of an international port that see many such cases will tend to impose sentences lower than that). Notwithstanding the fact that the maximum sentence for seeking to obtain leave to enter or remain by deception is two years, similar sentencing levels apply to this offence as to false passport offences[51].

---

48 *Makuwa* at [37].
49 [2004] EWCA Crim 3047.
50 See Chapter 3 for more details.
51 See *Ding* [2010] EWCA Crim 1979 and Chapter 4 for more details.

8.110

It is an open question as to whether, if a defendant is a refugee who cannot bring himself within the s 31 defence, account should be taken of his refugee status as a matter of mitigation. In *Kishientine*[52], it was held that the criminal courts should not involve themselves in an assessment of the genuineness of an asylum claim.

8.111

However, if refugee status has been granted, then this would appear to be something that should properly mitigate the sentence if it does not provide a defence, provided at least there is some nexus between the refugee status and the offending (the fact that someone had been trafficked into the UK was a proper matter to take into account in mitigation in a sham marriage case[53]).

Victims of trafficking

Introduction

8.112

The specific defence for victims of trafficking has historically been seen as an 'immigration defence' as it was often raised in relation to people who were smuggled into the United Kingdom from abroad for the purpose of exploitation. In fact, it would appear that most of the people who raise the defence are British citizens. However, a brief overview of the defence will be given here.

8.113

The trafficking offences and the definitions in the legislation are considered in Chapter 5 in relation to the trafficking offences.

Historical background

8.114

On 15 November 2000 the UN General Assembly adopted the Palmero Convention[54], an international instrument to tackle transnational organised crime. In addition, there were three Protocols dealing with specific issues that arose in that context, one being the Protocol to Prevent, Suppress and Punish

52 [2004] EWCA Crim 3352.

53 *G* [2011] EWCA Crim 491.

54 Formally 'The United Nations Convention Against Transnational Organized Crime' (Palmero, 2000).

Trafficking in Persons, Especially Women and Children, known generally as the 'Palmero Protocol' or the Trafficking Protocol/Trafficking Convention[55].

8.115

This was followed up by the Council of Europe Convention on Action against Trafficking in Human Beings ('ECAT'). This was ratified by the United Kingdom on 17 December 2008 (coming into force on 1 April 2009) and Directive 2011/36/EU on preventing and combating trafficking in human beings and protecting its victims (the 'Trafficking Directive'). The United Kingdom opted into this Directive, although following Brexit is no longer bound by it.

Definition of trafficking

8.116

The core definition of trafficking is set out in Art 3 of the Palmero Convention (and replicated in Art 4 ECAT):

> '**Article 3**
>
> *Use of terms*
>
> For the purposes of this Protocol:
>
> (a) "Trafficking in persons" shall mean the recruitment, transportation, transfer, harbouring or receipt of persons, by means of the threat or use of force or other forms of coercion, of abduction, of fraud, of deception, of the abuse of power or of a position of vulnerability or of the giving or receiving of payments or benefits to achieve the consent of a person having control over another person, for the purpose of exploitation. Exploitation shall include, at a minimum, the exploitation of the prostitution of others or other forms of sexual exploitation, forced labour or services, slavery or practices similar to slavery, servitude or the removal of organs;
>
> (b) The consent of a victim of trafficking in persons to the intended exploitation set forth in subparagraph (a) of this article shall be

---

55 The other two are 'Protocol Against the Smuggling of Migrants by Land, Sea and Air', with smuggling being distinct from trafficking because the people being smuggled are giving their consent) and 'Protocol Against the Illicit Manufacturing of and Trafficking in Firearms' (which has been signed, but not ratified, by the United Kingdom). The Smuggling Protocol (which was ratified by the United Kingdom on 09 February 2006) does have (at Art 5) a non-prosecution provision:

> **Article 5. Criminal liability of migrants**
>
> Migrants shall not become liable to criminal prosecution under this Protocol for the fact of having been the object of conduct set forth in article 6 of this Protocol.

However, this should be read with Article 6(4) – 'nothing in this Protocol shall prevent a State Party from taking measures against a person whose conduct constitutes an offence under its domestic law' which indicates that states are entitled to impose penalties on those who enter a country illegally. This has not yet been considered by the English and Welsh Courts, and it remains to be seen what approach would be taken.

irrelevant where any of the means set forth in subparagraph (a) have been used;

(c) The recruitment, transportation, transfer, harbouring or receipt of a child for the purpose of exploitation shall be considered "trafficking in persons" even if this does not involve any of the means set forth in subparagraph (a) of this article;

(d) "Child" shall mean any person under eighteen years of age.'

Adults

8.117

The definition is often split into three parts – actions, means and purpose. The terms are wide, and should be interpreted in accordance with the underlying purpose of the Conventions (the protection of fundamental human rights). Guidance on the meaning of terms can be found in the 'Council of Europe Convention on Action against Trafficking in Human Beings and its Explanatory Report' and 'Modern Slavery: statutory guidance for England and Wales (under s 49 of the Modern Slavery Act 2015)'.

Action

8.118

Action is the 'thing done' by the trafficker to the victim (there can be more than one action):

- Recruitment
- Transportation
- Transfer
- Harbouring
- Receipt

Means

8.119

This is the means whereby the trafficking ensure the compliance of the victim:

- threat or use of force or other forms of coercion
- abduction
- fraud or deception
- the abuse of power or of a position of vulnerability

- the giving or receiving of payments or benefits to achieve the consent of a person having control over another person

Purpose

8.120

The above must be done for the purpose of exploitation, which is defined as including:

- exploitation of the prostitution of others
- other forms of sexual exploitation
- forced labour or services
- slavery or practices similar to slavery
- servitude
- the removal of organs

8.121

The Directive (Art 2) specifically states that 'including begging' (in the context of 'forced labour or services'), and 'or the exploitation of criminal activities' are included within the definition of exploitation (appearing before the reference to the removal or organs). However, this should be seen as a specific example of forced labour, rather than introducing a further layer of protection absent from the Trafficking Convention. This was confirmed in *L and Othrs*[56] (at [13]):

> 'What, however, is clearly established, and numerous different papers, reports and decided cases have demonstrated, is that when there is evidence that victims of trafficking have been involved in criminal activities, the investigation and the decision whether there should be a prosecution, and, if so, any subsequent proceedings require to be approached with the greatest sensitivity. The reasoning is not always spelled out, and perhaps we should do so now. The criminality, or putting it another way, the culpability, of any victim of trafficking may be significantly diminished, and in some cases effectively extinguished, not merely because of age (always a relevant factor in the case of a child defendant) but because no realistic alternative was available to the exploited victim but to comply with the dominant force of another individual, or group of individuals.'

56 [2013] EWCA Crim 991, [2013] 2 Cr App R 23/

8.122

Further assistance can be found in the Home Office Guidance which states[57]:

> 'Forced criminality is understood as the exploitation of a person to commit activities that may include:
>
> - pick-pocketing
> - shop-lifting
> - drug trafficking or cultivation
> - begging
> - benefit fraud and/or other types of fraud
> - sham marriage
> - other similar activities which are subject to penalties and imply financial gain'

Children

8.123

It is recognised that the position of children is different. Crucially, for a child (defined as someone aged under 18) there is no requirement for the 'means' part. There are also a wider set of circumstances where a child may be exploited (for example, illegal adoption).

Consent

8.124

The consent of a victim of trafficking is irrelevant. With an adult, this will be because the 'means' part of the definition (for example, a threat) will override consent. The Convention recognises the different position of children who are unable legally to consent to their own exploitation.

Non-prosecution principle

8.125

As well as requiring action to be taken against those who traffic others, a critical element of the protection of victims is the principle that victims of trafficking who are forced or coerced into committing a criminal act should not be punished for doing so.

57 Modern Slavery: statutory guidance for England and Wales (under s 49 of the Modern Slavery Act 2015)' at [2.43].

8.126

The Palmero Protocol did not explicitly contain a non-prosecution provision, although it did contain a requirement 'to protect the victims of … trafficking' which was generally interpreted to include such a principle[58]. The first explicit reference in a treaty was in ECAT at Article 26:

> '**ARTICLE 26**
>
> *Non-punishment provision*
>
> Each Party shall, in accordance with the basic principles of its legal system, provide for the possibility of not imposing penalties on victims for their involvement in unlawful activities, to the extent that they have been compelled to do so.'

8.127

This was reflected in Art 8 Directive:

> '**Article 8**
>
> *Non-prosecution or non-application of penalties to the victim*
>
> Member States shall, in accordance with the basic principles of their legal systems, take the necessary measures to ensure that competent national authorities are entitled not to prosecute or impose penalties on victims of trafficking in human beings for their involvement in criminal activities which they have been compelled to commit as a direct consequence of being subjected to any of the acts referred to in Article 2.'

8.128

Prior to 31 July 2015, this was given effect in England and Wales by the exercise of prosecutorial discretion and, where applicable, the abuse of process jurisdiction.

58 The United High Commissioner for Human Rights issued 'Recommended Principles and Guidelines on Human Rights and Human Trafficking' in 2002 which stated (principle 7) that 'Trafficked persons shall not be detained, charged or prosecuted for the illegality of their entry into or residence in countries of transit and destination, or for their involvement in unlawful activities to the extent that such involvement is a direct consequence of their situation as trafficked persons' and (Guideline 4(5)) that states should ensure 'that legislation prevents trafficked persons from being prosecuted, detained or punished for the illegality of their entry or residence or for the activities they are involved in as a direct consequence of their situation as trafficked persons.'

Identification of victims of trafficking – the National Referral Mechanism

Introduction

8.129

The National Referral Mechanism ('NRM') is procedure whereby potential victims of trafficking are identified and referred for support. It is the role of the Competent Authority ('CA') to identify such potential and actual victims of trafficking. There are, in fact, actually two Competent Authorities, the now mis-named Single Competent Authority ('SCA') and the Immigration Enforcement Competent Authority ('IECA').

8.130

The IECA is responsible for considering all NRM referrals for all FNOs detained in prison and all people detained in an Immigration Removal Centre, as well as non-detained adult FNOs and those people without immigration status who are being considered for Third Country Removal or the inadmissible process. All other cases will be considered by the SCA.

First responder

8.131

Only a 'first responder' (sometimes referred to as FRO – 'First Responder Organisation') can make a referral to the SCA. The police and the Home Office (including Immigration Enforcement) are first responders. However, a defence solicitor is not, nor are the CPS, Prison Officers[59] or the Courts, and so they cannot make a referral.

8.132

However, a practitioner can (and should) make contact with a first responder and request a referral[60].

59 Prison Officers are often in a good position to identify potential victims of trafficking due to the greater degree of exposure to the people involved and that a significant part of their role involves observation of prisoner to identify (amongst other things) vulnerability. There is guidance for HMPPS – 'Modern Slavery Guidance' (13 February 2023) available online at – https://www.gov.uk/government/publications/modern-slavery-guidance.

60 A full list of first responders is contained in 'National referral mechanism guidance: adult' (19 May 2022) at [4].

Procedure

8.133

A referral is made through an online referral form. Once this is lodged, there is a two-stage process; a reasonable grounds decision ('RG') and then a conclusive grounds decision ('CG'). At the first stage the SCA will determine whether there are reasonable grounds to believe that the person is a victim of trafficking. The SCA is not bound to accept a person's account.

8.134

If there is a positive RG, then the next stage is a further investigation of the person's claim. There is a 'recovery and reflection period' of at least 45 days (in practice, the timescales are currently much longer due to resource issues)[61]. The purpose of this is to give the person time to access support and consider whether they are willing to support a prosecution, or to otherwise provide assistance to the authorities in relation to their experiences.

8.135

At this stage the burden of proof is the balance of probabilities (ie, 'is it more likely than not that the person is a victim of trafficking?').

8.136

Where there is a negative decision, then a request for reconsideration can be made on the grounds of further evidence and/or that the decision was not made in accordance with the guidance[62]. Beyond that, the remedy is Judicial Review.

Consent to a referral

8.137

The consent of an adult is required before a referral can be made (although where this is not given then the Home Office should still be notified). Whilst a child can be asked if they consent, there is no requirement for consent to be obtained before a referral is made.

Indicators of trafficking

8.138

By definition someone who has been trafficked will be vulnerable and will often be reluctant to disclose or discuss any past experiences. For that reason,

61 In the third quarter of 2022 the average wait for a Conclusive Grounds decision was 531 days (Illegal Migration Bill, Explanatory Notes at [14]).

62 'Modern Slavery: statutory guidance for England and Wales' at [14.126]-[14.230].

practitioners must not consider it sufficient to ask a client whether they have been trafficked, and then take a negative answer at face value. The Modern Slavery statutory guidance gives[63] a good overview of the possible indicators of trafficking that practitioners should be familiar with.

8.139

The Law Society had also issued a useful Practice Note[64] that includes the following:

> 'This non-exhaustive list of factors may help to identify possible victims:
>
> - suspected victim is from a place known to be a source of human trafficking*
> - possession of false identity or travel documents or having no identity documents
> - showing signs of fear or anxiety
> - suffering from STDs, pregnant or underaged
> - few, if any, personal possessions
> - exhibiting distrust of the authorities
> - evidence of violence or threats of violence
> - fear of revealing immigration status
> - lack of knowledge of home or work address
> - living in substandard conditions or a House of Multiple Occupation with many other people
> - signs that the individual's movements are being controlled or that they are taking instructions from a third party
> - inconsistent story or history
> - inconsistent about name and age
>
> *Based on the nationality of victims referred to in the National Referral Mechanism (NRM) in 2016, those countries are:
>
> - Albania
> - Vietnam
> - Nigeria
> - Afghanistan
> - Eritrea
> - Iran

63 'Modern Slavery: statutory guidance for England and Wales' at [3] and Annex A.
64 'Victims of modern slavery – guidance for solicitors' (Law Society, 30 April 2020).

- Slovakia
- Iraq
- Romania

The following people may be particularly vulnerable to the risks of modern slavery:

- unaccompanied, internally displaced children
- children accompanied by an adult who is not their relative or legal guardian
- young girls and women
- former victims of modern slavery, trafficking or other forms of serious abuse
- mothers and babies/children
- those who are in the care system or care leavers.'

8.140

The Practice Note makes the point that there are a number of good reasons why victims of trafficking will be reluctant to reveal their history. Where a practitioner has, for example, a Vietnamese national found in a cannabis factory, it would not be sufficient to take any denial of coercion at face value. Even outside of such 'stereotypical' examples, practitioners will need to give careful consideration to whether their client is a potential victim of trafficking in all cases.

Case management issues

8.141

In *R v D*[65] the Court of Appeal gave guidance as to the approach that should be taken in court:

> '19. In order to comply with the United Kingdom's international obligations with regard to the prosecution of victims of trafficking, the CPS issued the 2013 Guidance, highlighting the need for prosecutors to be alert to the indicators of trafficking and providing a detailed and structured approach to the decision on whether or not to prosecute in the public interest. The first question is whether there is reason to believe that the person has been trafficked. In determining this question the guidance requires the prosecutor to make proper enquiries and to utilise the National Referral Mechanism ("NRM"). A referral through the NRM will lead to a decision by the competent authority of which prosecutors should take into account.

65 [2018] EWCA Crim 2995.

20. This plainly did not happen in this case. However, as has previously been said by this court, the obligation to identify whether a suspect might be a victim of trafficking does not rest on the prosecutor alone. It is incumbent on a suspect's legal representatives in an appropriate case to take steps to ascertain if he had been trafficked and to advise him on the relevant provisions. The court should also be alert to ensure that this has been done. The failure of all parties and the court in this regard led to the potentially inappropriate prosecution and conviction of this applicant.

21. In the course of his submissions, Mr Douglas-Jones invited this court to clarify four points for the assistance of practitioners and courts faced with the prosecution of a potential VOT. With the caveat that we have not heard full argument, still less had the opportunity to canvass any views from others involved in the Criminal Justice System, we go some way towards doing so as follows:

1. The latest version of the CPS guidance on the non- prosecution of VOTs is dated 2018. This now sets out a four-stage test which requires inter alia the prosecutor to consider whether there is clear evidence of a statutory defence under section 45 of the Modern Slavery Act 2015. If the answer to that is "yes", then the case should not be charged or should be discontinued on evidential grounds. If not, the guidance requires the prosecutor to go on to decide whether it is in the public interest to prosecute. Thus the guidance still applies to all cases where the statutory defence is not available.

2. It is not always necessary, particularly in the context of domestic trafficking, for there to be movement before a person can be identified as a VOT. When considering the application of the public interest test and how the guidance should be applied, all concerned should consider the definition of "trafficking" in Article 2 of Directive 2011/36/EU of the European and Parliament and the Council (5 April 2011) which provides as far as material:

"This Directive is part of global action against trafficking in human beings, which includes action involving third countries as stated in the 'Action-oriented Paper on strengthening the Union external dimension on action against trafficking in human beings; towards global EU action against trafficking in human beings' approved by the Council on 30 November 2009. In this context action should be pursued in third countries of origin and transfer of victims, with a view to raising awareness reducing vulnerability, supporting and assisting victims fighting the root causes of trafficking and supporting those third countries in developing appropriate anti-trafficking legislation."

3. As a decision has to be taken whether or not to prosecute a VOT, it is of importance that wherever possible those who may be VOTs are identified before any plea is taken at court. Indeed in cases where there is a suspicion of trafficking or slavery, the CPS guidance requires prosecutors at the first hearing to request that a plea is not formally

entered and to apply for an adjournment for further investigation into the defendant's possible status as the victim of slavery or trafficking.

22.The court should be alive to the duties of the prosecution to comply with the guidance where a defendant is a potential credible VOT by reference to the indicators of trafficking published by the UN office on drugs and crime human trafficking and UN global initiative to fight trafficking.

23. Should the matter be raised at the first hearing the judge will need to determine, as a matter of judgment on the facts of the individual case, whether a defendant is a potential credible VOT. If he so determines, the case should be adjourned for an NRM referral to be made. This should take 45 days but in practice may be considerably longer.

24. In such cases we recognise that the usual stage timetable for case progression under Better Case Management in the Crown Court and Transforming Summary Justice in the Magistrates' Court cannot apply and stage dates will need to be altered to accommodate the referral. Courts will no doubt wish to ensure that VOT questions are not missed. Conversely, we anticipate that courts will be astute to guard against unfounded attempts to raise a VOT point and so cause delay and disruption. Because of the BCM ramifications, we will pass a copy of this judgment to the Senior Presiding Judge for consideration and, if necessary, action.

4.We remind all concerned of the need to be alert to the possibility of trafficking and re-trafficking which may arise in a number of different ways, as the present case demonstrates.'

8.142

In the Crown Court, the PTPH Form has a specific box asking 'Is the defendant said to be a victim of modern slavery?', which is under the heading of 'defence information'. In completing the form and drafting any defence statement practitioners will need to remember that a s 45 defence can only arise as an exclusion of liability for someone who has done the act. In other words, by relying on the defence, the defendant will effectively be admitting the elements of the offence.

8.143

Where the s 45 defence is to be advanced, it will need to be addressed in the defence statement. In this, requests for discourse for the NRM referral forms (including any attachments) and documents can be made.

Overview of the s 45 defence

8.144

The purpose of the defence is to give effect to the non-prosecution provision of the Palmero Protocol and provides protection to those who have been trafficked and, as a result of the trafficking commit offences, but who would not have the defence of duress. A further purpose is 'to provide further encouragement to victims to come forward and give evidence without fear of being convicted for offences connected to their slavery or trafficking situation'[66].

Legislation

8.145

The defence is set out in the Modern Slavery Act 2015, s 45:

> **'45 Defence for slavery or trafficking victims who commit an offence**
>
> (1) A person is not guilty of an offence if—
>
> (a) the person is aged 18 or over when the person does the act which constitutes the offence,
>
> (b) the person does that act because the person is compelled to do it,
>
> (c) the compulsion is attributable to slavery or to relevant exploitation, and
>
> (d) a reasonable person in the same situation as the person and having the person's relevant characteristics would have no realistic alternative to doing that act.
>
> (2) A person may be compelled to do something by another person or by the person's circumstances.
>
> (3) Compulsion is attributable to slavery or to relevant exploitation only if—
>
> (a) it is, or is part of, conduct which constitutes an offence under section 1 or conduct which constitutes relevant exploitation, or
>
> (b) it is a direct consequence of a person being, or having been, a victim of slavery or a victim of relevant exploitation.
>
> (4) A person is not guilty of an offence if—
>
> (a) the person is under the age of 18 when the person does the act which constitutes the offence,
>
> (b) the person does that act as a direct consequence of the person being, or having been, a victim of slavery or a victim of relevant exploitation, and

66 Explanatory Notes, MSA 2015 at [218]

(c) a reasonable person in the same situation as the person and having the person's relevant characteristics would do that act.

(5) For the purposes of this section—

"relevant characteristics" means age, sex and any physical or mental illness or disability;

"relevant exploitation" is exploitation (within the meaning of section 3) that is attributable to the exploited person being, or having been, a victim of human trafficking.

(6) In this section references to an act include an omission.

(7) Subsections (1) and (4) do not apply to an offence listed in Schedule 4.'

8.146

This came into force on 31 July 2015 and is not retrospective[67].

Adults v youths

8.147

As with the definition of trafficking, there is an important distinction in the legislation between those defendants who are adults, and those who were under 18 at the time of the offence.

8.148

For adults, once it has been proved that the defendant committed the offence, it is a defence if the defendant can show the following:

- Compulsion – the defendant was compelled to act in the way that they did
- Attribution – the compulsion follows from the relevant slavery/exploitation
- Reasonableness – a 'reasonable person' in the same situation as the defendant, and sharing their relevant characteristics would have 'no realistic alternative' to act in the way that they did

8.149

For a youth, the defence is the same, but there is no requirement to prove compulsion.

67 *CS & Le* [2021] EWCA Crim 134.

Burden of proof

8.150

The burden of proof is on the defendant, but is an evidential one[68]. Once sufficient evidence has been raised to put any aspect of the defence in issue, it is for the Prosecution to disprove it. That includes where there is an issue as to the defendant's age, it is for the prosecution to prove that they are an adult[69]

Meaning of compulsion/characteristics of the reasonable person

8.151

'Compulsion' is not the same as 'causation'[70], although it is a lower threshold that 'duress'[71].

8.152

As is noted in the Crown Court Compendium this has an overlap with the relevance of characteristics for the defence of duress, which would include their age and sex, as well as possibly any disability they are under[72]. It is unclear whether someone's history as a victim of trafficking is a relevant characteristic, although it is suggested that it may well be that a victim of trafficking would be in a category of people 'less able to resist pressure than people not within that category'.

Admissibility of the Competent Authority decision

8.153

The decision and reasoning of the Competent Authority is not admissible in a criminal trial[73], although the material underlying it can be adduced by either party in the usual way.

---

68 *MK & Gega* [2018] EWCA Crim 667, [2018] 2 Cr App R 14.

69 *MK & Gega* [44].

70 *VSJ* [2017] EWCA Crim 36 at [145].

71 The Crown Court Compendium Vol I at 18-6 contains further guidance and draft jury directions.

72 From *Bowen* [1996] 2 Cr App R 157:

> The defendant may be in a category of persons whom the jury may think less able to resist pressure than people not within that category. Obvious examples are age, where a young person may well not be so robust as a mature one; possibly sex, though many women would doubtless consider they had as much moral courage to resist pressure as men; pregnancy, where there is added fear for the unborn child; serious physical disability, which may inhibit self protection; recognised mental illness or psychiatric condition, such as post-traumatic stress disorder leading to learnt helplessness

73 *Brecani* [2021] EWCA Crim 731, [2021 2 Cr App R 12.

8.154

However, it can and should be used by the CPS in making a decision to prosecute, and can be used by a judge determining an abuse of process application. In addition, it is admissible on an appeal to the Court of Appeal to inform a decision in a case where someone is appealing on the basis that their status as a victim of trafficking has been overlooked.

8.155

Whilst a decision of the Competent Authority is not binding, there must be clear reasons for not following it[74].

The CPS Review – the four stage approach

Introduction

8.156

In reviewing a case where there are trafficking issues raised, the CPS have a specific policy[75] with a four stage approach.

8.157

The approach is as follows:

1. Is there a reason to believe that the person is a victim of trafficking[76]?
   - If yes, move to Question 2.
   - If not, you do not need to consider this assessment further.
2. Is there clear evidence of a credible common law defence of duress?
   - If yes, then the case should not be charged or should be discontinued on evidential grounds.
   - If not, move to Question 3.
3. Is there clear evidence of a statutory defence under Section 45 of the 2015 Act?
   - If yes, then the case should not be charged or should be discontinued on evidential grounds
   - If not, move to Question 4.
4. Is it in the public interest to prosecute? This must be considered even where there is no clear evidence of duress and no clear evidence of all of the elements of a section 45 defence or where section 45 does not apply (because the offence is excluded under Schedule 4).

---

74 *VCL v United Kingdom* (2021) 73 EHRR 9 and *BRP* [2023] EWCA Crim 40 at [51].

75 Modern Slavery, Human Trafficking and Smuggling (6 July 2022). This covers prosecutions for the slavery and trafficking offences, as well as question of prosecuting victims or potential victims of trafficking.

76 Including a victim of slavery.

> Prosecutors should consider all the circumstances of the case, including the seriousness of the offence and any direct or indirect compulsion arising from their trafficking situation.

8.158

Practitioners should be alive to the above and make representations based on it to the CPS. This can be pre-charge during a police investigation.

Excluded offences

8.159

The Modern Slavery Act 2015, Sch 4 sets out a list of the offences to which the s 45 offence does not apply. These include serious offences under the criminal law such as murder and rape, and the offences under ss 1 and 2. The only specific Immigration offence that is listed is the IA 1971, s 25 one (but not the s 25A offence, although the reason for that is unclear given the similarity and the fact that it has the same maximum sentence). Additional offences of relevance to immigration offence are the following:

- Modern Slavery Act 2015, s 1 (Slavery, Servitude and forced or compulsory labour)
- Modern Slavery Act 2015, s 2 (Human Trafficking)
- Perverting the course of justice

8.160

In *R v A*[77] it was concluded that s 45 effectively 'plugged the gap' that had previously existed by the failure to implement protections for victims of trafficking. The consequence is that whilst a stay is possible in theory, the 'cases in which duress and the s 45 defence are not available, but where it would not be in the public interest to prosecute on the basis of a victim of trafficking's status will, we think, be rare'. It was confirmed in *R v AAD*[78] that there was not a distinct approach in Sch 4 cases.

77 [2020] EWCA Crim 1408, [2021] 4 WLR 16.
78 [2022] EWCA Crim 106, [2022] 1 Cr App R 19.

9 Sentencing

Introduction

9.1

The law in relation to sentencing has got ever more complex over the years. This chapter aims to give an overview of how deportation works, as well as considering particular ancillary orders which arise in immigration offences, rather than an overview of the whole sentencing regime.

Sources of sentencing authority

Background

9.2

Whilst sentencing is still said to be an art rather than a science, it is fair to say that since the Criminal Justice Act 1972 it has become ever more scientific in approach. The Sentencing Act 2020 came into force on 1 December 2020. This creates a Sentencing Code that does not change the maximum sentences or ancillary orders for any offence, but its aim is to bring together in one place (almost all) the powers of a court when sentencing an offender. This applies to all people sentenced after 1 December 2020, whenever the offence was committed.

9.3

Running alongside this has been the development of Sentencing Guidelines, and latterly the creation of the Sentencing Council[1] which is a body tasked with preparing the guidelines. They create both guidelines in relation to specific classes of offences, as well as for overarching principles that apply in all cases. These are produced in draft, and only finalised after a consultation period.

9.4

Whilst there are currently guidelines in many of the commonly committed criminal offences, there are no Guidelines for immigration offences generally. Similarly, with the exception of the IA 1971, s 25 facilitation offence and the offence of using a false passport, there are no guideline cases for sentencing.

9.5

It follows that judges will have a much freer hand when sentencing most immigration offences, although in a number of cases there will be previous sentencing decisions that provide a guide.

---

1 Coroners and Justice Act 2009, Part 4.

9.6

In addition, the court will consider the 'Overarching Principles' guidance (which can be found on the Sentencing Council website). This provides guidance in all cases, whether or not there are specific guidelines for the offence.

9.7

This includes assessing the seriousness of the offence, which involves considering the harm caused by the offending, and the culpability of the offending. There are also a number of statutory and non-statutory aggravating and mitigating features, although it may be the case that many will not apply to any particular case.

Credit for a plea of guilty

9.8

Of particular note is the concept of 'credit' for a plea of guilty. This operates to reduce the sentence by up to a third where someone pleads guilty[2]. The level of discount depends on when the plea is entered (or indicated if a plea cannot be entered at that time because, for example, the offence is indictable only and so a plea cannot be entered in the magistrates' court). There is specific guidance ('Reduction in sentence for a guilty plea') which is also on the Sentencing Council website. A number of cases have reviewed and endorsed that approach[3].

9.9

There is a tension between the pressure for pleas of guilty to be indicated at the earliest opportunity with the requirement that someone receives full, and properly informed, legal advice. This is especially the case in an area of law such as immigration offences which can be complex and littered with potential pitfalls with specialist advice often being required[4]. Even where the existence of the s 31 defence is identified it would often be necessary for careful consideration to be given to the question of the applicability and viability of the defence which is unlikely to be able to be given at the first appearance (and often not at the PTPH). However, were that to happen, the defendant is likely to lose credit and end up with a longer sentence.

9.10

If a plea is not entered straight away, then an advocate may be able to rely on exception F1 Guidance;

---

2 This is on a statutory basis in Sentencing Act 2020, s 73.

3 See, most recently, *Plaku* [2021] EWCA Crim 568, [2021] 4 WLR 82 and *Dale* [2022] EWCA Crim 207, [2022] 2 Cr App R(S) 25.

4 See *Mateta & Othrs* [2014] 1 WLR 1516, [2013] EWCA Crim 1372 as one example among many where a specially convened Court quashed five convictions of asylum seekers prosecuted for using false passports to come to the UK.

'F1. Further information, assistance or advice necessary before indicating plea

Where the sentencing court is satisfied that there were particular circumstances which significantly reduced the defendant's ability to understand what was alleged or otherwise made it unreasonable to expect the defendant to indicate a guilty plea sooner than was done, a reduction of one-third should still be made.

In considering whether this exception applies, sentencers should distinguish between cases in which it is necessary to receive advice and/or have sight of evidence in order to understand whether the defendant is in fact and law guilty of the offence(s) charged, and cases in which a defendant merely delays guilty plea(s) in order to assess the strength of the prosecution evidence and the prospects of conviction or acquittal.'

9.11

Even then, this will often not be sufficient to ensure that credit is 'preserved.

Ancillary orders

9.12

It is important to note that there are a number of ancillary orders on sentencing that are either mandatory or discretionary. These are considered below.

Sentencing of youths

9.13

In relation to a youth (someone aged under 18) there is a different regime for sentencing, with different aims[5]. It is unusual for there to be prosecutions for immigration offences for youths, and so full consideration will not be given here.

5 Under Crime and Disorder Act 1998, s 37,

37 Aim of the youth justice system.

(1) It shall be the principal aim of the youth justice system to prevent offending by children and young persons.

(2) In addition to any other duty to which they are subject, it shall be the duty of all persons and bodies carrying out functions in relation to the youth justice system to have regard to that aim

In addition, s44 Children and Young Persons Act 1933 reads '*Principles to be observed by all Courts in dealing with Children and Young Persons.*

44 General considerations.

(1) Every court in dealing with a child or young person who is brought before it, either as … an offender or otherwise, shall have regard to the welfare of the child or young person and shall in a proper case take steps for removing him from undesirable surroundings, and for securing that proper provision is made for his education and training'

Deportation

Introduction

9.14

The law relating to deportation is, unsurprisingly, complex. It is also one where both the legislation, and the interpretation by the courts, change on a regular basis.

9.15

There tends to be a widespread misconception amongst criminal lawyers representing foreign nationals about what the consequences of a conviction are. Deportation (as opposed to a recommendation for deportation) is not actually a criminal sanction. However, as it is in this context that it is most likely to arise for practitioners, it is included in this chapter.

A deportation order

9.16

A deportation order is an order that the individual leaves the United Kingdom, and provides the power for him to be removed (and to be detained pending the removal). It operates to revoke any existing leave that the person has.

9.17

The court should operate with the legislative framework for deportation as set by Parliament, In *Williams*[6], a case from 1981, it was held that it was permissible, but generally inappropriate to make a *de facto* deportation order by making it a condition of a sentence or other order that the defendant leave the jurisdiction, at least unless the defendant consents (or 'acknowledges himself to be bound by it').

9.18

However, in *Dragoman v Camberwell Green Magistrates' Court*[7] it was held that there was no power to impose a condition requiring someone to leave the United Kingdom as part of a community penalty. This is the case whether or not the defendant consented. Whilst *Dragoman* relates to an EEA national (who had the benefit of much greater protection under EU law), there is no reason why this would not apply generally. The case of *Williams* is now old, and it is likely that it would not be followed given the prescriptive nature of the deportation regime.

---

6 See *Williams* (1982) 75 Cr App R 378 in relation to binding over orders.

7 [2012] EWHC 4105 (Admin).

Legislative framework for automatic deportation

9.19

There are various grounds on which deportation can be ordered[8], although for criminal practitioners the framework most likely to be seen is under the UK Borders Act 2007.

9.20

The power is at s 32;

> **'32 Automatic deportation**
>
> (1) In this section "foreign criminal" means a person—
>
> (a) who is not a British citizen or an Irish citizen,
>
> (b) who is convicted in the United Kingdom of an offence, and
>
> (c) to whom Condition 1 or 2 applies.
>
> (2) Condition 1 is that the person is sentenced to a period of imprisonment of at least 12 months.
>
> (3) Condition 2 is that—
>
> (a) the offence is specified by order of the Secretary of State under section 72(4)(a) of the Nationality, Immigration and Asylum Act 2002 (c. 41) (serious criminal), and
>
> (b) the person is sentenced to a period of imprisonment.
>
> (4) For the purpose of section 3(5)(a) of the Immigration Act 1971 (c. 77), the deportation of a foreign criminal is conducive to the public good.
>
> (5) The Secretary of State must make a deportation order in respect of a foreign criminal (subject to section 33).
>
> (6) The Secretary of State may not revoke a deportation order made in accordance with subsection (5) unless—

---

8 See IA 1971, s 3(5) –

(a) if, having only a limited leave to enter or remain, he does not observe a condition attached to the leave or remains beyond the time limited by the leave; or

(aa) if he has obtained leave to remain by deception; or

(b) if the Secretary of State deems his deportation to be conducive to the public good; or

(c) if another person to whose family he belongs is or has been ordered to be deported.

Also, s3(6) – 'a person who is not a British citizen shall also be liable to deportation from the United Kingdom if, after he has attained the age of seventeen, he is convicted of an offence for which he is punishable with imprisonment and on his conviction is recommended for deportation by a court empowered by this Act to do so.'

In relation to EEA cases the power is under Reg 27A Immigration (European Economic Area) Regulations 2016, which have been preserved by virtue of para 2, Sch 3 Immigration and Social Security Co-ordination (EU Withdrawal) Act 2020 (Consequential, Saving, Transitional and Transitory Provisions) (EU Exit) Regulations 2020 and Reg 8 Citizens' Rights (Application Deadline and Temporary Protection) (EU Exit) Regulations 2020.

(a) he thinks that an exception under section 33 applies,

(b) the application for revocation is made while the foreign criminal is outside the United Kingdom, or

(c) section 34(4) applies.'

Qualifying condition 1 – a sentence of more than 12 months

9.21

The basic requirement is that the person must not be a British Citizen[9], rather than being a foreign national (as in someone who is a national of a foreign country) and so someone who is stateless can be subject to the automatic deportation provisions[10]. Someone who is a dual national will be considered as British for these purposes (and therefore cannot be deported). If the defendant states that he is British or Irish, then the burden is him to show this, on the usual civil standard[11].

9.22

Condition 1 requires 'a period of imprisonment of at least 12 months'. This means at least one sentence of immediate imprisonment of at least 12 months, with 'at least' meaning 12 months or more[12]. Therefore, someone who receives a suspended sentence of 18 months will not qualify (although he would be if it was subsequently activated). Nor will someone who receives consecutive sentences totalling 12 months[13].

9.23

This can cause acute difficulties in terms of the structuring of the sentences. For example, a Judge may conclude that someone who commits two frauds six months apart, but sentenced at the same time, should be sentenced to 18 months immediate imprisonment. If she passes consecutive sentences of nine months, then the person will not fall within Condition 1. However, if she passes two concurrent sentences of 18 months imprisonment (which effectively amounts to the same sentence) then the same person will fulfil Condition 1.

9.24

The question of deportation (and the hardship that may follow from that) is not part of the sentence[14]. It therefore follows that a sentencer should not reduce a

---

9 Whilst Irish citizens can be deported, the situation is more complicated and outside the scope of this book.

10 *Johnson v SSHD* [2022] EWHC 3120 (KB).

11 IA 1971, s 3(8).

12 *Kluxen* [2010] EWCA Crim 1081, [2011] 1 WLR 218 at [7].

13 See *Ul-Haq* [2013] EWCA Crim 1478 for an example of a 12-month sentence made up of shorter consecutive sentences, but a recommendation for deportation was made, and upheld by the Court of Appeal

14 This has long been the case, starting with *Edgehill* (1963) 47 Cr App R 41 when the power to recommend deportation became available.

sentence in order to either account for deportation, or to avoid (or attempt to avoid) the deportation provisions[15].

9.25

However, can a sentencer structure a sentence in order to avoid that outcome? In *Hakimzadeh*[16] the Court of Appeal (on what was slightly out of the ordinary offending[17]) reduced a sentence of two years to 12 months due to other mitigation, but then went on to re-structure the sentence to two sets of concurrent sentences of nine months and three months, consecutive to each other. This was explicitly as:

> 'Having regard to the age of these offences, the very substantial period of residence here and the fact that deportation was clearly not in the judge's mind at all.'

9.26

This conclusion was doubted in *Turner*[18] (paras [27]–[28]) and *Mintchev* (paras 20-22). In *AG Ref (No 41 of 2013)*[19] the Court of Appeal confirmed that that was wrong and adopted the principle from previous references that:

> 'Judges should not, therefore, pass a shorter sentence or a sentence different in nature from one they would otherwise have passed on the basis they have been informed that the offender is liable to automatic deportation.'

9.27

That has been the position since. Whilst the principle that the proper sentence should not be reduced to avoid the provisions of the UK Borders Act 2007 is clearly a sound one, the question of the structuring is less straightforward. In the scenario above with two frauds, either way of passing the sentence is lawful, but they have potentially extremely different consequences. Unlike the situation where a shorter sentence is passed, the structuring of the sentence would not make the sentence unduly lenient just because it avoided the automatic deportation provisions.

9.28

It follows that a defence lawyer is perfectly entitled to suggest that consecutive sentences are passed, but as long as this is not on the basis of the deportation provisions, which may give the mitigation an air of unreality on occasions.

---

15 *Mintchev* [2011] EWCA Crim 499, [2011] 2 Cr App R(S) 81.

16 [2009] EWCA Crim 959, [2010] 1 Cr App R(S) 10.

17 Mr Hakimzadeh was a 'distinguished scholar' and a 'person of substance' with 'extremely [good] mitigation'. He was an American citizen, but had been in the United Kingdom for over 30 years (and so could presumably have obtained British citizenship).

18 [2010] EWCA Crim 2897, [2011] 2 Cr App R(S) 18.

19 [2013] EWCA Crim 1188.

9.29

One point that would need to be considered by a lawyer advising a client on appeal is that because the deportation provisions are not part of the sentence, the Criminal Appeal Act 1968, s 11(3)[20] will not apply. Therefore someone who was sentenced to nine months consecutive on two offences, and wishes to appeal the sentence, runs the risk of winning an appeal, but having a total sentence of 18 months replaced with one of 12 months concurrent on both counts (thereby triggering the automatic deportation provisions).

9.30

A sentence of detention in a Young Offenders Institute will count as a sentence of imprisonment[21], as will detention in a hospital after conviction[22] (but not after a verdict of not guilty by reason of insanity, or a finding that he did the act after a finding that he was unfit to plead)[23].

9.31

An indeterminate sentence will also count, provided 'provided that it may last for 12 months'[24]. This would appear to mean that there must be a tariff of at least 12 months, as anyone serving an indeterminate sentence may end up serving at least 12 months however short their tariff is. However, it is ambiguous and has not been resolved by the criminal courts. Given the current provision for life sentences, it would appear highly unlikely to ever be an issue as the tariff will likely be a lot longer than 12 months.

Qualifying condition 2

9.32

There are two limbs to condition 2. Firstly, the offence must be specified under the NIAA , 2002, s 72(4)(a).

9.33

However, whilst the Home Secretary has specified a large number of offences for the purposes of someone having committed a 'particularly serious crime', as set out in the Nationality, Immigration and Asylum Act 2002 (Specification of Particularly Serious Crimes) Order 2004, Schs 1–6, this has not been brought into force in relation to the UKBA 2007[25].

20 The provision that prohibits the Court of Appeal passing a sentence that ensures that 'taking the case as a whole, the appellant is not more severely dealt with on appeal than he was dealt with by the court below.'
21 UKBA 2007, s 38(1)(c).
22 UKBA 2007, s 38(1)(c).
23 UKBA 2007, s 38(3).
24 UKBA 2007, s 38(1)(d).
25 UKBA 2007, s 32 was brought into force in relation to Condition 1 only by UK Borders Act 2007 (Commencement No. 3 and Transitional Provisions) Order 2008.

9.34

The only offences under the IA 1971 included are ss 25 and 25A (and s 25B, although that has been repealed), but not the s 24 or s 24A offences. There are a large number of offences which include which could cover low level offending (such as theft and criminal damage) that cannot reasonably be said to be a particular serious crime[26].

9.35

As with the first qualifying condition, a suspended sentence will not count as a period of imprisonment (unless it is activated and imposed), but detention in a YOI or hospital (as part of a punishment, rather than after a verdict of not guilty by reason of insanity or unfitness to plead) will do[27].

Exceptions to automatic deportation

9.36

When a qualifying condition is met then the Home Secretary 'must' make a deportation order unless one of the exceptions in s 33 applies:

> **'33 Exceptions**
>
> (1) Section 32(4) and (5)–
>
> (a) do not apply where an exception in this section applies (subject to subsection (7) below), and
>
> (b) are subject to sections 7 and 8 of the Immigration Act 1971 (Commonwealth citizens, Irish citizens, crew and other exemptions).
>
> (2) Exception 1 is where removal of the foreign criminal in pursuance of the deportation order would breach–
>
> (a) a person's Convention rights, or
>
> (b) the United Kingdom's obligations under the Refugee Convention.
>
> (3) Exception 2 is where the Secretary of State thinks that the foreign criminal was under the age of 18 on the date of conviction.[28]
>
> (5) Exception 4 is where the foreign criminal–
>
> (a) is the subject of a certificate under section 2 or 70 of the Extradition Act 2003 (c. 41),

26 See the discussion in *EN (Serbia) v SSHD* [2009] EWCA Civ 630, [2010] QB 633 at [81]–[82].

27 UKBA 2007, s 38(2).

28 Exception 3 related to EEA citizens and was removed post-Brexit to be replaced with the exceptions at 6(A) and 6(C).

(b) is in custody pursuant to arrest under section 5 of that Act,

(c) is the subject of a provisional warrant under section 73 of that Act,

(ca) is the subject of a certificate under section 74B of that Act,

(d) is the subject of an authority to proceed under section 7 of the Extradition Act 1989 (c. 33) or an order under paragraph 4(2) of Schedule 1 to that Act, or

(e) is the subject of a provisional warrant under section 8 of that Act or of a warrant under paragraph 5(1)(b) of Schedule 1 to that Act.

(6) Exception 5 is where any of the following has effect in respect of the foreign criminal–

(a) a hospital order or guardianship order under section 37 of the Mental Health Act 1983 (c. 20),

(b) a hospital direction under section 45A of that Act,

(c) a transfer direction under section 47 of that Act,

(d) a compulsion order under section 57A of the Criminal Procedure (Scotland) Act 1995 (c. 46),

(e) a guardianship order under section 58 of that Act,

(f) a hospital direction under section 59A of that Act,

(g) a transfer for treatment direction under section 136 of the Mental Health (Care and Treatment) (Scotland) Act 2003 (asp 13), or

(h) an order or direction under a provision which corresponds to a provision specified in paragraphs (a) to (g) and which has effect in relation to Northern Ireland.

(6A) Exception 6 is where the Secretary of State thinks that the application of section 32(4) and (5) would contravene the United Kingdom's obligations under the Council of Europe Convention on Action against Trafficking in Human Beings (done at Warsaw on 16th May 2005).

(6B) Exception 7 is where—

(a) the foreign criminal is a relevant person, and

(b) the offence for which the foreign criminal was convicted as mentioned in section 32(1)(b) consisted of or included conduct that took place before IP completion day.

(6C) For the purposes of subsection (6B), a foreign criminal is a "relevant person"—

(a) if the foreign criminal is in the United Kingdom (whether or not they have entered within the meaning of section 11(1) of the Immigration Act 1971) having arrived with entry clearance granted by virtue of relevant entry clearance immigration rules,

(b) if the foreign criminal has leave to enter or remain in the United Kingdom granted by virtue of residence scheme immigration rules,

(ba) if the person is in the United Kingdom (whether or not they have entered within the meaning of section 11(1) of the Immigration Act 1971) having arrived with entry clearance granted by virtue of Article 23 of the Swiss citizens' rights agreement,

(c) if the foreign criminal may be granted leave to enter or remain in the United Kingdom as a person who has a right to enter the United Kingdom by virtue of—

(i) Article 32(1)(b) of the EU withdrawal agreement,

(ii) Article 31(1)(b) of the EEA EFTA separation agreement, or

(iii) Article 26a(1)(b) of the Swiss citizens' rights agreement,

whether or not the foreign criminal has been granted such leave, or

(d) if the foreign criminal may enter the United Kingdom by virtue of regulations made under section 8 of the European Union (Withdrawal Agreement) Act 2020 (frontier workers), whether or not the foreign criminal has entered by virtue of those regulations.

(6D) In this section—

"EEA EFTA separation agreement" and "Swiss citizens' rights agreement" have the same meanings as in the European Union (Withdrawal Agreement) Act 2020 (see section 39(1) of that Act);

"relevant entry clearance immigration rules" and "residence scheme immigration rules" have the meanings given by section 17of the European Union (Withdrawal Agreement) Act 2020.

(7) The application of an exception–

(a) does not prevent the making of a deportation order;

(b) results in it being assumed neither that deportation of the person concerned is conducive to the public good nor that it is not conducive to the public good;

but section 32(4) applies despite the application of Exception 1 or 4.'

Effect of the automatic deportation provisions

9.37

Once a Deportation Order is made, it will be for the Tribunal to make an independent assessment of these factors on an appeal. It is important to remember that the fact that either Condition applies does not mean that the defendant will be deported. The case will then go to the Home Secretary of State to consider the position. Because of the automatic nature of the UK Borders Act 2007, s 32 the criminal courts do not need to consider the s 33 factors. In addition, there is no need for a sentencer to state the effect of the sentence where a qualifying sentence is passed, although it would be good practice to explain this. An incorrect explanation would not impact on the outcome of the case given the mandatory nature of the UK Borders Act 2007, s 32.

The power to recommend deportation

9.38

A criminal court has long had a power to recommend deportation[29]. However, whilst the court still has the power to make a recommendation for deportation[30], this will be rare. It should not be done in a case where the automatic provisions apply[31].

9.39

Where a person does not receive any sentence of at least 12 months, whilst a court could recommend deportation, this is something that will be rare. The test for making a recommendation is high[32]:

> 'the court must consider whether the offender's conduct (including the instant offence and any earlier ones) constituted "a genuine and sufficiently serious threat to the requirements of public policy affecting one of the fundamental interests of society".'

---

29 The power was first granted in Aliens Act 1905, s 3, which came into force on 1 January 1906. That day, the first Expulsion Order (as it was then called) was made against Wilhelm Housmann, a German boy of 17 who appeared before the Sleaford Justices for an offence of theft. He pleaded guilty and was sentenced to 21 days and made the subject a recommendation. However, the Home Office declined to act on it as it was 'a trivial offence' and Wilhelm was 'of respectable parentage'.

30 The power appears in Sentencing Act 2020, s 386, but this refers back to the 1971 Act;
Deportation recommendations
See section 6 of the Immigration Act 1971 for provision about recommendations for deportation by a court dealing with an offender for an offence punishable with imprisonment where—
(a) the offender is not a British citizen, and
(b) is aged 17 or over when convicted.

31 *Kluxen* [2010] EWCA Crim 1081, [2011] 1 WLR 218.

32 *Kluxen* at [13].

9.40

It is unlikely that someone sentenced to less than 12 months will meet this test. In any event, it is open to the Home Secretary to instigate deportation in such a case with or without a recommendation. However, in relation to immigration offending which goes to the heart of the immigration system,[33] the situation is different, and a recommendation may be appropriate[34].

9.41

If a judge wishes to consider making a recommendation, they should *not* take account of the following[35]:

- The defendant's rights under the ECHR
- The impact of deportation on innocent third parties (such as family members)[36]
- The political situation in the receiving country

9.42

In addition, there were two factors relating to EEA nationals (the provisions of Directive 2004/38, art 28; the Immigration (European Economic Area) Regulations 2006) that should also not be taken into account.

9.43

However, if a judge is considering making a recommendation, then there must be a full enquiry into the question of whether or not one should be made[37]. In addition, the defendant must have had at least seven days' notice of the possibility of deportation[38], although a failure to do so will not be a ground of appeal[39]. The judge should give reasons for making the recommendation[40]. This is not just because of the general principles of criminal law and the defendant's

---

33 Examples of recommendations being upheld post the 2007 Act include;

- *Brown* [2010] EWCA Crim 1807, [2011] 1 Cr App R(S) 79 – 10 months for using a false passport to claim income support and housing and council tax benefit.
- *Junab* [2012] EWCA Crim 2660, [2013] 2 Cr App R(S) 23 – 6 months for producing a false passport and driving licence to get a national insurance number.

Against that, in *Owusu-Sekyere* [2012] EWCA Crim 334 – 8 months for using a false ILR stamp in a genuine passport in order to work, the recommendation was quashed on the grounds of a failure to warn the defence of the possibility or a recommendation and a lack of reasons, although it would have been substantively a proper order to have made.

34 A recommendation was also upheld in *Ul-Haq* [2013] EWCA Crim 1478 for a total sentence of 12 months (made up of shorter consecutive and current sentences) for a series of sexual assaults committed against lone women on the London transport network.

35 *Kluxen* [2010] EWCA Crim 1081, [2011] 1 WLR 218 at [29]

36 This was left open in relation to EEA cases given the potential for proportionality to be an issue in a recommendation

37 *Nasari* (1980) 71 Cr App R 87.

38 IA 1971, s 6(2). This will be done by the service of an 'IM3 Form', which is typically served at the time of charge. However, this is not always the case and prosecutors and practitioners should check in any relevant case that this has been.

39 *Abdi* [2007] EWCA Crim 1913, [2008] 1 Cr App R(S) 87.

40 The general duty is now set out at Sentencing Act 2020, s 52.

entitlement to know why the sentence was passed, but is also to assist the Home Secretary who will then have to decide whether to act on the recommendation.

9.44

A recommendation for deportation can be appealed to the Court of Appeal.

Procedure prior to making a deportation order

9.45

There is generally a two-stage procedure. First, at some point after the deadline for any appeal against conviction or sentence has passed (or the appeal dismissed), the Home Secretary will serve a notice of liability to deportation at the completion of sentence. This will set out the person's immigration and criminal history and the basis upon which deportation is conducive to the public good. The person will then have the opportunity to make representations, which will typically focus upon whether the test for deportation is met, as well as why he falls within any exceptions.

9.46

The Home Office will then consider the case as a whole, along with any representations that have been submitted. At this stage, consideration will be given to any human rights arguments raised. The Home Office will then determine whether a deportation order should be made. If it is, then it is that decision (rather than, counter-intuitively, the deportation order itself) that will be appealable (as would a refusal to revoke the order subsequently), with the grounds usually being that removal pursuant to the order would be a breach of the Refugee Convention and/or the ECHR[41].

9.47

If someone is facing further charges, then the Home Office will often pause any pending deportation process after the first stage until the new matter has been resolved, although that is not a fixed rule[42].

Effect of a deportation order

9.48

When a deportation is made, this requires the person named in it to leave the United Kingdom. It also provides legal authority to detain someone until they

---

41 In non-automatic deportation cases (under the Immigration Act 1971) where representations are made, a deportation order can only be made after any appeal has been concluded and the deadline for any further appeal has passed (unless the claim is certified).

42 Home Office – 'Pending prosecutions' v1.0 (10 August 2022), at pages 6-8.

are removed The order will generally remain in force unless and until it is revoked by the Home Secretary[43].

What happens after sentence

9.49

The question of what happens after sentence is for the Secretary of State and, potentially, the Immigration Tribunals. However, a brief overview is set out of 'what happens next'.

9.50

Those who are convicted of a criminal offence can be divided into three categories;

(a) Those sentenced to four or more years in prison

(b) Those sentenced to more than 12 months, but less than four years

(c) Other categories of offenders

Grounds of appeal

9.51

Any appeal must be couched in terms of the possible grounds of appeal. In practice this will likely be on the basis that the person is a refugee and/or that removal would breach their rights under Arts 3 and/or 8[44].

9.52

In most cases, the question for the Tribunal will be whether the appellant can be deported, or whether either the conditions in his home country, or his ties to the United Kingdom, precludes this. It is worth bearing in mind that, in relation to Foreign National Offenders where a deportation order is made (so not including those cases that the Home Office decide not to proceed with), almost 30% of appeals are allowed[45].

9.53

In relation to the first point, the law is relatively straightforward in that however serious the offending has been it is not possible to remove someone to a country where they will be at risk of Art 3 mistreatment (torture, or to inhuman or

43 Exceptions are rare and include when the person becomes a British Citizen or they were made subject of an order as a family member of someone who was the subject of an order, and that order falls away, or the relationship is no longer a qualifying one (eg, the child has turned 18, or the marriage ends).

44 It is possible to Judicially Review the decision to deport on the basis that that was not lawful.

45 Between 2008 and June 2021 6,042 out of 21,521 appeals were allowed by the First-tier Tribunal (Border Force transparency data; Q4 2022).

degrading treatment of punishment). Whether or not they will qualify for refugee status is more complicated. Even if there is a Convention Reason and they would otherwise be a refugee, then they will not qualify unless[46] (inter alia):

> '(iii) there are no reasonable grounds for regarding them as a danger to the security of the United Kingdom in accordance with Article 33(2) of the Refugee Convention; and
>
> (iv) having been convicted by a final judgment of a particularly serious crime, they do not constitute a danger to the community of the United Kingdom in accordance with Article 33(2) of the Refugee Convention as defined in Section 72 of the Nationality Immigration and Asylum Act 2002.'

9.54

However, for someone who is trying to resist deportation on the grounds of their private or family life, the situation is more complex. There is a vast amount of caselaw, with the issues being considered and reconsidered on a large number of occasions, so again this is a very brief overview (and will likely be out of date as soon as it is published).

9.55

The guiding legislation is in the NIAA 2002;

> **'117C Article 8: additional considerations in cases involving foreign criminals**
>
> (1) The deportation of foreign criminals is in the public interest.
>
> (2) The more serious the offence committed by a foreign criminal, the greater is the public interest in deportation of the criminal.
>
> (3) In the case of a foreign criminal ("C") who has not been sentenced to a period of imprisonment of four years or more, the public interest requires C's deportation unless Exception 1 or Exception 2 applies.
>
> (4) Exception 1 applies where—
>
> (a) C has been lawfully resident in the United Kingdom for most of C's life,
>
> (b) C is socially and culturally integrated in the United Kingdom, and
>
> (c) there would be very significant obstacles to C's integration into the country to which C is proposed to be deported.

46 Para 334 Immigration Rules.

(5) Exception 2 applies where C has a genuine and subsisting relationship with a qualifying partner, or a genuine and subsisting parental relationship with a qualifying child, and the effect of C's deportation on the partner or child would be unduly harsh.

(6) In the case of a foreign criminal who has been sentenced to a period of imprisonment of at least four years, the public interest requires deportation unless there are very compelling circumstances, over and above those described in Exceptions 1 and 2.

(7) The considerations in subsections (1) to (6) are to be taken into account where a court or tribunal is considering a decision to deport a foreign criminal only to the extent that the reason for the decision was the offence or offences for which the criminal has been convicted.'

The exceptions

9.56

There are two exceptions. Exception one protects those who have been in the UK lawfully for a long period of time and integrated themselves here, and who can show that there would be 'very significant obstacles' to him re-integrating in his home country.

9.57

Exception two protects someone who has a 'genuine and subsisting' relationship with either a qualifying partner[47] or a qualifying child[48] where the consequences on them of deportation would be 'unduly harsh'. To assess that, a decision maker should look at both the consequences if the partner or child goes to the deportee's home country, or they remain and the person leaves.

9.58

This test is a high one, especially where the sentence passed that triggered the deportation was four years or more when 'very compelling circumstance over and above those described' in the exceptions must be shown.

9.59

The decision is always a very fact specific one, with there often being a variety of different forms evidence not just from the appellant and his friends and family, but often psychologists, social workers and the like. As stated, and any list

---

47 A qualifying partner is a 'partner' who is either a British citizen or settled in the UK (s 117D(1)).

48 A qualifying child is someone aged under 18 who is either British or who has lived in the UK for at least seven years (s 117D(1)). See *R (RK) v SSHD (s117B(6); "parental relationship"* [2016] UKUT 00031 (IAC) for the meaning of 'parental relationship'.

of cases will likely be out of date as soon as it is prepared. Having said that, as of publication, a good overview (with reference to other cases of relevance) can be found from *Sanambar v SSHD*[49] and *HA (Iraq) & Othrs v SSHD*[50].

9.60

Whilst the deportation order gives the Home Secretary the power to remove the subject of it, the order does not expire once someone has been removed from the United Kingdom (or if they leave voluntarily). It will remain in force indefinitely, or until it is revoked. Leave to enter cannot be granted whilst it is extant, although an application can be made for its revocation at the same time as an application is made for entry clearance.

9.61

In those circumstances, the Secretary of State will consider all the circumstances of the case in deciding whether to revoke the order[51]. Where the person received a sentence of four years or more then 'the continuation of a deportation order against that person will be the proper course' forever (unless there are exceptional compelling circumstances, or a refusal would be a breach of the ECHR or the Refugee Convention)[52]. Where there was a sentence of less than four years then the period of time is ten years[53].

British citizens

9.62

As noted, British citizens cannot be deported, even if they are dual nationals. However, for those who have acquired nationality, there is power to remove someone's British citizenship. This can be on the basis that the grant was a nullity (usually on the basis that the applicant lied about their identity), or deprived of it on the grounds of fraud, false representations, concealment of a material fact or because it is conducive to the public good[54]. Although this is a power that has been used more frequently in recent years, it is still relatively uncommon.

EEA citizens

9.63

The situation with EEA citizens and their family members is complex and their position will depend on their history and what rights (if any) they had

49 [2021] UKSC 30.
50 [2022] UKSC 22.
51 Para 390 Immigration Rules.
52 Para 391(a) Immigration Rules.
53 Para 391(b) Immigration Rules.
54 BNA 1981, s 40 .

accrued prior to 31 December 2020. If they do not have immigration lawyers, then clients should be advised to seek such representation, who will be able to provide comprehensive advice on this point.

Early removal from the United Kingdom

9.64

There are two schemes under which a Foreign National Prisoner can be removed from the United Kingdom; TERS and ERS. These are distinct from deportation.

Tariff Expiry Removal Scheme ('TERS')

9.65

This scheme is for any prisoner serving an indeterminate sentence (Life or IPP). Someone will be eligible for removal at their Tariff Expiry Date. All foreign national prisoners who are liable to be removed[55] from the United Kingdom will be considered for TERS. The decision is made by PPCS (the Public Protection Casework Section, a division of the Ministry of Justice) rather than the Home Secretary.

9.66

This process can (and often will) run alongside the consideration by the Parole Board of a person's case, although these are two separate schemes with the Parole Board having no input into the decision under TERS. The following categories of people will usually not be approved for TERS:

- Someone who has a confiscation order made against them, or is subject to confiscation proceedings
- Someone who has outstanding criminal charges against them
- If there is clear evidence suggesting that the individual is actively planning to commit further criminal offences, including plans to evade immigration control and return to the UK unlawfully
- Someone serving a sentence for a terrorism or terrorism-related offence
- Where to allow removal of the individual from prison would undermine public confidence in the criminal justice system

9.67

In order for someone to be removed, there must have been a decision to deport made and, a signed deportation order created. In addition, there must not be

55 Defined in Criminal Justice Act 2003, s 259.

any outstanding immigration appeals and the prisoner must have the relevant travel documentation.

Early Removal Scheme ('ERS')

9.68

Almost all fixed-term prisoners[56] who are foreign nationals and are liable to be removed[57] from the United Kingdom can be removed before their earliest release date[58], provided that they have served the 'minimum pre-removal custodial period'. This is the longer of half of the requisite custodial period and the requisite custodial period less a year. The consequence of that is that someone serving a determinate sentence of less than four years will be eligible after serving a quarter of the sentence, whereas someone serving a sentence of over four years will be eligible after serving half, minus a year.

9.69

By way of example, someone serving a determinate sentence of two years would be eligible after six months (half of the 'requisite custodial period' which would be the year that they would normally serve), whilst someone serving a determinate sentence of ten years would be eligible after four years). Someone who is serving an extended sentence of nine years, consisting of a custodial period of six years and a three-year extended licence, would be eligible after three years (the four years that they would have to serve before being eligible for release, minus 12 months).

9.70

Someone who is a 'terrorist prisoner' is ineligible for the scheme, as will someone who has outstanding criminal cases or a confiscation order, but otherwise each case should be considered on its merits. However, there is no guarantee that it will be granted, although the presumption is that it will. The decision maker will be the Prison Governor who will consider public safety and a number of other factors. The following circumstances will be indicative of an 'exceptional case' where ERS should be refused[59]:

- clear evidence that the prisoner is planning further crime, including plans to evade immigration control and return to the UK unlawfully;
- evidence of violence or threats of violence, in prison, on a number of occasions;
- dealing in class A drugs in custody;

---

56 Defined in Criminal Justice Act 2003, s 237 as effectively meaning a prisoner who is not serving a life sentence or a sentence of IPP. This will include those serving extended sentences.

57 Defined in Criminal Justice Act 2003, s 259.

58 Criminal Justice Act 2003, s 260.

59 PSI 04/2013 – Early Removal of Foreign National Prisoners, at [2.13].

- serving a sentence for a terrorism or terrorism-connected offence (not being an offence listed in the Criminal Justice Act 2003, Sch 19ZA);
- other matters of similar gravity relating to public safety;
- where early removal under the ERS would undermine public confidence in the criminal justice system; or
- where there are extant extradition proceedings.

9.71

If the application is refused, then the prisoner will be eligible for release on Home Detention Curfew. There is no formal right of appeal to a court against the refusal, but the prisoner can appeal internally in the prison with the decision generally being reconsidered by another Governor of a higher grade that the original decision maker. The remedy thereafter is judicial review.

9.72

If someone returns to the United Kingdom following a removal under ERS then they will be liable to serve the outstanding custodial period.

Ancillary orders on sentencing

Forfeiture and Deprivation

Deprivation

9.73

Where a defendant is convicted of an offence, the court has the power to make a deprivation order in certain circumstances. As is clear from the name, the order deprives the defendant of the property but does not forfeit it (as is the case with a forfeiture order below).

9.74

This can only apply to property that was[60]:

- Lawfully seized from the defendant, or
- Was in the possession of the defendant when they were 'apprehended' for it, or
- When a summons to court was issued.

9.75

This is subject to the further requirement[61] that the property:

60 Sentencing Act 2020, s 153(2).
61 Sentencing Act 2020, s 153(3).

- Has been used to commit any offence, or
- Has been used to facilitate the commission of any offence, or
- Was intended to be used for either purpose

9.76

Facilitation has a wider meaning than it does in the IA 1971, s 25 offence, and includes[62]:

> 'taking any steps after the offence has been committed for the purpose of—
>
> (a) disposing of any property to which the offence relates, or
>
> (b) avoiding apprehension or detection.'

9.77

The court must take account of the value of the property and the likely impact on the defendant before making an order[63]. The order should be seen as part of the sentence and be taken into account in considering the overall sentence to be passed[64]. It is necessary for there to be a proper evidential foundation for any order including, if applicable, the calling of oral evidence[65].

9.78

An order can (probably[66]) be made even if the property does not belong to a defendant, although the criminal court is not generally the place to make a detailed assessment of complex civil matters and an order should only be made in a clear-cut case[67]. This would apply especially where there is a vehicle that is subject to a hire-purchase agreement[68], which is where the provisions of the IA 1971, s 25C would be applicable.

9.79

Taking an example of someone who brings a would be illegal entrant into the United Kingdom hidden in their car, where the car is owned by the defendant it would likely that a deprivation order would be suitable (subject to consideration of the other sentences passed). However, where the car was subject to a hire-purchase agreement, or the driver was in the course of his employment and the

62 Sentencing Act 2020, s 153(4).
63 Sentencing Act 2020, s 155(1).
64 *Price* [2015] EWCA Crim 318, [2015] 2 Cr App R(S) 8.
65 *Jones* [2017] EWCA Crim 2192, [2018] 1 Cr App R(S) 35.
66 *Hall* [2014] EWCA Crim 2413, [2015] RTR 9 – 'We do not have to decide, and it should not be understood that we have considered, whether there may be any circumstances in which s143 could be used to deprive an offender of possession of a vehicle, even if the offender does not have title to the vehicle. That may need to be examined on another day in another case'.
67 *Troth* (1980) 71 Cr App R 1; 'we consider that forfeiture orders ought not to be made except in simple, uncomplicated cases. If a person has an interest in an object which is not free from encumbrances then difficulties are likely to arise. Difficulties have arisen in this case'.
68 *Kearney* [2011] EWCA Crim 826, [2011] 2 Cr App R(S) 106.

car owned by his employer, it would likely be the case that a deprivation order is inappropriate (an order could be made under the IA 1971, s 25C in those circumstances).

9.80

When the court makes a deprivation order, it will be generally be for the police to take possession of the property, although there is provision in an immigration context for this to be changed to the Home Secretary;

> **'156 Deprivation order: property to be taken into possession of police or Secretary of State**
>
> (1) Where the court makes a deprivation order in respect of an offender for an offence, this section applies to the property to which the order relates.
>
> (2) If the court considers that the offence—
>
> (a) related to immigration or asylum, or
>
> (b) was committed for a purpose in connection with immigration or asylum,
>
> it may order that the property is to be taken into the possession of the Secretary of State.
>
> (3) Property that is taken into the possession of the Secretary of State by virtue of subsection (2) is to be treated for the purposes of section 26 of the UK Borders Act 2007 (disposal of property) as property that has come into the possession of the Secretary of State as mentioned in subsection (1)(b) of that section[69].
>
> (4) Unless the court makes an order under subsection (2), the property is to be taken into the possession of the police (if it is not already in their possession).'

9.81

A court should normally make an order under s 156(2) where the property was seized by an Immigration Officer, or by a police officer in a case that is an immigration one. Therefore with the example of the person smuggling in another in their own car, and a deprivation order is made, the Prosecution should invite the court to make this order.

69 This reads as follows;
Disposal of property
(1) In this section "property" means property which—
(a) has come into the possession of an immigration officer, or
(b) has come into the possession of the Secretary of State in the course of, or in connection with, a function under the Immigration Acts.

9.82

Where an order is made, a third party who wishes to establish a claim over the property can apply under the Police (Property) Act 1897 to establish ownership. In a case where a s 156(2) order is made then the third party can apply to the magistrates' court under the UK Borders Act 2007, s 26(2). The procedure is similar to that under the Police (Property) Act 1897, and the Secretary of State has made Regulations under s 26(5)[70]. There would appear to be power for an application for conversion in the civil court as an alternative[71], even where these are started more than six months after the order.

Forfeiture

9.83

The Sentencing Act preserves the power of forfeiture under a number of different Acts passed prior to 2020[72]. A forfeiture order not only deprives the defendant of their interest in the property, but transfers the ownership of the property. One such cases is in relation to a 'ship, vehicle or aircraft' connected with an offence under the [73] IA 1971, ss 25 and 25A where the power of forfeiture under the IA 1971, s 25C(2)(e) is preserved under the Sentencing Act 2020.

9.84

The power is limited to the following people for ships or aircrafts[74]:

(a) owned the ship or aircraft at the time the offence was committed,

(b) was at that time a director, secretary or manager of a company which owned the ship or aircraft,

(c) was at that time in possession of the ship or aircraft under a hire-purchase agreement,

(d) was at that time a director, secretary or manager of a company which was in possession of the ship or aircraft under a hire-purchase agreement,

(e) was at that time a charterer of the ship or aircraft, or

(f) committed the offence while acting as captain of the ship or aircraft.

---

70 Immigration (Disposal of Property) Regulations 2008/786.

71 *O'Leary International v Chief Constable of North Wales* [2012] EWHC 1516 (Admin), [2013] RTR 14

72 See the list at Sentencing Act 2020, s 160.

73 The Sentencing Act 2020 also refers to offences under s 25B, but this was repealed on 31 December 2020 for future offences. Whilst IA 1971, s 25C refers only to IA 1971, ss 25 and 25A, IA 1971, s 25B will continue to apply for orders made under the EEA Regulations 2016 (including when the order was made after 31 December 2020 under the preserved power in Reg 7(1)(a)(i) or (ii) Citizens' Rights (Application Deadline and Temporary Protection) (EU Exit) Regulations 2020, SI 2020/1209) by virtue of Reg 5(7)(b) Immigration and Social Security Co-ordination (EU Withdrawal) Act 2020 (Consequential, Saving, Transitional and Transitory Provisions) (EU Exit) Regulations 2020/1309.

74 IA 1971, s 25C(3).

9.85

Subsections (a)-(d) apply to a vehicle in the same terms but, instead of (e) and (f), it applies to someone who 'was driving the vehicle in the course of the commission of the offence'[75]. With ships and aircraft, there is a further restriction:

> '(4) But in a case to which subsection (3)(a) or (b) does not apply, forfeiture may be ordered only—
>
> (a) in the case of a ship, if subsection (5) or (6) applies;
>
> (b) in the case of an aircraft, if subsection (5) or (7) applies.
>
> (5) This subsection applies where—
>
> (a) in the course of the commission of the offence, the ship or aircraft carried more than 20 illegal entrants[76], and
>
> (b) a person who, at the time the offence was committed, owned the ship or aircraft or was a director, secretary or manager of a company which owned it, knew or ought to have known of the intention to use it in the course of the commission of an offence under section 25 or 25A.'

9.86

The effect of this is to recognise the fact that most ship and aircraft are operated commercially as part of a legitimate enterprise and to ensure a fair balance is drawn between having an effective enforcement regime whilst not causing financial loss to a legitimate business who are not culpable.

9.87

The power only exists if the defendant is 'convicted on indictment'[77]. If the plea is entered in the magistrates' court and sentenced there, then it would appear that a deprivation order would be the appropriate one (if applicable). However, where someone is committed for sentence, then the Crown Court has the power to 'deal with the offender in any way in which it could deal with the offender if the offender had been convicted of the offence on indictment before the court'[78], which includes by making a forfeiture order.

9.88

The court must give the opportunity to someone who claims an interest in the ship, aircraft or vehicle to be heard before making an order[79]. The magistrates' court will have jurisdiction over any property forfeited to determine an application under the UK Borders Act 2007, s 26.

---

75 IA 1971, s 25C(2).

76 As defined in IA 1971, s 25C(9).

77 IA 1971, s 25C(1).

78 Sentencing Act 2020, s 21(2)(b) (or s 22(2)(b) for youths).

79 IA 1971, s 25C(8) .

9.89

In *Cuthbertson*[80] the House of Lords held that there was no power under the Misuse of Drugs Act 1971 to order forfeiture where the offence indicted was a conspiracy, which would appear to apply to the IA 1971, s 25C provisions. However, with an attempt, the Criminal Attempts Act 1981, s 2(2)(h) provides that a forfeiture order can be made.

9.90

Where someone is arrested for an offence under the IA 1971, s 25 or 25A the ship, aircraft or vehicle can be lawfully held until the conclusion of any proceedings on the authority of an Immigration Officer of the rank of at least a Chief Immigration Officer or a constable. Application can be made by a person with an interest in the ship, aircraft or vehicle for its release. A court that grants the application can require a security or surety to ensure that if a forfeiture order is made then it will be made available to the court[81].

9.91

It can be seen that the power to order forfeiture is limited in terms of the venue where the plea was entered, but also as to when an order can be made, relative to a deprivation order. Care will need to be taken to ensure that there is actually power to make a forfeiture order, or whether the proper order is a deprivation order. The statute is silent as to what happens to property that is forfeited[82].

9.92

Practitioners should note that there is a similar power relating to the forfeiture of a 'ship, vehicle or aircraft' used for an offence under the Modern Slavery Act 2015, s 2 (human trafficking). This also only applies where the defendant is convicted on indictment.

Financial orders

Introduction

9.93

There are a number of financial orders that a court can make when sentencing someone. There are of both a mandatory and discretionary nature. A brief overview is set out below, but if further details are needed, then reference to a specialist criminal text should be made.

---

80 (1980) 2 Cr App R(S) 214.

81 IA 1971, s 25D.

82 Contrast with Misuse of Drugs Act 1971, s 27 where the court can order that anything forfeited can be ordered to be 'either destroyed or dealt with in such other manner as the court may order'.

9.94

As with other provisions, the rules relating to youths are different, and care should be taken if the defendant is under 18.

Surcharge

9.95

Whenever a court sentences someone, there is an automatic 'surcharge' (not, as it is often referred to, a 'victim surcharge') that must be imposed[83] in most circumstances. This applies in its current form to anyone sentenced after 14 April 2020.The amounts are set out in an SI (currently the Criminal Justice Act (2003) Surcharge Order 2012, although this will change from time to time).

9.96

The exact amount that will be ordered will depend on the details of the rest of the sentence. In addition, there are certain circumstances where the surcharge is not mandatory (for example, where a compensation order or confiscation order is made. This does not include the situation where a defendant is penniless and could not afford the order).

Costs

9.97

Where a defendant pleads guilty or is convicted after trial, it is likely that the prosecution will ask for 'costs'. The court can make an order in such sums as is thought to be 'just and reasonable'[84] and should generally make an order where a defendant can afford to pay.

9.98

Given that almost all defendants appearing before the courts are of limited means, the CPS website contains a 'scale of costs' setting out the typical amounts that will be charged[85]. Different considerations will apply where there is a defendant who is able to satisfy a large costs order.

Confiscation

9.99

Any offence from which a defendant receives a benefit can be subjected to confiscation proceedings under the Proceeds of Crime Act 2002. This is an

83 Sentencing Act 2020, s 42.

84 Prosecution of Offences Act 1985, s 18.

85 This is currently at – https://www.cps.gov.uk/legal-guidance/costs-annex-1.

extremely complex (and voluminous) area of law which is outside the scope of this book.

Prohibition on acting as an OISC advisor

9.100

Someone convicted of an offence under the IA 1971, s 25 or s 26(1)(d) or (g) is disqualified from registering as an immigration adviser with OISC[86].

9.101

Note that this does not apply to conviction under s 25A, or the dishonesty offences under s 24A, although it is not clear why that would be. It may be that this is surprising, especially in relation to the s 25A[87] offence where the conduct is similar, with the gravamen being arranging the circumvention of immigration controls by others. However, it is likely that the Immigration Commissioner would refuse an application for registration made by someone with a conviction for that offence, or for any of the imprisonable offences under the IA 1971.

Disqualification from driving

9.102

Whilst the power to disqualify someone from driving has historically been used against people convicted of driving offences, there is now power to disqualify anyone convicted of a criminal offence under the Sentencing Act 2020, s 163:

> **'163 Driving disqualification: availability for any offence**
>
> (1) A driving disqualification order is available to the court by or before which an offender is convicted of an offence if—
>
> (a) the offence was committed on or after 1 January 1998, and
>
> (b) the court has been notified by the Secretary of State that the power to make such orders is exercisable by the court (and the notice has not been withdrawn).
>
> (2) Where a driving disqualification order is available by virtue of this section, the court may make a driving disqualification order whether or not it also deals with the offender for the offence in any other way.'

86 IAA 1999, Sch 6, para 4A(c).

87 IA 1971, s 25A – helping asylum seekers arrive in the United Kingdom – see Chapter 5.

9.103

This makes a disqualification part of the overall sentence. There does not need to be any connection between the offence and driving, although that is generally the case[88]. Practitioners should be aware that there is a specific criminal offence under the IA1971, s 24C of driving whilst unlawfully in the United Kingdom. However, this is not yet in force, and it is not known when it will be.

88 See, as examples, *Cliff* [2004] EWCA Crim 3139, [2005] 2 Cr App R(S) 22 – affray, but where the defendant had admitted driving whilst under the influence of drugs and alcohol, and *Griffin* [2019] EWCA Crim 563, [2019] 2 Cr App R(S) 32 – perverting the course of justice by giving false names in order to avoid penalty points and disqualification.

10 Criminal procedure

Introduction

10.1

This chapter provides an overview of the points of procedure that may arise in immigration cases in particular.

Time limits for prosecution

10.2

The general rule is that there is no temporal limitation on bringing an either way or indictable only criminal offence[1]. However, the general rule for summary only offences is that a 'magistrates' court shall not try an information … unless the information was laid … within 6 months from the time when the offence was committed'[2]. This is a long-standing principle, although it is not easy to determine the rationale behind it. In another context, Lord Rodger stated that:

> 'It is not always easy to discern the policy behind the provisions limiting the time for bringing proceedings … Parliament takes the rather broader view that, if the offences are worth prosecuting at all at summary level, they are only worth prosecuting if they come to light and can be dealt with soon after they are committed, in accordance with the prescribed time-limit[3].'

10.3

However, there are exceptions in relation to certain summary only immigration offences set out in the IA 1971, s 28 as follows:

> **'28 Proceedings.**
>
> (1) Where the offence is one to which, under section 24(3) or 26 above, an extended time limit for prosecutions is to apply, then—
>
> (a) an information relating to the offence may in England and Wales be tried by a magistrates' court if it is laid within six months after the commission of the offence, or if it is laid

1 This is subject to any statutory exception. For example, Treason Act 1695, s 5 imposed a requirement that an indictment for certain offences of treason must be preferred within three years, although there may be earlier examples.

2 Magistrates' Courts Act 1980, s 127.

3 *R v J* [2004] UKHL 42, [2005] 1 Cr App R 19.

> within three years after the commission of the offence and not more than two months after the date certified by an officer of police above the rank of chief superintendent to be the date on which evidence sufficient to justify proceedings came to the notice of an officer of the police force to which he belongs.'

General exemption – s 28(1)

10.4

There are similar examples in a number of other statutes, mostly in relation to quasi-regulatory offences. The consequence is that the six-month time limit in the Magistrates' Courts Act 1980, s 127 does not apply. Instead, an offence can be prosecuted if the prosecution is started within six months of commission, or within three years of the offence, provided it is started no more than two months after the date certified by an officer of police above the rank of chief superintendent. Even though that investigations will now be led by the Home Office, this requirement for the police to sign has not been changed. It is unlikely that the court would allow the time limit to be extended by accepting an argument that the police force were not aware of the information as it was not presented to them by the Home Office and obtaining the benefit of the extension.

10.5

The word 'tried' in s 28(1)(a) means the trial itself, rather than when a plea of not guilty is entered. If there is a plea of not guilty, then a certificate signed after that will be valid[4].

10.6

By analogy with similar provisions in the Social Security Acts[5] and the Animal Welfare Regulations[6] that have been considered more recently, a valid certificate is likely to be conclusive of when sufficient evidence for a prosecution arose, subject to the ability to stay for an abuse of process in suitable cases[7]. The court in *R v Clerk to the Birmingham Justice, ex parte Offei* (1985) (unreported) proceeded on the basis that the magistrates would be bound by the certificate but would, in suitable cases, adjourn to allow a Judicial Review of the certificate. However, *Enaas v Dovey* [1986] CLY 1704 took the opposite view. This remains unresolved in the context of immigration offences, but it likely that the *Enaas v Dovey* would not be followed.

---

4 *Quazi v DPP* [1988] Crim LR 529.

5 *Azam v Epping Forest DC* [2009] EWHC 3177 (Admin).

6 *R (on the application of Chesterfield Poultry Ltd) v Sheffield Magistrates' Court* [2019] EWHC 2953 (Admin), [2020] 1 WLR 499.

7 The court in *ex parte Offei* proceeded on the basis that the magistrates would be bound by the certificate but would, in suitable cases, adjourn to allow a judicial review of the certificate. *Enaas v Dovey* [1986] CLY 1704 took the opposite view.

Evidence sufficient to justify a prosecution

10.7

This means more than information received or a belief that the person has committed the offence, but 'information which could be put before a court', and so a telephone call from a Home Office to a Police Officer (which would be inadmissible hearsay) was not sufficient, and the Officer was entitled to consider himself bound to wait for the evidence to be presented in writing[8].

10.8

Nowadays, if the investigation is triggered by the police receiving information about a suspect's immigration history from the Home Office, it is likely that sufficient material will be emailed to the police on the day of any conversation to satisfy the test. However, where someone is encountered by the police who suspect that a relevant offence may have been committed, that alone is unlikely to be sufficient.

10.9

In *ex parte Offei*, Mr Offei's valid leave expired on 11 April 1981 (and therefore, under the law as it then was[9], he committed the offence of overstaying contrary to s 24(1)(b)(i) the next day). Shortly after, he was interviewed by the police where he said that his leave had expired, but he had applied for an extension, which was still pending. He was not prosecuted until after his fresh application had been refused, whereafter there was further delay due to him moving address. A certificate was signed. However, the conviction was quashed as whilst the decision to await the outcome of the application may have been understandable, when Mr Offei stated in interview that his leave had expired, that was sufficient to evidence to justify a prosecution – 'The Act does not direct attention to whether it is justifiable to proceed, but to whether the evidence justifies proceedings'. This is important to consider in the situation where the CPS would, quite properly, wish there to be further investigations in relation to lines of enquiry that are raised to ensure that they comply with their obligations under the Code for Crown Prosecutors. That would not stop the clock running and an eye must be kept on the relevant time limits.

Offences to which the extended time limits apply

10.10

The time limit applies to the following offences: IA 1971, ss 24(1)(c) (remaining without leave), 26(1)(c) (false representation), and (d) (altering an official document).

---

8 *Enaas v Dovey* [1986] CLY 1704, applying *Osbourne* (1973) 57 Cr App R 297 which was decided in the context of the Judges Rules and the admissibility of confessions.

9 *Grant v Borg* [1982] 2 All ER 257, subsequently reversed by IA 1971, s 24(1A), brought in by IA 1988, s 6.

Other offences with different time limits

OISC

10.11

The OISC offence under IAA 1999, s 92B has an extended time limit in similar terms to the IA 1971, s 28(1). The extended period is two years rather than three years in s 28(1)(a), and the time period for action is then six months rather than two months in s 28(1)(a). In addition, it must by the Commissioner who certifies rather than a Chief Superintendent. Apart from the last requirement, it is unclear why there would be a difference.

10.12

A further difference is that the OISC offence requires the Commissioner to certify when the commission of the offence 'came to his notice', rather than the test under s 28(1)(a) which requires the Officer to determine when 'sufficient evidence to justify proceedings' came to the attention of one of his/her officers. Again, it is not clear why this difference exists (there is nothing in the explanatory notes, or the original Bill, to explain this) or whether, in practice, this will make any real difference.

Breach of immigration bail

10.13

There is a separate extended time limit for the offence under the IA 1971, s 24(1)(h) (breaching a condition of immigration bail without a reasonable excuse:

> '(1A) Where the offence is one to which, under section 24(3A), an extended time limit for prosecutions is to apply, then—
>
> (a) an information relating to the offence may in England and Wales be tried by a magistrates' court if it is laid—
>
> (i) within the period of six months beginning with the date of the commission of the offence, or
>
> (ii) within the period of three months beginning with the date when the person is first arrested for the offence or under paragraph 10 of Schedule 10 to the Immigration Act 2016 (arrest for breach of bail condition), if that period expires after the end of the period mentioned in sub-paragraph (i),'

10.14

The rationale for this is clear in that it may not be possible to determine whether there was a reasonable excuse until after the person has been arrested.

Geographical territorial limits

10.15

Historically, the general rule is that the courts of England and Wales exercises jurisdiction only over offences committed in England and Wales[10]:

> 'apart from those exceptional cases in which specific provision is made in regard to acts committed abroad, the whole body of the criminal law of England deals only with acts committed in England.'

10.16

However, as international travel has got more common, and modern technology has brought the world closer in ways that would have been unimaginable decades (let alone centuries) ago, crime will now routinely cross borders.

10.17

The sea surrounding the United Kingdom is UK 'territorial water'. The question of the exact point at which the land becomes the sea is complex, and unlikely to be of any significance in practice. Broadly, the boundary of the land and sea is typically taken as the place where the land meets the open sea according to the prevailing state of the tides. This is taken as the mean meridian tide line[11]. Any waters internal to that, are 'internal waters'.

10.18

Generally, the UK (and other states) territorial waters extend 12 nautical miles[12] from the low-water line around the coast[13]. Where this 'bumps up' against that of another state (as it does in the English Channel between the UK and France) then the dividing line is equidistant between the two states.

Jurisdiction over airplanes

10.19

The United Kingdom generally has jurisdiction over criminal offences committed on a aircraft in the following circumstances:

- Any aircraft in the airspace over the UK
- Any aircraft that has landed in the UK
- Any British-controlled aircraft outside

10 *Cox v Army Council* (1962) 46 Cr App R 258.

11 *Loose v Lynn Shellfish Ltd* [2016] UKSC 14, [2017] AC 599 at [62]–[67].

12 A nautical mile is 1,852 metres, rather than the 1,609 metres in the standard mile. So 12 nautical miles is 13.81 miles, or 22.22 km.

13 Territorial Sea Act 1987, s 1(1) and Territorial Sea (Baselines) Order 2014. This comes from the United Nations Convention on the Law of the Sea (Montego Bay, 1994).

- Any aircraft scheduled to land in the UK (but provided that it would be an offence both in the UK and in the country that the aircraft is registered)

10.20

In relation to the third and fourth case, the consent of the DPP is required.

Legislation

10.21

The main statute is the Civil Aviation Act 1982:

'92.— Application of criminal law to aircraft

(1) Any act or omission taking place on board a British-controlled aircraft or (subject to subsection (1A) below) a foreign aircraft while in flight elsewhere than in or over the United Kingdom which, if taking place in, or in a part of, the United Kingdom, would constitute an offence under the law in force in, or in that part of, the United Kingdom shall constitute that offence; but this subsection shall not apply to any act or omission which is expressly or impliedly authorised by or under that law when taking place outside the United Kingdom.

(1A) Subsection (1) above shall only apply to an act or omission which takes place on board a foreign aircraft where—

(a) the next landing of the aircraft is in the United Kingdom, and

(b) in the case of an aircraft registered in a country other than the United Kingdom, the act or omission would, if taking place there, also constitute an offence under the law in force in that country.

(1B) Any act or omission punishable under the law in force in any country is an offence under that law for the purposes of subsection (1A) above, however it is described in that law.

(2) Subject to any provision to the contrary in any Act passed after 14th July 1967, no proceedings for any offence under the law in force in, or in a part of, the United Kingdom committed on board an aircraft while in flight elsewhere than in or over the United Kingdom (other than an offence under, or under any instrument made under, any of the air navigation enactments) shall be instituted—

(a) in England and Wales, except by or with the consent of the Director of Public Prosecutions; or

(2A) The requirement in subsection (1A)(b) above shall be taken to be met unless, not later than the rules of court may provide, the defence serve on the prosecution a notice—

(a) stating that, on the facts as alleged with respect to the act or omission, the requirement is not in their opinion met;

(b) showing the grounds for their opinion; and

(c) requiring the prosecution to prove that it is met.

(2B) The court, if it thinks fit, may permit the defence to require the prosecution to prove that the requirement is met without the prior service of a notice under subsection (2A) above.

(2C) In the Crown Court the question whether the requirement is met is to be decided by the judge alone.

(3) For the purpose of conferring jurisdiction, any offence under the law in force in, or in a part of, the United Kingdom committed on board an aircraft in flight shall be deemed to have been committed in any place in the United Kingdom (or, as the case may be, in that part thereof) where the offender may for the time being be.

(4) For the purposes of this section the period during which an aircraft is in flight shall be deemed to include any period from the moment when power is applied for the purpose of the aircraft taking off on a flight until the moment when the landing run (if any) at the termination of that flight ends; and any reference in this section to an aircraft in flight shall include a reference to an aircraft during any period when it is on the surface of the sea or land but not within the territorial limits of any country.

(5) In this section, except where the context otherwise requires—

- *"aircraft"* means any aircraft, whether or not a British-controlled aircraft, other than—

  (a) a military aircraft; or

  (b) subject to section 101(1)(b) below, an aircraft which, not being a military aircraft, belongs to or is exclusively employed in the service of Her Majesty in right of the United Kingdom;

- *"the air navigation enactments"* mean the enactments contained in section 60 to 62, 72 to 77, 82 to 83, 87 and 97 of this Act;

- *"British-controlled aircraft"* means an aircraft—

  (a) which is for the time being registered in the United Kingdom; or

  (b) which is not for the time being registered in any country but in the case of which either the operator of the aircraft or each person entitled as owner to any legal or beneficial interest in it satisfies the following requirements, namely—

(i) that he is a person qualified to be the owner of a legal or beneficial interest in an aircraft registered in the United Kingdom; and

(ii) that he resides or has his principal place of business in the United Kingdom; or

(c) which, being for the time being registered in some other country, is for the time being chartered by demise to a person who, or to persons each of whom, satisfies the requirements aforesaid;

- *"foreign aircraft"* means any aircraft other than a British-controlled aircraft;
- *"military aircraft"* means—

(a) an aircraft of the naval, military or air forces of any country; or

(b) any other aircraft in respect of which there is in force a certificate issued in accordance with any Order in Council in force under section 60, 87, 89, 91, 101(1)(a) or 107(2) of this Act that the aircraft is to be treated for the purposes of that Order in Council as a military aircraft; and a certificate of the Secretary of State that any aircraft is or is not a military aircraft for the purposes of this section shall be conclusive evidence of the fact certified.'

10.22

Reference in this (and other) Acts to a place where a defendant 'may for the time being be', or 'is found' is likely to always be a reference to where he is at the time of trial[14].

Jurisdiction over spacecraft

10.23

There is also jurisdiction in England and Wales for criminal acts committed in a spacecraft launched from England and Wales[15]. For obvious reasons, this is a relatively niche provision that is unlikely to arise in practice.

14 'A man is 'found' wherever he is actually present, and the prisoner was found within the jurisdiction of the Central Criminal Court, and we are all of opinion that court had jurisdiction to try him' (Lopez (1858) 169 ER 1105).

15 Space Industry Act 2018, s 51.

Jurisdiction over offshore installations.

10.24

Any criminal act committed on an installation in the sea in UK territorial waters[16] or any designated areas of the continental shelf[17], or below or within 500 metres of it, is treated as being committed in the UK.

Jurisdiction over ships

Ships 'lying off the coast'

10.25

An English or Welsh court will have jurisdiction over a ship where it is[18]:

> 'situated on the coast of any sea or abuts on or projects into any bay, channel, lake, river or other navigable water the court shall have jurisdiction as respects offences under this Act over any vessel being on, or lying or passing off, that coast or being in or near that bay, channel, lake, river or navigable water and over all persons on board that vessel or for the time being belonging to it.'

General jurisdiction over offences committed on a ship

10.26

The Merchant Shipping Act 1995 provides for jurisdiction over crimes committed on a boat where the person is[19]:

> 'found within the jurisdiction of any court in any part of the United Kingdom which would have had jurisdiction in relation to the offence if it had been committed on board a United Kingdom ship within the limits of its ordinary jurisdiction to try the offence that court shall have jurisdiction to try the offence as if it had been so committed.'

10.27

If the person is a British citizen, then this will apply if they are charged with having committed an offence[20]:

---

16 Criminal Jurisdiction (Offshore Activities) Order 1987, art 3 (applies to acts within 500 metres of the installation) and Criminal Jurisdiction (Application to Offshore Renewable Energy Installations etc.) Order 2009, art 2 (applies to acts within a safety zone). This would include an offence of, for example, criminal damage to a windfarm or a common assault committed on board a ship as it was docking at the installation.

17 Continental Shelf Act 1964, s 1(7). A list of designated areas is contained in The Continental Shelf (Designation of Areas) Order 2013.

18 MSA 1995, s 280.

19 MSA 1995, s 281.

20 MSA 1995, s 281(a).

(i) on board any United Kingdom ship on the high seas,

(ii) in any foreign port or harbour, or

(iii) on board any foreign ship to which he does not belong[21];

10.28

For non-British citizens, there is a narrower jurisdiction – the English and Welsh courts will have jurisdiction where the offence is alleged to have been committed 'on board any United Kingdom ship on the high seas'[22].

10.29

'High Seas' in the context of jurisdiction over offences, means[23]:

> 'The expression 'high seas,' when used with reference to the jurisdiction of the Court of Admiralty, included all oceans, seas, bays, channels, rivers, creeks, and waters below low-water mark, and where great ships could go, with the exception only of such part of such oceans, etc., as were within the body of some county.'

British seamen

10.30

There is a separate jurisdiction to try British seaman in the following circumstances:

> **'282.— Offences committed by British seamen.**
>
> (1) Any act in relation to property or person done in or at any place (ashore or afloat) outside the United Kingdom by any master or seaman who at the time is employed in a United Kingdom ship, which, if done in any part of the United Kingdom, would be an offence under the law of any part of the United Kingdom, shall—
>
> (a) be an offence under that law, and
>
> (b) be treated for the purposes of jurisdiction and trial, as if it had been done within the jurisdiction of the Admiralty of England.
>
> (2) Subsection (1) above also applies in relation to a person who had been so employed within the period of three months expiring with the time when the act was done.
>
> (3) Subsections (1) and (2) above apply to omissions as they apply to acts.'

21 A person 'belongs' to the ship if they are a crew member, rather than being a passenger *Kelly* (1981) 73 Cr App R 310.

22 MSA 1995, s 281(b).

23 *The Mecca* [1895] P 95, at page 107.

Other instances of extra-territorial effect

10.31

As well as the general principles, some offences have specific jurisdictional extensions attached to them. For example, a drug trafficking offence committed on board any British ship will come within the jurisdiction of the British courts[24], with there being a wider jurisdiction over any offence of (broadly speaking) possessing or importing controlled drugs[25].

10.32

Specific examples of relevance in the immigration context are the facilitation offences (IA 1971, ss 25 and 25A) where the offence 'applies to things done whether inside or outside the United Kingdom'[26], and the ID Document offences[27] where any 'act or omission or other event (including any result of one or more acts or omissions) proof of which is required for conviction of the offence' 'occurred in England and Wales'[28].

Territorial Waters Jurisdiction Act 1878

Jurisdiction of the Admiralty – foreign nationals on foreign ships

10.33

Historically, offences committed on the seas outside of England and Wales fell within the jurisdiction of the Admiralty. This jurisdiction was similar to, but not the same as, the common law. There was an Admiralty Court that exercised that jurisdiction, although over time this waned.

10.34

The current position in relation to criminal cases is set out in the Senior Courts Act 1981:

> **'46.— Exclusive jurisdiction of Crown Court in trial on indictment.**
>
> (1) All proceedings on indictment shall be brought before the Crown Court.

---

24 CJ(IC)A 1990, s 18.

25 CJ(IC)A 1990, s 19. This applies to any British ship, any unregistered ship, or any ship registered under Art 17 United Nations Convention against Illicit Traffic in Narcotic Drugs and Psychotropic Substances (Vienna, 20 December 1988).

26 IA 1971, ss 25(4) and 25A(4). See also the Criminal Law Consolidation Act 1861 which extended jurisdiction for a number of offences including some under the Offences Against the Person Act 1861 and what is now the Theft Act 1968 and the Criminal Damage Act 1971.

27 CJA 1993, ss 1(2)(ca) and 2. Section 1 contains a number of other offences that are 'Group A' offences.

28 CJA 1993, s 2(1) and (3).

(2) The jurisdiction of the Crown Court with respect to proceedings on indictment shall include jurisdiction in proceedings on indictment for offences wherever committed, and in particular proceedings on indictment for offences within the jurisdiction of the Admiralty of England.

46A.— Offences committed on ships and abroad.

(1) Sections 280, 281 and 282 of the Merchant Shipping Act 1995 (offences on ships and abroad by British citizens and others) apply in relation to other offences under the law of England and Wales as they apply in relation to offences under that Act or instruments under that Act.'

10.35

It is an open question as to whether the reference to the 'jurisdiction of the Admiralty' in s 46(2) means that the Crown Court is the *sole* court that can arbitrate on offences within the jurisdiction of the Admiralty or whether, when a court is called upon to arbitrate on a matter within the jurisdiction of the Admiralty that is to be heard on indictment, this has to be heard by the Crown Court. The current version of the Territorial Waters Jurisdiction Act 1878, s 4 (see below) appears to be clear that there is a jurisdiction in the magistrates' court, although this has not been ruled upon yet by the courts.

10.36

The importance of the distinction is that if the former is correct, then the magistrates' court would have no jurisdiction to try a summary or either way matter.

The 1878 Act

10.37

On 17 February 1876 the Franconia (a German ship carrying mail from Germany to the West Indies) crashed into the Strathclyde (a British ship travelling to India) a short while after the latter had set off from Dover, and whilst it was within UK Territorial Waters. Just over half of the seventy passengers and crew of the Strathclyde drowned.

10.38

The German skipper of The Franconia stood trial at the Central Criminal Court for the Manslaughter of one of the Strathclyde's passengers[29], and was convicted. However, his conviction was subsequently overturned[30] on the basis that as a foreign national on a foreign ship within UK territorial waters, the English court had no jurisdiction over his offending.

29 The proceedings are available at 'Old Bailey Online'.
30 *R v Keyn (The Franconia)* (1876) 2 Ex D 63.

10.39

To close this lacuna, Parliament quickly passed the Territorial Waters Jurisdiction Act 1878. As amended, the relevant parts read as follows:

> '**2. Amendment of law as to jurisdiction of the Admiral.**
>
> An offence committed by a person, whether he is or is not a subject of Her Majesty, on the open sea within the territorial waters of Her Majesty's dominions, is an offence within the jurisdiction of the Admiral, although it may have been committed on board or by means of a foreign ship, and the person who committed such offence may be arrested, tried, and punished accordingly.
>
> **3. Restriction on institution of proceedings for punishment of offence.**
>
> Proceedings for the trial and punishment of a person who is not a subject of Her Majesty, and who is charged with any such offence as is declared by this Act to be within the jurisdiction of the Admiral, shall not be instituted in any court of the United Kingdom, except with the consent of one of Her Majesty's Principal Secretaries of State, and on his certificate that the institution of such proceedings is in his opinion expedient …
>
> **4. Provisions as to procedure.**
>
> On the trial of any person who is not a subject of Her Majesty for an offence declared by this Act to be within the jurisdiction of the Admiral, it shall not be necessary to aver in any indictment or information on such trial that such consent or certificate of the Secretary of State … as is required by this Act has been given, and the fact of the same having been given shall be presumed unless disputed by the defendant at the trial; and the production of a document purporting to be signed by one of Her Majesty's Principal Secretaries of State as respects the United Kingdom … shall be sufficient evidence for all the purposes of this Act of the consent and certificate required by this Act.
>
> Any stage of proceedings—
>
> (a) before the summary trial of the offence; or
>
> (b) before the offender has been sent for trial for the offence,
>
> shall not be deemed proceedings for the trial of the offence committed by such offender for the purposes of the said consent and certificate under this Act.
>
> **7. Definitions.**
>
> In this Act, unless there is something inconsistent in the context, the following expressions shall respectively have the meanings herein-after assigned to them; (that is to say,)

> "*The jurisdiction of the Admiral,*" as used in this Act, includes the jurisdiction of the Admiralty of England and Ireland, or either of such jurisdictions as used in any Act of Parliament; and for the purpose of arresting any person charged with an offence declared by this Act to be within the jurisdiction of the Admiral, the territorial waters adjacent to the United Kingdom, or any other part of Her Majesty's dominions, shall be deemed to be within the jurisdiction of any judge, magistrate, or officer having power within such United Kingdom, or other part of Her Majesty's dominions, to issue warrants for arresting or to arrest persons charged with offences committed within the jurisdiction of such judge, magistrate, or officer:
>
> "*United Kingdom*" includes the Isle of Man, the Channel Islands, and other adjacent islands:
>
> "*Offence*" as used in this Act means an act neglect or default of such a description as would, if committed within the body of a county in England, be punishable on indictment according to the law of England for the time being in force;
>
> "*Ship*" includes every description of ship, boat, or other floating craft:
>
> "*Foreign ship*" means any ship which is not a British ship.'

10.40

Section 2 and 3 struck a balance between the need for people such as Captain Keyn to be prosecuted, whilst respecting the general principle that the courts will be cautious about assuming jurisdiction over foreign nationals, whether from friendly countries or not. Section 3 provides a 'safety-valve' that ensures that a person will not be prosecuted unless there is consideration by someone who is able to take account of the wider political context and any potential damage to international relations that may follow.

10.41

This is not a provision that has been considered much by the courts of England and Wales. It is not clear if the requirement for consent is derogable[31], or what the consequence of a failure to obtain consent may be. From the words of the statute, it would appear that the DPP or Attorney-General cannot give consent (as they would do in the vast majority of cases where consent is required).

10.42

Practitioners will need to consider this wherever they have a client who is a foreign national on board a foreign ship, whatever offence they are charged with.

31 See *Carltona Ltd v Commissioners of Works* [1943] 2 All ER 560 for the origin of the 'Carltona Principle' that in many cases a consent vested in a Secretary of State can be exercised by 'responsible officials of the department'.

What offences are covered?

10.43

The definition of 'offence' in the Territorial Waters Jurisdiction Act 1878, s7 makes it clear that it only applies to indicatable (ie, either way and indictable only) offences. This does not include offences such as common assault, which are only triable on indictment in specific circumstances[32]. In those cases, it is likely that it would be concluded that the English and Welsh courts have no jurisdiction over a summary only offence committed by a non-British national in a non-British boat.

Attempts and conspiracy

10.44

If the substantive offence is one for which consent is required, then it will be required before an attempt is prosecuted (and vice versa)[33]. However, with a conspiracy the situation is different and even if the substantive offence does not require consent, then a conspiracy will do[34].

10.45

On that basis, if two people without entry clearance are in United Kingdom territorial waters on a foreign boat and decide to come to the UK then it would appear that consent would not be needed for the attempted s 24(D1) offence[35], but it would be for any conspiracy charge.

Historical note

10.46

In relation to immigration offences under the IA 1971 the timeline for which offences do not require consent is as follows:

- Prior to 31 May 2016 – all offences required consent
- 31 May 2016 – 23 August 2022 – ss 25, 25A and 25B (as was)
- 24 August 2022 – 11 April 2023 – any offence under Part 3 (IA 1971, ss 24–27)

---

32 Interpretation Act 1978, Sch 1 – '"offence triable either way" means an offence, other than an offence triable on indictment only by virtue of CJA 1988, Part V which, if committed by an adult, is triable either on indictment or summarily;'

33 CAA 1981, s 2(2).

34 Criminal Law Act 1977, s 4(2) contains a similar deeming provision to that in CAA 1981, s2(2), however that only applies to conspiracies to commit offences where the consent of the DPP or AG is required.

35 Unlawful Arrival, for which the consent of a Secretary of State is not required since 24 August 2022 – NABA 2022, Sch 6, para 4(b) and (Commencement No. 2) Regulations 2022, reg 2(b).

- 12 April 2023 onwards – as above, plus the Part 3 offences are 'onshored'[36]

10.47

For other offences, practitioners (both prosecution and defence) will need to consider what exception (if any) to the requirement for consent there is and, if there is none, whether the requisite consent has been given.

Control zone/Channel Tunnel

10.48

Whilst an offence committed in a foreign country would normally be outside the jurisdiction of the English and Welsh courts, the development of the Channel Tunnel, the procedure whereby the border controls are prior to embarkation rather than after arrival in the United Kingdom, and greater cross-border traffic in general, lead to the need for specific exceptions for these scenarios.

10.49

Since 1 March 2012 the Border Force (a branch of the Home Office) has been responsible for staffing and maintaining the border controls at the various air, sea and rail ports of entry to the United Kingdom. In addition, there are a small number of border control points in France[37], Belgium[38] and the Netherlands[39] where Border Force Officers operate in a UK Control Zone ('UKCZ') to check passengers before they embark rather than, as would normally be the case, when they disembark in the UK[40].

10.50

By virtue of the Nationality, Immigration and Asylum Act 2002 (Juxtaposed Controls) Order 2002, SI 2002/2818, art 12(1):

---

36 A new IA 1971, s 28(A1) is introduced (NABA 2022 (Commencement No. 5 and Transitional Provisions) Regulations 2023, reg 3):

> (A1) Proceedings for an offence under this Part that is committed in the territorial sea adjacent to the United Kingdom may be taken, and the offence may for all incidental purposes be treated as having been committed, in any place in the United Kingdom.

37 These are at Paris (Gare du Nord), Marne-le-Vallée, Lille, Fréthun and Coquelles rail ports, and Calais and Dunkirk sea ports. Coquelles operates a customs post as well as immigration control. There are 'Short-Term Holding Facilities' in Coquelles, Calais and Dunkirk.

38 At Brussels.

39 At Rotterdam and Amsterdam.

40 Reciprocal arrangements are in place in the UK in the rail ports of St Pancras International, Ebbsfleet International, Ashford International and Cheriton, and at the sea port of Dover. These are operated by French Immigration Officers as the frontier of the Schengen Area.

'12.— Application of criminal law to a Control Zone in France[41]

(1) An act or omission which constitutes an offence under an immigration control enactment shall also be an offence if it takes place in a Control Zone in France.

(2) An act or omission which constitutes an offence under the law of England and Wales if committed by a constable or an immigration officer in the exercise of his functions shall also be an offence if it takes place in a Control Zone in France by such an officer in the exercise of his functions.

(5) A provision of the criminal law in force in England and Wales for the protection of constables or immigration officers, or their property (including property in their possession or control), shall apply also in a Control Zone in France.

(6) Summary proceedings for an offence committed in a Control Zone in France by virtue of this article and which is an offence triable summarily or triable either way may be taken, and the offence may for all incidental purposes be treated as having been committed, in the county of Kent or in the area consisting of the inner London boroughs

(7) Any jurisdiction conferred by virtue of this article on any court is without prejudice to any jurisdiction exercisable apart from this article by any French court.'

10.51

An 'immigration control enactment' is defined as[42]:

> 'an Act of Parliament, or an instrument made under such an Act, which contains provision relating to immigration controls.'

10.52

There is a separate deeming provision in relation to the Channel Tunnel, in the Channel Tunnel (International Arrangements) Order 1993, SI 1993/1813:

'5.— Application of criminal law

(1) Any act or omission which–

(a) takes place outside the United Kingdom in a control zone, and

(b) would, if taking place in England, constitute an offence under a frontier control enactment,

41 A similar arrangement is in place with the Netherlands –The Channel Tunnel (Arrangements with the Kingdom of the Netherlands) Order 2020, art 5.

42 NIAA 2002 (Juxtaposed Controls) Order 2002, SI 2002/2818, art 2.

or any act or omission which—

(c) takes place outside the United Kingdom in a supplementary control zone, and

(d) would, if taking place in England, constitute an offence under an immigration control enactment,

shall be treated for the purposes of that enactment as taking place in England.

(1A) Summary proceedings for anything that is by virtue of paragraph (1) or (1ZA) an offence triable summarily or triable either way may be taken, and the offence may for all incidental purposes be treated as having been committed, in the county of Kent or in the area comprising the inner London boroughs.

(2) Any jurisdiction conferred by virtue of paragraphs (1), (1ZA) and (1A)] on any court is without prejudice to any jurisdiction exercisable apart from this article by that or any other court.

(3) Where it is proposed to institute proceedings in respect of an alleged offence in any court and a question as to the court's jurisdiction arises under Article 38(2)(a) of the international articles, it shall be presumed, unless the contrary is proved, that the court has jurisdiction by virtue of that Article.'

10.53

'Immigration Control Enactment' has the same meaning as it does in the 2002 Order. There are separate provisions in the Orders extending the powers of arrest, etc.

10.54

In addition to extensions to the general criminal law, The Channel Tunnel (Security) Order 1994, SI 1994/570 creates a number of different criminal offences:

- Art 4 – Hijacking a train – indictable only, life imprisonment
- Art 5 – 'Seizing the tunnel system' – indictable only, life imprisonment
- Art 6(1)(a) and (b) – Damaging or destroying a train or tunnel system (or goods located there) endangering the safety of it – indictable only, life imprisonment
- Art 6(1)(c) – Committing an 'act of violence'[43] likely to endanger the safety of the train or tunnel system – indictable only, life imprisonment

43 Defined in Art 6(5) as 'an act which constitutes—

(a) the offence of murder, attempted murder, manslaughter, culpable homicide or assault,

(b) an offence under section 18, 20, 21, 22, 23, 24, 28 or 29 of the Offences against the Person Act 1861 or

(c) an offence under section 2 of the Explosive Substances Act 1883, or which if committed in England and Wales, Scotland or Northern Ireland would constitute such an offence.'

- Art 7(1) – intentionally damaging, destroying or interfering with property related to a train or tunnel system – indictable only, life imprisonment
- Art 7(3) – intentionally communicating false information that endangers the safety of a train or tunnel – indictable only, life imprisonment
- Art 8(1) – threatening to commit an offence under Art 6(1) or 7(1) in order to another to do (or not do) an act – indictable only, life imprisonment
- Art 29 – false statements relating to goods – summary only, level 5 fine
- Art 30 – false statements relating to ID documents – summary only, level 5 fine
- Art 31 – unauthorised present in restricted zone – summary only, level 5 fine
- Art 32(1)(a) – obstructing an person – either way, maximum sentence two years imprisonment
- Art 32(1)(b) – impersonating an authorised person – summary only, level 5 fine

10.55

The indictable only offences require the consent of the Attorney-General to prosecute (although there do not appear to have been any prosecutions to date).

Age disputes

10.56

In the current age of computer records, it is extremely unlikely that practitioners will come across a British (or EU) national where there is a genuine dispute over when he or she was born.

10.57

With foreign nationals (and asylum seekers in particular) however, this is far from uncommon. A cynical view would be because people are aware of the benefits that accrue if someone is found to be under 18 both in terms of the availability of support as well as a lower likelihood of prosecution and a much lower likelihood of detention[44].

10.58

However, there are a number of other reasons, including; language difficulties, some genuinely do not know when they were born and others may accidently give a wrong age for cultural reasons as the way an age is stated is different.

44 The general power of detention in IA 1971, Sch 2, para 16 is subject to strict limitations as set out in IA 1971, Sch 2, paras 16(2A) and 18B

10.59

For this reason, with young defendants there is always a possibility that the age given in the CPS or Home Officer papers is inaccurate. Once an age has been determined, it can be difficult to challenge and, as we are used to that information being accurate, it is easy to miss. A mistake as to age can make a vast difference to sentence as well as potentially to jurisdiction.

10.60

It is not only a question of getting the age wrong by a year or so. For example, in *R v JF*[45] the appellant was sentenced to ten months for entering the UK on a false passport on the basis that she was 26. This age was supported by a Social Services age assessment. However, after expert evidence was obtained by a paediatrician, it was accepted that she was in fact only 16. In light of that, the sentence was quashed and replaced by a conditional discharge.

10.61

This highlights the importance of not accepting an age assessment on its face if the client states that s/he is younger than that, as even an age gap of ten years is not necessarily fatal.

Procedure

10.62

The procedure for the determination of age is set out at the Sentencing Act 2020, s 405, although not in any real detail:

> **405 Age of the offender**
>
> (1) This section applies for the purposes of any provision of this Code which requires a person's age to be determined by the court or the Secretary of State.
>
> (2) The person is to be deemed to be whatever age the person appears to the court, or, as the case may be, the Secretary of State, to be.
>
> (3) For this purpose, the court or Secretary of State must consider any available evidence.

10.63

Further guidance is contained in the Children and Young Persons Act 1933, s 99:

45 [2008] EWCA Crim 1838.

'99 Presumption and determination of age.

(1) Where a person, whether charged with an offence or not, is brought before any court otherwise than for the purpose of giving evidence, and it appears to the court that he is a child or young person, the court shall make due inquiry as to the age of that person, and for that purpose shall take such evidence as may be forthcoming at the hearing of the case, but an order or judgment of the court shall not be invalidated by any subsequent proof that the age of that person has not been correctly stated to the court, and the age presumed or declared by the court to be the age of the person so brought before it shall, for the purposes of this Act, be deemed to be the true age of that person, and, where it appears to the court that the person so brought before it has attained the age of eighteen years, that person shall for the purposes of this Act be deemed not to be a child or young person.'

10.64

Where there is a dispute about the correct age of the defendant, the court should adjourn for a hearing to determine that question. It is unlikely ever to be sufficient for a judge to make a conclusion based on his or her observation of the defendant[46].

10.65

It is likely that the Home Office will have carried out an age assessment. This will be recorded on a 'BP7' form which will record the basis on which the assessment is made. It is important that this document is obtained by the prosecution and defence as a starting point.

10.66

Assessing age is not an exact science, with there not being any particular way of determining the age of someone. Anyone representing a defendant in those circumstances should arrange for a 'Merton compliant'[47] assessment to be conducted. The principles underlying such an assessment were set out at para 21 of *MVN v London Borough of Greenwich*[48]:

(1) The assessment must be a holistic one and must start with an open mind, with no imposition on the child to prove his age to the assessing social workers.

(2) Physical appearance and demeanour are notoriously unreliable factors not determinative of age.

(3) Cultural, ethnic and racial context of the young person being assessed must be considered as these may reflect in their presentation as well as their descriptions of their lives.

---

46 *L and Others* [2013] EWCA Crim 991, [2013] 2 Cr App R 23 at [22].

47 From *R (B) v Merton LBC* [2003] EWHC 1689 (Admin), [2003] 4 All ER 280.

48 [2015] EWHC 1942 (Admin).

(4) General credibility is not to be determinative of age. It is more likely that a young person who tells a consistent account of his life which supports his claimed age will be the age he claims to be. Conversely, young people may lie for reasons unrelated to age but related to their claims for protection or the reasons they had to leave their country of origin.

(5) The child should be afforded the benefit of the doubt where evidence can tip one way or the other.

10.67

It is open to a court to direct an assessment itself in appropriate cases[49], although it is not mandatory for there to be one before the court makes an assessment.

10.68

A good example of the procedural difficulties is given in *Mohammed*[50]. The appellant had stated that he was a youth on arrest for one offence of sexual assault and, on the basis that he was 16, his case was kept in the Youth Court. However, the Crown challenged the assessment of age which prompted a hearing where a Youth Justice Worker gave evidence. The DJ found him to be 22, continued with a summary trial and, after convicting him, committed him for sentence.

10.69

Prior to sentence he was charged with two further sexual assaults and committed for trial to the Crown Court on the basis of the DJ's age assessment. The Youth Justice Worker gave a signed witness statement and the defence obtained an age assessment stating that the defendant was aged under 18. Following this, the CPS conceded the appellant's age was 16 for the purpose of the matters on indictment and the first matter (which had been appealed to the Crown Court) was remitted back to the Youth Court in front of the same DJ.

10.70

That DJ concluded that there was no power to re-visit the age question and returned the case to the Crown Court. Whilst waiting for the trial in the Crown Court, the appellant committed a further sexual assault which was joined up with the others. The trial proceeded on the basis that he was a youth with the question of age being reserved to the end of the trial. After he was convicted the case was adjourned during which the appellant provided a report from a psychologist that concluded that his presentation was consistent with a 16 year old. The judge made a determination (without hearing evidence or submissions) that the appellant was an adult. The appellant appealed the sentence on the basis that this assessment was flawed (and was also unreasonable).

---

49 *M v Hammersmith Magistrates' Court, Hammersmith Youth Offending Team* [2017] EWHC 1359 (Admin), at [16]

50 [2021] EWCA Crim 1375.

10.71

The Court of Appeal upheld the assessment. It concluded that had that not been the case, then they (having no power to remit) would have had to have had a further hearing at which a fresh determination could be made.

Impact of an incorrect age assessment

10.72

The consequence of the Children and Young Persons Act 1933, s 99 and the Sentencing Act 2022, s 405 is that where an age assessment turns out to be incorrect then this will not, of itself, be a ground of appeal against conviction. It may be that it would form part of wider grounds.

10.73

It is unclear whether there is a burden and standard of proof as such, or whether the court must make an assessment in the round[51] (which would appear to be the most likely reading of s 99) or whether the burden falls on the party asserting an age as it would with other matters[52]. Where both parties agree, then it would likely still be open to the judge to conclude that the stated age should not be accepted.

Resolution of age disputes in immigration proceedings

10.74

Historically, age assessments were conducted by individual local authorities, with the remedy for an applicant who disagreed with the assessment being judicial review. The Nationality and Borders Act 2022[53] introduced a new statutory scheme with a 'National Age Assessment Board'[54], whose role is to undertake age assessments, being established. NABA also contains When provision for the transfer of the jurisdiction for the resolution of age disputes to the First-tier Tribunal (IAC)[55].

Application to the CCRC/Court of Appeal

10.75

Many of the cases that have shaped the law in relation to immigration offences are ones that have gone to the Court of Appeal out of time (often by a number

---

51 *R (HAM) v London Borough of Brent* [2022] EWHC 1924 (Admin)

52 See, in an immigration appeal, *Rawofi* [2012] UKUT 197 (IAC) and, when it is in force, NABA 2022, s 54 (see below). This is the case in relation to the s 45 defence – see Chapter 8. In the unlikely case where the defendant is asserting that he is an adult, then the standard would be the usual civil one.

53 NABA 2022, Part 4, ss 49–57.

54 In force as of 31 March 2023.

55 NABA 2022, s 54.

of years) and following a guilty plea. Whilst both of these factors are normally bars to a successful appeal, the Court of Appeal have often been willing to look behind this due to the complexity of the law and the fact that that complexity, and the potential defences, are often overlooked by the lawyers and judges in the trial court.

10.76

The Court of Appeal issue a helpful document 'The Court of Appeal Criminal Division Guide to Commencing Proceedings', which any practitioner should have regard to. This is updated regularly and is available online[56].

Legal aid

10.77

For in time appeals the representation order in the Crown Court covers an advice on appeal from the advocate at trial. If an appeal is lodged, and permission is granted, then legal aid will usually be granted.

10.78

In out of time cases, funding will be available in certain cases to provide advice on applications to the Court of Appeal as well as to the CCRC. This is under the LAA's 'Advice and Assistance' Scheme:

> '11.5 If the Client has received an adverse opinion on appeal and wishes to obtain a further opinion, you must consider how long it was since the first opinion was given. If recent, and it appears that all issues have been considered, no further work may be undertaken.
>
> 11.6 Where there is further evidence or the Solicitor can point to some defect in the opinion or the proceedings, then further work may be justified for a further opinion, regardless of when the first opinion was obtained.'

10.79

The relevant forms are the CRM1 and CRM.2 A client will have to pass the 'Means Test'[57] and the 'Sufficient Benefit Test'[58]. In practice, a successful appeal

56 The current version is July 2021, and is available here – https://www.judiciary.uk/wp-content/uploads/2021/07/Blue-guide-July-2021-Final-1.pdf.

57 The LAA 'Keycard No 46' contains a useful summary (it can be found at – https://assets.publishing.service.gov.uk/government/uploads/system/uploads/attachment_data/file/1127538/Criminal_Keycard_46_Jan_23_Update.pdf).

58 As set out in Standard Crime Contract 2022, para 3.10 – 'Advice and Assistance may only be provided on legal issues concerning English (or Welsh) law and where there is sufficient benefit to the Client, having regard to the circumstances of the matter, including the personal circumstances of the Client, to justify work or further work being carried out'.

against conviction or sentence will be a 'sufficient benefit' for the purposes of the Scheme. In addition, a provider cannot claim if someone has had advice and assistance from another provider in the last six months unless[59]:

(a) there is a gap in time and circumstances have changed materially between the first and second occasions when the advice and assistance was sought; or

(b) the client has reasonable cause to transfer from the first provider; or

(c) the first provider has confirmed to you that they will be making no claim for payment for the advice and assistance.

10.80

The Upper Limit for advice and assistance for appeals is £314.81 and for CCRC applications is £524.69, with the following being (currently) the applicable rates[60]:

	London (£)	National (£)
Routine letters written and routine telephone calls per item	4.04	3.89
Preparation hourly rate	52.15	49.22
Travel and waiting hourly rate	27.60	27.60

10.81

Application can be made (using the CRM5 form) to extend the amount, which requires it to be shown that the proposed further work is reasonable[61].

Appeals out of time ('OOT'[62]) in the Court of Appeal

10.82

The time limit for an appeal against conviction in the Crown Court is 28 days from conviction[63] (this is calculated from the date of the verdict of the jury or plea of guilty, not from sentence), although there is power for this to be extended both before and after the 28 days have expired[64]. The Court of Appeal guide sets out the procedure to be followed.

59 Standard Crime Contract 2022, para 11.26.
60 Criminal Legal Aid (Remuneration) Regulations 2013, Sch 4, para 8.
61 Standard Crime Contract 2022, paras 5.8-5.19.
62 'OOT', for 'out of time' is the acronym that will often be seen.
63 CAA 1968, s 18(2).
64 CAA 1968, s 18(3).

Fresh evidence

10.83

In the context of out of time immigration appeals it is often the case that fresh evidence or other material (such as medical reports, decisions of the Competent Authority, etc) evidence is relied on. The test for the admission of fresh evidence is at the Criminal Appeal Act 1968, s 23:

> '**23.— Evidence.**
>
> (1) For the purposes of an appeal, or an application for leave to appeal, under this Part of this Act the Court of Appeal may, if they think it necessary or expedient in the interests of justice—
>
> (a) order the production of any document, exhibit or other thing connected with the proceedings, the production of which appears to them necessary for the determination of the case;
>
> (b) order any witness to attend for examination and be examined before the Court (whether or not he was called in the proceedings from which the appeal lies); and
>
> (c) receive any evidence which was not adduced in the proceedings from which the appeal lies.
>
> …
>
> (2) The Court of Appeal shall, in considering whether to receive any evidence, have regard in particular to—
>
> (a) whether the evidence appears to the Court to be capable of belief;
>
> (b) whether it appears to the Court that the evidence may afford any ground for allowing the appeal;
>
> (c) whether the evidence would have been admissible in the proceedings from which the appeal lies on an issue which is the subject of the appeal; and
>
> (d) whether there is a reasonable explanation for the failure to adduce the evidence in those proceedings.
>
> …
>
> (4) For the purposes of an appeal, or an application for leave to appeal, under this Part of this Act, the Court of Appeal may, if they think it necessary or expedient in the interests of justice, order the examination of any witness whose attendance might be required under subsection (1)(b) above to be conducted, in manner provided by rules of court, before any judge or officer of the Court or other person appointed by the Court for the purpose, and allow the admission of any depositions so taken as evidence before the Court.'

10.84

In practice the Court of Appeal will often admit the evidence '*de benne esse*' – ie, they will read the documentary evidence and/or hear from the witnesses, whilst reserving the question of admissibility until the end of the proceedings.

10.85

On a practical level, the Form NG (appeal form) should be accompanied by a separate 'Form W' in relation to each witness. In addition, a '*Gogana* statement'[65] should be produced by the applicant's solicitor.

10.86

In appeals against conviction where there was a guilty plea it will almost always be necessary for the applicant themselves to produce a statement. This should include confirmation of a waiver of privilege, as well as the reasons why they are not guilty of the offence and a full explanation of what happened at court that led them to plead guilty.

10.87

Even where fresh material is not strictly evidence (such as a determination from an Immigration Judge) it is still prudent to identify such material and make an application to adduce it.

10.88

Some of the material will be in the hands of a prospective applicant, but it is possible to make a Subject Access Request[66] to the relevant body (eg, police, CPS, Home Office and Ministry of Justice) to seek further material.

10.89

Practitioners in 'second appeal' or 'second advice' cases, where they did not conduct the original trial, are obliged to follow the procedure set out in *McCook*[67] and other cases, and summarised in the Court of Appeal Guidance:

> '(i) New legal representatives are required to confirm within the grounds of appeal that the duties set out in *R v McCook* ibid and associated authorities have been complied with.

---

65 Named for *Gogana* (1999) Times, July 12 1999, although the report has no details of what was decided. It was next considered in *James* [2000] CLR 571 where it was said that 'where fresh evidence was tendered from a witness who was said not to have been available at the trial, it was essential that an affidavit should be sworn by the defendant's solicitor describing the circumstances in which the witness came forward to make the statement and the circumstances in which that statement was made'.

66 Data Protection Act 1998, s 7. The Information Commissioner's Office website contains guidance on how to make an application – https://ico.org.uk/for-the-public/your-right-to-get-copies-of-your-data/preparing-and-submitting-your-subject-access-request/. Those organisations are familiar with such requests.

67 [2014] EWCA Crim 734.

(ii) If these queries result in privileged information being included within, or as an attachment, to the grounds of appeal (including but not limited to, explicit or implied complaints about the conduct of trial representatives), then a signed waiver of privilege must also be lodged with the grounds of appeal. Failure to lodge a signed waiver of privilege may mean that the Single Judge and/or the court will not have sufficient information to determine whether the grounds of appeal are arguable. Grounds of appeal may be dismissed on that basis; *R v Frost-Helmsing* [2010] EWCA Crim 1200.

(iii) If trial representatives have failed to respond to these inquiries within a reasonable time, fresh representatives should instead seek other objective independent evidence to substantiate the factual basis for the grounds as far as they are able. A statement confirming that the trial representatives have failed to respond to their McCook inquiries should be lodged with the grounds of appeal, along with a signed waiver of privilege.

(iv) Fresh representatives also should consider obtaining other objective independent evidence if the information provided by the trial representatives contradicts the appellant's instructions.'

Uncontested appeals

10.90

Although proceedings in the Court of Appeal are adversarial in nature, as the court have repeatedly stated, the question of the safety of the conviction is for the court rather than the parties. However, for obvious reasons, it will be rare for a conviction to be upheld where both sides say that it is unsafe.

10.91

The procedure to be followed has been set out helpfully in a recent IA 1971, s 25 (pre-NABA 2022 so the issue was 'enter' – see Chapter 5) case[68]:

> '12. The court is asked to exercise its power under section 18(3) to grant an extension of time in many different circumstances and neither the Criminal Appeal Act 1968 nor the Criminal Procedure Rules limit the discretion of the court on the issue whether an extension of time should be granted (see *Thorsby & Ors* [2015] EWCA Crim 1 and *Patterson* [2022] EWCA Crim 456 at [26]). The following guidance has been given by the Court of Appeal in *Thorsby* and *Patterson*, see in particular *Patterson* at [27]:

68 *Khodamoradi* [2023] EWCA Crim 37 – as published, the citation is given as [2022] but as the case was heard and judgment given in January 2023, this would appear to be an error.

> (1) The principled approach to extensions of time is that the court will grant an extension if it is in the interests of justice to do so. The judgment is judicial and nor merely administrative.
>
> (2) The court will have in mind finality, the interests of the parties, the efficient use of resources and good administration. The public interest also critically embraces the justice of the case and the liberty of the individual.
>
> (3) Where there is no good reason why the time limits were not complied with, the court is unlikely to grant an extension unless injustice would be caused in consequence. The merits of the underlying grounds will be examined. It is not the case, however, that an arguable case on the merits is simply a trump card without more.
>
> (4) The court will be more likely closely to examine the merits of an outoftime appeal when it is argued that some principle of law or legal requirement has been ignored or overlooked.
>
> (5) Applicants would be expected to demonstrate with particularity when and in what circumstances they became aware of the entitlement for the first time, that no further delay had occurred after then, and if there had been delay by the applicant himself, the court would be likely to refuse the extension of time.
>
> 13. We would add one further point. This is that an applicant who seeks an extension of time should give a detailed description of the delay and the reasons for it. In all but an exceptional case, the information should be provided in a witness statement which complies with the requirements of section 9 of the Criminal Justice Act 1967.
>
> 16. We were informed by the applicant's counsel that a practice has developed in cases such as these of no evidence being provided in support of an application for extension of time where the prosecution does not oppose the appeal or the extension of time. In so far as such a practice exists, it should cease.'

10.92

There is a clear tension in that a lawyer acting for an appellant may be reluctant to incur a potentially relatively large amount of costs complying with the above in a case where the appeal will be not opposed (and will, in fact, often be supported) by the Prosecution, and is therefore highly likely to be allowed. This will be the case whether their client is privately paying or on legal aid.

10.93

However, given the clear steer from the Court of Appeal, a practitioner should generally ensure that they comply with all the relevant procedural requirements, even if this means that the legal aid order will need to be extended to cover a solicitor.

10.94

The caveat would be that in clear cases where the prosecution have confirmed that the appeal will not be opposed, it is open to a practitioner to correspond with the Registrar to raise this fact, and point out the potential costs that may be incurred with a view to directions been sought to exempt them from further compliance. Whether this succeeds will depend on a number of factors, but it is unlikely that a lawyer will be criticised for making the application.

Appeals from guilty pleas

Introduction

10.95

Unlike in an appeal to the Crown Court from the magistrates' court where there are strict limits on the jurisdiction of the Crown Court to hear an appeal, the power in the Court of Appeal is not as restricted. The court 'shall allow an appeal against conviction if they think that the conviction is unsafe'[69].

10.96

However, for obvious reasons, the generally rule is that a guilty plea is taken as a freely entered admission of guilt and would preclude an appeal against conviction:

> '19. A defendant who pleads guilty is making a formal admission in open court that he is guilty of the offence. He may of course by a written basis of plea limit his admissions to only some of the facts alleged by the Crown, so long as he is admitting facts which constitute the offence [...]. But ordinarily, once he has admitted such facts by an unambiguous and deliberately intended plea of guilty, there cannot then be an appeal against his conviction, for the simple reason that there is nothing unsafe about a conviction based on the defendant's own voluntary confession in open court. A defendant will not normally be permitted in this court to say that he has changed his mind and now wishes to deny what he has previously thus admitted in the Crown Court.[70]'

10.97

However, there are a number of cases where the court will consider an appeal against conviction, notwithstanding that there was a guilty plea.

10.98

These have been summarised in *Tredget*[71] as broadly falling into three categories:

69 CAA 1968, s 2.
70 *Asiedu* [2015] EWCA Crim 714, [2015] 2 Cr App R 8.
71 [2022] EWCA Crim 108, [2022] 2 Cr App R 1.

i. Cases where the plea is vitiated

ii. Cases where there is a legal obstacle to the person being tried

iii. Cases where it is shown that the plea cannot be considered to be a proper one as it can be shown that the defendant did not commit the offence

Category 1 – vitiated pleas

10.99

This can arise in a number of cases, but the essential point is that the circumstances in which the plea was entered was not one where it can be said to be proper for a court to continue to rely on it. These can be broken down into cases where the plea was a nullity and those where it is not a nullity but the conviction is still unsafe. It is fair to say that the courts have not always been entirely consistent in relation to drawing the distinction between the two and it is not always easy to establish clearly the relevant principles.

10.100

For example, erroneous legal advice is capable of falling into both categories depending on the circumstances of the case. So, in *Saik*[72] it was said[73]:

> 'For an appeal against conviction to succeed on the basis that the plea was tendered following erroneous advice it seems to us that the facts must be so strong as to show that the plea of guilty was not a true acknowledgment of guilt. The advice must go to the heart of the plea, so that as in the cases of *Inns* and *Turner* the plea would not be a free plea and what followed would be a nullity.'

10.101

However, where the advice given did not cover an available defence (such as the s31 defence) then[74]:

> 'The test for a plea to be held a nullity was elaborated (per Scott Baker LJ in *R v Saik* [2004] EWCA Crim 2936) as requiring the facts to be so strong as to demonstrate that there is no true acknowledgment of guilt with the advice going to the heart of the plea so that it was not "a free plea". It is, however, important not to water down the underlying concept of the jurisdiction so as to bring nullity into play purely on the basis of advice alleged to be wrong. For those circumstances, there remains a basis on which this Court can intervene which is firmly grounded in the safety of the conviction.'

72 [2004] EWCA Crim 2936.

73 At [57]. The case was successfully appealed to the Supreme Court – [2006] UKHL 18, [2006] 2 Cr App R 26, but not on this point.

74 *Mohamed (Abdalla) & Othrs* [2010] EWCA Crim 2400, [2011] 1 Cr App R 35, at [12]. This was a number of false passport cases that were co-joined to consider the effect of a failure to advise on a s 31 defence.

10.102

In those circumstances it has to be shown that the defence 'would quite probably have succeeded' with the consequence that a 'clear injustice was done'[75]. It is clearly a fine line between the two and will be very fact specific, although it may be thought that someone who is not advised about a defence that, objectively, obviously arises on the facts of their case cannot be said to entering a 'free plea' when they are told that there is no defence and they have no choice but to plead guilty.

10.103

In assessing whether a defence would 'quite probably have succeeded' it is appropriate to have regard to a decision of the First-tier Tribunal (or other judicial finding) on a relevant question (such as whether a person is a refugee or a victim of trafficking)[76].

10.104

Other examples include an incorrect ruling by the trial Judge that leaves the defendant with no defence (rather than a much weakened one)[77] or applies improper pressure on a defendant to plead guilty[78], as well as more unusual situations such as where a defendant changes their plea to guilty because they are under the influence of LSD[79].

The 'Dastjerdi Checklist'

10.105

This will be relevant where the issue is the advice (or lack thereof) as to a defence. *Dastjerdi*[80] was a false passport case where the applicant was an Iranian man who was arrested in Gatwick airport in transit to Canada with a false Romanian ID Card, to which he pleaded guilty and was sentenced to 12 months. He appealed out of time on the basis that he had not been advised of the availability of the s 31 defence. The appeal was conceded by the Crown, and was allowed. At para 9 the court set out and adopted a 'checklist' as to how such cases should be approached.

---

75 *Mohamed (Abdalla)* at [13] referring to *Boal* (1992) 95 Cr App R 272 which was the first of this line of cases. Mr Boal pleaded guilty to offences under Fire Precautions Act 1971, s 23 committed when he was the temporary assistant manager (providing holiday cover) of Foyles Bookshop. His application to appeal against sentence was refused by the Single Judge but renewed where Lord Lane (the then LCJ) raised the question (which ultimately succeeded) of whether Mr Boal was, as required 'a manager of the body corporate'.

76 *Sadighpour* [2012] EWCA Crim 2669, [2013] 1 Cr App R 20.

77 *Asiedu* at [20].

78 See *Nightingale* [2013] EWCA Crim 405, [2013] 2 Cr App R 7. This was the famous case of a soldier who was convicted at a Court Martial after pleading guilty to firearms offences following an unrequested sentence indication that had the effect of narrowing 'the proper ambit of [the] freedom of choice' of the defendant.

79 *Swain* [1986] CLR 480.

80 [2011] EWCA Crim 365.

10.106

This has been considered and approved in a number of cases, and is applicable to both the s 31 defence[81] and the s 45 VOT one[82]:

- Should the applicant have been advised about the possibility of availing himself of a s 31 or s 45 defence? If so,
- Was he, in fact, so advised?
- Was it open to the applicant, had he been so advised, to advance the defence?
- Was it (at least) quite probable that the applicant would have been able successfully to advance such a defence?[83]

Change of law cases – injustice or significant injustice or substantial injustice?

10.107

In *Ordu* [84] the appellant applied eight years out of time to the Court of Appeal for permission to appeal against her conviction for a false passport offence on the basis that she was not advised about the s 31 defence.

10.108

The court approached the application on the basis that the defence would probably have succeeded. However, the conviction was from October 2007 and the availability of the s 31 defence on the facts of the case was 'clarified' by *Asfaw*[85]. On that basis, the appeal of Ms Ordu was based on there being a 'change of law'. In those circumstances, the court stated that an extension of time should only be granted if a substantial injustice will occur if the appeal is not allowed to proceed. This was said to be a higher threshold than that set out in *Boal.*

10.109

It is fair to say that the Court of Appeal has not shown a great enthusiasm for the *Ordu* test in subsequent cases, which is perhaps unsurprising as it involves leaving in place a conviction that is recognised as being an unsafe one. It does not appear that there is another case where an application for permission to appeal in an immigration case has been refused on the basis that it is a change in

81 *Elmi* [2022] EWCA Crim 1428, [2023] 1 Cr App R 7.

82 See, most recently, *AFU* [2023] EWCA Crim 23, at [99].

83 In *AFU* there was reference to the situation in *Kakaei* [2021] EWCA Crim 503 (which was a small boat crossing case) where a 'legal heresy' as to the meaning of s 11 entry had been allowed to develop which meant that it 'may be unjust' to require a defendant in those circumstances to show that a defence may well have succeeded.

84 [2017] EWCA Crim 4, [2017] 1 Cr App R 21.

85 [2008] UKHL 31, [2008] 1 AC 1061.

law case, but one where no substantial injustice occurred. The court has either found that it was not a change of law case at all[86] and/or there was substantial injustice[87].

10.110

In any event, in many cases the appellant has no convictions before or after the false passport (or other offence) being appealed. In those circumstances it is likely that there will be an ongoing impact on the person's immigration position in the United Kingdom. Even where they have overcome that, it will impact (for example) on an application for citizenship, an application to travel to the USA, or a DBS check for employment[88].

Category 2 – legal obstacle

10.111

This will cover cases such as where there should never have been a trial at all (such as where proceedings are an abuse of process[89]) or the proceedings are so unfair that there is a fundamental breach of a person's Art 6 rights (such as where there was a real possibility of jury bias)[90].

10.112

Although different constitutions of the Court of Appeal have taken different views as to the applicability of Category 2 cases in immigration appeals (in the sense of the possible s 31 or s 45 defence), it is now confirmed that even where a person's guilty plea is not vitiated, the abuse of process jurisdiction remains. In those circumstances where, on the facts and law as they are now known, a prosecution would not have been brought (or, if brought, would have been stayed as an abuse of process) then a conviction appeal may still be successful.

Category 3 – Other reason

10.113

These cases will typically be where new evidence since the trial shows that person who pleaded guilty was, in fact, innocent (rather than there being some other good reason to doubt their guilt). These will be few in number. Examples include where another person subsequently pleaded guilty and it was accepted that the appellant's confession (which was followed by a plea of guilty) was 'an

86 *Abdulahi* [2021] EWCA Crim 1629.

87 *GS* [2018] EWCA Crim 1824, [2019] 1 Cr App R 7.

88 See *JM* [2021] EWCA Crim 1137 at [40].

89 See, as an example, *Mullen* [1999] EWCA Crim 278, [1999] 2 Cr App R 143, where the British authorities sidestepped extradition proceedings by assisting in the person's deportation from another country in breach of Pubic International Law.

90 *Abdroikof & Othrs* [2007] UKHL 37, [2008] 1 Cr App R 21.

appalling lie about himself'[91], where there was clear evidence that the appellant was in prison at the time of the offence[92] and DNA evidence showed that a person's plea of guilty to manslaughter was incorrect and someone else was responsible[93]. This will be likely to have little application in an immigration case.

Criminal Cases Review Commission

Background

10.114

The large number of high profile miscarriage of justice cases in the late 1980s and early 1990s exposed the need for a proper framework for investigating and analysing such cases. This led to the establishment of the Criminal Cases Review Commission, a statutory body, that was set up under the Criminal Appeal Act 1995.

10.115

Their remit is to investigate cases where an individual complains that they have been wrongly convicted or sentenced. They do not quash the conviction or sentence themselves, but have the power to refer the case to the Court of Appeal who then deal with the case.

10.116

Whilst there have been a number of critical views of the CCRC that have been expressed, there are distinct advantages in such an application. For the client, it is free to apply and there is no risk to making an application in terms of costs or loss of time. In addition, the CCRC have far greater resources and powers to investigate than an individual solicitor has. In particular, they can far more readily obtain information from the police, courts and CPS.

Procedure

10.117

The CCRC is supposed to be accessible to all, and so lawyers are not needed to submit an application. However, legal aid is available in appropriate cases, and many applicants would wish to use a lawyer.

10.118

Generally, the CCRC will only consider a case where the applicant has previously applied to the Court of Appeal and either been refused at the permission stage

91 *Foster* (1984) 79 Cr App R 61.
92 *Verney* (1909) 2 Cr App R 107.
93 *Jones* [2019] EWCA Crim 1059.

by the Single Judge or by the Full Court on an appeal. There is a power for the CCRC to consider an application when that has not happened, but only when there are 'Exceptional Circumstances'[94]. This not defined, and will be very fact specific, although the CCRC are relatively flexible in appropriate cases. This will apply even in cases where an appeal would not be out of time due to the power of the Court of Appeal to extend time. If, however, there is an application or appeal pending, then the CCRC cannot get involved.

10.119

The CCRC website has an application form that can be completed online or downloaded and filled in before being posted.

10.120

Historically, the CCRC have referred a number of immigration cases to the Court of Appeal[95]. These are mostly, but not exclusively, false passport cases.

In the Court of Appeal

10.121

When the CCRC refers a case to the Court of Appeal this has a similar effect as to a grant of permission by the Single Judge, and the case would generally proceed in the same way. This means that a loss of time direction cannot be made, but costs can.

10.122

Where permission has been granted, the Full Court is then solely looking at the question of whether the conviction is 'safe' and cannot generally dismiss an appeal on the basis that permission should not have been given, despite that being a ground on which permission could be refused[96].

10.123

However, on a CCRC reference on a change of law case the Court of Appeal can dismiss the appeal if they conclude that even though they would have to allow the appeal, they would not have granted permission[97]:

94 See 'Casework Policy – Exceptional Circumstances' (CW-POL-06).

95 There is a 'Topic: Asylum and Immigration' page on the CCRC website (https://ccrc.gov.uk/category/referrals/asylum-and-immigration/) which has a list of some (but not all) of these cases.

96 As to the difference see, as an example, *Welsh* [2015] EWCA Crim 1516, [2016] 1 Cr App R 9 which concerned the failure to obtain consent from the AG for a conspiracy out of the jurisdiction (which was required under Criminal Law Act 1977, s 1A). In relation to seventeen of the applicants, the court concluded that there was no injustice, and therefore it would be proper to refuse permission to appeal out of time, notwithstanding that 'Had an appeal been issued within 28 days of conviction this court would have quashed the convictions and ordered retrials (or perhaps granted a writ of *venire de novo*), [57]'.

97 CAA 1968, s 16C(2) and (3).

'(2) Notwithstanding anything in section 2, 13 or 16 of this Act, the Court of Appeal may dismiss the appeal if—

(a) the only ground for allowing it would be that there has been a development in the law since the date of the conviction, verdict or finding that is the subject of the appeal, and

(b) the condition in subsection (3) is met.

(3) The condition in this subsection is that if—

(a) the reference had not been made, but

(b) the appellant had made (and had been entitled to make) an application for an extension of time within which to seek leave to appeal on the ground of the development in the law,

the Court would not think it appropriate to grant the application by exercising the power conferred by section 18(3).'

Challenge to a CCRC refusal

10.124

There is no appeal against a CCRC decision, with the only route being by Judicial Review. However, there is no bar on asking for a review or making a further application (although the CCRC are not obliged to consider afresh arguments already raised and dealt with).

Anonymity in criminal/immigration cases

10.125

The usual rule in criminal proceedings (at least for adults) is open justice. One consequence is that there are generally no reporting restrictions. This can be contrasted to the position in asylum appeals where it is often the case that judgments will be anonymised[98].

10.126

The reason for this is that where someone is claiming asylum, to publish their name in a news report (or law report) may put them at risk in their home country if they were to be returned (as well as any family members who have remained behind).

98 See para 22-23 Presidential Guidance Note No 2 of 2022: Anonymity Orders and Directions regarding the use of documents and information in the First-tier Tribunal (Immigration and Asylum Chamber) for the First-tier Tribunal and paras 27-30 'GUIDANCE NOTE 2022 No 2: Anonymity Orders and Hearings in Private' in the Upper Tribunal.

10.127

The balance between the principles of open justice and the risk to individuals is not an easy one to strike. However, in asylum (and other protection cases) the Court of Appeal (Criminal Division) have recognised that it will often be the case that the usual principles do not apply. In *R v L & N* [99]it was said (at [15]):

> 'In the light of that evidence, the need for consistency and the UK's obligations generally, we accept that it would, in principle, be desirable for the Court of Appeal Criminal Division to follow the practice adopted by the Civil Division and the Tribunals of anonymising the applicant in cases raising asylum and international protection issues. However, we are concerned that other important issues are at stake for example the principle of open justice in the context of criminal trials and appeals; we have not had the benefit of representations from the press. Moreover, we note that in criminal appeals, different considerations may arise in relation to the risk on return or the background facts relied upon may be different from those in the associated asylum case. We can also envisage circumstances where there may be less restrictive means (short of an anonymity order) of addressing the risk of harm. In these circumstances, we decline the invitation to give general guidance. We shall consider the question of anonymity on the specific facts in the context of each of the appeals before us.'

10.128

Practitioners will want to consider whether include an application for anonymity in any application for permission to the Court of Appeal.

Crown and magistrates' courts

10.129

Whilst there is less likely to be media interest or publicity in trial courts, it would appear that a similar principle would apply in the Crown Court.

CPS guide to immigration offences

CPS guidance on immigration cases

10.130

As well as the CPS Code for Crown Prosecutors, the CPS issue specific guidance for the prosecution of immigration offences[100] that all practitioners will need to be aware of. This gives an overview of the main immigration offences and

99 [2017] EWCA Crim 2129.

100 This is published online. The latest version (revised 06 December 2022) is at – https://www.cps.gov.uk/legal-guidance/immigration.

defences, as well as setting out the way that cases will be investigated (including the 'prosecution strategy'). This contains a useful checklist of 'potential sources of evidence'.

10.131

The document also contains a further, and more comprehensive, guide to the public interest factors in the decision to prosecute in immigration offences (in particular the s 24(A1)-(D1) and s 25 offences).

10.132

Practitioners are able to make representations at any time both pre and post-charge, which is an opportunity that should generally be taken. This is both in relation to whether there is sufficient evidence as well as the public interest.

10.133

The CPS guidance specifically covers the Art 31 protection, and this is something that should be traversed in any representations (if that is potentially applicable). Depending on the content of the police interview, it may be necessary to give fuller details about the journey to the United Kingdom and the basis of the asylum claim.

10.134

A tactical decision will need to be made by a prospective defendant as to how much information is given. However, if it is decided that the best interests of the client is by disclosing his account, then it is generally better to give as much information as possible. Particularly in cases where it is said that the client is a refugee, reference should be made to the background country conditions and the reasons why a recognition of refugee status is likely.

Memorandum of understanding

10.135

The CPS publish[101] a 'Memorandum of Understanding between The Crown Prosecution Service, Immigration Enforcement and National Policing on Immigration Crime' (the 'MOU'). The current version came into force from 28 June 2022 (the same day as many of the new criminal offences in the NABA 2022).

10.136

The stated aim is to describe 'the co-operation arrangements between the Parties in respect of the investigation, the institution and prosecution of offences and the recovery of assets in respect of Immigration Enforcement Casework in

101 This is available online from the CPS website.

England and Wales'. This applies alongside the Code for Crown Prosecutors and, where applicable, the CPS Guidance on Immigration Offences.

10.137

The format, if not the exact detail, will be familiar to practitioners from a general criminal background. Significant points to be aware of are that a Chief Immigration Officer (or higher grade) can appeal against a CPS decision[102] and the MOU has not been update alongside the CPS Immigration Guidance, so the summary contained at paras 67–70 is now out of date and should not be relied on (to the extent that there is any difference).

10.138

All practitioners should be aware of Annex A that sets and the roles and responsibilities of the various professionals on the prosecution team at all stages of the investigation (including at appeals post-conviction).

Alternative disposals

Administrative removal

10.139

Where somebody who is suspected of a criminal offence is in the United Kingdom unlawfully, and they agree to be removed, then in some cases it would be in the public interest to simply remove them rather than take any formal action. This would not be appropriate for someone suspected of the the Asylum and Immigration (Treatment of Claimants, etc) Act 2004, s 2, or is likely to be seeking leave to remain in the United Kingdom (whether on the basis of an asylum or human rights claim or otherwise).

10.140

The CPS Immigration Guidance states that the public interest factors set out in that document, as well as whether the likely sentence is less than 12 months imprisonment, are applicable in determining whether some form of action other than prosecution. This is a course of action that is more likely to be followed where the offence is summary only or either way.

10.141

In many cases, this will be a pragmatic and straightforward way of proceeding. Where a client wishes for this, then a practitioner should make representations to the CPS as to why this would be the appropriate disposal (with a conditional

102 MOU, [13]-[17].

caution as an alternative)[103]. A sentence of less than 12 months will cover a large number of offences, including a large number of immigration offences. Practitioners will need to ensure that the client would be making a fully informed decision to be removed, and is not simply doing this to avoid a prosecution.

Conditional cautions

Introduction

10.142

The power of the police to issue a caution, a formal warning as an alternative to a prosecution, has existed on a non-statutory basis since at least the mid-nineteenth century[104]. These would be an official marking of the fact that an admission to a criminal offence had been made. However, once the caution had been administered, that was the end of the matter.

10.143

There is now power, under the Criminal Justice Act 2003 (CJA), Part 3[105], to issue a 'conditional caution'. This is governed by a Statutory Code – 'Code of Practice for Adult Conditional Cautions 2013 ('Code of Practice')'[106], which apply in all cases. Reference should also be made to the DPP Guidance[107].

10.144

The regime applies to almost all offenders who have committed a summary only or either way offence. This includes foreign nationals who may also, in certain circumstances, be conditionally cautioned for an indictable only offence (although the suitability for a conditional caution in those circumstances must be determined by a District Crown Prosecutor rather than the police[108]). The case should be referred by the police to the Head of the local Crown Court Unit[109].

---

103 Reference can also be made to the 'Decision and Disposal' section of 'Dealing with potential criminality (ICE teams) (v2.0, 13 February 2023) which indicates that 'administrative removal will normally be appropriate' where:
- an immigration offender can be removed within a reasonable time period
- the immigration offender has previously complied with directions such as temporary release and the re-documentation process
- there are no outstanding applications for leave to remain or enter which require consideration or outstanding applications can be resolved within a reasonable time period
- the immigration offender is not suspected of having committed an offence which would attract a prison sentence of 12 months or more

104 *R (Stratton) v Chief Constable of Thames Valley Police* [2013] EWHC 1561 (Admin), at [21]. This case contains a useful overview and history of the cautioning process.

105 CJA 2003, ss 22-27.

106 Available online, and issued under CJA 2003, s 25. There is specific guidance on conditional cautions for foreign nationals at relevant points in the guidance.

107 'Conditional Cautioning: Adults – DPP Guidance' 03 October 2022. This is statutory guidance issued CJA 2003, s37A.

108 A Sergeant can authorise a conditional caution for a case where the offence is summary only or for an either way offence that is not usually tried in the Crown Court.

109 The Code of Practice DPP Guidance at [16] sets out the procedure to be followed.

10.145

The aim of a conditional caution is to divert someone who would otherwise be subject to a criminal prosecution away from court and, provided they comply with any conditions attached, the case will not proceed as a prosecution.

Requirements

10.146

A conditional caution can only be given to a person if the following conditions are satisfied[110]:

- There is sufficient evidence that that person has committed an offence to charge them[111]
- The person has admitted the offence (normally in a formal PACE interview on tape, although this is not necessary)
- The conditions, and consequences of a breach, are fully explained
- The person signs a formal document accepting the above

Application to foreign nationals

10.147

There is a specific provision relating to foreign nationals (who are adults) where a conditional caution can be administered requiring them to leave the United Kingdom and not return[112], provided that the likely sentence imposed by a court would not exceed two years' imprisonment.

10.148

It can only be administered where the person has no leave to enter or remain in the United Kingdom, or there is otherwise a power to force their removal[113].

---

110 CJA 2003, s 23.

111 This is separated in the legislation into a requirement that the prosecutor has sufficient evidence that the person has committed the offence, and that there is sufficient evidence to charge them. In practice the person's admissions are likely themselves to be sufficient evidence.

112 As set out in CJA 2003, s 22(3D) the conditions attach to achieve the 'objects' of the caution, defined in s 22(3E) as:
(a) bringing about the departure of the relevant foreign offender from the United Kingdom;
(b) ensuring that the relevant foreign offender does not return to the United Kingdom for a period of time.

113 CJA 2003, s 22(3G):
'In this section "relevant foreign offender" means—
(a) an offender directions for whose removal from the United Kingdom have been, or may be, given under—
(i) Schedule 2 to the Immigration Act 1971, or
(ii) section 10 of the Immigration and Asylum Act 1999, or
(b) an offender against whom a deportation order under section 5 of the Immigration Act 1971 is in force.'

When a 'foreign offender' is detained by the police, then the Custody Officer should contact the UKBA to see if they are someone who may fall with the category of people who could receive a conditional caution.

10.149

However, a conditional caution cannot be made where:

- The person has made an asylum or human rights claim which is still outstanding[114]
- The person is a suspected victim of trafficking
- There is no prospect of removal in a reasonable period of time

10.150

A conditional caution can be offered after a decision to charge has been made if it is considered to be more appropriate. If that occurs, the criminal proceedings should be adjourned whilst this is resolved.This specifically includes the situation where an asylum or human rights claim (which would normally preclude a conditional caution) is withdrawn after a decision to charge has been made[115].

10.151

For that reason, practitioners should be alive to this and make representations for a conditional caution in a suitable case, even if the client has already been charged.

10.152

Practitioners will need to be aware of the risk that their client will consent to removal in cases where they have a valid claim to stay in the UK in order to avoid a prosecution, and must make steps to ensure that their agreement is a valid one. This will be particularly acute where an asylum or human rights claim has been withdrawn. The Police and prosecutors will also need to ensure that the decision made by a suspect is a valid one and that they have had access to legal advice where appropriate.

10.153

The DPP Guidance suggests that in such a case once the caution has been administered, the case should be discontinued, although this may not be possible in many cases, particularly in the Crown Court (one consequence of the expectation that pleas will be entered as soon as possible is that it allows for

---

114 Although the DPP Guidance states that a conditional caution 'cannot be offered where the offender makes or has an outstanding asylum or Human rights claim to remain in the UK or where the offender admits to committing a document or identity fraud offence in order to make a claim for asylum' ([15.2.1]), the Code of Practice states that such a person may be offered a caution once any asylum or Human rights claim has been concluded ([2.20]) which would appear to be more consistent with the statutory scheme.

115 DPP Guidance, [9.1]-[9.2].

less room for manoeuvre to obtain a more pragmatic outcome). The difficulty with offering no evidence is, of course, that then there is no recourse if the offender changes his mind and declines to co-operate with removal.

Conditions

10.154

The exact conditions will depend on the circumstances of the case, but typical ones suggested include:

- Report regularly to an immigration office, reporting centre, police station or other similar place, pending removal;
- Obtain or assist authorities in obtaining a valid national travel document;
- Comply with removal directions and any lawful directions given to effect departure (usually within 16 weeks, but generally no more than 24 weeks);
- Not to return to the UK within a specified period of time, normally five years (but can be up to ten years in more serious cases) as set out in the Immigration Rules[116].

10.155

In addition, other conditions unrelated to immigration can be added[117], provided that they are compatible with the immigration position and would not delay removal. In determining the conditions, it is possible for the prosecutor to consult with the UKBA[118].

10.156

Where the conditions for any caution would not involve the 'foreign offender conditions', then the same approach as would be taken with any other offender. In those circumstances, a conditional caution is unlikely to be issued if the offence is one that is likely to attract a high community order or custodial sentence.

10.157

Conditions can be varied with the consent of the person[119].

116 It is possible to impose a longer time period, but this would be an exceptional course, and only if the offence is a particularly serious one (Code of Practice at [2.32]).

117 As set out in CJA 2003, s 22. The Code of Practice contains a helpful summary at [2.14]-[2.20].

118 Code of Practice at [2.22] and [2.45].

119 Code of Practice at [3.23].

Breach of conditions

10.158

Where a conditional caution has been given, and the person breaches the conditions, then the reasons for the non-compliance must be assessed and, if there is no reasonable excuse then the prosecutor must decide to either deem the caution as completed, deem it as incomplete but not requiring any further action, vary the conditions, or prosecute for the offence (it is not an offence to break the conditions of the caution itself). A breach of conditions may include making an asylum or human rights claim after accepting the caution, but prior to removal[120].

10.159

There is power for a police officer to arrest without warrant someone they have reasonable grounds to believe has failed (without a reasonable excuse) to comply with the conditions of a caution[121]. Where a decision cannot be made whilst they are detained, there is power to release them (either on bail or not), until a charging decision is made.

120 Code of Practice at [3.21].
121 CJA 2003, s 24A.

11 Evidence

Introduction

11.1

This chapter provides an overview of some of the common evidential issues that arise in relation to prosecution for immigration offences. Some apply generally under the criminal law, some to specific parts of the Immigration Acts, whilst some only relate to specific offences.

Foreign law

Introduction

11.2

The general rule is that foreign law is a question of fact (not law) that would require expert evidence[1]. However, in the Crown Court this will be decided by the judge rather than the jury[2]. It is not sufficient to provide extracts of foreign law without more[3].

Foreign Convictions

11.3

If disputed, foreign convictions of an individual can only be proved under the Evidence Act 1851, s 7[4]. This would involve producing a copy of the relevant

1 *Okolie* [2000] CLY 941.

2 Administration of Justice Act 1920, s 15. To the extent that there is an issue about the burden and standard of proof it is likely to follow the usual rule; namely if the prosecution seek to adduce it, then it must be shown to the criminal standard, whereas if it would be to the civil standard if the defence are relying on it – *R v B* [2018] EWCA Crim 73, at [24].

3 *Dalrymple v Dalrymple* (1811) 161 ER 665.

4 This reads:

> 7. Foreign and colonial acts of state, judgments, &c. provable by certified copies, without proof of seal or signature or judicial character of person signing the same.
>
> All proclamations, treaties, and other acts of state of any foreign state or of any British colony, and all judgments, decrees, orders, and other judicial proceedings of any court of justice in any foreign state or in any British colony, and all affidavits, pleadings, and other legal documents filed or deposited in any such court, may be proved in any court of justice, or before any person having by law or by consent of parties authority to hear, receive, and examine evidence, either by examined copies or by copies authenticated as herein-after mentioned; that is to say, if the document sought to be proved be a proclamation, treaty, or other act of state, the authenticated copy to be admissible in evidence must purport to be sealed with the seal of the foreign state or British colony to which the original document belongs; and if the document sought to be proved be a judgment, decree, order,

certificate of conviction sealed by the foreign court (or, if there is no seal, then signed by the judge with a statement certifying that there is no seal). There is no further requirement to prove the seal or the official status of the judge.

11.4

However, once that has been established, then there is no specific way that identity (namely that the person in the dock or witness box is the person named in the documentation) must be proved, although nowadays fingerprints would be the standard procedure[5].

The IA 1971

Introduction

11.5

The IA 1971 makes some specific evidential rules for criminal offences (and immigration matters that may impact on the prosecution of immigration offences).

Burden of proof for British nationality/exemption

11.6

In relation to the operation of the IA 1971, s 3(8) provides:

> 'When any question arises under this Act whether or not a person is a British citizen, or is entitled to any exemption under this Act, it shall lie on the person asserting it to prove that he is.'

11.7

This will apply to any of the offences in the IA 1971, Part III (ss 24–27), but not in relation to immigration offences in other statutes. The statute does not state the standard of proof, but would again presumably be to the criminal standard if the prosecution raise it and the civil standard if raised by a defendant.

---

or other judicial proceeding of any foreign or colonial court, or an affidavit, pleading, or other legal document filed or deposited in any such court, the authenticated copy to be admissible in evidence must purport either to be sealed with the seal of the foreign or colonial court to which the original document belongs, or, in the event of such court having no seal, to be signed by the judge, or, if there be more than one judge, by any one of the judges of the said court, and such judge shall attach to his signature a statement in writing on the said copy that the court whereof he is a judge has no seal; but if any of the aforesaid authenticated copies shall purport to be sealed or signed as hereinbefore respectively directed, the same shall respectively be admitted in evidence in every case in which the original document could have been received in evidence, without any proof of the seal where a seal is necessary, or of the signature, or of the truth of the statement attached thereto, where such signature and statement are necessary, or of the judicial character of the person appearing to have made such signature and statement.

5 See *Kordasinski* [2006] EWCA Crim 2984, [2007] 1 Cr App R 17 and *Mauricia* [2002] EWCA Crim 676.

Documents in arrival and entry offences

11.8

There are specific evidential presumptions for the entry and leave offences in the IA 1971, s 24[6], that are considered in Chapter 4.

Facilitation offence – the IA 1971, s 25

11.9

Specific provision is made for the admissibility of foreign law in relation to the s 25 offence (which can be committed by breaches of immigration law in member states rather than just in the United Kingdom):

> '(3) A document issued by the government of a member State certifying a matter of law in that State—
>
> (a) shall be admissible in proceedings for an offence under this section, and
>
> (b) shall be conclusive as to the matter certified.'

11.10

This does not apply to the other offences in Part III, including the s 25A offence (which has always related to asylum seekers coming to the United Kingdom rather than any other EU state).

11.11

The IA 1971, s 25(3) does not mean that this is the only way that foreign law may be proved. In *Bina*[7] it was said[8] that s 25(3) was:

> 'an example of a well-known legislative device whereby some fact of foreign law (perhaps of diplomatic or other status) may be admitted or proved in evidence. However, compliance with this particular legislative device is not, in our judgment, the only manner in which the content of a relevant foreign law may be proved. It may be proved by way of expert evidence. Alternatively, as appears in this case, it may be proved by an admission as to what the foreign law is …
>
> Compliance with the precise mechanics of s.25(3) is permissive only. It is not, in our judgment, the only manner in which conspiracy to breach the law of a member state could be proved on the facts of the case.'

---

6 These are in relation to the s 24(B1) offence – entering without leave, and the s 24(D1) offence – arriving without an entry clearance where it is required.

7 [2014] 2 Cr App R 30.

8 At [25].

11.12

It is likely that in most cases there will be an agreement between the parties as to what the relevant law is (not least as it will likely be similar to UK law, even if not identical).

Secretary of State Documents

Admissibility under the IA 1971

11.13

Specific provision is made in the IA 1971, s 32(2)–(4) for the admissibility of certain documents issued by the Secretary of State:

> **'32.— General provisions as to Orders in Council, etc.**
>
> (1) Any power conferred by Part I of this Act to make an Order in Council or order (other than a deportation order) or to give any directions includes power to revoke or vary the Order in Council, order or directions.
>
> (2) Any document purporting to be an order, notice or direction made or given by the Secretary of State for the purposes of the Immigration Acts and to be signed by him or on his behalf, and any document purporting to be a certificate of the Secretary of State so given and to be signed by him or on his behalf, shall be received in evidence, and shall, until the contrary is proved, be deemed to be made or issued by him.
>
> (3) Prima facie evidence of any such order, notice, direction or certificate as aforesaid may, in any legal proceedings or other proceedings under the Immigration Acts, be given by the production of a document bearing a certificate purporting to be signed by or on behalf of the Secretary of State and stating that the document is a true copy of the order, notice, direction or certificate.
>
> (4) Where an order under section 8(2) above applies to persons specified in a schedule to the order, or any directions of the Secretary of State given for the purposes of the Immigration Acts apply to persons specified in a schedule to the directions, prima facie evidence of the provisions of the order or directions other than the schedule and of any entry contained in the schedule may, in any legal proceedings or other proceedings under the Immigration Acts, be given by the production of a document purporting to be signed by or on behalf of the Secretary of State and stating that the document is a true copy of the said provisions and of the relevant entry.'

11.14

This would appear to cover all the formal documents that are issued by the Home Office that would of relevance in a criminal prosecution, such as a deportation order for the purposes of the IA 1971, s 24(A1) offence. It does not appear that it would apply to the letters that are issued with it (such as any letter giving the reasons for a deportation order). However, if such evidence is admissible (and it would frequently not be in a criminal prosecution as not being of relevance) then s 32 does not provide a complete code of admissibility and that evidence would be admissible under other routes. This would not apply to mixed documents such as a letter granting an extension of leave to remain, which would be admissible via this route.

11.15

Where someone is subject to immigration bail and is being prosecuted for breaching it, then the notice of bail would fall under this section, but it would be necessary to prove the breach with evidence from Immigration Officers.

Documentary Evidence Act 1868

11.16

This Act contains further provisions relating to the admissibility of documents[9]:

> **'2. Mode of proving certain documents.**
>
> Prima facie evidence of any proclamation, order, or regulation issued before or after the passing of this Act by Her Majesty, or by the Privy Council, also of any proclamation, order, or regulation issued before or after the passing of this Act by or under the authority of any such department of the Government or officer or office-holder in the Scottish Administration as is mentioned in the first column of the schedule hereto, may be given in all courts of justice, and in all legal proceedings whatsoever, in all or any of the modes herein-after mentioned; that is to say:
>
> (1) By the production of a copy of the Gazette purporting to contain such proclamation, order, or regulation.
>
> (2) By the production of a copy of such proclamation, order, or regulation, purporting to be printed by the Government printer, or, where the question arises in a court in any British colony or possession, of a copy purporting to be printed under the authority of the legislature of such British colony or possession.

9 This is explicitly stated as being in addition to any other means of admissibility – Documentary Evidence Act 1868, s 6.

(3) By the production, in the case of any proclamation, order or regulation issued by Her Majesty or by the Privy Council, of a copy or extract purporting to be certified to be true by the clerk of the Privy Council, or by any one of the lords or others of the Privy Council, and, in the case of any proclamation, order, or regulation issued by or under the authority of any of the said departments or officers or office-holders , by the production of a copy or extract purporting to be certified to be true by the person or persons specified in the second column of the said schedule in connexion with such department or officer or office-holder.

Any copy or extract made in pursuance of this Act may be in print or in writing, or partly in print and partly in writing.

No proof shall be required of the handwriting or official position of any person certifying, in pursuance of this Act, to the truth of any copy of or extract from any proclamation, order, or regulation.'

11.17

This covers a wide range of documents, with 'order' being given a wide meaning[10]:

> 'covering at any rate any executive act of Government performed by the bringing into existence of a public document for the purpose of giving effect to an Act of Parliament. This is all the more so when the Acts in question are merely designed to facilitate proof of matters which can be clearly proved otherwise, albeit in a less convenient manner.'

11.18

This is wide enough to include a probation licence relating to someone released into the community whilst serving a custodial sentence[11].

Criminal Justice Act 2003

11.19

The above rules run alongside the usual rules in relation to hearsay evidence that criminal practitioners will be familiar with. Home Office documents (such as correspondence to an immigrant or a Reasons for Refusal Letter) are likely to be business documents admissible under the hearsay provisions of the general criminal law[12].

---

10 *Clarke* (1969) 53 Cr App R 251.

11 *West Midlands Probation Board v French* [2008] EWHC 2631 (Admin), [2009] 1 Cr App R 29.

12 See CJA 2003, ss 117 and 118.

11.20

The Criminal Justice Act 2003 (CJA 2003), s 117 makes provision for the admissibility of documents that are 'created or received by a person in the course of a trade, business, profession or other occupation, or as the holder of a paid or unpaid office' where certain conditions are satisfied. The purpose of this section is to make admissible those records that were prepared by people who could be presumed to be relatively neutral and disinterested in the outcome of any court case. Immigration Officers who may be dealing with a number of different people that they do not know would likely fall into this category.

11.21

The CJA 2003, s 118 preserves various common law rules relating to admissibility, with the most relevant likely to be the first:

> ***'Public information etc***
>
> 1 Any rule of law under which in criminal proceedings—
>
> (a) published works dealing with matters of a public nature (such as histories, scientific works, dictionaries and maps) are admissible as evidence of facts of a public nature stated in them,
>
> (b) public documents (such as public registers, and returns made under public authority with respect to matters of public interest) are admissible as evidence of facts stated in them,
>
> (c) records (such as the records of certain courts, treaties, Crown grants, pardons and commissions) are admissible as evidence of facts stated in them, or
>
> (d) evidence relating to a person's age or date or place of birth may be given by a person without personal knowledge of the matter.'

11.22

A 'public document' is 'a document that is made for the purpose of the public making use of it, and being able to refer to it. It is meant to be where there is a judicial, or *quasi*-judicial, duty to inquire'[13], which includes a register of births and marriages (although this will also be admissible under other provisions). This is the case, even with a foreign register[14].

11.23

The primary route to admissibility will now be under the 2003 Act, and it is of course the case that a document may be admissible in a number of different ways. The inclusion of the above is to show that practitioners (whether prosecution or defence) must not rely solely on the CJA 2003.

---

13 *Sturla v Freccia* (1880) 5 App Cas 623, per Lord Blackburn.

14 *Lyell v Kennedy* (1889) 14 App Cas 437.

11.24

In *DPP v Leigh*[15] the respondent was charged with failing to provide the details of the registered keeper of a car[16]. In proving this, the prosecution were entitled to rely on the evidence of a civilian employee that he had checked the relevant correspondence logs and was satisfied that there was no response as required as this was not hearsay evidence at all. This was said to be consistent with the case of *Patel*[17], which was a case that held that Home Officer records that showed the lack of a relevant entry to show that someone was an illegal entrant for the purpose of a facilitation offence. However, in order to rely on such evidence, the person seeking to rely on it will need to ensure that the person who gives the evidence sets out in detail how the lists were prepared (see *DPP v Leigh* at [4]–[5]).

11.25

In practice, the prosecution will serve a statement from an Immigration Officer saying that they have checked the relevant records and there is nothing to say that Mr X ever applied for entry clearance (or whatever the case may be). It would be then up to the defence to decide to what extent, if any, that could be put in issue.

Admissibility of immigration interviews

Introduction

11.26

It is the case that there is often a considerable overlap between evidence that the Home Secretary would use to make an immigration decision, and evidence that could be used to prosecute a criminal offence. This raises the question of to what extent any evidence gained from an immigration investigation can be used in a criminal prosecution.

Application of PACE

11.27

It is not uncommon that someone who is facing a criminal allegation will have been interviewed by Immigration Officers previously. This may be where the criminality alleged is as a result of the previous contact, such as a false statement in an interview, or it may be the case that the person has previously had contact with an Immigration Officer in relation to the matter which is later charged.

---

15 [2010] EWHC 345 (Admin).
16 A summary only offence under Road Traffic Act 1988, s 172.
17 (1981) 73 Cr App R 117.

11.28

A paradigm example would be in relation to someone accused of an arrival or entry offence who has claimed asylum. There would have been a Screening Interview and, depending on the progress of the asylum claim, a full asylum interview. Other common examples would be someone who is encountered by an Immigration Officer during a 'raid' and is interviewed as to their immigration history and presence at the place of detention, but is subsequently charged with illegal working, or a person charged with a 'sham marriage' offence who has previously been interviewed as to whether the marriage is one of convenience to ascertain his immigration position.

11.29

There is a difficulty caused by the fact that in the vast majority of cases of interactions with Immigration Officers the sole purpose is in relation to immigration enforcement, and checking whether someone has status in the United Kingdom, or is otherwise complying with any restrictions on them. A criminal prosecution is not in the minds (or certainly not in the forefront of their minds) of any of the Immigration Officers and the reality is that a prosecution is not contemplated. For that reason, much of the training and operational procedure is geared towards immigration and civil enforcement rather than criminal proceedings.

11.30

The distinction is important because of the much higher safeguards that operate in a criminal case. This creates a tension between the importance of not watering down those safeguards for someone who is prosecuted, whilst ensuring that evidence which is relevant (and often highly probative) is not ruled inadmissible. The starting point is that the Police and Criminal Evidence Act 1984 does not apply to anyone other than Police Officers, which includes Immigration Officers.

11.31

However, the IAA 1999, s 145 provides:

> **'145.— Codes of practice.**
>
> (1) An immigration officer exercising any specified power to—
>
> (a) arrest, question, search or take fingerprints from a person,
>
> (b) enter and search premises, or
>
> (c) seize property found on persons or premises,
>
> must have regard to such provisions of a code as may be specified.
>
> (6) "Code" means—
>
> (a) in relation to England and Wales, any code of practice for the time being in force under the Police and Criminal Evidence Act 1984;'

11.32

The stated intention for this was that[18]:

> 'This section allows the Secretary of State to direct that immigration officers must have regard to relevant provisions of the existing PACE codes of practice in England Wales and Northern Ireland when exercising specified powers to arrest, question, search persons, enter and search premises, take fingerprints or seize property. The direction issued under this section must specify which powers are covered, which provisions of the existing PACE codes of practice are relevant and list any modifications necessary to ensure consistency of approach. The section will reinforce the existing commitment under section 67(9) of PACE which requires any person charged with the duty to investigate offences to have regard to the relevant PACE codes of practice. It will extend this commitment to immigration officers when they are exercising specified powers under Schedule 2 to the 1971 Act and also to any authorised person exercising the power to take fingerprints conferred by section 141 of this Act.'

11.33

The relevant Direction is the Immigration (PACE Codes of Practice) Direction 2013[19]. This states explicitly that nothing within it 'affects the operations of PACE, s 67(9)[20].

Elsakhawy and the applicability of PACE to Immigration Officers

11.34

This has been considered in an immigration context by the Upper Tribunal in *Elsakhawy (immigration officers: PACE)*[21]. This concerned an appeal in an EEA case where the Home Office alleged that there was a 'sham marriage'. This allegation followed an enforcement visit to the appellant's address where questions were asked of the appellant that were subsequently relied on (in part) to seek to remove the appellant.

11.35

The focus of the Tribunal was on the use of such questions and answers in immigration proceedings and it was noted that[22]:

18 Explanatory notes, para 399.
19 This is different from The Police and Criminal Evidence Act 1984 (Application to immigration officers and designated customs officials in England and Wales) Order 2013, which is considered in Chapter 12.
20 Para 4, PACE Codes of Practice Direction.
21 [2018] UKUT 00086 (IAC).
22 At [149].

> 'The admissibility in criminal proceedings of evidence obtained contrary to PACE is to be determined in accordance with section 78 of that Act (see above). What fairness demands is highly context-specific. The fact that a judge in a criminal trial may decide that certain evidence ought to be excluded, as having an adverse effect on the fairness of the proceedings, has little to say about the task facing a Tribunal, in civil proceedings, which must determine a person's entitlement under the EU Treaties to be in the United Kingdom. Plainly, a grossly abusive set of failures may incline the Tribunal, in such proceedings, to the view that – for *its* purposes – admission of the evidence would be inappropriate; for example, if admission would be seen as endorsing highly problematic behaviour on the part of immigration officers.'

11.36

The Tribunal upheld the distinction between administrative enquiries as to breaches of the Immigration Acts and enquiries as to whether there has been a breach of the criminal law. It also accepted the reality of the situation 'on the ground' that only an extremely small number of people who are illegal entrants or overstayers are prosecuted[23]. The conclusion was that Immigration Officers investigating a sham marriage would not be (in the words of PACE, s 67(9)) 'acting in the discharge of any duty they may have of investigating offences or charging offenders'[24].

Immigration v criminal arrest

11.37

There is a distinction between an immigration arrest, where someone is arrested on suspicion of being someone who may be removed from the United Kingdom as someone not lawfully present here[25], and someone arrested for a criminal offence. The former should be told[26]:

- that they are under arrest and not free to leave
- the reason for the arrest
- the reason why it is necessary to arrest them

11.38

They should also be given what is described as an 'administrative caution', in the following terms[27]:

23 At [141].

24 At [139]. It was also said that entering into a sham marriage only 'may' involve the commission of a criminal offence, although it is hard to see how someone who has entered a sham marriage, and used that to make an application to the Home Office, is not committing an offence.

25 This would typically be under IA 1971, Sch 2, para 17, which sits alongside the power to detain in para 16.

26 Home Office Guidance 'Arrest and Restraint', v2 (November 2021), at page 11.

27 'Arrest and Restraint' guidance at page 11.

> 'I am an Immigration Officer. I am arresting you on suspicion that you are a person liable to immigration detention. This is because I suspect you [*give reason, eg "have entered the UK illegally", "have overstayed your leave", "have breached a condition of your leave", and so on*]. This is not an arrest for a criminal offence. Do you understand?'

11.39

The difficulty that can be seen here is that all the examples given also amount to criminal offences[28]. The Guidance also addresses[29] the question of an arrest for a suspected criminal offence where, as would be expected, there is a requirement to give the warning against self-incrimination that is familiar to criminal practitioners. However, PACE does not apply in non-criminal cases[30].

Requirement to caution

11.40

Whereas a police officer would normally caution someone prior to any substantive interaction with them, the obligation to give an administrative caution arises only on an immigration arrest (where there is reasonable suspicion that an administrative breach of the immigration law or a criminal offence has been committed), and not on any initial questioning[31], although the distinction may not matter in practice.

11.41

That does not cover the situation in the criminal courts, and the fact that evidence collected by an Immigration Officer may be used in an immigration case, even where the consequences are as serious as cancelling somebody's leave to remain, does not make it admissible in a criminal case. It is likely that a criminal court will approach matters in a different way to the Tribunal would an immigration case given the higher safeguards in place (particular in relation to confessions).

11.42

A further point of significance, and which is different to statements made to people such as Probation Officers or Social Workers, is that where someone is specifically told that they are *not* being arrested for a criminal offence, it may be considered to be even more unfair to rely on anything then said.

---

28 Contrary to IA 1971, s 24(B1), (C1), (1)(b) respectively.
29 'Arrest and Restraint' guidance at page 28-29.
30 *Campos v SSHD* [2022] EWHC 3299 (Admin), at [112].
31 *Campos* at [111].

Exploratory questioning and Initial examination interview

11.43

These will be conducted, as the name suggests, when an Immigration Officer first encounters someone in circumstances that indicate that they may be an illegal entrant or otherwise someone who is in breach of immigration law. The Home Office have produced guidance on 'Enforcement interviews'[32], which sets out the procedure to be followed.

11.44

In short form, this envisages a two-stage initial process. Firstly, this is to establish whether there are reasonable grounds to consider that the person is someone who may be removed from the UK. If so, then the process moves to what is an examination under the IA 1971, Sch 2, para 2 or 2A. This is a formal interview, and the questions and asked should be logged (nowadays likely on the PRONTO system). Immigration Officers typically do not have body worn footage, and there is no obligation to make an audio recording of these interviews. At the end of the interview, it should be given to the person to sign.

Applicability of CODE C to Immigration Officers

11.45

Two particular difficulties that arise here is that most Immigration Officers do not have the relevant training to conduct criminal arrests and criminal interviews and that all of their interactions are likely to be with people who have, or at the least there are grounds to suspect have, committed a criminal offence. The guidance[33] is that if 'information is discovered that gives rise to a reasonable suspicion that a criminal offence has been committed *that is likely to be pursued to prosecution*[34] you should suspend the interview and take advice from the police (if present) or Criminal and Financial Investigations (CFI)'. A decision would then be made as to whether a criminal investigation should start and, if so, the person should be arrested and given the criminal caution.

11.46

A criminal court will be looking at the case from the other end of the telescope, in the sense that they will have someone in front of them charged with a criminal offence who will be one of the many thousands of people who have been stopped and spoken to by Immigration Officers. Whilst it may be understandable that Immigration Officers cannot routinely caution everyone they encounter, that would not relieve them of the obligation to caution as far as the criminal case is concerned.

---

32 Currently, v2.0 (22 December 2020).

33 Page 14.

34 Emphasis added.

11.47

The 2013 Direction has, at Sch 1, a table of the relevant powers that an Immigration Officer may exercise and which powers of PACE are applicable. The relevant one is:

Column 1 (powers exercised under the following provisions)	**Column 2 (code provisions for England and Wales)**
Interview under caution to establish an offence or breach.	**Code C** – 1 (not 1.1A – 1.3, 1.9, 1.11, 1.13 – 1.17); 2.6, 2.6A; 6.1, 6.4, 6.6-6.17; 10 (not 10(c), 10.11A); 11; 12; 13; 16 (not 16.1A, 16.1B, 16.2, 16.3, 16.6, 16.10); Annex B, C, D and G **Code E** – All provisions (not 1.6(a), 1.6(b), 1.8, 1.9, 3.2) **Code F** – All provisions (not 1.6(a), 1.6(b), 3.2)

11.48

In relation to this, the Direction has not been amended to take account of the amendments to Code C, so it will be necessary to go to the original one to trace the above if needed[35].

11.49

In *Elsakhawy* the Upper Tribunal concluded that an 'interview under caution to establish an offence or breach' referred, in both cases, to the criminal law[36], and so the obligation to administer a criminal caution would only arise where there is an active investigation and real contemplation of criminal proceedings.

11.50

It must be doubted whether that conclusion would be followed by a criminal court. At the least it is certainly arguable that (as was recognised in *Elsakhawy* at [144]) that 'offence or breach' must refer to different things (or else there would be no need to use two terms), with this realistically referring to either a criminal offence or a breach of the immigration law. If that is the case, then the protections of Code C would apply and the likelihood of any interview being excluded is high.

35 Archived at https://webarchive.nationalarchives.gov.uk/ukgwa/20200729053712/https://www.gov.uk/government/publications/pace-code-c-2012
36 At [142-144].

When is there a requirement to caution?

11.51

The fact that the Immigration Officer has not been trained in PACE would not appear to be a relevant consideration. Further, it is likely that the fact that a prosecution for an offence is unlikely does not change the test that would be applied in the criminal courts. For example, where a Customs Officer is speaking to someone coming in to the United Kingdom:

> 'The appropriate time to administer the caution in a situation such as this is when, on an objective test, there are grounds for suspicion, falling short of evidence which would support a prima facie case of guilt, not simply that an offence has been committed, but committed by the person who is being questioned.[37]'

11.52

Even if that is not the case and the criminal court were to hold that an Immigration Officer is not covered by PACE, s 67(9), that will not be the end of the matter as the judge will still have to consider whether to exclude the evidence under PACE, s 78. Here, given that anyone who is liable for administrative removal is likely to be committing a criminal offence, then many judges would conclude that a failure to caution (even if made in good faith and in accordance with published Home Office Guidance) would mean that 'the admission of the evidence would have such an adverse effect on the fairness of the proceedings that the court ought not to admit it'.

11.53

Whilst it is arguable, and it will always be a fact specific, prosecutors should think carefully before trying to adduce such evidence given the risk of legal challenge (including on an appeal if the evidence is admitted). Defence representatives should make representations as to the admissibility of any such evidence.

Application to witnesses

11.54

Similar considerations also apply to potential witnesses, particularly those who are nominally the victims of an offence (such as someone who is being facilitated for the purpose of an IA 1971, s 25 or 25A offence).

11.55

For example, where a lorry is stopped going through a port with illegal entrants hidden in it, the driver could be expected to be arrested for facilitation. Those people on board may be spoken to both as witnesses to that offence, but also

37 *Nelson* [1998] 2 Cr App R 399.

as suspects in the IA 1971, s 24(B1) offence in their own right. However, even if it is always unlikely that the passengers would be prosecuted, it is likely that the court would conclude that all involved should be cautioned (although this would no render their evidence inadmissible in a facilitation trial of the driver).

Screening Interviews

11.56

When an asylum claim is made (either at the border or in-country) all applicants will have a Screening Interview, and some will also receive a Preliminary Information Questionnaire[38].

11.57

At the start of a Screening Interview there will be a rubric that is read out. This includes the following (or similar):

> 'The officer is going to ask you some questions about your identity, family, background, travel history and some health and welfare questions. The officer will only ask you for a brief outline of why you are claiming asylum today. The officer will not be making the decision on your asylum claim. You must answer all the questions fully and truthfully. Making false statements may:
>
> - Constitute a criminal offence
> - Damage your credibility
> - Make you liable for prosecution and imprisonment.
>
> At the end of the interview it will be given to the Applicant to sign, and the following declaration will be read out:
>
> By signing this application you are declaring that all your personal details are correct and that you understand that it is a criminal offence to seek to obtain leave to remain in the UK by deception.'

11.58

A Preliminary information Questionnaire includes the following (or similar):

> 'You must not provide information that you know to be false to support your claim or omit facts that you think may harm your claim. Doing so may affect the credibility of your claim. You may be prosecuted for providing false information to support an unfounded claim and may face up to 2 years in prison.'

38 See Chapter 1 for more details.

11.59

The potential problem can be immediately seen, in that as well as a failure to caution, there is effectively a requirement to answer questions in breach of the right to silence. This is compounded by the fact that given that such interviews often occur shortly after someone has arrived in the United Kingdom, which means that they would be unfamiliar with the procedure and it would be unlikely that they would have legal representation and.

11.60

Whilst these interviews are undoubtedly carried out for the purposes of the immigration case and not for a criminal investigation, given the above it is likely that a court would decline to admit evidence obtained as a result of these questioning[39].

Substantive asylum interview (SEF Asylum Interview)

11.61

The substantive asylum interview will occur in almost all asylum claims. Again, the purpose is to assess the person's immigration case and not for the purpose of any criminal offence.

11.62

Here, the interview will start with something along the lines of:

> **'Compulsory Statements – to be read out at every interview**
>
> This interview is your opportunity to tell us your reasons for claiming asylum. It is very important you do not withhold any information you believe to be relevant to support your claim. I will help you by asking you questions so that we have the information we need to make a decision in your case.'

39 Against that, there is a statutory bar in relation to the categories of interviews set out in Youth Justice and Criminal Evidence Act 1999, s 59, Sch 3 where there is a criminal penalty for not responding, which is not the case for immigration interviews. In addition, there are cases such as *Elleray* [2003] EWCA Crim 553, [2003] 2 Cr App R 11 where an admission to a Probation Officer was held to be admissible, although the court did say that:

> 'So in the case of an admission the prosecution should first carefully consider whether it is right to rely upon evidence provided by a conversation between a probation officer and an offender and only rely upon it if they decide it is in the public interests so to do. If they do decide to rely upon that evidence, having taken into account the considerations of public interest to which we have made reference, then the court still has a discretion under s. 78 of the 1984 Act to ensure that no unfairness will occur because of the reliance on the admissions which an offender is alleged to have made. In deciding whether to exclude the evidence it is perfectly appropriate for the court to have in mind the contrast between the position that exists where an offender is interviewed by the police and that which exists when the offender is interviewed by a probation officer. The court should bear in mind the need for frankness between the offender and the probation officer; the fact that there may not be a reliable record of what was said; that the offender has not been cautioned; and that the offender has not had the benefit of legal representation. The protection which the court can provide under s. 78 in the majority of cases should be sufficient to ensure that no unfairness occurs to an offender.'

11.63

An asylum interview is less likely to be problematic as, although they are longer, it will normally be questions about the applicant's experiences in their home country, and will therefore be less likely to be relevant. However, similar considerations as above would likely apply.

Admissions in Tribunal proceedings

11.64

In many cases evidence will be called during an immigration appeal (especially one where it relates to events in-country) which shows the appellant's guilt of a criminal offence (for example, that they are an over-stayer or that they have been working without permission). It would be impracticable to provide a warning against self-incrimination in every case, and appellants do not generally give evidence under oath. It is unlikely that there would ever be a prosecution relying on anything said before a Tribunal.

12 Investigatory powers

Introduction

12.1

This chapter provides an overview of the main investigatory and enforcement powers of Immigration Officers, as they relate to immigration offences. Immigration Officers have a number of different powers both in relation to immigration (civil) powers, as well as in relation to criminal cases. This Chapter will focus on the criminal powers that can be exercised, but practitioners will need to be aware of the fact that most of the time Immigration Officers will be exercising their civil powers.

12.2

Immigration Officers are told that they 'must only use criminal powers when there is a genuine intention to prosecute an individual for immigration related criminal offences. These powers directly relate to the investigation of a suspected immigration offence. They are not about establishing immigration status and are distinct and separate from your administrative powers'. Further, 'Investigation of an offence involves the process of examining whether an offence has been committed and if so by whom. The usual purpose of investigation where a criminal offence is detected is prosecution; however, in the context of immigration investigations it is often a more proportionate approach to pursue administrative removal action and this remains the policy for most cases detected'[1].

Application of PACE

12.3

The Police and Criminal Evidence Act 1984 (Application to immigration officers and designated customs officials in England and Wales) Order 2013 ('PACE Order 2013') sets out how PACE applies to accredited Immigration Officers in a modified form[2].

---

1 'Dealing with potential criminality (ICE Teams)', v2.0 (13 February 2023).

2 This is distinct from the Immigration (PACE Codes of Practice) Direction 2013, and arises from Borders, Citizenship and Immigration Act 2009, s 23.

12.4

The structure is that the Order sets out a number of powers that an Immigration Officer will have when conducting an investigation[3], that a police officer in the same circumstances would have. There are also limitations put in place[4], with one notable one being that this Order does not give the power to bail or charge someone.

12.5

The Order also sets out what the equivalent rank of an Immigration Officer to a police officer[5]:

Rank of Constable	Grade of Immigration Officer
Sergeant	Immigration Officer
Inspector	Chief Immigration Officer
Chief Inspector	Chief Immigration Officer
Superintendent	Immigration Inspector

12.6

The Home Office publishes guidance[6] on the Order in general, as well as guidance on a number of different topics in more detail[7]. The guidance makes clear that this only gives power to 'criminal investigators in Immigration Enforcement (IE) and suitably trained and accredited criminal investigators within the Home Office'. Further, it is stated that where an Immigration Officer can rely on the Order, they should do so in preference to any powers that they may have under the Immigration Acts or other legislation[8], which is set out below.

Powers of arrest

Arrest without warrant

12.7

An Immigration Officer can arrest without warrant someone who has, or they have reasonable grounds for suspecting has, committed, or is about to commit one (or more) of the following offences[9]:

3 Arts 3, 5-11, with reference to Part 1, Sch 1.
4 Art 4.
5 PACE Order, Sch 1, Part 1.
6 Criminal investigation guidance to the PACE (1984) Order 2013 (version 9.0)
7 These are collected online 'Enforcement and criminal investigations (immigration staff guidance)'.
8 Criminal investigation guidance, page 3.
9 There are further powers to arrest for Scottish criminal offences (AI(TC)A 2004, s 14).

Common Law Offences[10]

- Conspiracy to Defraud

Offences Against the Person Act 1861[11]

- Section 57 (Bigamy)

Perjury Act 1911[12]

- Section 3 (False Statement with regards to marriages)
- Section 4 (False Statement with regards to births and deaths)
- Section 7 (Aiding, abetting, counselling, procuring, or suborning another to commit the section 3 or 4 offence)

Theft Act 1968[13]

- Section 1 (Theft)
- Section 17 (False Accounting)
- Section 22 (Handling Stolen Goods)

Immigration Act 1971[14]

- Section 24 (Entry/Leave offence, apart from the offence under s 24(1)(d)[15])
- Section 24A (Leave to enter by deception)
- Section 24B (Illegal Working – employee offence)
- Section 25 (Facilitation the breach of immigration law)
- Section 25A (Facilitating the arrival of asylum seekers)
- Section 26(1)(g) (Obstructing an Immigration Officer/other person[16])
- Section 26A (Offences relating to Registration Cards)
- Section 26B (Possessing an Immigration Stamp)

10 AI(TC)A 2004, s 14. This has an additional requirement that the Immigration Officer is 'in the course of exercising a function under the Immigration Acts' for the power to arrest to be authorised. As a matter of policy (if not law) this can only be exercised by 'appropriately trained officers' – 'Dealing with potential criminality (ICE Teams)', v2.0 (13 February 2023).

11 AI(TC)A 2004, s 14.

12 AI(TC)A 2004, s 14.

13 AI(TC)A 2004, s 14.

14 IA 1971, s 28A.

15 Failing to comply with a direction to report to, or to submit to a test as directed by, a medical officer of health – see below for powers or arrest with a warrant.

16 This is limited to the case where either the service of a summons was impracticable or inappropriate for the reasons set out in s 28A(7)(a)-(d) and (9), or the Immigration Officer has reasonable grounds for believing that arrest is necessary to prevent the suspect either causing physical injury to himself or to other people, suffering physical injury himself, or causing loss of damage to property (s 28A(8)).

Forgery and Counterfeiting Act 1981[17]

- Section 1 (Forgery)
- Section 2 (Copying a False Instrument)
- Section 3 (Using a False Instrument)
- Section 4 (Using a Copy of a False Instrument)
- Section 5(1) (Possessing a False Instrument with Intent)
- Section 5(3) (Possessing material to make a False Instrument with Intent)

Immigration and Asylum Act 1999[18]

- Sections 105 and 106 (Asylum Support Offences)

Asylum and Immigration (Treatment of Claimants, etc) Act 2004

- Section 2 (Failing to have an immigration document)
- Section 35 (Failing to co-operate with removal)[19]

Proceeds of Crime Act 2002

- Section 453C (Obstructing an Immigration Officer exercising a power under POCA 2002)[20]

Immigration, Asylum and Nationality Act 2006[21]

- Section 21 (Illegal Working – employers offence)

Fraud 2006[22]

- Section 1 (Fraud)
- Section 11 (Obtaining Services Dishonestly)

UK Borders Act 2007[23]

- Section 22 (Assaulting an Immigration Officer)

Identity Documents Act 2010[24]

- Section 4 (Possessing a False ID document with intent)
- Section 5 (Possessing apparatus to make a False ID document)
- Section 6 (Possessing a False ID document)

---

17 AI(TC)A 2004, s 14.
18 UKBA 2007, s 18.
19 AI(TC)A 2004, s 35(5).
20 POCA 2002, s 453C(4). This is subject to the same limitation as exists for IA 1971, s 26(1)(g).
21 IA 1971, s 28A.
22 AI(TC)A 2004, s 14.
23 UKBA 2007, s 23.
24 AI(TC)A 2004, s 14.

Immigration Act 2014

- Section 33A (Landlord Offences)
- Section 33B (Letting Agency Offences)

Modern Slavery Act 2015[25]

- Section 2 (Human Trafficking)

12.8

As and when the illegal driving offence under the IA 1971, s 24C is in force, then this will be arrestable without a warrant, but with the same caveats applicable to the IA 1971, s 26(1)(g) offence.

Arrest with warrant

12.9

An Immigration Officer can apply to a Justice of the Peace for an arrest warrant if there are reasonable grounds to suspect that they have committed the following offence[26]: IA 1971, s 24(1)(d). (Failing to comply with a direction to report to, or to submit to a test as directed by, a medical officer of health.)

12.10

This offence is rarely charged, and it is not clear how often this power has been exercised. There were offences that were previously arrestable only with a warrant (such as the landlord offences relating to illegal letting).

Search of a person after arrest

Otherwise than at a police station

12.11

Where someone is arrested (other than at a police station) for an offence under the IA 1971, Part 3[27] (or a number of other offences[28]) then, if an Immigration Officer has reasonable grounds to believe that they present a

25 AI(TC)A 2004, s 14.
26 IA 1971, s 28AA.
27 Ie, any offence under IA 1971, ss 24, 24A, 25, 25A, 25B and 26.
28 These offences are:

- AI(TC)A 2004, s 2
- AI(TC)A 2004, s 35
- IANA 2006, s 21 (Illegal working – employers offence)
- Borders Act 2007, s 22 (Assaulting an Immigration Officer)
- IA 2014, s 33A – (Landlord Offences)
- IA 2014, s 33B – (Letting Agency Offences)

danger to themselves or others, they may search them[29]. If the Immigration Officer has reasonable grounds to believe that the person may have anything in the following categories concealed on them, then they can search them to find:

- Anything that might be used to assist an escape, or
- Anything which might be evidence relating to the offence for which he was arrested

12.12

This is subject to the limitation that it is only to the extent that it is reasonably required to discover it.

12.13

Anything that is seized that falls into the above categories can be retained. A search of the mouth is authorised, but not of clothing in public (other than a coat, gloves and jacket).

Arrest at a police station

12.14

Where someone is arrested for a Part 3 offence, the asylum support offences[30] (or any of the other offences that the IA 1971, s 28G applies to), and is in police detention[31], an Immigration Officer may search them[32]. There are two separate powers for a search, but both require that the custody officer[33] considers it necessary to find material that falls within this section. Anything found that the Immigration Officer has reasonable grounds for believing falls into either category may be seized. The power to search under this section does not include the power to conduct an intimate search[34]. Any search must be carried out by someone of the same sex as the detainee.

12.15

There are a number of purposes of a search of a suspect. Firstly, this is to find things which might be used to:

- Cause physical injury to himself or others

29 IA 1971, s 28G. In *R(HM) v SSHD* [2022] EWHC 695 (Admin), [2022] 1 WLR 5030 it was said that those words (in the context or IA 1971, Sch 2, para 25B, 'set a low bar for the exercise of the power. The immigration officer considering whether to carry out search has an obligation to consider his own safety and that of others who may encounter the arrested person while he is in custody'.

30 IAA 1999, ss 104 and 105.

31 As defined in PACE 1984, s 118(2) and (2). In brief this is if he is under arrest at a police station, or being transferred, or is at, another location (other than a court). This includes someone being transferred by a private contractor as well as a constable.

32 IA 1971, s 28H.

33 See PACE 1984, Part IV.

34 As defined in PACE 1984 – 'a search which consists of the physical examination of a person's body orifices other than the mouth'

- Damage property
- Interfere with evidence
- Assist his escape

12.16

Secondly, this relates to items that the Immigration Officer has reasonable grounds for believing is evidence relating to the offence.

12.17

The difference between the two is that something in the first category will be retained by the police, whereas something in the second category would be retained by the Immigration Officer.

Powers of entry to premises

Powers of entry in order to arrest

Introduction

12.18

Immigration Officers have a number of powers to enter and search 'premises'. Premises are defined as follows[35]:

> 'Premises" includes any place and, in particular, includes—
>
> (a) any vehicle, vessel, aircraft or hovercraft;
>
> (b) any offshore installation;
>
> (ba) any renewable energy installation;
>
> (c) any tent or movable structure;'

12.19

In *R(HM) v SSHD*[36], the court approved[37] Home Office guidance that:

> 'Although "any place" can include any place in the open air, that place should itself be capable of amounting to "premises" in the ordinary sense of the word. That is, it should be a distinct piece of land in single occupation or ownership and therefore, for example, the middle of the high street would not constitute "premises".

35 As defined in IA 1971, s 28L, referring back to the definition in PACE 1984, s 23.

36 [2022] EWHC 695 (Admin), [2022] 1 WLR 5030.

37 *R(HM) v SSHD at* [80]-[81]. See also, guidance in 'Dealing with potential criminality (ICE Teams)', v2.0 (13 February 2023).

12.20

"Business Premises" is defined at s 28L(2) as: 'premises (or any part of premises) not used as a dwelling'.

12.21

'Relevant evidence' is a term that appears in various provisions. It is not defined in the definitions section, and is at various points defined slightly differently as the context requires. In essence, it means evidence relating the offence in question other than material that is covered by legal privilege (or that the Immigration Officer has reasonable ground for believing is).

General powers and responsibilities in relation to warrants

12.22

The courts will strictly enforce the requirements and procedural safeguards for search of premises and consequential seizure of material, with the consequences that a breach may lead to a court ordering the material be returned.[38]

12.23

There are specific procedural safeguards set out in the IA 1971, s 28K in relation to the execution of a warrant. The IA 1971, s 28J states that an entry or search pursuant to a warrant is unlawful unless it complies with the requirements set out there[39]. Of particular note is the requirement for the application for a warrant to 'identify, so far as is practicable' the persons or articles to be sought'[40].

12.24

A good summary of what is required by a JP in considering an application (in relation to PACE, s 8) is set out in *R (Glenn & Co (Essex) Ltd & Others) v HMRC*[41]:

> 'i) as has been repeatedly stressed, the safeguard against the unlawful invasion of premises is the strict application of the statutory criteria;
>
> ii) there is nothing in PACE which requires the court to give reasons why it is satisfied that there are reasonable grounds for believing the matters set out in s.8(1)(a)–(e) and in some cases, it may be unnecessary to do so. One 300 example would be where the written Information was compelling as to the grounds for a belief, and clearly addressed the specific matters which are required to

38 Most authorities in relation to this are concerning search and seizures under PACE, but the terminology in relation to the powers under IA 1971 often track the wording of PACE, and it is likely that similar principals will apply.

39 There are in similar terms to the safeguards in PACE, ss 15 and 16.

40 IA 1971, s 28J(2)(b).

41 [2011] EWHC 2998 (Admin), [2012]1 Cr App R 22.

be addressed in s.8(1)(a)–(d), see for example Lord Woolf C.J. in Cronin (above) at [15]:

> "… On examination of the information it would be possible to say, if the matter had to be reviewed by a court, whether there was material on which a justice could be satisfied. Therefore, without any more, it would be possible for a court to scrutinise the question whether this was a case where, prima facie, the warrant had or had not been lawfully issued" ;

iii) in most cases, and particularly where the information is given or supplemented orally, magistrates should ensure that:

a) reasons for their decision are given, see for example *R. v Lewes Crown Court Ex p. Nigel Weller & Co* [1999] EWHC Admin 424 Kennedy L.J. at [6]:

> "The reality is that (1) the person or persons against whom an order is made are entitled to know why it is made; (2) the requirement to give reasons should help ensure that a judge does, as he must, address each of the statutory requirements before making the order, and (3) if it is necessary to review an order in this court reasons will be of great assistance. We will know why the judge decided as he did";

b) those reasons are recorded at the time, see *R (Wood) v North Avon Magistrates' Court* [2009] EWHC 3614 (Admin), Moses LJ at [25]:

> "If reasons are recorded at the time, then not only a complainant will be in a position to understand why his premises had been raided, but also there will exist the powerful discipline for the decision-maker of knowing and having to record why the warrant was issued.'"

12.25

There is power for a warrant to name people other than Immigration Officers to accompany Immigration Officers on a search. Such people then have the same powers, including the same powers of seizure and retention, provided that they are with, and under the supervision of, an Immigration Officer.

12.26

There are a number of other requirements for an Immigration Officer to follow, with additional safeguards in relation to 'all premises' warrants. This include that an entry and search must be undertaken within three months of the warrant being issued and 'at a reasonable hour' unless that would frustrate the purpose of the search[42].

42 IA 1971, s 28K(3)–(13).

12.27

The same provisions apply to a warrant issued under the IA 1971, Sch 2, para 17(2) or 25A(6A) (power to issue a warrant to enter and search business premises).

Entry without a warrant – business premises

12.28

An Immigration Officer (or Police Officer) can enter and search a business premises to arrest someone for the following offences under the IA 1971[43]:

- Section 24 (Entry/Leave offences, apart from the offence under s 24(1)(d)[44])
- Section 24A (Leave to enter by deception)
- Section 24B (Illegal Working – employee offence)

12.29

This also applies to any of the other offences that the IA 1971, s 28G applies to.

12.30

There is also power to enter a business premises to arrest someone liable to be detained under the IA 1971, Sch 2, para 16. This power can only be exercised[45]:

- To the extent that it is reasonably required
- If the Immigration Officer or Police Officer has reasonable grounds for believing that the person that they are looking for is on the premises
- If the Immigration Officer or Police Officer shows identification (whether or not he is asked to do so)
- With the authority of a Chief Superintendent (for a Police Officer), or the Home Secretary or a civil servant of the rank of at least Assistant Director (for an Immigration Officer). Any authority lapses after seven days.

12.31

Where someone is detained, then a detainee custody officer may enter the premises in order to search them prior to escorting them to a custodial setting[46].

43 IA 1971, s 28CA.
44 Failing to comply with a direction to report to, or to submit to a test as directed by, a medical officer of health – see below for powers or arrest with a warrant.
45 IA 1971, s 28CA(2).
46 IA 1971, s 28CA(6). A detainee custody officer is defined in IAA 1999, s 154.

Entry without warrant to arrest – any premises

12.32

An Immigration Officer may enter and search any premises without a warrant where they have reasonable grounds for believing that a person is on the premises who they are seeking to arrest for the following offences under the IA 1971[47]:

- Section 25 (Facilitating the breach of immigration law)
- Section 25A (Facilitating the arrival of asylum seekers)

12.33

The power to enter and search can only be exercised to the extent that it is reasonably required[48]. The Immigration Officer must produce identification (even if they are not asked to do so)[49].

12.34

Where the premises consist of 'two or more separate dwellings', the power does not extend beyond the power to enter and search[50]:

(a) any parts of the premises which the occupiers of any dwelling comprised in the premises use in common with the occupiers of any such other dwelling; and

(b) any such dwelling in which the officer has reasonable grounds for believing that the person whom he is seeking may be.

Entry with a warrant to arrest – any premises

12.35

Where a Justice of the Peace is satisfied (by written information on oath) that an Immigration Officer who has reasonable grounds to suspect that a person who is liable to arrested for a relevant offence is 'to be found on any premises' then they can grant a warrant permitting the Immigration Officer to enter (by using force if necessary) the premises named in the warrant to search for and arrest the suspect[51].

12.36

The relevant offences are mostly under the IA 1971[52]:

47 IA 1971, s 28C.
48 IA 1971, s 28C(2)(a).
49 IA 1971, s 28C(4).
50 IA 1971, s 28C(3).
51 IA 1971, s 28B.
52 IA 1971, s 28B(5).

- Section 24(A1)-(E1) – Entry/Arrival Offences
- Section 24(1)(b),(c),(d), (f) or (h) (Summary Only Entry/Leave offences)
- Section 24A (Leave to enter by deception)
- Section 24B (Illegal Working – employee offence)
- Section 26A (Offences relating to Registration Cards)
- Section 26B (Possessing an Immigration Stamp)
- IAA 1999, ss 105 and 106 (asylum support offences)
- Asylum and Immigration (Treatment of Claimants, etc) Act 2004, s 2[53]
- IANA 2006, s 21 (Illegal working – employers offence)[54]
- UK Borders Act 2007, s 22 (Assaulting an Immigration Officer)[55]
- IA 2014, s 33A (Landlord Offences)[56]
- IA 2014, s 33B (Letting Agency Offences)

12.37

This warrant can authorise an Immigration Officer or a constable to enter and search.

General powers of entry to search

Entry with a warrant

12.38

A Justice of the Peace can issue a warrant to enter and search a premises under the IA 1971, s 28D(4) on application by an Immigration Officer, where there are reasonable grounds to believe that[57]:

(a) A relevant offence has been committed

(b) There is material on the premises that is likely to be of substantial value to the investigation of the offence and likely to be relevant evidence

(c) The material does not consist of include items subject to legal privilege, excluded material or special procedure material, and

(d) Either –

    i. It is not practicable to communicate with anyone entitled to grant entry

53 AI(TC)A 2004, s 2.
54 IANA 2006, s 21(3)(a).
55 UKBA 2007, s 23(2).
56 IA 2014, s 33(6)
57 IA 1971, s 28D.

ii. It is not practicable to communicate with anyone entitled to grant access to the evidence

iii. Entry will not be granted unless there is a warrant

iv. The purposes of a search may be frustrated or seriously prejudiced unless an Immigration Officer can secure immediate entry.

12.39

In practice, it is the last of these exceptions that are most likely to arise.

Definitions

12.40

Premises should be strictly construed, and so a car park belonging to a flat may well not be part of the 'premises'[58].

12.41

The relevant offences are those specified under the IA 1971, s 28B(5), as well as the two facilitation offences :

- Section 25 (Facilitation the breach of immigration law)
- Section 25A (Facilitating the arrival of asylum seekers)

All premises warrant

12.42

'Premises' is further defined as being any premises (singular or plural) specified in the application. However, there is also power to grant the application to cover any premises occupied or controlled by a person specified in the application (an 'all premises warrant'). This will not be granted unless there are reasonable grounds to believe that it is necessary to search other premises occupied or controlled by the person in order to find the material, and it is not reasonably practicable to specify all the premises which the person occupies or controls and which may need to be searched[59].

Multiple entry warrants

12.43

A warrant can authorise entry and search of the premises on more than one occasion if the Justice of the Peace is satisfied that that is necessary in order to

58 *R (Wood) v North Avon Magistrates' Court* [2009] EWHC 3614 (Admin).
59 IA 1971, s 28D(1B).

achieve the purpose for which the warrant is authorised. This can be granted for an unlimited number of entries, or subject to a maximum number[60].

Entry to premises after arrest

General power after arrest for Immigration Officers

12.44

When someone is arrested (other than at a police station) for any offence under the IA 1971, Part 3 (or the asylum support offence, or any of the other offences that the IA 1971, s 28G applies to) then if an Immigration Officer has reasonable grounds for believing that there is 'relevant evidence' in any premises where the detainee was when he was arrested, or immediately before he was arrested, they may enter and search that premises[61].

12.45

The power can only be exercised if it is reasonably required to discover the evidence. Where the premises consist of two or more separate dwellings then the power can only be exercised in the dwelling where the arrest took place (or where the detainee was immediately before arrest) and any communal areas.

12.46

Anything found which the Immigration Officer has reasonable grounds for believing is 'relevant evidence', unless they believe that it is subject to legal privilege, may be seized and retained.

Entry after arrest for serious offences

12.47

When someone is arrested for the IA 1971, s 25 or s 25A offence (the two offences in Part 3 that carry a sentence life imprisonment) then an Immigration Officer may enter and search any premises 'occupied or controlled' by them[62], provided that the Immigration Officer has reasonable grounds for suspecting that there is relevant evidence there.

12.48

This power can only be exercised to the extent that it is reasonably required to discover the relevant evidence. It must be authorised in writing by a 'senior officer' (a Chief Immigration Officer, or one of higher rank) unless 'the

60 IA 1971, s 28D(1C)-(1D).
61 IA 1971, s 28E.
62 IA 1971, s 28F.

presence of that person at a place other than one where he is to be detained is necessary for the effective investigation of the offence', in which case a search can be carried out without authorisation. If that is the case, then the Immigration Officer carrying out the search must inform a senior officer as soon as practicable.

12.49

The senior officer (whether authorising in advance or being informed afterwards) must make a written record of the grounds for the search and the nature of the evidence searched.

12.50

As above, anything found by the Immigration Officer which they believe is relevant evidence not subject to legal privilege, may be seized and retained.

Difference between the two powers

12.51

The difference between the two powers is that the power under s 28F is wider, in that it can apply to any premises 'occupied or controlled' by the suspect, but there is a greater level of safeguards against abuse in the requirement to have an authorisation.

12.52

The power to search without a warrant arises after someone is arrested for one of a number of offences. There is no need for the s 25 and s 25A offences to be included given the wider powers of search that attach to them.

Search of premises for nationality documents

Search without warrant after arrest

12.53

Where someone is arrested for any offence and an Immigration Officer or Police Officer suspects that:

(a) that the individual may not be a British citizen, and

(b) that nationality documents relating to the individual may be found on–

 (i) premises occupied or controlled by the individual,

 (ii) premises on which the individual was arrested, or

 (iii) premises on which the individual was, immediately before being arrested.

12.54

Then there is power under the UK Borders Act 2007 to enter and search the premises in order to find these documents[63].

12.55

The definition of 'nationality documents' is wider than may be thought, being a document showing:

(a) the individual's identity, nationality or citizenship,

(b) the place from which the individual travelled to the United Kingdom, or

(c) a place to which the individual is proposing to go from the United Kingdom.

12.56

This needs the written authority of a 'senior officer' (a Chief Immigration Officer or Police Inspector) who must also arrange for a written record to be made of the nature of the documents sought and the grounds for the suspicion. If the suspect is released without charge, then this power lapses.

Search with warrant

12.57

Where the above conditions apply in relation to arrest, an Immigration Officer or a police officer can apply to a Justice of the Peace who can grant a warrant to search one or more named premises, or an all premises warrant[64], if they are satisfied that there are reasonable grounds for believing that the relevant documents may be found, that the documents are not covered by legal privilege[65], and:

(a) it is not practicable to communicate with any person entitled to grant entry to the premises;

(b) it is practicable to communicate with a person entitled to grant entry to the premises but it is not practicable to communicate with any person entitled to grant access to the nationality documents;

(c) entry to the premises will not be granted unless a warrant is produced;

(d) the purpose of a search may be frustrated or seriously prejudiced unless an immigration officer or constable arriving at the premises can secure immediate entry.

---

63 UKBA 2007, s 44.
64 UKBA 2007, s 45.
65 UKBA 2007, s 46(2)

12.58

The same safeguards that apply to searches under the Immigration Act 1971 apply to searches under the UK Borders Act 2007, ss 44 and 45.

Retention of documents

12.59

An Immigration Officer or police officer may seize any document which they think is a 'nationality document' relating to the person arrested. Any document seized can be retained if:

(a) the individual to whom the document relates may be liable to removal from the United Kingdom in accordance with a provision of the Immigration Acts, and

(b) retention of the document may facilitate the individual's removal.

Search of premises for personnel records

Search for personnel records without warrant

12.60

This applies to someone arrested for, or where an Immigration Officer or constable reasonably believe is liable to arrest for the following offences[66]:

IA 1971

- Section 24 (Entry/Leave offences)
- Section 24A (Leave to enter by deception
- Section 24B (Illegal Working – employee offence)

Or they are liable to be arrested under Sch 2, para 17 (arrest for someone liable to be detained under para 16 for the purposes of examination)

12.61

It also applies where an Immigration Officer or constable reasonably believe someone is liable to arrest for the following offences:

IA 1971

- Section 24 (Entry/Leave offences)
- Section 24A (Leave to enter by deception

Or they are liable to be arrested under Sch 2, para 17

66 IA 1971, s 28FA.

12.62

In those circumstances the Immigration Officer or constable can search any business premises where the arrest is made or, as the case may be, if they reasonably believe the person who is liable to arrest is present, ***and*** 'employee records' will be found on the premises that will be of 'substantial value' (either standing alone of with other material) to the investigation of an illegal worker employer offence[67]. Any such material that the searcher reasonably suspects will be of substantial value to either the illegal worker employer offence **or** the asylum support offence[68] can be seized. The Immigration Officer or constable must produce identification whether or not asked.

12.63

Again, this does not apply to items subject to legal privilege. In addition, to the requirement that the search must be reasonably required to discover the evidence, the Immigration Officer or constable must reasonably believe that one of the following apply:

i. Permission to search has been refused

ii. Permission to search would be refused if requested

iii. It is not practicable to communicate with anyone entitled to grant access to the records

iv. The purposes of a search may be frustrated or seriously prejudiced if it is not carried out at that point

Search for personnel records with warrant

12.64

An Immigration Officer can apply to a Justice of the Peace for a warrant[69] in relation to premises (or sets of premises). A JP can authorise a warrant if they are satisfied that there are reasonable grounds for believing that:

a) An employer has provided inaccurate or incomplete information under the NIAA 2002, s 134,

b) On the premises there will be employee records (that are not subject to legal privilege) that will 'enable deduction of some or all of the information which the employer was required to provide', and

c) One of the following apply:

    i. It is not practicable to communicate with anyone entitled to grant entry

    ii. It is not practicable to communicate with anyone entitled to grant access to the records

---

67 IANA 2006, s 21.

68 IAA 1999, ss 105-106 – see Chapter 7.

69 IA 1971, s 28FB.

iii. Entry to the premises or access to the records will not be granted unless there is a warrant

iv. The purposes of a search may be frustrated or seriously prejudiced unless an Immigration Officer can secure immediate entry

12.65

Whilst on the premises pursuant to a warrant, the Immigration Officer can seize and retain employee records (that are not covered by legal privilege) which they reasonably suspect 'will be of substantial value (whether on their own or together with other material) in the investigation of the disclosure offence under NIAA 2002, s 137 or an asylum support offence.

All premises warrant

12.66

There is also power to grant the application to cover any premises occupied or controlled by a person specified in the application (an 'all premises warrant'). This will not be granted unless there are reasonable grounds to believe that it is necessary to search other premises occupied or controlled by the person in order to find the records and it is not reasonably practicable to specify all the premises which the person occupies or controls and which may need to be searched[70].

Multiple entry warrants

12.67

A warrant can authorise entry and search of the premises on more than one occasion if the Justice of the Peace is satisfied that that this is necessary in order to achieve the purpose for which the warrant is authorised. This can be granted for an unlimited number of entries, or subject to a maximum number[71]. This is a similar power, with similar conditions, to the power under the IA 1971, s 28D.

Retention of material

Under the IA 1971

12.68

Where any material is seized by an Immigration Officer under the IA 1971, Part 3 then it may be retained 'so long as is necessary in all the circumstances'[72].

70 IA 1971, s 28D(1B).
71 IA 1971, s 28D(1C)-(1D).
72 IA 1971, s 28ZI.

In particular, this includes the power to retain it to conduct forensic analysis, for use as evidence in any trial and, where there are reasonable grounds to believe that it has been obtained as a result of a criminal offence, to establish its lawful owner[73].

12.69

There is no power to retain an item where a copy or photograph would be sufficient[74]. Further, for someone who is the occupier of the premises where the items were seized or had custody of control of it before it was seized, the Immigration Officer must provide them with a written record of what was seized on request[75]. The above duties are subject to the caveat that permission need not be granted if that would prejudice an investigation, court case or 'the exercise of any functions in connection with which the material was seized'.

12.70

Similarly, if such a person, or someone acting on their behalf, requests access to the seized material then this must be arranged under the supervision of an Immigration Officer (or Officer if the material was retained by the police). If the person wishes to have a copy or photograph of it then the Immigration Officer can arrange for them to be granted access, or they can provide a copy within a reasonable time[76].

The IA 2016

12.71

The IA 2016, s 48 gives an Immigration Officer wide ranging powers of retention:

> **'48 Seizure and retention in relation to offences**
>
> (1) This section applies if an immigration officer is lawfully on any premises.
>
> (2) The immigration officer may seize anything which the officer finds in the course of exercising a function under the Immigration Acts if the officer has reasonable grounds for believing—
>
> (a) that it has been obtained in consequence of the commission of an offence, and

73 The consequences of s 28H are that if the Immigration Officer seizes a weapon or similar then it will be retained by a police who have a wider power to keep it, see PACE 1984, s 22.

74 IA 1971, s 28ZI(3).

75 IA 1971, s 28I. This also applies to anything seized under s 47 (civil power to search) or IA 2016, s 48, or under the powers relating to searches for the asylum support offences, or assaulting an Immigration Officer under UKBA 2007, s 22, or documents or material seized under UKBA 2007, s 46 or s 46B.

76 IA 1971, s 28I.

(b) that it is necessary to seize it in order to prevent it being concealed, lost, damaged, altered or destroyed.

(3) The immigration officer may seize anything which the officer finds in the course of exercising a function under the Immigration Acts if the officer has reasonable grounds for believing—

(a) that it is evidence in relation to an offence, and

(b) that it is necessary to seize it in order to prevent the evidence being concealed, lost, altered or destroyed.

(4) The immigration officer may require any information which is stored in any electronic form and is accessible from the premises to be produced if the officer has reasonable grounds for believing—

(a) that—

(i) it is evidence in relation to an offence, or

(ii) it has been obtained in consequence of the commission of an offence, and

(b) that it is necessary to seize it in order to prevent it being concealed, lost, tampered with or destroyed.

(5) The reference in subsection (4) to information which is stored in any electronic form being produced is to such information being produced in a form—

(a) in which it can be taken away, and

(b) in which it is visible and legible or from which it can readily be produced in a visible and legible form.

(6) This section does not authorise an immigration officer to seize an item which the officer has reasonable grounds for believing is an item subject to legal privilege.

(7) Anything seized by an immigration officer under this section which relates to an immigration offence may be retained so long as is necessary in all the circumstances and in particular—

(a) may be retained, except as provided for by subsection (8)—

(i) for use as evidence at a trial for an offence, or

(ii) for forensic examination or for investigation in connection with an offence, and

(b) may be retained in order to establish its lawful owner, where there are reasonable grounds for believing that it has been obtained in consequence of the commission of an offence.

(8) Nothing may be retained for a purpose mentioned in subsection (7)(a) if a photograph or copy would be sufficient for that purpose.

(9) Section 28I of the Immigration Act 1971 (seized material: access and copying) applies to anything seized and retained under this section which relates to an immigration offence as it applies to anything seized and retained by an immigration officer under Part 3 of that Act.

(10) This section does not apply in relation to anything which may be seized by an immigration officer under—

(a) section 19 of the Police and Criminal Evidence Act 1984 as applied by an order under section 23 of the Borders, Citizenship and Immigration Act 2009, or

(b) Article 21 of the Police and Criminal Evidence (Northern Ireland) Order 1989 (SI 1989/1341 (NI 12) as applied by that section.

(11) In this section and section 49 "immigration offence" means an offence which relates to an immigration or nationality matter.'

12.72

The case of *R(HM) v SSHD*[77] gives extensive consideration to this section and the interplay with powers under the IA 1971 and PACE.

12.73

The power in the IA 2016, s 48(3) applies when an Immigration Officer is exercising a power under the Immigration Acts and does not give a freestanding power to undertake a search. The power only arises where the Immigration Officer has reasonable grounds for believing that the item seized is 'evidence in relation to an offence'[78].

Consequences of an unlawful search and seizure

12.74

Where material is obtained as a result of an unlawful search, a trial Judge has a discretion (but not an obligation) to stay the proceedings as an abuse of process[79] or, if not, to exclude any illegally obtained evidence[80]. However, the reality is that both courses of action are unusual, and that court will routinely admit evidence from an unlawful search whether of a person[81] or of premises[82]. This is so even when the ECHR is taken into account[83].

77 [2022] EWHC 695 (Admin), [2022] 1 WLR 5030.
78 *R(HM) v SSHD* [107]-[109].
79 *Warren v AG for Jersey* [2011] UKPC 10, [2012] 1 AC 22.
80 Pace Code B (that deals with searches states (at B1.5) –

> If the provisions of PACE and this Code are not observed, evidence obtained from a search may be open to question.

81 *Kuruma* [1955] AC 197.
82 *Jeffrey v Black* (1978) 66 Cr App R 81.
83 *Abdurahman* [2019] EWCA Crim 2239, [2020] 1 Cr App R 27.

12.75

The exception to this is in relation to confessions, where courts are much more ready to exclude evidence (see Chapter 11 for more details).

Use of force

12.76

In addition to the common law powers that every citizen has, an Immigration Officer has the power to use reasonable force in a number of different circumstances[84]. The IAA 1999, s 146 contains a general power to do so when 'exercising any power conferred on him by the Immigration Acts[85]'.

12.77

In addition, the PACE Order 2013, art 6 states:

> '**6.** Where any provision of the Act as applied by article 3—
>
> (a) confers a power on an immigration officer, and
>
> (b) does not provide that the power may only be exercised with the consent of some person other than the immigration officer upon whom the power is conferred, the immigration officer may use reasonable force, if necessary, in the exercise of the power.'

12.78

The exercise of these powers are reserved to specially trained Immigration Officers[86].

12.79

In relation to other Acts, there is often a specific provision in the legislation (for example, see below in relation to Illegal Working Closure Notices).

---

84 Guidance is contained in 'Use of force: Guidance for Immigration Enforcement Officers' (v3.0), May 2022

85 This is defined in UK Borders Act 2007, s 61(2) as any of the following thirteen Acts:
(a) the Immigration Act 1971
(b) the Immigration Act 1988
(c) the Asylum and Immigration Appeals Act 1993
(d) the Asylum and Immigration Act 1996
(e) the Immigration and Asylum Act 1999
(f) the Nationality, Immigration and Asylum Act 2002
(g) the Asylum and Immigration (Treatment of Claimants, etc.) Act 2004
(h) the Immigration, Asylum and Nationality Act 2006
(i) [the UK Borders] Act 2007
(j) the Immigration Act 2014
(k) the Immigration Act 2016
(l) Part 1 of the Immigration and Social Security Co-ordination (EU Withdrawal) Act 2020 (and Part 3 so far as relating to that Part) and
(m) the Nationality and Borders Act 2022.

86 Criminal investigation guidance, page 9.

Powers at sea

Introduction

12.80

Prior to the NABA 2022 there were a number of powers for different agencies to intercept boats in the sea surrounding the United Kingdom[87] in a variety of circumstances. This included Police Officers and Customs Officers, but the full powers did not extend to Immigration Officers.

12.81

Immigration Officers did have powers[88] to stop, board, search and, if needed, divert to port, a ship in UK territorial waters[89] if they had reasonable grounds to believe that a facilitation offence[90] was being committed. However, this would only apply to those specific offences, and would only apply in UK waters.

12.82

In order to fill the gap, there were further powers introduced (as of 28 June 2022) by the NABA 2022, s 45 (implementing Sch 7). This provides that in relation to any ship an Immigration Officer[91] has all the powers set out in the IA 1971, Sch 4A, Part A1, in order to prevent, detect, investigate or prosecute an offence under the IANA 2006, ss24(A1), (B1), (D1), (E1), 24B, 25 or 25A, or s 21[92], as well as attempt to commit these offences[93]. There is a further restriction in that the Secretary of State must give authority to exercise these powers in all cases other than a UK ship in UK or international waters[94].

The IA 1971, Sch 4A Powers

12.83

The Schedule should be consulted for the full details of the powers, but as a rough guide includes the power to:

- Stop, board and search a ship (including the cargo)
- Direct the ship to go to anywhere in the UK

87 Modern Slavery Act 2015, ss 35-39 and Policing and Crime Act 2017, ss 84–95.

88 Granted under IA 2016, s 75 and Sch 14, which made amendments to the IA 1971.

89 Different provisions are set out in relation to Scotland and Northern Ireland, which will not be considered here.

90 An offence under s 25, 25A or, prior to its repeal, IA 1971, s 25B.

91 Some of the powers can be exercised by a Police Officer acting in 'hot pursuit' of a relevant ship – IA 1971, s 28P.

92 IA 1971, s 28Q. See also the Part A1 powers introduced as of 12 April 2023 by virtue of The Nationality and Borders Act 2022 (Commencement No. 5 and Transitional Provisions) Regulations 2023.

93 This would not extend to the s 24B offence due to the Criminal Attempts Act 1981 not applying to summary only offences. A conspiracy to commit these offences is not included, although any conspiracy would likely include an attempt or the substantive offences.

94 IA 1971, s 28LA(2).

- Direct the ship to eave UK waters
- Search anyone on board for evidence (and to find anything that might be used to cause injury or damage)
- Require production of a nationality document (and search them if not forthcoming)
- Arrest anyone suspected of committing a relevant offence
- Seize material that appears to be evidence

12.84

There is a similar (but not quite identical) set of powers in the IA 1971, Sch 4A, Part 1 in relation to ships in English and Welsh waters where the relevant offence is the s 25 or s 25A one. These powers can be exercised by an English or Welsh Police Officer as well as an Immigration Officer (or an 'enforcement officer'[95]).

12.85

In exercising these powers, an Immigration Officer may use reasonable force if necessary.

Criminal Offences

12.86

Several criminal offences are created in Sch 4A, Part K1 of obstructing an Immigration Officer, failing to comply with a requirement made by an Immigration Officer (without a reasonable excuse), providing false information or failing to disclose relevant information when required. These are summary only offences with a maximum sentence of six months. The s 31 defence does not apply to any of the offences. Whilst Art 31 would not apply to obstructing, given that s 31 applies to the s 24A and s 26(1)(d) offences, it is unclear why (in principle) it was not extended to the remaining offences, unless it was considered that where an Immigration Officer was present the person could be said to have finished their journey.

Seizure of ships

12.87

An Immigration Officer, acting with the authority of the Secretary of State, may seize a ship (and any property relating to it) that is in the UK or UK

95 This is defined in IA 1971, s 28Q as being a 'commissioned officer of any of Her Majesty's ships' or someone in command of a Navy or RAF aircraft of hovercraft.

waters, where there are reasonable grounds to suspect that it has been used in the commission of a relevant offence[96].

12.88

What happens to the ship depends on whether it is a ship without nationality. If so, the procedure is as set out in the IA 1971, s 28PA(7)–(12) which gives the Secretary of State the power to return it to its owner, retain it or dispose of (which includes the power to sell, destroy or donate it to charity).

12.89

Where the ship is registered to a state, then that state must be notified. The relevant power is at the UK Borders Act 2007, s 26 which gives the magistrates' court (exercising its civil jurisdiction) the power to determine what happens next.

12.90

As an example, where a RHIB (or other boat) is found abandoned on a beach where an Immigration Officer would have reasonable grounds to suspect that it has been used to cross the Channel, perhaps due to the presence of a French document and lack of identifying features or indication of ownership, the Immigration Officer would likely then have reasonable grounds to suspect that it has been used in the commission of a relevant offence, and it can be seized under this section. Given that, it is unlikely that the owner will be identified, or would wish to be identified. After 31 days they can then dispose of it by selling it or donating it or, if it is unsuitable to be used, destroying it.

Powers of disclosure

12.91

The Secretary of State has the power to require banks (and other financial institutions) and employers to provide her with information about a customer or employee if she reasonably suspects that they have committed a number of immigration offences[97].

Employers

12.92

In relation to employers, the relevant offences are[98]:

- IA 1971, s 24(A1)-(E1) (illegal entry and similar offences)
- IA 1971, s 24A(1) (leave to remain by deception)

96 IA 1971, s 28PA
97 NIAA 2002, ss 134-139.
98 NIAA 2002, s 134(1).

- IA 1971, s 26(1)(c) and (d) (false representation/alteration of documents)
- IAA 1999, s 105(1)(a)-(c) and s106(1)(a)-(c) (asylum support offences)

12.93

It is not clear why the power would not extend to, for example, the s 24A(2) offence (avoiding enforcement action by deception). The power can only be exercised in order to establish where the person is or 'relates to [his] earnings or to the history of his employment)[99].

12.94

A reference to 'employer' includes someone who is a former employee. In determining who an employee is, reference should be made to the AIA 1996, s 8(8). Where someone's services are provided through an employment agency, then (if they are not, legally speaking, employed by either) the agency is deemed to be the 'employer' at the relevant time[100].

Financial institution

12.95

The definition of financial institution is at the NIAA 2002, s 135(2). The relevant offences[101] are solely the asylum support offences. However, the test is wider than for employers in that what is required is that (as well as reasonable suspicion that the offence has been committed) the Secretary of State reasonably suspects that the information is 'relevant to the offence', and that the institution has it[102].

Procedure

12.96

The procedure in relation to both is the same. A notice must be served in writing and must specify what information should be provided, how it should be and the time limit for compliance (which must be no less than ten working days)[103]. The person who received the notice must then provide the information in the required time frame.

12.97

There is no appeal against the order (so any challenge would be by way of Judicial Review), and it is a criminal offence (summary only, with a maximum sentence of three months) to fail to comply without a reasonable excuse[104]. Provision is made for liability for a corporate body, and its officers[105].

---

99 NIAA 2002, s 134(2).
100 NIAA 2002, s 134(4).
101 NIAA 2002, s 135(1)(a).
102 NIAA 2002, s 135(1)(b) and (c).
103 NIAA 2002, s 136(3)
104 NIAA 2002, s 137(1)
105 NIAA 2002, s 138

12.98

Any material received under this section cannot be used in criminal proceedings against that person (other than for proceedings for an offence under this section)[106].

Disruption of illegal working

Illegal Working Closure Notice

12.99

In order to tackle 'rogue employers' and disrupt those who repeatedly employ 'disqualified' people (those who are working illegally, as defined in the IANA 2006, s 21(1B)), there is power in the IA 2016, s 38[107] for a Chief Immigration Officer to issue an Illegal Working Closure Notice. This is supposed to provide a rapid response, with the effect of a notice being that the premises must shut for 24 hours[108]. This can be extended to 48 hours by an officer of the rank of Immigration Inspector[109] (if they made the initial Order, then this can be for 48 hours[110]).

12.100

The Notice can be issued if the relevant Officer is satisfied on reasonable grounds that a premises is employing someone who is a disqualified person or is on bail with a condition prohibiting them from working, *and* the employer (or someone connected to the employer as defined in the IA 2016, Sch 6, para 1(9)) has been convicted of the illegal employment offence at any time, or received a civil penalty (under the IANA 2006, s 15) in the last three years, or received a civil penalty at any time that they have not paid[111].

12.101

An Immigration Officer or police officer can use reasonable force to enter the premises and fix the notice or secure the premises[112].

Statutory Guidance

12.102

Statutory Guidance is in force[113]. This states that the power is not one that will be routinely used[114]:

---

106 NIAA 2002, s 139

107 This implements IA 2016, Sch 6 which contains the substantive provisions.

108 IA 2016, Sch 6, para 2(2).

109 IA 2016, Sch 6, para 2(5).

110 IA 2016, Sch 6, para 2(3).

111 The full definitions are in IA 2016, Sch 6, para 1(8).

112 IA 2016, Sch 6, para 4.

113 This is issued under IA 2016, Sch 6, para 16. The current version is 'Illegal Working Closure Notices and Compliance Order', dated 17 January 2017, and is available online https://assets.publishing.service.gov.uk/government/uploads/system/uploads/attachment_data/file/608708/Closure_notice_and_compliance_order_guidance_Jan_17.pdf.

114 Page 9, Guidance.

> 'In practice, a closure notice would generally be served in the most serious cases, where a high proportion of the workforce encountered is working illegally and where it is considered that this course of action is required to prevent continuing illegal working. As a matter of policy, it would also be used as a tool to provide an appropriate response where such behaviour has been combined with 'phoenixism'. This is where a business has closed to evade sanctions, re-opened in a new identity and continued with the non compliant activity.'

Illegal Working Compliance Order

12.103

Unless the Immigration Officer considers that the Notice should be cancelled (either because they consider that the conditions for issuing it are not met, or they are satisfied that the employer has a statutory excuse for each disqualified person), then an application must be made to the magistrates' court for an Illegal Working Compliance Order[115]. This can be issued for up to 12 months[116] and can contain a number of different provisions to[117]:

> '(a) prohibit or restrict access to the premises,
>
> (b) require a person specified in the order to carry out, at such times as may be specified, such right to work checks as prescribed in regulations,
>
> (c) require a person specified in the order to produce to an immigration officer, at such times and such places as may be [..] specified [by the court], right to work documents as prescribed by the Secretary of State in regulations,
>
> (d) specify the times at which and the circumstances in which an immigration officer may enter the premises to carry out such investigations or inspections as may be specified in the order, and
>
> (e) make such other provision as the court considers appropriate[118].'

---

115 IA 2016, Sch 6, para 5(6).

116 IA 2016, Sch 6, para 5(8). This can be extended by no more than 6 months at a time, up to a total of 24 months (para 7).

117 IA 2016, Sch 6, para 5(1).

118 Examples given in the guidance are:

- any employee must promptly co-operate with the request for documents as part of any right to work checks imposed on the employer;
- document copies retained as a result of right to work checks be held on the premises for the duration of the order for ease of inspection;
- an immigration officer conducting an inspection may require any person he or she reasonably suspects to be working at the premises to co-operate with a biometric scan of their finger prints;
- where the court orders the continued closure of the premises, that the closure notice is replaced by a notice detailing the terms of the illegal working closure order concerning the closure;
- that the employer must inform immigration officers if they intend to move the operation of the business to another premises;
- if an immigration officer considers it necessary, they may be accompanied by a constable for the purpose of an inspection visit; and
- the court may also consider extending checks and inspections to other premises within the ownership of the same employer where there is evidence that these are required to prevent illegal working.

12.104

The employer, or anyone with an interest in the premises, can attend the court to make representations. A court can adjourn for up to 14 days to allow someone with an interest in the premises the opportunity to be heard[119]. A hearing can proceed if the respondent (or one of a number of respondents) does not attend. There is a right of appeal to the Crown Court that can be exercised by both sides[120]. As well as an appeal, either side can apply to vary or discharge an order.

Reimbursement and compensation

12.105

As well as the usual provision for litigation costs, there is also power for the Home Secretary to apply within three months of the Order expiring for an order for reimbursement costs[121], to cover the costs of securing and maintain the premises.

12.106

There is a complementary power[122] for someone who has incurred financial loss by a Closure Notice (other than one that is cancelled due to them showing a statutory excuse) to apply for compensation for that loss no later than three months after the expiration of the notice, provided that:

(a) at the time the closure notice was applied, the test was not met (i.e. the employer was not employing illegal workers or had not previously failed to comply with illegal working legislation);

(b) the applicant has incurred financial loss as a result of the notice; and

(c) having regard to all the circumstances, the court considers it appropriate to order the payment of compensation in respect of that loss.

Offence

12.107

It is a criminal offence to (without reasonable excuse) access the premises in breach of a Closure Notice, or obstruct an Immigration Officer or police officer who is issuing an Order or securing premises, or contravening a Compliance Order. This is summary only, with a maximum sentence of six months.

---

119 IA 2016, Sch 6, para 6.
120 IA 2016, Sch 6, para 9(1)–(3).
121 IA 2016, Sch 6, para 13.
122 IA 2016, Sch 6, para 15.

Index

[All references are to paragraph numbers]

E

V

Y

www.ingramcontent.com/pod-product-compliance
Lightning Source LLC
LaVergne TN
LVHW080011210926
848481LV00011B/2990
* 9 7 8 1 5 2 6 5 2 5 5 1 2 *